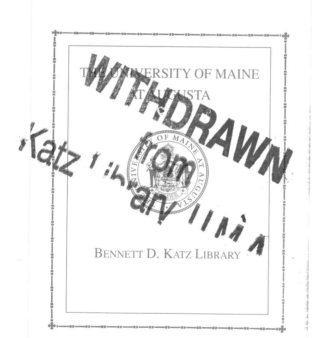

Hazel Wolf

FIGHTING THE ESTABLISHMENT

For my friend Hazel
at 100 years, with
my great admiration,
Olaus Argyll

Hazel Wolf

FIGHTING THE ESTABLISHMENT

Susan Starbuck

Susan Starbuck

UNIVERSITY OF WASHINGTON PRESS

Seattle and London

Copyright © 2002 by the University of Washington Press
Designed by Pamela Canell
Printed in the United States of America

Frontispiece: *The Brown Creeper.* Original painting by Tony Angell.
Facing page 275: Hazel Wolf at the Seattle Arboretum, 1995.
Photo by Natalie B. Fobes.
Excerpt from "Joe Hill" on p. 189 copyright © 1938 by Bob Miller, Inc.;
lyrics by Alfred Hayes, music by Earl Robinson.

Library of Congress Cataloging-in-Publication Data
Starbuck, Susan.
Hazel Wolf : fighting the establishment / Susan Starbuck.
p. cm.
Includes bibliographical references and index.
ISBN 0-295-98222-5 (alk. paper)
1. Wolf, Hazel, 1898–2000.
2. Environmentalists—United States—Biography.
I. Title.
GE56.W65 S73   2002   363.7'0092—dc21   2002002546

The paper used in this publication is acid-free and recycled from 10 percent post-
consumer and at least 50 percent pre-consumer waste. It meets the minimum
requirements of American National Standard for Information Sciences—
Permanence of Paper for Printed Library Materials, ANSI z39.48–1984. ♾ⓞ

To Hazel Wolf;

Nydia Levick, her daughter;

and Ann Sargent and Juanita Commeree,

her granddaughters

To my daughters:

Madeleine, Elinor, and Emily Frey

Contents

Preface

I can organize things I don't even know anything about.
I can get people going. If it is a good project,
I can find the right people and sell it to them.

*H*azel Wolf's adventures began in the salt water of "the inlet" that thrusts three miles into the city of Victoria, British Columbia. Where the inlet narrows at the Gorge, she played and swam with the gang nearly every day of her young life. She sustained her action-packed lifestyle as a young person fighting deportation, as an adult organizing for the environment, and as an elder traveling to Nicaragua and connecting to global politics. At the end of her life, she constructed her autobiography as she had lived it—as a series of adventure stories. Her goal was to make her adventures sound like so much fun that the reader would be compelled to emulate her.

This book is the result of my twenty-year collaboration with Hazel Wolf. I met her in January 1980, four months after the birth of my twin girls, Madeleine and Elinor. With their older sister, Emily, I had three girl babies under three and one-half years old. Hazel Wolf was eighty-one years old, and I was to complete her oral history for the Washington Women's Heritage Project at the University of Washington. She was the Northwest's premier environmentalist, the organizer of twenty-one Audubon Society chapters in Washington State, and the hub of a vast network of activists. The usual two-hour oral history format hardly scratched the surface of her life, so for many months I found myself laboring up Seattle's Capitol Hill on my bicycle to tape-record her story. Months became years. Absorbed by the three children, the house, and the husband, my sense of self, once solidly centered on my career as teacher and historian, was vanishing.

I was astounded that Wolf, though a highly social person, rooted her identity not in human organizations or roles but in the larger life of nature. She was feminist by birth, not by theory, a woman who knew already as a child swimming in the bays and inlets of Victoria that she was a free and equal, female part of nature. History came alive as she told me stories about her childhood in the industrial slums of turn-of-the-twentieth-century Victoria, her rebellion against harsh public school authorities, her emigration to Seattle in the 1920s, and her union organizing. I listened; the power of her stories moved and shaped me toward reclaiming my self. A "devout atheist," Wolf would not call herself a spiritual teacher, yet my own spiritual journey was launched by the tape recording of her life story.

Over the years, we became quite friendly, though I told her only a little about my life and she was extremely discreet about family members' and friends' personal affairs, which were "nobody's business." We enjoyed trading insider jokes based on the details of her life, and sometimes we went out to dinner together. I was one of the many who, at her 100th birthday party, on March 14, 1998, wore on my lapel the little red car designating those who had driven Hazel to a meeting of some sort.

In 1996 she asked me to take her shopping for an outfit that would be suitable to wear at Governor Lowry's reception for her. We visited five stores on two separate occasions. Finally we slogged to the top floor of Nordstrom's department store, and she invested a considerable amount of money (saved from various awards) in a bright, handsome, periwinkle-blue suede suit. Six months later, she decided she didn't like the color: she preferred her thirty-year-old green wool. She invited me to try the blue one on: I was to buy it from her. I told her that I couldn't afford it. Week after week, she insisted: I could pay in monthly installments. So, okay, now I own a swank blue suede suit. Perhaps it's her personal legacy to me, or perhaps I just got conned by a very thrifty householder.

By the time my children had grown and I was ready to write, Hazel Wolf had become famous as an environmental activist. Media attention exploded as she gathered awards and approached her 100th birthday party.

I had taped more than two hundred hours of conversations. My basement contained many boxes of her correspondence and clippings files, her 1916 diary, her two one-act plays, and three legal-size file folders of documents on her deportation case. I had interviewed family members and friends. I was searching for the form for the biography of a working-class activist whose highest post in sixty-five years had been secretary, save for a two-year stint as president of the Federation of Western Outdoor Clubs. First I wrote in the voice of an academic biographer, injecting Hazel Wolf's voice into the text in long quotations. But I liked the quotations better than the text, so I tried stringing her stories together in one long "as told to" autobiography and relegated my voice to historical footnotes. Readers complained about the way it fell into a series of anecdotes and one-liners instead of developing a sustained narrative. When I confronted Wolf with the problem, she said, "I don't know what we can do about this dilemma unless we write a book about somebody else. And these friends of yours—if I could think of a good one-liner, we'd fax it to them."

I pressed her for an explanation. "You have a certain style of telling short stories that end with a punch line. How can we make this into a single, connected story, an autobiography?"

She countered, "I knew I was stylish, but I didn't know I had a style. In fact, I've often wondered where those one-liners come from. They just pop into my head and out. I laugh at them myself because I haven't heard them before. It's part of fighting the establishment, I think.

"Take the speech I wrote for the Seattle University commencement exercise in June 1997. Who ever heard of a speech like that? The idea was that the graduates are running into a tough world and they better be prepared for it, get ready to see the funny side of it, and laugh. Some of the things I elaborated were really tough things, like their job's going to be forty hours a week. That's bad news. Making someone laugh about that is quite a trick. Some of the things I elaborated were ridiculous, like rain on the Fourth of July year after year after year. And so the message gets through while they're laughing."

Hazel Wolf told short stories that got everyone laughing; that was her style. The laughter translated into less ego investment and more flexibility on both sides of an issue—more opportunities for Wolf to attain her political ends. In life, Hazel Wolf turned thoughts and feelings into actions. In her stories, she dramatized her actions with humor. Through storytelling, she constructed her image and strengthened her activist style by making it conscious, from the very first story of the bogeyman to the last one predicting her return as a mushroom. Through storytelling, rather than through reflection, Wolf created her self, her power, and her myth, and she furthered her agenda.

Once I recognized the function of her storytelling, I let it form the book. I wanted readers to hear and be changed by her stories, as I had been. My role was listener, preserver of her oral style, editor, and organizer. I arranged the stories in six parts—corresponding to the major periods of her life, beginning with her childhood—each part consisting of subsections with collections of Hazel Wolf's stories on that topic. The fast pace of the anecdotes, mimicking that of her life, provides the momentum for jumping from one story to the next, linking them in the illusion of narrative. The book can be read without consulting the endnotes, which contain historical context and commentary.

While writing this book, I grew frazzled trying to include every funny story and comment Wolf ever made. Her friends trade "Hazel stories," incidents when they saw her transform a nasty confrontation at a demonstration into dialogue, or when they heard her upend a stuffy bureaucrat with one of her "smart-aleck one-liners." At her many birthday parties—even at her memorial celebration, on February 11, 2000—there was always an open mike for affectionate "roasts" of Wolf. I realized that "Hazel" stories were multiplying faster than the incidents that gave rise to them. I had to select.

Why did Hazel Wolf, a formidable writer and an editor of newsletters since the age of twelve, not collect her own stories and write her own autobiography? She wanted direct action. She did not think about her life as a narrative with a plot and themes; rather, she thought about the causes to which she had devoted it. Many born at the turn of the twentieth century who endured the Depression and two world wars would say with her that they did what had to be done; more precisely, in Wolf's case, she knew what she needed to do. She said that writing her autobiography seemed too self-centered and, besides, she was too busy with the environmental movement. Yet she wanted her story published, knowing that it would be a powerful argument for the cause of social and environmental justice.

I must have seemed like a willing victim, someone who would do it her way—but it was a collaboration. I listened, the best way to help shape a story, but I also stopped the tape recorder to argue history, politics, philosophy, religion, feminism, communism, and environmentalism. Together we teased out the lines of her life. When we went over the text together, we mostly laughed. We also wrangled about the transition from oral to written language. For example, I was in favor of all of the "damns," "okays," and "you guys," and she, an experienced editor, wanted to omit these, as well as anything she considered embarrassing. Later, when I tried to sneak expurgated text back in, she'd always find it.

Although she didn't stop the Northern Tier Pipeline project or write the judicial opinion on old-growth forests, Hazel Wolf organized hundreds of organizers in hundreds of environmental projects and thus touched thousands; she sowed the seeds of a grassroots environmental consciousness that will surely prevent us from enduring another century of mindless plunder. I arranged Wolf's stories to show how, with immense physical and intellectual energy, she realized her talent for organizing and welded it to a vision of democracy that includes mutually respectful relationships among peoples and between people and land.

In Parts I and II, I include many childhood stories. Wolf did not romanticize her childhood, nor did she view it as a short prologue to the real story of her adult contributions to society. She told the childhood stories often—they were guides and motivations for action. They provided an outline of her modus operandi as an organizer later in her life, for Hazel the child and Hazel the adult were nearly the same person. To those who have read of her typical days at the age of sixteen, it should seem less miraculous that she was editing *Outdoors West* on the day she died, at the age of 101.

Part III, "Communist," on her 1930s activism in the Communist Party, shows Hazel Wolf in her prime, having fun. In the notes, I provide background material on the Communist Party USA to demonstrate that Wolf and her friends were ordinary Americans using democratic processes to meet the crisis of the Depression, not conspirators or dupes controlled from Moscow. I have witnessed too many of her admirers looking askance at her and asking, "Now, what about this Communist business?" as if her involvement were an aberration in an otherwise glorious career, whereas in fact there is continuity and consistency. She never changed her core beliefs, she told a friend a few months before she died; rather, she expanded her arena.

When she told me about her deportation case of the 1950s, I realized that her story and hundreds like it were missing from U.S. history books. She opened my eyes to the concentrated doses of good and evil that coexisted during the McCarthy period, and to the role of ordinary, unsung citizens like Hazel Wolf who had worked to "stop the nonsense." In order that a general reader might appreciate her contribution to our democracy, I included the legal and political context of her case in the notes to Part IV, "Fighting Back."

Parts V and VI contain the highlights of Wolf's activism in the environmental movement. I had to ignore many "Hazel stories," boxes of letters, memos, resolutions, clippings, notes, and photographs in order to delineate what she considered her major contributions to the movement: her role in building membership for the Seattle Audubon Society, beginning in 1965; her coalition-building activities; the reports she brought back from Nicaragua in the late 1980s; and her efforts to globalize environmental consciousness in the 1990s.

In the past twenty-five years we have seen an exponential increase in the devastation of wild environments, the suffering of indigenous peoples, the loss of species, cultures, and languages, and the loss of a view of life as sacred. All this has led many in industrialized nations to seek a renewed understanding of our human sense of place in nature. While finding one's sense of place in nature is a deeply spiritual endeavor, Hazel Wolf's way of life was framed by neither religion nor science. She lived with her mind and senses open to the moment, when particular movements, colors, shapes, or sounds suddenly pulled her into the living universe. As a child, she did this through her adventures swimming, canoeing, running in vacant lots, playing games in the street. As an elder, Wolf experienced kinship with creatures, the way both animals and humans take moments to acknowledge their connection with the universe:

> I look out my kitchen window. Every morning the pigeons, and sometimes crows, get on the wire across the street and just sit there. When I've been out camping, I've noticed that very early the birds will get someplace and sit, enjoying the morning. It's quiet. They have to spend all the rest of the day finding food. So when they get up in the morning, they just relax and enjoy the sun. I don't know what they're thinking about. I, too, like to sit, look at things. This is the side of animal life that Darwin overlooked. He didn't understand that birds have souls. I say it's a spiritual thing for them to sit and just bathe in the sun in the morning, whereas if they were true Darwinians they would be out foraging for food.

In almost every section of her autobiography, Wolf circles back to memories of herself and her neighborhood when she was a child. Neighborhood was the key experience and concept of her environmental practice. In her neighborhood, everything connected: water, beaches, hillsides, factory bosses, single mothers, prostitutes, drunks, stars, stones, herons, logs, mosses, fish. Wolf framed environmental issues by asking, "Who is my neighbor?" She acknowledged that it takes practice to remember to ask that:

> You get pretty proud. Arrogant. Egotistical. But, you know, everybody's pretty special, even heads of corporations. People panhandle up on Broadway. Sometimes I give them something. Sometimes I just smile at them and walk on. This time I was approached while I was waiting for a bus by the most disreputable-looking guy you ever saw. Old. Dirty. Blood on his face. Filthy hands. And he wanted some money. So in my haphazard way, I thought: "I'll give him a few coins." I picked a quarter and a couple of dimes out of my purse. I held them in my hand. He held out his hand. And I'm not going to touch that filthy hand, see. I'm just going to let those coins drop into it. And then, just as I was about to do it, it came to me in a flash:

"Who in hell do I think I am that I can't touch this man's hand?" So I opened my fingers and grasped his hands, and put my other hand underneath. And then he looked at me, for the first time he looked at me. We looked at each other, with our eyes, and we started to talk. I missed three buses talking to the guy.

Acknowledgments

$\mathcal{M}$any of Hazel Wolf's friends gave me interviews, read the manuscript, and provided anecdotes and insights.[1] I thank all of you who, devoted to Wolf and to conservation, encouraged and helped me. To Nydia Levick and Ann Sargent, Hazel Wolf's daughter and granddaughter, I owe the greatest thanks for their time, patience, and trust. Karen Blair encouraged me to begin this project, and then, twenty years later, gave it her crucial support. Jody Burns, Julie Mello, Brian Price, Marilyn Smith, and Trileigh Stroh prodded me and read early drafts. A stay at Hedgebrook Women Writers' Retreat, in Langley, Washington, made a book seem possible. Bob Grant guided me through the Seattle Audubon Society, and Helen Engle of the National Audubon Board never lost faith. Margaret and John Scarborough, Deborah Greene, and Karl Thuneman helped me craft my writing, as did the Hedgebrook Women Writers' Group (Judy Bentley, Rosemary Gordon, Terry Miller, Janine Shinkoskey Brodine, and Kate Willette). Pat Coburn, James Jack Johnston, Laura Kaluba, Lorraine McConaghy, Melanie Noel, and Steve Zander transcribed or read chapters. Anna Balint's talented engagement with the text helped me shape a long narrative into stories. Stanley Rosenberg edited an early version of the manuscript and even knew the Communist Party songs. Chris Peterson, the executive director of the Seattle Audubon Society, inspired me with her love for Hazel Wolf and for this project. Marilyn Trueblood, Xavier Callahan, and Kris Fulsaas, on behalf of the University of Washington Press, gave their disciplined attention to the project. Finally, my parents, Mr. and Mrs. Fletcher P. Thornton, gave me support when it was most needed.

1. [Although Hazel Wolf died in January 2000, the interviews in the appendixes retain the speakers' present-tense narratives.—Ed.]

Hazel Wolf

FIGHTING THE ESTABLISHMENT

PART I

Ready for Adventures: 1898–1914

If anyone told me "no" when I was growing up,
that's when I was most apt to do it.

Hazel Wolf was born on March 10, 1898, in a Victoria, British Columbia, hotel. Her mother was an American, born in Paoli, Indiana, and her father was an immigrant to Canada from Scotland. The couple had left their home in Tacoma, Washington, just two weeks earlier to ferry the seventeen miles to Victoria. Wolf's birth in Canada made citizenship an issue for her from the start.

Wolf begins her autobiography with her signature story, "The Bogeyman," in which as a child she defeated the scare tactics of her Victorian parents and set off on a life of jaunty fearlessness. For 101 years, she challenged barriers and threats, right up to her confident confrontation with the ultimate bogeyman, death, on January 19, 2000.

Political, not psychological, theory informs Wolf's childhood stories: she was not in the least interested in analyzing her family-of-origin issues. For insights into human nature, she relied on the British poetry she had memorized in Canadian public schools. Rather than a journey of self-discovery, Wolf's life unfolds as the application of principles she gained early in life. From her family and neighborhood she learned her responsibility for the community, her freedom and playfulness, her understanding of the role of the working class in history, and her experience of unconditional love.

Water was Wolf's medium: diving, swimming, paddling, rowing, active, fluid, present, quick, constantly in motion at the center of a gang of friends. On land she was running across vacant lots in search of blackberries, clambering over fences to steal peas and potatoes, biking all over the city, or hiking to the lakes and beaches of Vancouver Island. Wolf's unromantic wholeness with nature makes Part I key to her autobiography. She experienced as a child what she later articulated as an environmentalist: there is no split between nature and culture. We humans cannot "save" wilderness or the environment as if they were entities separate from us. There is no "intelligent" human fundamentally distinct from other forms of life. We are part of nature, and it is us.

Wolf spent much of the first sixteen years of her life running with her gang in immediate, sensuous contact with water, earth, wind, and rain. Her sense of self was rooted in her confident physical presence in the social and natural worlds. Knowing herself as creature of both nature and the working poor, she never let her social status interfere with her ultimate sense of her possibilities.

In her childhood stories, we see Wolf the mature activist who kept the interconnected universe in mind: everyone she worked with on both sides of an issue became her friend. There was no separation in Wolf's practice between the personal and the political, the spiritual and the practical, or between individual and community interests.

1 / My Family

THE BOGEYMAN

I was born fighting the establishment: I was told I tried to bite the doctor when he smacked my behind to start my breathing. Hazel Anna Cummings Anderson—I never did like being named after a nut.

As a child, I was very self-willed. In the first picture taken of me as a baby, I am old enough to stand up and hang on to the edge of my crib, and I look real perky. My father wrote on the back of this picture in Spencerian script—it was supposed to be very elegant—"Ye sow the wind, ye reap the whirlwind,"[1] which indicates to me that, one, my father had a sense of humor and, two, I must have been a hell of a kid!

My mother, like all parents at that time, tried to discipline me with the Bogeyman. I remember this stormy night. I was real small, maybe four or five, and I don't know what I did, probably wouldn't go to bed or something awful like that. She said the Bogeyman was out on the front porch with a big sack and was going to take me away if I didn't do this and this and this. And I'd had it, that night I'd had it with this Bogeyman. I opened the door to check it out and there's nothing out there, nothing. And that taught me something that I needed to know: the Bogeyman is never there. So I open all the doors.

I remember I was scared, and I half expected he might be out there, see. It was a real act of courage that night. But it really destroyed any effect of my mother's threats from then on. I called her bluff, or I just paid no attention to her.

She tried spooking me again when I was a little bit older. I liked to sleep out on the beach in the summertime when we were camping. I'd make a little place in the sand, well away from our tent on the edge of the beach. My mother was worried about my sleeping out there and she tried to get me not to do it. I wouldn't pay any attention to her. So she cooked it up that one of the neighbors would put on her husband's clothes and come in the dark to menace me. I woke up, and here's this "guy." I grabbed a bunch of rocks and yelled, "You better get out of here or I'll throw all these rocks at you." Well, the impostor didn't want to be stoned, so she left. Pretty near sent her to her death. I went back to sleep. I wasn't letting people spook me. I wouldn't tolerate it.

I must have been a terrible child. I was into all kinds of mischief, but not bad mischief like stealing. In the rough neighborhood where I grew up, a lot of the kids ended up in reform schools and penitentiaries. I ran with that gang, but I never got into serious trouble.

I never was afraid of spankings, but I didn't like to be physically mauled like that. To me, they were an outrage.[2] And they inspired me to ever higher heights of misbehavior, to show that it didn't do any good at all. My brother, on the other hand, was so sentimental that when he got a spanking he felt really bad about it and he was a good boy for a long time afterward. My sister was a timid person, afraid of spankings. To avoid them, she would tell lies and do all kinds of sneaky little things. I grew up with this fabulous reputation for never telling lies, and I was above telling lies, not because I was noble, but because I wasn't the least bit afraid of what would happen to me if they knew the truth. That's my cynical way of looking at my morals and virtues as a child.

I decided to put an end to my mother spanking me. I thought: "I'm not going to cry. Let her swack away." So I stood there. She spanked and spanked and spanked. No tears, no emotion. Boy, that took the heart out of her. And she never tried again. She was a reasonable woman. She could see that I didn't give a damn whether she spanked me or not, and that spanking wasn't going to deter me from future crimes. There was nothing she could do to stop me, nothing.

There were times when I would come into conflict with my mother, and I would come to the conclusion, as children often will, that I really wasn't her child—that I was adopted, or found on the doorstep. I wanted nothing to do with the whole crowd, and I'd run away. But I always fled in such a way that I would soon be found. And I never came back on my own. I was always brought back with my honor intact. Basically, I wanted to throw a scare into her.

One time I left, and I was not ever going to come back home again as long as I lived. I knew what I was going to do, because I'd been reading G. A. Hente stories. G. A. Hente was a popular English writer for children, presumably for boys, and the boys in these stories had tremendous adventures. They went right across South America, trapping birds, picking berries, and making little tree shelters. So I always daydreamed about catching fish and living off the land and having these adventures. This time I really was going to do it. It was late in the afternoon but still broad daylight. I thought, "No, I'll start out in the morning. No use starting out now." I was over in the big field in back of our place, waiting for darkness. And darkness began to come. Instead of seeing shining roads and beautiful sunlight filtering down through the trees, it looked kind of foggy. I was getting hungry, too. Just about that time, my brother came over and told me, "Our mother says if you want to eat dinner, you better come home." I said, "All right," and thought to myself, "I'll still start out tomorrow in the morning." That ended that episode. I guess I was what they called a tomboy.[3]

MY MOTHER

Now I'll tell about my mother, Nellie Frayne Anderson, because my orientation was toward my mother, and I grew up in a woman-centered culture. Nellie. She hated that name. She said every cow and horse in the country was named Nellie. I know her birthday: January 4, 1872. It's about the only birthday that I remember. We used to save our money to buy her a present—something very impractical, as I look back on it, like a hair ornament that you'd wear in court. I always remember, when I wake up on January 4, "Oh, it's my mother's birthday."

My father was injured at sea. I have no recollection of the catastrophe that hit the family. I was only five when he became an invalid. It was an accident, and in those days there was no insurance for injured workers, no widow's pensions, no nothing. They just threw you ashore and that was the end of it. So my mother was left with this crippled husband, and she just got busy earning the living. She didn't have any education or any particular skill, but she did all kinds of things, from scrubbing floors to keeping boarders and nursing.[4]

As for my father, I always remember him in a wheelchair, or he walked with crutches. He lived five years after the accident and died in 1908, when I was ten years old. To me, childhood was fun, you know, but it must have been a bad time for my mother. We were very poor. I can only imagine that the poverty must have been pretty profound.

My mother was always moving, trying to find a better place. The more we moved, the more it was the same thing: miserable houses, prostitutes and drunks, very young and very old people left to their own devices in the streets. I was ragged and shabby, I'm sure, but I was robust and strong, a kind of leader with the kids. And I always felt secure because my mother was there. Even though she was out working, I knew she'd come home. It's important that children have a feeling of security. I think that money has very little to do with that, very little to do with that.

Oh, she did all kinds of things, all kinds of different things to make a living. She wasn't a nurse, but if they needed somebody to take care of an invalid, she'd do it. She would do housework. She worked in factories. I remember she was a salesperson in a cigar stand. She was always saying, "I want to keep the family together," because there was always the danger of having to send us away. And I remember thinking, "Why does she bother? I wonder what it would be like in a foster home or an orphanage?" I thought it would be an adventure, and I was ready for any kind of an adventure. But we were together, and as I grew older, I realized that was a tremendous gift. I told my brother and sister many times, "That's the legacy our mother left us."

Once I almost slipped away from my mother. Her sister, Sarah, my Aunt Sally, lived in Seattle and was quite well-to-do. I spent my summers with her. She had four children who were adults as far as I was concerned, because they were so much older than I was, and they lived in luxury compared to my beat-up old home. They even had a servant who at mealtime appeared out of the blue. I always wondered how he knew that something was wanted. The truth was that my aunt had a bell under the carpet that she would push with her foot, but I didn't find that out for a long time. They were very genteel, so every summer I had to change my personality completely when I went there. I couldn't use four-letter words. Not modern four-letter words, but the slang of those days: gosh, heck, gee-whiz, golly, and darn. She wouldn't tolerate that kind of vulgarity. I quickly adapted because I liked my aunt and my cousins. This family all doted on me, made a pet of me.

When things got really tough for my mother, there was talk about my aunt adopting me. So, okay, I went over to Seattle. I was all thrilled with the idea of being adopted by my aunt and basking in the love and admiration of these four cousins. I should have known, or they should have known from past experience, that I would get homesick sooner or later: on the summer visits, I would wake up one morning after a couple of weeks and want to go home. This time, I was there for much longer. I went to school—I was in the fourth grade—I don't know how many weeks. Then I fell in the schoolyard and sprained my shoulder. I really wanted to go home! And home I went.

My mother wanted me home, too: she had made this sacrifice, letting me go. I remember her telling me how often while I was away she had taken out a plaid skirt that I hadn't taken with me and put it up to her face and wept. Anyway, I was home, and my mother kept the family together. I shudder to think what would have happened had I stayed with my aunt and become genteel. An awful fate.

My mother was different. She came out into the street on summer evenings and played ball—no other kid's parent did that! Maybe she'd had a hard day's work, but she could still play with us. After dinner we played cards. We had a very short attention span and would start giggling and poking each other, and cheating, and it would annoy her to no end, so she would make cocoa and toast. And we were permitted to dunk the toast. I can picture her in front of the fireplace, down on her knees playing marbles on the rug that had a beautiful big dog woven into the pattern—it must have been hideous.

The fact that we didn't have much money didn't come into it. I didn't know anything about money when I was a kid. If I wanted any, my brother and I went around the neighborhood and collected beer bottles and sold them back to the brewery.

My mother had dark blue eyes and a beautiful voice. She sang when she was working around the house, so I know all those old ballads: "I'll Take You Home Again, Kathleen." What a nice guy he was in that song. She was homesick, and he was going to take her home. "Do You Remember Sweet Alice, Ben Bolt?" and "Annie Laurie . . . with a neck like a swan," and I could just see this long neck of the swan.

She earned some money singing, too. It was during the Klondike gold rush [from 1896–97 to 1907–09]. There was a saloon in Victoria, and in back of it was a theater, with box seats. The gold diggers would come back with all their gold from Alaska to this saloon. She often sang there with her lovely red hair and black dress—what a gorgeous dress, long! It flared out at the bottom from the whalebone that made it stiff. She was completely covered, and she looked beautiful. Now, this was a rowdy bunch, but she was totally different, and that's the kind of woman that guys liked to see, so they would throw money up on the stage. Once or twice I was allowed to go up in the balcony. All the women there were prostitutes—not that I had to avoid prostitutes. It was just no place for a kid.

For a while she worked in an overalls factory and was secretary of the iww [Industrial Workers of the World] union.[5] I'd go to meetings with her when I was seven, eight, and nine years old. When she got up to read the minutes and came to a word she couldn't pronounce, she'd spell it, and everybody would laugh. I come from a long line of secretaries.[6]

Mother was there. She was really with us. It's just a feeling inside, not a fact to be documented. We children didn't pay any attention to her jobs, and she never complained about the hard work. She was a social person, a live-and-let-live person. Lively, red-haired, left with three children, a disabled husband, and, finally, widowed, she simply rose to the occasion. I don't know why.

MY FATHER

I wasn't particularly fond of my father. Because he was an invalid for quite a while before he died, he didn't loom very large in my life except for certain things that he told me that I remember very vividly and that affected my thinking. Apparently he went a little deeper than a lot of people, somewhat of a brain. I can remember them saying, "He's never without a book in his hands." I have a certificate from the high school in Sterling, Scotland, where he got an award in English literature and physiology. He told me about the middle class, and I carried a grudge against the middle class for quite some time, until much later, when I realized I was probably in it. He laid a foundation for a global look at things. He believed in socialism, and he explained it to me. And I believe in socialism—believe me, I believe in socialism, despite the Soviet Union's failure. I hang on to that theory like grim death—but it's got to be democratic. Eventually, that's what we'll have.

My mother was a socialist, too. Well, I don't know that she believed in socialism, because she never voted. She said, "They're all a bunch of scalawags." She didn't worry about theoretical things, but he did.

He admired China. He thought it would be the agent of great good in the world at some future time, but that at the present time China was a great monster, asleep. When it turned over and woke up, we would see changes for the better. I had a vision of this yellow monster with a big grin on his face turning over, saying, "Here I am!"

Another thing he talked about was religion. I have an image of my father by an open window in a room that was sparsely furnished. I was quite young. I don't remember what he looked like, but I can see his hand, the fingers spread out. He was telling me how many people there were in the world. At that time there were probably a billion. On his hand he pointed to one finger and he said, "Just a very small group are Christians, a very small group. The rest of them all believe in something else: they're Muslims and Buddhists and Confucians and other things. And this minority of Christians are in turn split into many different factions. There's the big split between Catholics and Protestants. And the Catholics have a split between the Roman Catholics and the Greek Catholics. The Protestants are split into Methodists and Baptists and all the other denominations, each one thinking that if you do not follow their theory you won't get to heaven." Then he summed it up by saying, "So what makes you think that some little sect in a minority religion has the truth, to the exclusion of all the rest of the human race?" And I thought, "Well, the arrogance of one of these little tiny sects thinking that they have all the knowledge!" That shattered my belief in Christianity forever. So I grew up like he was, an atheist.

Nobody in my family went to church. My mother had no time for fussing around with religion. She just worked all the time. Besides, I don't think she was even remotely interested, not a reverent person. When things got tough, she would chant, "Oh, don't it beat hell how Jesus loves me." Another thing she used to say was, "God said to Moses, 'Come forth,' and he came fifth and lost his job." So I was never sent to church. In fact, I grew up without prejudice against religion, which is a nice way to grow up. "Each to his own."

When my father came home injured, in 1903, he had a very short fuse and was in such pain that he took laudanum [tincture of opium] to ease it. He tried to beat us children from his wheelchair with a cane. My mother threatened him: "If you touch one of those children, you're out of here."

She separated from him around 1907, and he got his own place down the street. I saw even less of him. When he got bedridden, in 1908, she let him come home and nursed him until he died that year.

I barely remember my father's funeral, though if my mother had died I would surely have remembered hers. In those days, death was really pretty exciting. People put a black thing on their door, a rosette with long ribbons. The men wore a black band on their sleeve. The women wore black dresses for a year, then they graduated to purple, and then finally they came out of it. When there was a death in the family, you just retired out of sight, presumably to grieve.

Now, I wasn't particularly grieving about the death of my father. I wanted to go out and play. My mother wouldn't let me, and I was chafing at the bit because I had to stay in. I remember the people going up and looking in the coffin, but my mother had me stay there in my seat and not go through that.

He had been a sick man and cranky. Undoubtedly I didn't like him too well. One time he wanted me to bring home a newspaper. We might have been having some trouble, so I was mad at him. He couldn't get it himself because he couldn't walk, and I wouldn't bring it to him. I just wouldn't bring it to him. I must have been stubborn—I wasn't that easy a child to raise. Later I realized that was very cruel, and it gnawed on me. I regretted it. So after he died and was buried, in order to appease my conscience, I took a newspaper out and laid it on his grave.

MY ANCESTORS

My Great-Grandmother Anderson was probably born in the early 1800s, and I think it is very remarkable that I have had physical contact with her and also with my great-great-grandchildren, who will probably live to the late twenty-first century. I've touched seven generations, spanning almost three centuries. It's a long stretch, isn't it, that I reach that far back from those days and then beyond it? I was born March 10, 1898, in the Dominion of Canada, during the reign of Queen Victoria. I'm not sure, but I think

Thomas Jefferson was president of the United States: I haven't finished the research.

I was conceived in Tacoma but born in a hotel in Victoria, British Columbia, under "Old Glory," as my mother called it, because she was an American woman and very patriotic. She didn't like the idea of her child being born on foreign soil, so she had a flag hung over the bed. Not many people are born under the American flag.

My mother lost her citizenship when she married my father, a Scottish immigrant to Canada. Both in Canada and in the United States, women lost their citizenship if they married foreigners, and that law prevailed right up until 1922. After that, women could marry without losing their citizenship, and they could get their lost citizenship restored very easily with a simple application. My mother had hers restored when our family moved back to the United States, in the 1920s. They did all kinds of things to women in those days: identity, citizenship, all wiped out when they married.

I was born Canadian, but on the matter of nationality, I always contended I was half Scotch and half soda water. My mother didn't like me to say that, because she was the half soda water. She considered herself an Irish American because her father considered himself an Irish American. They always go by the male line and forget that there is all this female coming in, which could be all kinds of things.

I had always understood that this Irish American father of hers was born at sea. It was hearsay. Recently, I found out from a long-lost cousin that this guy was born at sea in 1830 on the way from Ireland to the United States. I began thinking about that. The name was originally DeFrayne, and they were Huguenots from France.[7] They fled France to Ireland in 1685, penniless. For the next century and a half, they must have been ganging up with the native Irish, fighting the British. Now, in 1830 it was a long and very perilous trip across the Atlantic. Nobody in his right mind would bring a pregnant woman onto a ship, knowing full well that the child was going to be born at sea. So they weren't escaping starvation—no—they were escaping persecution. I figure that's why they left in a hurry. They were on the lam.

That was my grandfather, Richard Frayne, born on the ocean. They dropped the "De" somewhere in the middle of the Atlantic. Legend has it that he became a doctor who left the South before the Civil War because his leanings toward the Northern cause made him unpopular there. I do know as a fact that he was a soldier in the Union army, a captain, and that he came from Kentucky.

After the Civil War, Capt. Richard Frayne settled in Paoli, Indiana. Nellie, my mother, was born there on January 4, 1872, the youngest child after her three siblings, Sarah, Howard, and Robert.[8] Nellie's mother, Eugenia Frayne, died in June of that year as a result of my mother's birth, so my knowledge of my grandmother Eugenia was stopped cold. I suppose she kept house and took care of her children. Women did that in those days.

The motherless Nellie was farmed out among relatives in Kansas and Kentucky. She used to tell us that in Kansas cyclones would come, and the people would all go down in cellars. And in Kentucky she had a mammy that tucked her into bed and kissed her goodnight. My mother's education was restricted to fourth-grade level, not unusual for women in those days.

After his wife, my grandmother, died, Captain Frayne came west in the early 1890s, bringing all four children and settling in Puyallup, Washington, where he opened up a hardware business in partnership with Ezra Meeker.[9] Captain Frayne died and was buried in Coupeville, on Whidbey Island, in 1893, so I never knew him.

Sarah was fifteen years older than Nellie and looked after her. I think my mother was repelled by the stern moral stance taken by Aunt Sally, as I called her. Apparently, they drifted apart. Nellie supported herself as a waitress in Tacoma, where she met and married George Anderson.

Now for my father's side, the Scotch half of my Scotch and soda. My father's father, George William Cummings Anderson, was a marine cook.[10] Unfortunately, I didn't inherit his skill. He died before I was born. He had the rank of sergeant, and he cooked for the 43rd Highland Regiment that traditionally staffed (I refuse to say "manned") the Fort of Gibraltar. His son, my father, was born on Gibraltar, May 24, 1869. My father and his brother and two sisters were christened by the Presbyterian chaplain: I have the certificate. When he was a young child they returned to Sterling, Scotland, their home castle, where he grew up. The whole family migrated to Victoria, British Columbia, from Scotland when my father was about twenty years old. Isn't it funny that I can dig these things out?

My father was a seaman, too, a sergeant in the merchant marine, and he, too, was named George William Cummings Anderson. He must have shipped into Tacoma and met my mother at her job as a waitress. They were married in 1894. He was at sea when my birth was hard upon them, so my mother crossed over the border and stayed with my father's parents in Victoria to have someone to care for her.

I remember that grandmother in an apron, a very white, clean apron, tied in the back. I didn't like her. She was kind of harsh. She died, fortunately. Pretty soon my mother had a falling out with these relatives of my father's, and I never knew them, although I dimly remember my great-grandmother, a real old lady, who spoke entirely in Gaelic. She never said "cry," she said *greet*—I remember that one word of Gaelic. My father knew a lot of Gaelic. He called me his little *cuddie,* which is "donkey." I must have been stubborn.

All good Scottish people were baptized—even I was baptized, my grandmother saw to that. She died before the other two children were born: my brother, George William Cummings Anderson, in 1901, and my sister, Dorothy Patience Cummings Anderson, in 1903. So they weren't baptized, and they are not going to go anywhere in the hereafter, just me.

SONNY AND DOT

*M*y brother's name was George William, but he was always called Sonny. He and I were pretty much inseparable. We quarreled, but between quarrels we were real buddies sharing adventures. We would build a ship in the kitchen with chairs, then we'd sail along for a while until we met a disaster and had to jump off the ship, shouting, "Aberdoon the ship," because we didn't know how to say "abandon." When we pretended that we were loggers, both of us wanted to be called "Bill." "Bill" seemed like a good working-class name to me. He would say, "Let go of the hose, Bill" or "Take this ax, Bill," and so would I. Fortunately, the name stuck with him, not with me.

He was very handy as a young kid, and he made a lot of money fixing bicycles. He picked up old bicycle frames in all kinds of places, straightened them out, painted them, put wheels on them, and sold them. His workshop was in his bedroom. A big frame up on the wall was made into a toolbox and filled with all kinds of tools. He was always fixing my bicycle, but I never paid him. It wasn't a matter of principle. I just had other things to do with my money. I would say, "If you fix this once more, I'll pay you," and I never did. On the day of his death he said, "You know, you owe me a lot of money."

My brother was three years younger than me, and my sister was five years younger. Five years when you're little puts them out of your game altogether. So I ignored her. I never had to look after her, probably because I refused to do it. I remember her saying after she grew up that she never remembered my striking her. I said, "Well, Dot, you were beneath my notice, that's why." I didn't mind pounding my brother, but I was not going to hit a little kid five years younger than myself.

She was born premature. There was a big stirring in the family that I was only vaguely aware of as she was between life and death. She was a seven-month-old baby when we almost lost her to whooping cough. She couldn't get her breath. She'd whoop and get blue in the face. I can remember them swinging her by the heels, the way they did it in those days. Maybe she didn't die in spite of it. She was kind of fearful because of her frailty.

She grew up liking fine clothes and dancing. As we grew older, her friends were not my friends. I had contempt for people who dressed up and went to dances. She was very artistic and created marvelous dresses. I remember one: it was dark, with a huge embroidered cobweb and a little spider up on the shoulder, beautiful on her, but on me it looked funny. If I wanted to get a laugh, I'd put on one of my sister's dresses.

She also made pretty things, like lampshades and a whole series with driftwood—a lot of potential talent that was utterly undeveloped. I think she would have gone a long way had she been in a walk of life that would have sent her off to art school. Dorothy was the spitting image of my mother, with really red hair, blue eyes, and a sense of humor, too. And my brother, well, nobody had ears that stuck out like that.

MY WOMEN'S LIB PHILOSOPHY

I never wanted to help my mother in the house, doing women's work, and never wanted to cook anything for my little brother, but I did anything in that line for my sister because she was a girl. Here's an example of my women's lib philosophy. It's a disgraceful episode, and I hate to tell it. My mother left home one morning and told me to cook breakfast for my little brother. She never should have done that, because I didn't think that was a woman's work, to cook breakfast for her brother. Why didn't he cook for me? I never spelled that out in my mind, but I knew that I just didn't want to cook for that guy. So I sent him to the store for something. Then I sent him back again, but he wouldn't go. I said, "All right, then, I won't cook your breakfast." There was a woman, Stella, who had housekeeping rooms in our house. One door of her apartment led into our pantry, and the other door led out into the hall. She looked in and took pity on my brother. She said, "You come in here and have breakfast with me. I have some trout." My scheme to keep my brother from having breakfast was falling apart at the seams. I was frustrated, lounging in the doorway of the pantry, watching them eat, and suddenly I got a fiendish idea. I grabbed a whole handful of salt, and I ran in there and dumped it on this trout. Then I ran out the other door and escaped. My mother came home and told me that I would have to tell Stella that I was sorry, or else. So I went in and said, "My mother told me to come in and tell you I was sorry or else she'd beat me up."

I remember another incident that sort of fixed my women's lib philosophy. It was Halloween, and we were all disguised. I was with a gang in the neighborhood, going around. It wasn't "trick or treat" in those days. It was just tricks, and some of them were pretty bad—taking off people's gates, rocks through windows—and people got injured. That's why the adults changed it to "trick or treat." For some reason, this bunch I was with had to run, and all the girls screamed. I noticed: girls scream, boys don't scream. And I never screamed again. I had no idea of leading a big fight for women's rights, or anything of that sort, no idea at all. I'd heard about suffragettes, and I wasn't tremendously interested, but I've fought my little individual battles all my life.

There was another very important incident while I was a young child. This was in Seattle, while I was with my Aunt Sally. My aunt had a friend visiting her whose name I don't remember, but who had a memorable influence on me. She and I were picking blackberries in my aunt's yard. An enormous big spider appeared, and I said, "Ugh, look at that ugly spider." She said, "Now, now, I wouldn't say that. Amongst spiders she might be a very handsome creature." And I never forgot that. I never see a spider but what I don't sit back and admire it, especially if it's a big one.

2 / The Gang

THE GORGE

I looked like my father. His brother was a barber and looked just like him. After my father's death, I went to the barbershop. When I saw my uncle, I was looking right into my own eyes. I was like my father temperamentally, too. I wanted to be a seaman—crazy about boats—just like he was. I would get out of bed at night and sleep on the floor because I thought sailors slept on the deck. I liked to be in the water, even just my hands: I didn't like to cook, but I loved washing dishes.

I loved storms. Victoria faces the ocean: it's a straight shot for the wind, from the west through the Strait of Juan de Fuca and, bang, into the city. Great big rollers of storms would come up and, oh, would I get excited. I would go down to the place where the waves crashed onto the rocks, and as they receded, I'd run after them, watch to see when the next ones were coming, and then run back to the shore. I was challenged to see if they could catch me. How I ever survived my childhood, I'll never know.

It was hard to avoid swimming if you were a child in Victoria then. Sooner or later, you'd fall into the water and learn how to swim. Three miles from the harbor, the inlet that goes up through the city becomes very narrow. It is called the Gorge, the French word for "throat." It was very special to us children, with a bridge across it. We swam on both sides of the Gorge, and sometimes we went through it on the riptides. There were maybe eight or nine of us, and we were great swimmers. We'd go to the Gorge every day after school. I'd take the streetcar or go out on my bicycle. We even swam in the winter. It was fearfully cold. Sometimes the water was frozen up at the other end. We just jumped in and out again.

I avoided boys my age and went around with my brother and a gang of younger boys. I remember this gang best when I was about twelve, in 1910. People my own age were too mature. I was small for my age and looked much younger, and I didn't develop early. I actually liked girls better, but their ways bored me—sitting around, playing with jacks or dolls.[11] I liked the things that boys did, though I never, I repeat, never wanted to be a boy.

The Gorge was way out of the city and very beautiful. The tourists used to come out by streetcar and head down to the lovely beach. On the way down, there was a Japanese tea garden where they could get tea and ham sandwiches for twenty cents. Then, before they went down to the beach, they would walk onto the bridge and see this very lovely current that went under it. The whole streetcar would empty of tourists, and as soon as they arrived at the bridge, Billy Muir and Buck Calder, who were great divers, would be standing on the railing making ready to dive—but "Augh," they had to get back, it was frightening. They dared not dive. We'd be down below to egg them on: "Come on, now, you know you can do it." "Okay, okay," so they'd get up on the railing again, but "Oh no," they were scared. So then we'd say, "Look, we'll give you a dime if you jump off that bridge." "Okay." They'd get up there, but "Naw," they couldn't do it—they were scared, they were scared. "Come on," one of the tourists would say, "I'll give you a dime." Pretty soon we'd get the crowd interested in this dime business, and after we got all that we could shake out of that bunch, the boys would make one of their beautiful dives. Then we'd work the next streetcar, until we each had twenty cents to go and buy a ham sandwich and a cup of tea at the tea garden.

When the tide was low, we'd go out on the rocks under the bridge and inflict ourselves with little teeny cuts on the barnacles. Now, when you get cuts in salt water, they bleed profusely. We would come up from the rocks streaming with blood, horrifying the tourists on the bridge with this gory mess. We had a certain amount of contempt for them. Then there was an old canoe. I don't know whom it belonged to. We'd turn it over, and four or five of us would get underneath it, and of course there's space underneath, so we could stay there a long time. All the tourists could see was a canoe drifting down, and there's singing coming from nowhere.

And the mudhole. Sometimes we'd cover ourselves with mud as a disguise, then we'd get buckets of water and make a charge and throw the water on the people sunbathing on the raft tied under the bridge. Then we'd dive into the water, which was full of swimmers, and the mud would all wash off. When we came up, nobody could tell who did it. I was always ready for adventures.

Not so many years ago, I read that they don't swim at the Gorge anymore. It's polluted. Something fell out of me when I read that they polluted the place where I played as a child! I don't think any pollution I ever heard of anyplace affected me like the pollution of that inlet in Victoria, because that was my very own, you know, that was where I grew up and had my being for so many years. I have a feeling that if I had stayed there, I could have seen to it that it didn't happen.

CLIFF-HANGERS

After a day in the water, in the evening the gang played wild games like Kick the Can and baseball, rough things that girls didn't indulge in, in those days. There was this empty field, a couple of back lots—it seemed like a vast prairie to me. We'd play cowboys and Indians. I was always an

Indian, and I always escaped. I was physically strong, good at the high jump and the broad jump, and I could run 100 yards in eleven seconds, which few boys could equal.

One of the things about survival in this world, I think, is knowing when to run. I had that timing down. It helped keep me out of real serious trouble. I remember one of the boys went around trapping butterflies with a long pole that had a loop and a net on it. Then he stuck pins in them and saved them in boxes. He was much older than I was. One day he was chasing this butterfly and I interfered so he couldn't catch it. Then he was after me. He didn't catch me, either. I could run like a deer. But every day, coming home from school, I had to watch out for this guy because I had cheated him out of one of his prizes. So I was willing to risk my life for nature.

Now, I didn't know one bird from another, one flower from another, one rock from another, and I never read nature books. I didn't learn anything about the particulars, but I wasn't afraid of anything, and I was concerned about living things. I didn't like to step on flowers. I released spiders when I came across them and they needed rescuing. I felt sorry for the worms that got washed out of the soil and onto the pavement when it rained. I used to pick them up, dig a little hole, and put them back into the earth.

> I would not enter on my list of friends
> (Tho' grac'd with polish'd manners and fine sense,
> Yet wanted sensibility) the man
> Who needlessly sets foot upon a worm.[12]

We had to memorize lots of poems in elementary school.

I didn't want to take life. I didn't even want to slap mosquitoes, but I did. Like the Indians, who always apologized to the animals they killed, I had those impulses.

Just a block or so away from our house there was a foundry. The gang had good relationships with the men who worked there. We would sneak bottles of beer from someplace and hand them up to the men through the windows. But there was an antagonism between the mill boss and our neighborhood gang. We were always teasing him, and he would chase us.

We had a curfew. We'd be out in the street after hours, then the cops would chase us home. There wasn't a cop on the beat who could pull up along behind me and catch me. And besides, we had all kinds of holes we could dive into, fences to go through, and cracks in the walls. We were very poor and lived in the downtrodden part of town. If we had been in the wealthy district, we would have been gently taken home to our parents. The cops were looking for trouble, so we figured we'd give them all we could, so as not to disappoint them. Some of the kids did things like stealing and breaking into places and damaging things, so they landed in jail.

When they planned an adventure that had a penalty attached to it, I'd always wiggle out before it started. My mother was a cut above the other mothers in the neighborhood as far as propriety was concerned, and that influenced me in knowing right from wrong and consciously making decisions. She was an upright woman with a lot of self-respect. Having this middle-class background, she had all kinds of ideas about things such as table manners. You didn't drink your soup from the bowl. You tilted your bowl back. You always left a little soup, just a little. Now, out from under my mother's tyranny, I can eat my soup any way I want.

My mother had to work away from the home, and there were no "day people" looking after us. I think it was a good thing that we were neglected somewhat. She was not a strict disciplinarian. She vacillated, so we had to learn to be tough. It gave us a chance to grow, and we knew we weren't going to be clobbered.

My mother worried. She thought I'd come a-cropper, but what could she do? I remember there was a cliff about 300 feet high on the beach along the sound. A little dog landed on a ledge—I don't know how it got up there. I went up to rescue that dog. It was very dangerous, but everything would have gone fine if my mother hadn't come walking along the beach at that moment, and here's her darling daughter up there with this dog hanging around her neck, happily trying to bring it down from the cliff. It was things like this that worried my mother more than anything else. She would have worried if my brother did that sort of thing, too.

Another time that same dog—it wasn't even my dog—got caught in the tide and couldn't get back in, so I went out after it. On the other side of the bay was a fort, and the soldiers kept yelling at me, "Go back, go back!" But I couldn't—I had to get that dog. It just added a little spice to it, being able to show the soldiers that I could do it. So I swam out and started towing him back, and it was a real struggle, a real struggle to get out of that current. I didn't think anything would happen to me if I had got caught in the current, you know. After all, I wasn't going to go down. I would just have been swept out to sea, and surely somebody would have come along with a boat. Anyway, I got the dog.

Our most dangerous game was on the logs. There were big log booms in the bay [outside Victoria Harbor], and, of course, if a log rolled and you fell underneath, it would be the end of you. One day we were playing down there, and a woman called us over and said that she had lost a son on those logs, and would we please never play there again. We were just overcome, and we never did. But we still made boats out of them. That was the best fun. My brother and I would get a log, and with a piece of driftwood we'd paddle into the bay, our feet dangling in the water, out to the big ships moored [at a naval dockyard] in the Esquimalt basin's Royal Roads. The ships' cooks would throw us oranges.

The YMCA was looking for talent, and they heard about a bunch of rag-tail kids that were swimming all the time around the waterfront and the Gorge. So they invited the gang to join as a group. The gang was delighted—it was free tuition, use of the swimming pool, and all sorts of things—but they said, "What about Hazel?" "Oh, no way could Hazel come." The kids said, "Well, then, we're not taking it. You take Hazel, you take us all." So they had to take me. I was on the boys' 110-pound basketball team, and the only thing I couldn't participate in was swimming in the pool because the boys went in without their bathing suits.

We called ourselves the Y-O-U Club, but I can't remember what that stood for. Everybody paid twenty cents' dues. We brought cans of beans to eat and had weekly team meetings. I was the editor, my first editorial job, of a little newspaper at the YMCA, which consisted mostly of insults among the people in the Y-O-U Club. I also ran a continuous story. It was one of those cliff-hangers. I'd carry the story on until someone was literally hanging from a cliff or lashed to a railroad tie, one little episode every month, a preposterous story that nobody could take seriously.

I liked to skate on thin ice, reckless in a lot of ways. My mother told me later, "I worried more about you than you could imagine. I never, never understood you. But, really, I didn't have anything to worry about."

PROSTITUTES, NUNS, AND MUSIC

As a child, my first concern was swimming, biking, and playing, and I let nothing interfere with it. But I had other interests as well. I got my love for classical music early on from a boyfriend of a prostitute, Willetta, who lived at our house. He came up and brought records for her, not really for her but for himself, to play while he was there. He talked to me about the worth of this kind of music, and he gave me three records. One was Galli Curci singing "Brilliant Bird"—I could sing right along with her, no matter how high she went—and Mussorgsky's "Pictures at an Exhibition." I don't remember the other one. I played them and played them and played them. Later, when I was able to buy records, I bought those kind, and occasionally went to a concert.

The boyfriend had a bulldog. He paid me to exercise it, but I was not to let it go into the water. Now, the dog wanted to go in the water, so I let him. Then I would dry him all off. It was kind of mean of me. The boyfriend was a photographer. He took a picture of the dog alongside of me, and I'm doing exactly like the dog, pulling a scowl. I have on my black-and-white checkered jacket, which I put on in the morning when I got up and took off at night when I went to bed. I loved that jacket. One time I had a little padlock that I was fooling around with. I got it locked in the buttonhole of that jacket and couldn't get it out. So there it was, part of the jacket.

We lived in a tough neighborhood. The county broke up the red-light district and scattered the prostitutes all over the city. A lot of them came to live in our neighborhood, in housekeeping rooms, and they paid my mother walloping good money for them. They went to hotels when they had their clients, so we didn't have a lot of trade going on in our house. They just lived there. I was surrounded by these women and a lot of rough elements.

I remember their names: Willetta, Irene, Mary, Stella, and Dutch Violet. Prostitutes don't see children very much, and everybody likes young things. They were very sentimental women, and they made a big pet of me. I have a book up on my shelf that Willetta gave me: Lamb's *Tales of Shakespeare.* She wasn't so uneducated that she had failed to hear of Shakespeare. Later, her gift prompted me to read the original plays. The prostitutes at our house were very fine women and were attractive to men just as intelligent people.[13]

My education with the prostitutes was going along fine, but I had to go to kindergarten. My mother sent me to the Sisters of St. Anne, a French order. They had a boarding school as part of the convent,[14] but they also took day scholars. I'd be at St. Anne's only four or five months at a stretch, then my mother couldn't afford it, and back I'd go to public school. I had to change my whole approach, switching back and forth from one to the other, a skill that I've never lost.

Of course they had a Christmas festival at St. Anne's. The Sisters used to do what they called "tableaux," nativity scenes. They would put some kind of powder in a frying pan, set it on fire backstage, and that would light the whole scene up in red smoke. Then they'd put some other powder in the pan, and beautiful green lights would come over the scene. There would be the cradle, and the infant Jesus would be a doll, of course. There'd be angels standing around, and shepherds, and the three wise men. The curtain would open, and the pan would flare up backstage, and here's this beautiful nativity scene. I was an angel: big white wings, and a long white robe. I was so thrilled.

Right in the middle of all the rehearsals, news came that a bishop was going to visit the kindergarten tableau, so they were going to heat up the program a little bit on his behalf. Unfortunately, I had an unusually nice singing voice as a child. Sister decided that I would sing a solo, and I wouldn't be an angel—couldn't do both. Oh, I was upset. I wanted to be an angel so badly, stand there with these wings and that long white robe. They took my angel role away from me, for which I never forgave them. I must have known that was the closest I'd ever get to heaven.

I didn't want to sing for the bishop. The act consisted of my pacing up and down on the stage, holding a doll, supposedly my baby brother, and singing him to sleep with a lullaby. I was pigeon-toed, born with clubfeet, which my mother massaged into place somewhat. I'd worn braces as an infant and as a toddler. Eventually, I overcame this condition by roller-skating—you can't roller-skate pigeon-toed. But at this point, I wasn't cured. I'd walk up and down the stage, and the nun standing in the wings would put her hands together with her fingers pointed sideways to remind me to turn my toes out.

I was so rebellious, so rebellious, though I finally learned the song. The bishop was a big fat guy, and he sat in the front seat. I don't know what was so hilarious about my performance, but evidently it amused him to no end. I can just see him right there in front of me, just laughing with his great mouth and teeth. One of those minor tragedies. That's life, starting with kindergarten.

LEO

I went to a jillion schools. One time I went to a public school in Tacoma. I was over there visiting my Uncle Bob and Aunt Rose, my mother's brother and sister-in-law, and it was during school session, for some reason. I was bored and had nobody to play with all day by myself, just my aunt. I thought, "I'm going to be here two weeks, I will go to school." In those days, when you wanted to change schools, you just went in and sat down, told the teacher your name, and you were in. It's not that simple anymore. You have to have a serial number and a computerized résumé and God knows what all. I went in and sat down, and the teacher came right over to ask my name. Now, as I mentioned earlier, I never liked the name Hazel. I didn't like being called after a nut. I wanted to be called Rosemary, something pretty. I thought, "Here's a chance to change it," and it had to be done fast. Uncle Bob and Aunt Rose had a daughter named Leona, who was older than I was, and whom I worshipped. I probably had my cousin Leona's name on the edge of my consciousness, but I only got as far as "Leo." The teacher looked at me and said, "Leo?" "Yes." I said it, so I was going to say that was my name. She said, "That's a boy's name." I said,

"Yeah, I know, but that's my name." So I was Leo for the two weeks and I got to like it.

When I got home, I decided that I was going to change my name to Leo. My sister cooperated right away. I bullied and bribed and flattered my brother, but he still wouldn't cooperate at all. What really turned it around was that we moved. I went to the new school with my new name. When the kids came over and called for me to come out and play, they all called "Leo," and so my brother had to call me Leo. My mother was the last to give up, and she would have a throwback every once in a while. She'd say "Hazel!" and, oh God, I'd know I was in trouble when she reverted to Hazel. That's the story of my name.

VERY INTELLIGENT

*M*y cousins in Tacoma and Seattle were all older than I was, and they were very important to me. I visited them all the time. I came to the age when you become conscious of the fact that people have personal beauty or don't have it, and you wonder where you fit in: you realize it's important to be good-looking. I had a cousin, Lois, one of Aunt Sally's daughters. She was probably a senior in high school. I adored her. My nickname with that family was "Zed" because as a Canadian I always say "X, Y, Zed," like the English, and they thought that was funny. I distinctly remember asking her, "Lois, am I pretty?" And I can remember her looking at me critically and saying, "Zed, not exactly, Zed. But you look very intelligent." And from then on, I never wanted to be beautiful. I wanted to look intelligent because Lois obviously thought that was much more important than looking pretty. I think that was good to have somebody to set a kid on the right trail, not to be worrying about what they look like. I don't think I've worried since!

Things went fairly smoothly until 1914, when I was sixteen. I reached the age when little girls were to transform into young women. One was suddenly supposed to become sexy. At this age, one donned an array of clothing equipment: corsets, which were strangling garments reinforced by bone ribs, with really heavy steel ones in front and back; high-heeled and pointed shoes; long skirts flowing to floor length; and hair no longer blown in the wind but held under control, piled high on the head with dozens of hairpins.

My mother bought me a corset, insisting that without it I looked like a sack tied in the middle. "What would a man think if he touched you and encountered uncorseted flesh beneath your dress?" she asked pointedly. I said, "I'd punch him in the jaw." Though I was very skinny, I buckled it on. I was so miserable. I climbed over a fence, and I broke one of those steel things. Then pretty soon I broke another one, and another one. And pretty soon I pulled them all out and stuck the lump of material in the drawer. It rested there peacefully for a while. My mother looked at me one day and said, "You have no idea how much better you look since you started wearing that corset." So I went into the drawer and pulled it out and said, "Oh, do I?" That was the end of that.

My mother and I had a running battle about shoes. Remember Sir John Suckling's verse describing the perfect woman?

> Her feet beneath her petticoat
> Like little mice, stole in and out,
> As if they fear'd the light.[15]

I can also remember Sir Walter Scott in "The Lady of the Lake":

> E'en the slight hairbell raised its head,
> Elastic from her airy tread.[16]

In an age when women were supposed to have tiny feet, I wanted only comfort. But here I was, stuck with these high-heeled shoes. They weren't spikes, but they were high. I was hobbling and unhappy. I started to school with them on for the first time, went through the gate in the backyard, and past the woodshed. Suddenly I had an inspiration. I went back to the shed, took the ax, and chopped off both heels. It ruined the shoes. So my mother didn't try that one again, either.

Floor-length skirts were another problem. For a long time I had worn my skirts about six inches below the knee—I could climb a fence with little trouble. Girls avoided me, their mothers frowned, and I knew I would have to give in and wear long skirts if I were not to become a social outcast. About the time I was reaching my point of despair came a gleam of hope. The fashions, under French leadership, suddenly decided to shorten skirts, not to thigh length as now, but to just below the knee. When I read this in the newspapers, I knew the fashions in the United States and Canada would soon follow suit if I could just hold out. And they did! Skirt lengths went up. Like the river song, "Men may come, and men may go, but I go on forever," fashions may come and fashions may go, but my skirts stay just below my knee.

No problem with my hair. The hairpins fell out, and my hair just flopped around my face. Hair was supposed to be women's crowning glory. "If God didn't want women to have long hair, He wouldn't have let it grow"—it went something like that. It was a moral issue. Then came the time when women cut their hair short. I was in the hospital with a boil that looked kind of dangerous. A snowstorm locked us in there. I wasn't sick, so I was running around helping the nurses. They wanted to bob their hair, but the superintendent said any girl who bobbed her hair was out. That threw them for a while. Then, one morning, the nurses came clattering, clattering in with bedpans and cans of water for the washbasins, and they all had their hair bobbed. Every one. They had bobbed each other's hair. The poor superintendent was stuck. She couldn't fire the whole bunch. So I cut mine, too. I wasn't burdened with too much hair, anyway. It never grew much below my shoulders.

Despite my rebellion against clothing, I think I was popular with the boys. The kids used to play kissing games at parties. My mother didn't approve of such games, and she wouldn't let me go to the parties unless I promised not to engage in kissing. Okay, so I go to a party. The boys all know that I'm not the kissing type, because I don't play the games. I hear them arguing at the foot of the stairs. "No, I want to take Hazel home." "No, I want to take Hazel home." Something about what I was doing they liked. I was pleased when I overheard this, but I was surprised. I had no idea that they would vie to take home a girl they knew they couldn't kiss. They could only get her home.

BASKETBALL

None of that deflected me from my real interest, however, which was basketball. When I was in elementary school, which went to the eighth grade at that time, girls were discouraged from doing anything along the line of athletics. I was all for outdoors and sports, and I thought we should be able to play basketball like the boys. So I went to the principal, Mr. Campbell, and asked him why girls couldn't play basketball. He said, "Girls don't play basketball." I said, "They don't have a ball, and they don't have any standards, that's why they don't play basketball." That kind of threw him. He said, "If you can find two teams, I'll provide the ball and standards. Come back and see me again sometime." That was in the morning. I had done quite a bit of planning before I went up on this thing, and at two o'clock that afternoon we knocked on his door. We had two teams. So he had to provide the ball and standards. Total victory. That was my first definite bit of organizing on behalf of women's liberation.

I remember the first game. It was raining, and the girls weren't used to holding a dirty old basketball—or any muddy old thing—and the ball was coming at them, and they were backing away from it. They had no idea of teamwork. If they got the ball, they would shoot regardless of where they were on the field, not pass it to a player who was more favorably positioned. Boys started in right away on basketball, so they knew teamwork. The girls were used to acting as individuals.

THE NEIGHBORHOOD

Our neighborhood in Victoria was kind of mixed. There were working people and there were people not producing very much. We children were running in the streets, but it wasn't because all of our mothers were working. Some were home—we just played in the streets and, later, all over the city. This was the dark ages: there were no electric lights, no Coleman lamps even, but it wasn't all bad. There were no automobiles, either, so we didn't have traffic to contend with. We played a lot of community-type games like Run Sheep Run, Fox and Goose, and Paper Chase, which took us scurrying around for blocks. Nobody came down to bother us. We didn't have anything worth stealing, I guess. We probably lived in the poorest part of the city, but it was still livable, a safe place, not like a real slum.

In our neighborhood we had plenty of immigrants from the old countries, quite a lot of Scandinavians. But, oh, we used to tease the Chinese. Really tease them. We threw snowballs at the windows of the Chinese laundry and took off running when one of the windows broke. Then, one time, the Chinese laundry sent back a very expensive pearl-and-diamond brooch that one of our renters had left on her blouse. It was tied right on top of the bundle. They could have kept it. I was impressed. I thought, "I'll never tease the Chinese again, they are so honest." And since I was a leader, nobody else teased them, either. I saw to that.[17]

We had no African Americans. None. In Victoria at that time, we discriminated against East Indians and against the French Canadians. Since India belonged to the British Empire, East Indians could travel anywhere within it. I remember when I was quite young a whole bunch of very tall East Indians came by with their turbans. They were hungry. They'd go from door to door asking for food. They were dark, black, great big guys. People were scared of them. My mother was, too, but she always gave them food. It was a long time before they melted into the economy. I don't know if they ever melted into the social structure. They seemed to gather around selling coal and ice, little businesses all over, just like the Japanese people went in for landscape gardening.

I stayed in touch with a lot of my childhood friends until they died, like Pinky. I have so many pictures of Pinky. She had very pale, pale gold hair. We visited with each other from the time we were about eight years old until she died, in the early 1990s. Our family lived at 626 Princess Avenue, in a row of houses, and Pinky's family lived in one of them. Her father, Mr. Tippy, was a subcontractor who put asphalt on all the streets of Victoria. Pinky had a brother, Claude, so Pinky and her brother and I and my brother used to play all the time with Mr. Tippy's truck drivers, who boarded at their house. When the streets of Victoria were all paved,

Pinky's family settled in Tacoma, where I had an aunt and uncle and some cousins, so I visited her over there.

Audrey Griffin and I visited each other until she died, in 1995. There's a set of pictures in which Audrey and I staged a three-act play at her family's farm, not too far outside of Victoria.

May Neilsson was another one. We used to go to the stock theater together every Saturday. We wrote and visited until she died. Her daughter, Andrea, and I exchange Christmas cards.

Neighborhood is the people of the community. All these kids in the neighborhood played together. Then we went to school together. And then we went to work and knew each other all our lives. We were very close. I always was coming back to the neighborhood. Most of the people were poverty-stricken and uneducated. A lot of them were heavy drinkers, and there were sick people and old shabby houses and things like that. I used to daydream about getting an education, learning how to build houses, then coming back to this neighborhood and redesigning all the houses and fixing them all up, you know. I'd just look up and down and gloat at these nice houses. Those are the kinds of daydreams I used to have.

And I often dreamed that I was saving somebody's life: people were in a burning ship, and I'd swim out with a rope and bring them all to shore. Or I'd save somebody from drowning. There was a background of an admiring crowd while I did this. Although I outgrew that solitary-hero business, I still wanted to be doing something for humankind. I wanted to be an architect, or a doctor, so that I could come back and cure all the people in my neighborhood. I wanted to go out into the big world and bring all these goodies back. Those people were my people. I respected them, and the neighborhood was home to me.

Why didn't I dream, "I'm going out in the world and I'm gonna learn how to become a great architect and, gee, I'll make a pot of money and then I'll have the great big house?" Why didn't I go down that avenue? No, I dreamed about going out and becoming a doctor, a person who knows how to deal with alcoholism, then going back and reforming all these alcoholic people. Of course, I couldn't ever dream in reality of becoming a doctor. The nearest thing I could ever be was a nurse, because no women were doctors.

The dreams I had as a child, I lived out in my adult life, just on a different level. I didn't go out in the world and become a great physician, but I worked on issues like health insurance. And I didn't become a great architect, but I worked on issues like low-income housing and welfare for the unemployed. So you see, I lived to realize all of my dreams.

PART II

Fighting for Survival: 1914–1931

... Switching from one world to the other, just like shifting on the typewriter, uppercase and lowercase. I got so there was nothing to it.

I wanted to steer. Charlie did not want me to, so I sat in the bow of the
boat. He had to let me steer as he could not see with me there.

I ended up being Hazel Wolf.

This section covers the years from Hazel Wolf's elementary-school
graduation through her emigration to Seattle, from adolescence to independent adulthood. There were several Hazels: one kept on adventuring,
another was a bookworm who valued education, and work was entirely
separate, engaging neither the adventurer nor the thinker. She was
"Hazel" to her teachers and employers, and "Leo" to her family and close
friends. All of these Hazels show up in her diary, a $4 \times 8 \times 1.5$-inch lined,
leather-bound volume written in a neat, round hand, chronicling every
movement of every waking day from June 1 to August 31, 1916, when she
was eighteen years old. This diary and photographs are the only artifacts
remaining from her early life.

In the prevailing style of the period, she wrote what she did and saw,
and excised feelings and reflections. With profound attention to detail,
Wolf recorded every event, person talked to, and shop visited, as well as
how many miles she traveled, the names of roads, bays, and beaches, and

how long she stayed in swimming. She wrote in short, strong, single-action sentences with active verbs. Though each day brought a new jumble of adventures and lost items, her life as revealed in the diary was as structured as a nun's.

3 / From School to Work

SCHOOL

I didn't get along with the public schools. They were very harsh, and I was opposed to this harshness. I fought them from the minute I got in there till the second I got out.

I was an indifferent speller, four or five errors a day. Some of the students got fifteen errors out of twenty-five words. Miss Dowler said that she was going to give them the strap the first time they did it, two slaps the second time they did it, and so on. I had never gotten fifteen errors, but from then on I did, every day—fifteen, sixteen, or seventeen errors. The first day, she gave me one slap, then two slaps the next day, and she knew that wasn't my normal pattern. When she got up to eight slaps, she could see that a year from then I'd be getting 365 slaps, and she wouldn't have time for anything else. So what did she do? Lifted her ridiculous law. I went back to my usual four or five errors. I beat the system, although I had to take some abuse from the rubber strap. It was about four inches wide, and Miss Dowler would just wang it down on your palms. But I'd perfected the technique of cupping my hands so it didn't hurt too much.

I wouldn't take my books home. I had this theory that people work eight hours a day, then they have a six-pack and put their feet up. I saw all the adults doing that. But no, I had to study after dinner. Well, I wouldn't do it, so I was a terrible scholar. I took the eighth grade twice.

I remember Mr. Campbell, the principal, who was also the teacher of the eighth grade. He'd give me my books and say, "Take these home now and study them." I'd say, "Okay," and I'd walk out of there, put them down on the bench in the schoolyard, and walk off and leave them. Some kid would pick them up and take them in to Mr. Campbell. I'd get strapped for that, but it didn't make any difference.

We all hated Old Man Campbell, so we got back at him with our taunts:

> There was an eagle going south,
> He had Old Campbell in his mouth.
> And when he saw he had a fool,
> He dropped him in the North Woods school.

Another one was:

> Old Man Cam, a fine old man,
> He goes to church on Sunday
> And prays the Lord to give him strength
> To lick the kids on Monday.

We'd tease him by murdering the British anthem. Instead of "God save our gracious king, Long live our noble king! God save the king," we used to sing, "God save our old tomcat! Feed it on bacon fat! God save the cat!"

Boys received harder and more frequent lickings from Old Man Cam than girls did, so I challenged the roughest boy in the school to a competition to see which of us could get the most lickings in a week. We both prowled around the school, doing various forms of mischief, and publicly totaled up the lickings we received. Still, Old Man Cam was giving that guy more lickings, and I was losing. At the end of the week, I took a bucket of water up to the third-floor window over the entrance of the school and dumped it on the students sitting on the steps below. The principal was right there looking. Well, the other guy still won, but I felt that I had really earned mine and just didn't get as many because I was a girl.

Much later, I actually met Mr. Campbell on the street. I apologized because I was such a nuisance to him when I was in school. He said, "Don't worry. I just couldn't deal with you. I was so packed with overwork that

I had no time to spend with individual students." There was no such thing as counseling in those days. Apparently he liked me. I was just one of these kids he didn't have time for. He was never a bad guy. He's the one who gave us [girls] the basketball and the standards.

Whenever my mother could afford it, she sent me back to St. Anne's Convent school. They accepted any student who could pay. She wanted to get me out of that rough neighborhood and away from all those prostitutes and whatnot. I could walk there, but it was a different world, a peaceful place where people spoke gently, softly. I just loved those Sisters. I wouldn't do anything to make it hard for them, but I had certain transitions to go through. I learned to say "good morning" to the Sisters when I saw them and bow my head courteously when I passed. You waited your turn. You didn't swear. I learned that was unacceptable in certain places. It's a survival technique, blending in with the scenery. Sometimes I even boarded. We slept in little beds lined up in a dormitory. The Sister would come in the morning with holy water and sprinkle it on you to wake you up for Mass. You got dressed and washed in the little basin, then you went down to the chapel. Now, the women in the Catholic Church had to wear hats. In the Jewish religion, the men wore the hats and the women didn't, because they were inferior. That's the way religion worked.

The nuns were disciplinarians, but they knew how to do it without demeaning the pupils. I was angry when students were disobedient. I couldn't see how they would act up with these nice women who were so different from the teachers in public school. I came home loaded with medals for good conduct, I was so good. I'm sure not all Catholic schools are that way, but that's the way it was at St. Anne's.

Then hard times would descend on my mother, and I would come back to the neighborhood. I had another transition to go through. I never had to say "good morning" to anybody—teachers of all people. I had to learn to swear again. I went back and forth like that several times, switching from one world to the other, just like shifting on the typewriter, uppercase and lowercase. I got so there was nothing to it.

I loved the nuns and the prostitutes, and I've thought since then that they have a lot in common. At one time, nuns were considered the leftovers of society, the rejects. They saw that they weren't going to get married, so after a certain length of time, if they were religious, they'd go into the convent. It was also used as a punishment for disobedience. Prostitution was another alternative to marriage. The prostitutes came from orphanages or poverty-stricken, miserable home lives. It was a very, very hard way to earn a living, and prostitutes didn't live long. They were constantly on the alert, police always breathing down their necks. If there had been a better way to earn a living, I'd say ninety percent of them would have taken it. From their point of view, scrubbing floors wouldn't have been a better way. It might have been from mine, because I couldn't have imagined submitting to all of those sexual abuses.

Getting from the eighth grade to high school was a terrible ordeal. All the eighth graders in the city, hundreds of students, assembled in a big high school auditorium for a public examination. With my record, a bunch of Ds and Cs and C-minuses, Mr. Campbell naturally told me, "It's no use your taking that examination. You can be excused." I decided that I would show him. I said, "I don't want to be excused. I want to take it." So I took my books home and studied every night until two or three o'clock in the morning, for two weeks. I remember laughing to the kids walking with me up the steps of the high school: "Don't anybody jostle me, or all this stuff that my head's poked full of will get knocked out." I came out fifth highest in the city.

There was no question about my going to high school. It was just understood that I had to go to work. Hardly anybody in my walk of life went to high school. My mother couldn't support me, and she needed the money. I suspect that the grade schools turned out better scholars then than they do now. We had just a few subjects—reading, writing, arithmetic, history, composition, grammar—but they really drilled us in those areas. I was fairly well educated coming out of the eighth grade, despite all my poor grades.

Deep down, I always had a desire for more education and a career that was more than a menial job, but I wasn't ready to settle down and become a student. That's an important point: that I aspired to higher education, but that I wasn't willing at that time to do anything about it. I was too busy having fun, playing basketball.

LEGAL SECRETARY

*W*hen I was fifteen years old, my mother remarried. My stepdad was Jacob Hughes, a Welshman whose ancestors ran away from the American Revolution up to Canada. They were called the United Empire Loyalists and highly honored up there. So now I was "Leo Hughes." Jacob was a salesman for a wholesale grocer, a German firm, so we were lifted out of some of that poverty.

Just after my graduation from elementary school, my stepfather got me a job in a candy factory. I was supposed to go and get an interview, but I kept putting it off and putting it off. I thought if I put it off long enough, they'd hire someone else. Under all this pressure from my parents, and with only two weeks left of the summer, I finally had to go to the interview. I sabotaged it but good. I said I'd be glad to take the job, but that when school started, in two weeks, I'd have to quit the factory to attend classes. I came home acting all crestfallen because I didn't get the job.

So my stepfather paid my tuition to a business college at St. Anne's Convent. He was really a very good person. It was a six-month course that began in fall 1913. That I liked, and I worked at it. I learned shorthand and typing, a foot in the door. I still couldn't spell, and I couldn't add up two and two. I was born left-handed, but the nuns tied my left hand behind my back and forced me to write with my right hand, so I couldn't write properly.

Sometime toward the beginning of the year 1914, my stepfather got me a job with a firm of attorneys for twenty-five dollars a month. In those days, you didn't have to have a Ph.D. to work in an office. If you could type and had a smattering of shorthand and a dictionary handy, you were equipped. Clerical work was a real step ahead of factory work in every respect: prestige, wages, interesting work, and the possibility of progressing.

I don't know why they paid me the twenty-five dollars a month, because I couldn't write a letter, and I typed forty words a minute, with frequent erasures. If it hadn't been for the two law clerks, I wouldn't have lasted a week. They would piece together what my shorthand notes were supposed to be telling me. My first dictation tape ended with the following sentence: "The defendant denies each and every allegation contained in the plaintiff's complaint." I didn't know what a defendant was. I'd never heard the word "allegation." I kind of knew what a plaintiff was. I had a terrible time, but it didn't disturb me very much. That job was just an intrusion.

I do remember one case: a young African American who tried to go to the Pantages Theater, and they wouldn't sell him a ticket. He hired the law firm where I worked, and he sued the theater. This Pantages outfit was American, and so tried to enforce the same segregation policies in Canada that they did in the United States. Our client won. There were laws against discrimination in Canada, so we got him a good solid settlement, too. I was interested in that. Otherwise, all I thought about was "When I get out of here, I'm going to get my bicycle and go swimming."

Next door to my office, an African American ran a shoe-shine thing, and he lived in my neighborhood. Sometimes I walked home with him at night. My mother found out and, ah, she was upset. She forbid me to do it. I just laughed at her. I said, "Look, all our lives you've been telling us about your mammy, how she tucked you in bed every night. Now, I'm not asking this guy to kiss me good night and tuck me in bed. I'm just walking home with him, and I'm going to continue to walk home with him." That quieted her down.

Out of the twenty-five dollars in wages from the law firm, I paid fifteen dollars to my mother for room and board, a five-dollar payment on a bicycle, and the rest for candy, no doubt. It didn't cost anything to swim, and it didn't cost anything to read, and it didn't cost anything to play basketball. And clothing was the least of my troubles, as long as I had a good bathing suit. It had a high neck, long sleeves, a little skirt, and bathing slippers. I was sixteen and quite childlike. From an adult point of view, I don't know that I'd have liked myself particularly.

SUMMER CAMP

*I*n the summer, people closed up their town houses and commuted to their work in the city from tents on the beaches. I didn't know families who had regular buildings for summer homes, not in my walk of life. I remember one summer we went out to Esquimalt, on the west side of Victoria Harbor. We had one big tent for our kitchen and living room, and two small ones for bedrooms. The beaches were just filled with tents.

On Sunday, people from the city would come out on the streetcar for picnics. They'd come down the steps onto the beach, and they'd stare at all these camps. People had names for their camps, so my mother made a big sign: CAMP TAKE A GOOD LOOK. The neighbor next to us saw it and made a sign that said CAMP TAKE ANOTHER GOOD LOOK. The third one down had a sign: TAKE A LOOK AT US TOO. Then we'd all sit there and watch the tourists come down. They'd look into the first camp, they'd see the first sign, and they'd be embarrassed, you know, they'd look away. But they'd look into the next one and see the second sign and get more embarrassed, and on down.

Some summers we'd camp on the beach on the far side of Esquimalt Harbor, on the Strait of Juan de Fuca. We'd see ships anchored out there. Every morning a fisherman named Art Featherbarrow would come and pick me up at the beach and row me across the harbor to the city side, where I'd catch a streetcar [into Victoria] to work. Then, in the late afternoon, he'd pick me up and row me back to camp. When it was too rough, he would phone me at work to warn me to take the streetcar all the way around. Well, I wanted it to be rough. There wasn't any place that I couldn't swim. I'd see the wind was blowing and know he was going to phone me, so I would lift the phone off the hook. He'd feel obliged to meet me on the city side to try to get across Esquimalt Harbor, and I'd get to ride in the waves.

SNICKLE FRITZ

They fired me from the law offices in early spring 1916. For thirty-five dollars a month, another girl agreed to do my job as well as keep the books of the law firm. I was not bitter about it. Unemployment was my chance to go back to night school to speed up my typing and take a little bit of

Latin—everyone studied Latin in those days. I worked at a great handicap because I had so little education. I was ignorant of mathematics, for example. The only thing I had going for me was my reading. I had acquired a knowledge of the English language, but I had a very poor opinion of myself.

My stepfather got me a temporary job in the Parliament of British Columbia, next to the Empress Hotel. I was in the basement, in a big pool of stenographers. When a legislator wanted to dictate, he'd send for one of us. Mrs. McAllester was in charge of the pool. She was passing by my desk one day and she said, "You insert the paper in your machine and manipulate your machine so cleverly. You just keep building on your natural gift, and you'll become a great secretary." Then I realized I was in a learning process. It was a turning point.

Only a couple of months later, my stepfather found me a job as secretary with the Dominion Public Works Department. The office had responsibility for maintenance of all of the public buildings that belonged to the Canadian government. It was a big barn of an office, with black Underwood typewriters lined up on the desks. Mr. Henderson was the resident architect. He was well over seventy years, appointed by an ancient prime minister at a time when retirement at a certain age was not mandatory, so he was there for life. Mr. Brown, his assistant, would step up into Mr. Henderson's shoes if and when Mr. Henderson ever stepped out of them. I don't know what Mr. Brown did meanwhile. Those government jobs were filled with political appointees, and that's what we were. We had absolutely nothing to do except get a big report out, which didn't take any time at all. Just little dabs of work. Everything came from Ottawa, all our supplies, even the ink. And because it would freeze on the way across the continent, it came in powder form. We'd have to mix water with it.

Mr. Henderson was a crotchety old Scotsman who didn't believe in eating lunch. We worked from nine to five, and every day when we ate our lunch, he'd say something mean about it. Finally I agreed with him. He was right—we shouldn't eat a lunch. I would forgo my lunch and leave at four o'clock instead of five o'clock. Well, I ate my lunch as I worked anyway. What could he do? We had made this bargain. He had to let me go at four o'clock, but I knew he really didn't want to.

I got a fabulous wage, fifty-eight dollars and thirty-three cents a month. Back in Ottawa they had made a mistake and given me the salary of the woman who left my position. She had taken eight years to work up to it. Mr. Henderson found out about this mistake and told me not to tell anybody. Then Thelma Gowan was hired and started at the bottom, probably twenty-five dollars. I didn't tell Thelma what I was getting, because they would just knock me down to twenty-five dollars, and she would gain nothing. Thelma was a socialite, really clothes-conscious. She and her friends dressed beautifully and went to dances and parties. At first I didn't like her because she was so fancy, and because her way of life was so different from mine. We sat opposite each other, and in a little while I realized that she wasn't stuck up. You wouldn't think we would have anything to talk about, but we did. We were great friends.

She thought I looked deplorable. In order to improve me, she designed two dresses and took the material and patterns to her dressmaker. I offended the dressmakers to some extent by insisting on having pockets put in. When they were finished, Thelma took me home with her, zipped me up in one of the new ones, did my hair, and put makeup on my face. She said I looked beautiful, but I couldn't stand that junk: felt just like someone had spread molasses all over me. I went right home and washed my face.

Somehow Thelma found out about my wages. She didn't talk to Mr. Henderson about it. She wrote to Ottawa. Instead of docking my wages, they upped hers, a happy ending. But Mr. Henderson was just furious. He detested Thelma after that. You know, you go through channels, and she should have gone through him. He always favored me anyway. He had a pet name for me: Snickle Fritz. I would threaten to quit if things didn't come out to my liking. I'd start to walk out of the place. Once I even got as far as the elevator before he called, "Snickle Fritz, come back in here." I'd come back, and we'd settle our differences.

4 / Not the Slightest Bit Boy-Struck

LEAVING HOME

I had nothing to do at the Public Works Department. I didn't want to knit, so I just started to write diaries, but either I got rid of them or lost them. The one remaining is just an endless round of activities. Up at 4 A.M. to go pick berries and to bed after midnight, having gone to work, gone swimming and rowing, practiced the piano, argued with my stepdad about the war [World War I], and then of course cleaned and whitened my shoes, which suffered tremendously during all these strenuous activities. The next morning I'd wake up and write: "I was a little tired."

Every so often I made entries like this: "The *Newington* came in today" or "Didn't see the *Newington*." The *Newington* was my first love affair, but it was all in my head. During the war, just outside of the [Victoria] harbor in the big Esquimalt basin, there was a Canadian navy cruiser, the *Newington,* on patrol all the time, I guess to keep out spies. When I was commuting to [the family's summer tent] camp with Art [Featherbarrow], we'd throw a line up to this huge boat, and it would steam over as close to the other shore as it could, dragging our little boat behind. Then Art would row the rest of the way to camp. We never got on board, but I saw a young crew member, a sailor. I had romantic ideas about him. I only spoke to him once, but I daydreamed about him, calling him "the little cabin boy." Really, I had a crush on him.

Thursday, June 1, 1916

Got up 8:00 A.M., went to work. Worked fairly hard. Came for lunch. On my way back I called at Dalziels'[1] and persuaded Ella to go swimming. Didn't see the *Newington.* Late for work. Got my check for $58.33. Met Ella and bought a pair of shoes to be stretched. Went to a store and put a $3.00 deposit on an ugly green coat. Walked to Ella's. Her mother did not want her to go so I fooled around and played ball with Bob and Harry and little Dorothy Jennings. Got out to the Gorge at 8:30 and found ladies' bathing house unlocked. Got undressed and I went in first and Ella followed. Was dressing when some kids locked us in but we got out a window. Started back to Ella's and I lost my small diary. I went home on the car and arrived at 11:30. Had some lunch and washed my hair. Was asleep about 12:00 A.M.

Wednesday, June 7, 1916
Yorkey [a friend of the Dalziel brothers] had a frisky horse but he let me try it around the block and then he said Ella and I could go by ourselves for an hour. My horse ran away but I managed to hang on. Some dogs frightened it. . . . The horses were tired out. Yorkey was not mad. He came home part of the way with me. I went to bed as soon as I got home; was tired out.

Sunday, June 25, 1916
Met the deaconess of the Centennial Church and she invited me to the launch picnic next week. . . . Went over to the Convent to see the Sisters. Went to Benediction with the nuns. Miss Sweeney took us to see the Convent Art Exhibit. Left about four.

Wednesday, Aug. 30, 1916
I wanted to steer. Charlie [one of the gang that gathered at the Dalziels'] did not want me to, so I sat at the bow of the boat. He had to let me steer as he could not see with me there. Nearly bumped into two logs. Went away out the harbor. It was rolling a bit on the water. Turned back nearly at Albert Rd. Coming back I nearly ran the bow into a tug. Got back to Pt. Ellice Boat House without mishap.

I wanted to stay out late, but my mother was always worrying about me. There was my big solo canoe trip to Esquimalt. I started home too late, and it got rough in the open sea of the Strait of Juan de Fuca. The wind was blowing, so I had to put a rock in the bow of the canoe to keep it from swamping. Darkness overtook me just as I got back into the mouth of the harbor; that was when the real trouble came. I couldn't tell where the land was. The harbor was just filled with lights, some were moving and some were fixed, and I couldn't tell which was which. I was paddling in darkness in this little canoe without a light, and I got panicky, real panicky. I was afraid that if I kept on going I would be bumped into by the hundreds of tugs and big ships going back and forth in all directions in the busy harbor.

I came up to a buoy and just grabbed it and clung to it. I thought, "I'll stay here till daylight. I just can't go on." Then I remembered my family wondering all night long what had happened to me. They would be terrified. They'd think I was dead. So I knew I had to go on. Fortunately, nothing bumped into me, and I got to the place underneath the bridge where I had rented the canoe. Well, half the neighborhood was waiting at the Dalziels'. My relatives, especially my mother, were frantic and more than a little displeased when I finally showed up. They thought I was a goner.

People who have reddish hair have a tendency for freckles, and I had a lot. Most people try to get rid of them. I loved them, just a passion for freckles, but all I'd do was burn and peel, burn and peel. On that canoe ride, with the sun blazing down on my face and arms all day, I thought, "Great, my freckles will grow and move just a little bit closer to each other, and I will have a nice tan."

I got a third-degree sunburn. When the peeling took place, all the freckles came off, and they never did come back. My mother phoned Mr. Henderson to say that I could not come to work till Monday. This led to my leaving home.

Friday, June 16, 1916
Ella phoned me up and asked me to get up at 4:00 Sunday morning to go swimming with her and Jim. I said yes. Mother said if I went I had to stay away all the time.

Saturday, June 17, 1916
In town we had ice cream at Stevenson's and on the way home I asked Mrs. Dalziel if I could board at her place. She said yes. After supper I phoned mother and said I was going to stay all night.

Sunday, June 18, 1916
It was so windy at 4:00 A.M. that we did not want to go swimming so we stayed in bed till 9:30. After breakfast phoned Mother and said I *had* gone

swimming so she said that I could not come back and to come and get my clothes.

I went to live at Dalziels' and there was pressure to come back home.

Wednesday, June 21, 1916
Mother phoned me and said Dad got a letter from the Executive Committee asking why I was not living at home as they have received a report to that effect. I think it was a put-up job between Dad and the Secretary to get me home.

Friday, June 23, 1916
Mother phoned and said the expressman was up for my trunk and she wanted to know if I thought I was doing right leaving home, but I said to send the trunk anyway. I felt pretty bad about it but I don't want to go home while Dad is there.

DAD AND MOTHER

*E*ven though I wrote in my diary, "I don't want to go home while Dad is there," my hatred of Jacob Hughes, my stepdad, wasn't going to cause me to leave home. He never had much to say about the three of us kids. My mother ruled the roost.

Jacob didn't abuse me. I abused him, from the day of their marriage up until long past this diary. He was a really good man, and he did his damnedest to make a friend of me. He financed my stenography training, and he found me jobs. But I hated him.

I was eighteen or nineteen years old when I realized what a creep I had been! We were at the beach. Jacob and I had a terrible fight. He said something derogatory about my father. I threw a cup of tea at him, then ran up the beach and hid behind a log. Now, I depended on him for a ride to work, but I was emotionally upset. He came out to the beach and kept calling me: "Jack. Where are you, Jack?" He used to call me Jack the Sailor, his pet name for me because I wanted to be a sailor. "Come on," he called again. "You've got to go to town. I'm going to take you to town."

And that's when I got it: after all I'd done to him that morning, he was still concerned about getting me to town! I didn't answer him. I just let him go, but I was conscience-stricken. For the first time, I could see what a good man he was to me. When I met him at lunch that day, I was going to tell him I was sorry. I was all primed. I felt kind of good about it, too. But before I could get it out of myself—because it wasn't easy—he started to tell me how wrong he had been. And that really got me, that really got me. I burst out into tears, and we became reconciled, and there was never any problem between me and my stepdad after that.

I was attached to my mother, and she to me. I was always getting home-sick. It was a traumatic experience, to leave the nest. I think it always is for young people. On Wednesday, July 26, I "sat down on the rocks for a while eating blackberries." This is the only time I sat down in the whole three-month diary. I wonder what I was thinking. I didn't know that much about my mother. I never asked her a lot of things that I wish I had. But whatever I was thinking wouldn't have shown up in this diary.

THE RACE TO THE GORGE

*O*ne of the things that amuses me in my diary is the day I made the three-mile swim from the harbor to the Gorge. That water was cold. It got warmer as you swam up the inlet. I always claimed I came in fifth. Everybody else said I came last because only five made it. I got a medal but I lost it. I probably would have come in first if it had been a longer race. I could just swim all day, it would be no effort—the water was just another element for me. Billy Muir and Buck Calder and I were like sea otters, in and out of water all the time. Billy was a champion diver, and Buck raced and also was a diver. He was a skinny little kid, black from the sun.

For many years they still held that annual three-mile swim up from the inner harbor. Now the swimmers grease their bodies, whereas we didn't have any such sophisticated goings-on. We plunged into that cold water and swam those three miles.

Saturday, August 12, 1916

The *Newington* is in. Practiced. Went out in the back and boxed with Ed [another member of the Dalziel gang]. Played baseball with Yorkey and Ed. Rode to work. The elevator man said my name was in the paper to swim from the Empress Landing to the Gorge Bridge. I then made up my mind to go in it. There were twenty-one in the race. Audrey [Griffin], Winnie [Painter], and I went to the phone and Ella said Ted and Curly Develin [a friend of the Dalziel brothers] would meet me on the way down from the Pt. Ellice Boat House. We all lined up. The man fired the pistol and we all jumped off. Audrey led. I had no one to guide me so I followed Winnie but dropped back. I went a long way out of course and only six were behind me. I nearly went into a boom of logs, and two boys in a canoe said they would come with me. I got along all right then. Robin Grey, [who] I was afraid might beat Audrey, dropped out. Several more dropped out, as the water was cold and they had three miles to go. At the Point Ellice Bridge, Ted and Curly met me in a canoe. A man came past in a rowboat and said only five were ahead of me and three behind. I talked to the kids and dived down to the bottom every once in a while. Three dropped out and Audrey, Gordon Young, Winnie Painter, Ben Robinson, and I were all who were left. Audrey got in first in one hour, twenty-two minutes; Gordon Young, one hour, forty-five minutes; Winnie Painter next; Ben Robinson in one hour, fifty-two minutes; and me in one hour, fifty-five minutes. Met Ella and Nellie Jennings [the Jenningses lived next door to the Dalziels]. Curly wanted to go swimming so Ella and I went in with him at the Pay B. Hse [pay bathhouse]. Stayed in about an hour. Walked home. Had supper. After supper Curly took me for a motorcycle ride out the Dallas Road till 10:00 when we went down to the Nanaimo train to see some kids off but missed it. Ella and I went to bed at 12:15.

"ELLA HAS CHANGED A LOT"

I was eighteen years old in 1916, although all through that diary I sounded like I was twelve. Here I'm running around with all these Dalziel boys— Jim, Bob, Harry, Ted, and Buns—and I'm not the slightest bit boy-struck.

I was interested in their sister, Ella. She couldn't look sideways at any-body. All these brothers watched her like a hawk. I had all my other friends, too: Curly Develin, Pete Flynn, Johnny Bates, Charlie with the launch, and I was writing to Bert, Art, Archie Hughes, and Harry Parker over-seas, and I was friends with Audrey Griffin, Verna Elves, Kate Parker, and Maymie Hare and Thelma at work, and many more. I had strong friend-ships among both girls and boys, but I didn't know which was which. I didn't distinguish between them.

Johnny Wardle, a boyfriend of Ella's, died. When she came back from his funeral in Nanaimo, I wrote in my diary, "Ella has changed a lot," but she had been different for quite a while. I felt that she had betrayed me, because we had vowed that we were going to live happily ever after. We weren't going to get married, we were just going to swim and be together. Then she began dating and going on picnics. She was getting into these guys who were just playmates to me. That's what separated us. We had a big fight and got reconciled, but it was looser after that. She was no longer devoted to me for lifelong friendship.

Tuesday, June 20, 1916

Had supper, and Ella and I had a fight about me phoning some kids who I never phoned, but we went for a walk and made up. Passed a haunted house and went in to explore and found a lot of pieces of paper with writ-ing on them hidden in the rafters. They had a lot of stuff about a tomb and a lady getting beaten to death and burglars and all kinds of creepy things. Ella and I are going to be detectives and find a couple of fortunes.

Saturday, July 1, 1916
Dominion Day

Ella was packing her suitcase to go to Nanaimo to Johnny's funeral, so I went in the kitchen and talked to Harry and Yorkey, who were stewed, till about 11:30 when we all went to bed.

Friday, July 7, 1916

. . . got a card from Ella. . . . Wrote to Ella.

Saturday, July 15, 1916
Left at 6:00. Went to E. & N. Station to meet Ella and Ted. Was glad to see Ella. Got home and made an awful noise as I was in high spirits about Ella coming home. We all went in the parlor and sang, but Ella has changed a lot. She does not like me anymore since she came back. And I am glad I am going home Monday, only I like Mrs. Dalziel.

Friday, July 21, 1916
Ella went for a ride on my bike. Ella and I went to bed at 12 and talked a long time.

Wednesday, August 9, 1916
Went to the arena to hear Rev. Billy Sunday, a great Prohibition speaker who was once a baseball player. He gave a good speech but he was so funny and used so much slang that Ella and I laughed all the time. Sang "God save the King" and left. Started home and got as far as Discovery St. when the Interurban came along at a quarter to eleven. We ran and jumped on the back, but the fender started to fall off, so I jumped off. Ella kept on right across the bridge. I ran after it. Ella jumped off when the car slowed up at the fountain and waited for me.

Sunday, August 20, 1916
Ella and I started home. Sat down on the pavement and finished our lunch. Heard some sailors singing in a house, so we climbed up on the fence and listened. A man came out so we ran . . . Ella and I lay down on the sofa.

Incidentally, Ella and I were lifelong friends. She came quite often to visit, and when she died left me a lovely necklace and earrings that I wear often. I led Ella around by the nose, but I found a soulmate in Audrey Griffin. Audrey and I were equals. She was a Canadian national swimming champion.

I was mischievous, but I was a survivor. I didn't land in the slammer or get raped. I was pretty independent and creative, didn't scare easily, didn't panic.

Sunday, August 13, 1916

Pete Flynn was going to take Nellie Jennings on his motorcycle and Curly
Develin was going to take me out to the Lake. We started out together,
but Pete was such a bad rider that Curly and I went ahead and Pete wob-
bled all over the road. At the pumping station Curly's wheel-drive broke.
Pete stopped and helped him fix it. When he got started up again with
Nellie on the back, he turned off the road up over a pile of eighteen-inch
pipes. Nellie jumped off and Curly helped him start off again. We started
and passed Pete. Turned off the main road up the narrow road that led
to camp. It twists an awful lot and is overgrown with salal bushes. We took
a wrong fork and found ourselves in someone's backyard, so turned back
to the fork and took the other turning but could not go far on account of
the salals. In the meantime Pete started up the bad road, and going up a
hill Nellie fell off. Pete noticed it after a while and left his bike and came
back. She was not hurt so they walked along the road and saw Curly's
motorcycle standing. . . . Curly started and went about ten feet when his
motor-drive broke. We had to look for the clip, and Pete in the meantime, seeing we did not catch up to him, turned back and left Nellie. He
helped us fix up and we started off again. Passed Nellie walking up a hill. . . .
Just as we turned back, their chain broke and they shouted to us to stop,
but we did not hear them but went right on. We got home without further accidents.

HARRY PARKER

Saturday, July 15, 1916

Went to Mr. Bantley's and had my [piano] lesson. Did not know it very
well. At about 2:00 the 103rd Regiment came past Mr. Bantley's on their
way down to the boat. Stood on the steps. Saw the two Campbell boys, Harry
Parker, S[e]rgeant Major Black, Ernie Cruise, and Frank Setterington. Ran
home to Mother's, ate a bit of egg, and Mother and Dorothy and I went
down to the boat to see the soldiers off to England. Harry Parker gave me
his swagger stick with his regiment colors on it. Norma Black was crying
on account of her father going to war.

I know one boy embarrassed me—scared the hell out of me—and that was Harry Parker. When he left with his regiment for England, he gave me his swagger stick all decorated with his regiment colors. I had no idea I was accepting a love token. I just liked the swagger stick.

He actually proposed to me after he got overseas. I felt just terrible about it. I was great friends with the whole [Parker] family. I visited them on their farm near where we camped on the beach. My particular friend in that family was a girl about my own age, Kate. Harry was just a nice kid, a little older than I was. I guess he was shy and didn't have nerve enough, so he got overseas and wrote me a letter. I had no idea he had those leanings. I didn't feel that way about him, not for a minute. I liked him very, very much, but to have him write from overseas from the middle of the trenches and all that was devastating. What was I going to say? I hated to say no to him, I really hated to say no. Finally I wrote him and told him no.

I think it would have been a brave person who would proposition me, any kind of proposition! I didn't want to marry Harry Parker or anybody else. I used up every bit of my energy in athletics, nothing left over for sexual energy, nothing. I didn't start to menstruate until I was sixteen. My mother was about to take me to a doctor when I finally started, and then I stopped when I was only forty-two, so I didn't have a very long reproductive period.

Tuesday, August 15, 1916
The kids got all packed up and an auto came up at 11:00 to take us to the boat. Mrs. Dalziel, Nellie, Bessie, Ted, Yorkey, Johnny, Harry [Dalziel], Buns, Bob, Ella, and I all piled in. Went down to the boat. They put their things aboard while I watched them load. It was nearly time for the boat to go, so I kissed Ted and Yorkey good-bye and shook hands with Johnny, George, and Tommy Rogers. . . . There was a letter from Kate [Parker] with her brother Harry's picture.

That must have been a big concession on my part. I kissed nobody! Obviously, it was a friendly kiss, or I wouldn't have written it in there. I didn't have any kind of a romantic idea about any of these guys. Even if

I had, they wouldn't have turned up in this diary. Most people write a diary to put their feelings in, then they have to lock it up for fear somebody will get it. Anybody could read my diary. I edited out any feeling. I just wanted to keep a record of my activities. Too bad I didn't put more feeling into it, but I know I just definitely didn't. I didn't want people to know what I was thinking. I still am private. Interesting to have a diary without anything in it.

THE CLASSICS

I read all kinds of things, and my mother played a role in this. She read romantic novels, but she would lecture me about how I shouldn't read that trashy stuff. I should read classics. Now, I never paid much attention to what my mother said I could and couldn't do, but for some strange reason I bought that whole package and never read anything but classics. My mother didn't know what classics were, and neither did I. So I went snooping around in the libraries, trying to pick out classics. I'd ask the librarian, "Is this a classic?" If she said it was, I took it home. I read all kinds of improbable books, some of them terribly boring. One was Edmund Burke's *The Sublime and Beautiful.*[2] I'll never forget that book. I read it from one end to the other, and I learned the difference between what is sublime and what is beautiful, but since then they've become blurred in my mind. I read about Greek architecture and about artists' lives, all in the local library. I didn't know anybody who read the kind of books I read, or could discuss them with me, though I tried once with Ella.

Friday, June 9, 1916
Went to Lane's [where Ella was employed] to see Ella on my way home from lunch. Wrote an essay on "Youth's Head" [a painting] by Murillo. Ella thought it was crazy, which is not very encouraging for a budding genius. After work went to library with Ella. Got a book on Reynold's and Landseer's paintings.

Saturday, July 29, 1916
It was very calm on the water and I read a history of France.

It was a pretty raggedy education, but at least the books weren't spoiled for me. I was the only person I knew who loved *Ivanhoe.* Everyone else studied it in high school. I remember the opening words: "The curse of St. Swithin on these infernal porters," followed by a discussion about using the Anglo-Saxon word "pig" when the animal had to be taken care of, but when it was on the table and ready to eat, then it was "pork," the French word. The librarian in Victoria gave the nod to authors like Dickens and Thackeray and Jane Austen, whom I read all the time. And the Bröntes. I loved *Jane Eyre,* she's so independent. I've read that a couple, three times.

I had a double existence, two different worlds: an activity world and an intellectual world. The world of intense activity was full of people. I was never one to go on solo swims or hikes. I wanted at least two people so I could say, "Look at that!" and share the beauty and the adventure. So I was not a loner. But my other world, the intellectual world, was a side of my nature I couldn't share with anybody.

Although I was surrounded by jazz, that sort of thing, I studied classical music. My mother bought a beat-up old piano and paid for my lessons. I had to practice an hour a day. My teacher was a German, Mr. Bantley, and I was his favorite pupil. I was such a dirty, grubby little kid that he had his wife wash my hands, neck, and ears before I could play. Then he would have her listen to me. He said I had tremendous temperament—whatever that was—and would make a great pianist. He was going to send me to Germany to finish my training and see me through financially. He had two pianos, one for the great unwashed—and that was me. The other one was from the German city of Leipzig. If I could learn to play Beethoven's "Moonlight Sonata," he would let me play on the Leipzig piano.

Fortunately, I didn't become a great pianist. The First World War interfered with that. They persecuted Germans, and my teacher had to leave the country. But I still know the "Moonlight Sonata," and I spent last New Year's Eve dutifully in church listening to a Bach recital.

WORLD WAR I

Sunday, June 18, 1916

I went next door to Jennings' to see if they were coming down to the boat with us to see some soldiers off. . . . I nearly went to sleep. At 11:00 we went down to the boat, and Buns and I made a heck of a noise. At the boat we could not find Mr. Huff, but saw Mr. Johnson and said good-bye to him. Ella and I saw Mr. Paul off on the HMS *Shearwater*. The boat pulled out and we went back and got home after 12:00.

Tuesday, June 20, 1916

The 11th H.M.R.s [His Majesty's Regiments] were going to England so I met Mrs. Dalziel and we went down to the boat, and there was an awfully big crowd. I saw Jimmie McPherson, Percy Wills, and Bill Reid, who were going away. They left at 4:30.

Monday, August 7, 1916

Saw George Dempsey off on the *Rainbow* on Bay St. . . . We got a letter from Archie saying he was not going back in the trenches.

When the First World War broke out, I was sixteen. It seemed like a great adventure, a romantic idea. The thought of killing somebody was not part of it. I wanted to drive a truck, to bring around the munitions. I never thought of it in terms of human suffering: deaths of soldiers, the effect on their families, killing people whom you didn't even hate. When they had a regiment of recruits ready to go, the boat would come in, and we'd go down to the harbor to see them off and cheer.

Gradually, the ranks of my friends were thinned. Not everybody wanted to go. One boy who was in the eighth grade with me, a handsome, popular young kid, claimed he was a conscientious objector. He wouldn't go, so they put him in a camp. I was shook up, because I was intensely patriotic. None of the Dalziel boys went overseas. Harry, the oldest one, heard that if you ate a lot of soap, your heart would beat like crazy and they wouldn't take you. So he did, and his heart beat like crazy, and they refused him. He died of heart failure some years later, so I suspect he had a bad heart. Soap had nothing to do with it!

I have photographs of some of the soldiers going away. Ah, the poor devils. I knew a lot of them. In my diary, I kept track of the boats coming in and going out of the harbor to take them away, and I noted when I sent and received letters to Bert [a cab driver], Archie Hughes, Art Featherbarrow, and Harry Parker. Everybody got drafted.

The British Empire had a great policy in regard to its armies: they recruited their troops from Australia and Canada and their different colonies, and they put those regiments on the front lines. British troops stayed back. They had recruited a whole regiment out of Toronto into what was called the Princess Patricia Regiment and sent it over to France, where it was wiped out. The city of Toronto was drawn into deep mourning because the load of death fell on this one city. So the British cut that out. They scattered the people from one city into all different regiments. Still, there was a tremendous death roll of Canadians in France. They were either killed in action, gassed, or wounded. Not many escaped.

You see, the war went on and on and on, from 1914 to 1918. That's four years! And all the young men were gone, and all the wounded were coming back with nothing to show for it. The morale of the nation got very low, and mine along with it.[3] "What are we fighting this war about?" I finally asked myself. We were told the Germans were mean people—Huns, they were called—who tortured babies and cut their hands off.

The war destroyed my stepfather, to a large extent. The wholesale grocery where he had worked for years and years was owned by a German, so it was looted during the war hysteria. They raided all German businesses and destroyed them. German children were looked down on, ridiculed, and hated. They did the same thing in the United States. It was a terrible thing, very much like what they did to the Japanese in the Second World War. Finally, we all stopped believing the lies that the government spread around about the Germans and why we were fighting the war.

Toward the end of the war, the Russians held back half the German army on the Eastern Front, and the Allies held off the other half of the German army in the trenches on the Western Front. It was a stalemate, the suppliers were getting rich, and all the soldiers were getting killed or living in the mud, their bodies covered with lice. Then came the dreadful news that the Russians had surrendered. That was really a blow because if we couldn't beat the German army, split in half on two fronts, then what chance did we have against the whole German army once they shifted it to one front? So I went around all day mad at the Russian army, especially at the Russian generals who gave the orders to surrender. After a few days, the news began to seep through that it had nothing to do with the government or the generals. The soldiers had simply gone home. They weren't getting paid, had no shoes, no equipment. Their farms were neglected. And I remember so clearly in the kitchen saying to my mother, "Why don't they all go home? Why don't our people come home?"

That's where I got my love for the Russian Revolution. It did end the war, definitely ended the war. That was in 1918. Morale went down on the Western Front, the German soldiers began to exchange cigarettes with the British soldiers, and rebellion broke out in Finland and Germany. The Allies, defending the interests of the ruling class, began to think they'd better settle these revolutions or they were going to lose the whole bit. So they quit the trench fighting—ended the war, but quick—and sent armies up to suppress the revolution in Finland, where they were successful, and also in Russia, where they were not successful. But they kept fighting to crush the revolution. They were fighting it when they dropped the bomb on Hiroshima in 1945, making sure the Russians didn't get to Japan first.

When the Russians went home, it completely changed my thinking about war. It made me feel how foolish it all was. It affected my unity with the soldiers and my consciousness of world politics. I have very strong, dark feelings about war. War is unacceptable, a terrible thing, a terrible thing. I can't understand how anybody would want to go into the army or have anything to do with it.

That's the end of my diary. I never put anything in it that I thought, just the things that I did. And I didn't want anyone prying into my mind, either.

5 / Two Separate Lives

MARRIAGE

Let's skip over this marriage business. It is a sensitive area of my life, and I'm not going to go into it too much except to say that I felt trapped. Definitely trapped. You see, I developed very late. I was afraid that boys my age would make sexual overtures, so I avoided them. When I was eighteen and nineteen, I looked younger, and I was still playing with the kids, boys about fifteen and sixteen. Up to that time, boys were just playmates to me, a kind of protection, so sex was never a problem with me. But eventually it catches up with you. One day I looked at a person and I was in love, just like that. I was almost twenty years old. I married the first guy who kissed me, and that was Ted Dalziel. He was such a nice guy.

One night we stayed out all night, you know, the way lovers do. I started home, but the family was up early—it was Christmas morning! So I went over to Mrs. Dalziel and asked her to tell my mother I'd spent the night at her place.

When the young kids I played with heard that I was going to get married to Ted, they said, "What's he want to marry a boy for?" I remember the wedding: February 9, 1918. It was a simple business. We went to the home of the clergyman, the same one who had baptized me twenty years earlier. When we came back, there was a little reception at my parents' home. After I was married, the boys came up to the house and whistled and called for me to come out and play. They looked on me as one of the gang. I'd go canoeing, hiking, and swimming, just as before. My husband said he felt he was surrounded by a bunch of schoolkids. I had two separate lives. One was this intense athletic activity, and then this marriage business. And it didn't last long, as you can imagine. I wasn't conscious of conflicts after I was married, though there probably were some.

I left the job with Mr. Henderson in early summer 1918 because I was three or four months pregnant.[4] Nydia Audrey Dalziel[5] was born December 1 of that year in the front room of 1033 Burdette Avenue, my mother's and Jacob Hughes's house. Ted was in the army over in North Vancouver, so he could come to visit. He had been drafted after we got married, but he didn't get sent over because I was pregnant. Nydia saved his life, but I didn't do it so he wouldn't be killed. I didn't want to be pregnant. After she was born, then they would have sent him, but the war was over on November 11, 1918, so he came back, and we set up our own place in Victoria.

There were lots of Dalziels around to make a fuss over Nydia. Everybody made a fuss over Nydia. She should have been rotten spoiled, but she wasn't. When Billy Muir and Buck Calder came over to see the baby, Billy said he would marry her when she grew up, provided she didn't turn out like me.

That same clergyman who christened and married me christened my daughter, Nydia Audrey, in 1919, on the same date (May 4) and in the same dress I'd been christened in, and I professed to be upset because he didn't recognize the dress. Audrey Griffin was there as Nydia's godmother. The clergyman, Reverend Clay, wasn't a particular friend of the family's. If he hadn't been alive to do it, and if the dress hadn't still been kicking around, I never would have done it. So I had Nydia's christening on the anniversary of mine, with no religious meaning.

Twenty years later, Nydia and I went over to Victoria to the big old church in the middle of town and looked up the records. There was the document for her christening. We got photostatic copies. It interested her a great deal—people are attached to the past. You like to know what the past was all about, so you can use it as a guideline for the way you're going, but I don't think it should be something that you worry about particularly. It's gone.

SEPARATION

I was pretty much shut in with this child and no particular community to help me raise it except my mother. I've never been one to look inward, to see what's going on in there, but at the time Nydia was an infant I became aware that I was subject to fits of depression. I think most young people are. I found out that the fits were phony, and here's how I discovered it:

when I'd feel down in the dumps, I'd test myself by saying, "Now suppose that someone offered you a trip to India. Would you feel happy?" "Nope," I said to myself. "I wouldn't be happy." Nothing I could tempt myself with would get me out of the depression. Then one morning I'd wake up and be all right again. Nothing had changed in the night. I'd test myself again by saying, "Suppose some sad thing existed, suppose your friend died, would you be sad?" "No," I said to myself, "I wouldn't be sad. I'd grieve, but I wouldn't be depressed." That's how I realized that the moods were physical, purely physical, based on some laws that I didn't understand, like the cycles of the sun or the moon, and I lost confidence in them. When you have something physical, you have some control over it, so when the depressions would come, I'd talk myself out of them. They were phony, not based on what was happening to me. Pretty soon I outgrew them.

I thought a lot about moods and depressions at that time. You could be in real danger, out of a job and all kinds of bad things happening to you, but you might not be depressed about it. You'd worry, but you wouldn't fall into depression. And even if you were depressed because of your situation, you'd have a chance to overcome it with your mind, because your mind has considerable power over your body—not absolute, but a lot. I never get those depressions now, haven't for years. You understand it, you can control it.

Meanwhile, I had a lot of decisions to make about raising a child. I went against the whole world on the matter of clothing, for example. They had fearful garments to put on a newborn baby: a band about six inches wide, almost the length of the child's torso, went around the middle with four or five little safety pins, tight. They called it a belly band. And of course a diaper. Then came the "baracoat," which was flannelette, tied around the chest. It had a band at the top all crisscrossed to make it quite stiff. That tied and cinched down. Then they put on a long, flannel petticoat, and a dress, and a little woolen shirt on top of that. And socks and shoes. And a jacket. The poor little kid was like a board.

I thought how I'd feel if I had all that clothing tied and pinned, couldn't move hand or foot, and uncomfortably hot. It seemed to me that a baby wants to wiggle, like it does when it's naked. That's the way it grows. I didn't read about all this, because there were no books on how to raise children, just books on how to teach them good manners. I said to my mother, "I'm only going to put a diaper and jacket on the baby. Then I'll cover it up with blankets and keep it warm that way." "Oh, no," she said. "You can't do that. It will hurt its back when people pick it up." I said, "If you can't pick a baby up without breaking its back, don't pick it up." I had all the old wives in the county screaming their lungs out at me. I'm happy to say that I didn't break her back.

Marriage was a custom I couldn't stay with. I wasn't going to sit there and take it. I will say, looking back, that I had very good taste in marrying people who never abused me. If anybody was abused, they were: I wasn't fit for anybody to marry! I made people unhappy. I took Nydia and moved out of Ted's life. She was about one and a half years old, probably the summer of 1920. He didn't want me to leave him.

It had nothing to do with my husband, his personality, or any of those things, because he was a truly fine person, but we had hardly anything in common. He found a better wife later on and had a family. I moved back over to Mother's, and I took my daughter with me. Mothers are responsible for bringing children into the world, and she was my responsibility. I told her father that I'd never ask for any support money, and I never did. Once she got older, he started sending her money, though. She visited him, and he took her to dinner occasionally, so she knew her dad.

When Ted died [in 1949], he never mentioned Nydia in his will. When a parent dies and omits to mention one of the direct descendants in the will, it is assumed that it was just an oversight. Ella tried to get Nydia to sue to break the will. Nydia turned to me and said, "What'll I do?" I said, "You tell Ella to get lost!" Why should we do something he didn't intend? He had two children by his second marriage, and Nydia was long gone out of his life, so why should she come back into it again? She didn't need the money.

THE PLUNGE FOR DISTANCE

I went to work for a real estate agent in Victoria sometime in late 1919 or early 1920. I don't remember what I did, although I was there two years.

Jobs were not the be-all and end-all of my life, as anyone could probably have concluded by this time. Al Davis, the man who owned the business, was a sports promoter with a wheeler-dealer reputation. He got hold of a piece of property with buildings up at the Gorge. He built an athletic club there, the Vancouver Island Athletic Association (VIAA), and I belonged.

Through VIAA I went into competitive sports. The VIAA promoted swim meets and water festivals with other clubs in Victoria and with other cities along the coast, such as Seattle and Vancouver. It was a big deal. We all carried amateur cards. I did my best work when I was on a swimming relay or water polo team. We were competing, but I felt part of a gang, which was different from the individual glory, you see.

I entered into a decathlon—broad jump, high jump, canoeing, bicycling, 100-meter race, and more—and won it citywide. I was good in most events, but the only thing that I excelled in was the plunge for distance, which is no longer used in swimming competition. I won a Pacific Coast championship to equal the women's world record. My name was in Spaulding's record book.

To do the plunge for distance, we stood on the edge of the tank and gave ourselves a great dive, but a very shallow one so that we just skimmed through the water, then stayed there, floating along face down just below the surface for as long as a minute. The time I won the championship, I had not practiced a great deal, but I was going to get all the mileage I could out of that minute. Before it was up, I ran out of oxygen. I was still moving but I wouldn't put my head up. If you're in that position you can't help but breathe, so I started to breathe and my lungs began to fill up with water. They said, "Time." I put my head up but I was really half drowned. I crawled out of the tank and went into the bathhouse and just heaved. I could hear them calling me to come out for my second try. No way. I could hardly walk.

I coughed and coughed until I got it all out and got myself under control. Finally, after about twenty minutes, when I figured I looked normal, I came walking out and everybody said, "Hey, where ya been? We've been looking for you. You equaled the women's world record." I didn't tell anyone what happened. I wouldn't want them to know I was that stupid. That was my one big triumph in the field of athletics.

One time we were sitting on a raft waiting our turn, each of us wanting to win the next race. There was a big bunch of people in the grandstand, all watching. I thought to myself, "It probably isn't important whether I win or lose because what we're all doing here is furnishing a diversion for those people in the grandstand. They have all kinds of problems, their children home with the measles, or a big light bill that they can't pay. They're all going to go home to the sick child or the unpaid bill, and they couldn't care less who wins." Maybe that's when I shed my illusion about being important.

ORGANIZING FOR ATHLETICS

This talent for organizing, such as I have, was exerted in my early years on behalf of athletics. After I started working and had a child, I continued to play basketball. There's a great picture of Nydia sitting in front of the team in 1921 as our mascot. By that time, there were a lot of teams: churches and one of the newspapers had teams. So I decided we should have a citywide league of women's basketball teams. We'd hold a series of games, charge admission, and give out medals and all this good stuff. I thought we needed somebody of importance, a big name, to be head of the league and draw people in. I went to see Miss DeWolf, the director of the YWCA. She agreed to be the president. That was all I needed. With this name in my little hot hands, I went to work and organized the league.

Now, Miss DeWolf was a very strict Methodist. In those days, the big moral issues were the cutting of hair and the wearing of bobby socks. So in our league constitution and bylaws, Miss DeWolf insisted on a clause banning bobby socks and short shorts. But I liked her. The fact that she would be president of a league of women's basketball teams showed her liberal trend.

Crowds of people came to the games. We charged ten cents, and we had a real following, much like women's baseball teams have in small towns today. Some kindly person donated a silver pin for each person on the winning team, and there was a [trophy] cup. My team didn't win, so I didn't get one. It would have been lost by now anyway, but I can still see those neat little pins with the silver basketballs on them.

Al Davis, my employer and the owner of the VIAA club, erected a 100-foot tower for the boys to dive from. He was quite a promoter. The two young divers, Billy Muir and Buck Calder, would dive off this tower on the occasion of athletic meets. I was always opposed to this diving. I thought it was dangerous, and I expressed myself very forcefully in this regard. I would never watch them dive. That was my part, you know, refusing to watch them. This particular day, there was a huge crowd out at the Gorge at a big gala swimming event. I put my head down. Billy dived, and I realized that something had happened. He broke his back. Audrey Griffin fished him out.

As you can imagine, Al Davis felt terrible when this thing happened to Billy, and he started to raise money to pay all the expenses, but he ran into problems because people didn't trust him. He had this wheeler-dealer reputation. I could see that he wasn't going to get anywhere raising funds, so Audrey Griffin and I decided we'd have to get different sponsorship. I went around to all kinds of athletic clubs, and to people in the community, and got them all to come to a meeting to set up a fund-raising committee for Billy. Al Davis showed up at this meeting, along with the mayor, and they hadn't even been invited. Al was just furious. He wanted to know who called the meeting together. Nobody seemed to know. I was kind of a shabby, nondescript sort of person, and I had no particular standing in the community. Al was up there on the stage, shouting. I thought, "Well, I better speak up." Finally, I said, "I called the meeting together." Somebody had to take responsibility for it.

Then Al Davis charged that I was libeling him, saying he was untrustworthy. I replied that I did not think for one minute that he would do anything crooked with regard to Billy Muir, and I believed that. But I also said that he, Al Davis, didn't have the trust of the community, and that's why I had set up this other organization. After I spoke, a responsible citizens' committee was formed, with one of the trustees from a bank and all these good people on it. The fund-raising went ahead great blazes. Audrey and I held dances, we charged exorbitant fees at basketball exhibition games, and we went around door-to-door. But I was out of a job, naturally. Al was also going to get me expelled from the athletic club, but people came to my rescue, and he didn't get to do that. The mayor was mad at me too. Imagine having a mayor mad at you!

After Billy was released from the hospital, we paid his doctor bills and bought his water bed, a whole new set of chairs designed for him, and an ancient radio. We raised enough money to hire a full-time registered nurse so that he could live at home. He lived for two years. Billy was a very popular athlete, and a wonderful boy he was, too. I wrote to the Rev. Billy Sunday, the evangelist preacher. I thought he could do something to help Billy Muir. I went to see him every day until I left the country, for about a year. All we ever did was insult each other.

6 / Immigrant

HAND-TO-MOUTH

When I immigrated to Seattle, Washington, in 1921, I was up against a lot of things, and sort of living hand-to-mouth. After the First World War came the Depression [beginning in Canada in 1919]. That's why I came to the United States. People poured out of Canada.

I wanted to become a nurse, that's what I really wanted. When I had applied at the hospitals in Victoria, they wouldn't take me because I was a married woman, even though I was separated. And I had a child: they wouldn't hire married people, divorced people, or people with children. It was almost impossible to get any job as a married woman in Canada, and that's the truth. You have to have lived in those days to know what we were up against.

I said, "Okay, I'm not going to be married." I left my daughter with my mother in Victoria, I came to Seattle, and I posed as a single woman. I was going to get a job and save enough money to go into one of those nursing hospitals to train. The discrimination against women wasn't as bad in Seattle as it was in Canada. That's really why I came here to the United States. Maybe I wouldn't have left Victoria had I not been frustrated in that ambition.

The first job I got in Seattle was putting MADE IN JAPAN stickers on Easter bunnies. Funny little job. That only lasted a day or so. Then I had a job in a mailing bureau owned by a guy named Hayden. The building is still there. Of course, they did everything by hand in those days, none of this computer business, no machines that lick stamps and tie up bundles, so many little iron fingers coming up and tying knots—they didn't even have one of those. At Hayden's I would work like crazy all morning. After lunch, I would get bored and start up all kinds of antics, full of jokes and tricks, making people laugh and diverting people from their work. When a crew of kids came in from the university in the afternoons, it didn't take much to get them going. Hayden finally had to fire me. I bargained: "I'll come to work in the morning, and in the afternoon, as soon as I feel one of these playful urges coming on, I'll leave." He agreed.

I got my afternoon job at a restaurant that opened for lunch, but I had this problem of not remembering what people ordered. I found it takes real skill to be a waitress, and nobody can tell me any differently. The men customers would make risqué remarks to me. I'd practically spit at them when they did, and that doesn't go over, you know. A waitress has to take a lot of that garbage, but not me. I would just tell them to shut up, or I'd say whatever happened to come handy. So I was very unpopular with the men. They didn't tip me. But I was popular with the women because I would do anything for them. They left me tips. This job hadn't been going on very long when there was a hullabaloo up at the front desk between the boss and a young man from the mailing bureau, asking for me. The boss insulted the young man, and that made me pretty mad, so I quit.

I had another moonlighting job in a soda fountain. At first I didn't know how to make these fancy dishes—you know, banana splits with nuts and bolts and all kinds of things on them. I got by because when people ordered things, I'd say, "You tell me how to make it, and I'll do it for you." I was supposed to work until midnight. It was on 1st Avenue where the Exchange Building is now, down at the foot of the hill. No problems of danger at night in those days.

But they wouldn't close the doors until fifteen minutes before midnight. Consequently, customers would still be sitting there at midnight. I was supposed to clean up, wash the dishes, and put the cream in the refrigerator, all of which took me until way after midnight, and I didn't get paid for that. I complained about working overtime without pay, but it didn't do any good. So I just walked out at midnight. The next day they said, "You forgot to put the cream back." I said, "Unless you close your doors earlier, it's always going to be left out because I'm going home at midnight. That's all you're paying me for." That was the end of that job.

UPROOTED

I felt trapped in Seattle. I yearned for the water. I just yearned for the water. I used to walk along 2nd and 1st Avenues, and when I came to the intersections I could look through and see Puget Sound. You get that way living on an island: in Victoria, you were always by the water, but in Seattle you're divorced from it. Another big problem when I came to this country was that I had no place to continue my athletic life. I'd get a friend, we'd take the streetcar, plan to go out, build a fire someplace on the beach, and swim. But we found that people lived all along the shore, and we couldn't get to it, and places like Alki were paved over. I didn't like Lake Washington because I couldn't stand freshwater: it was slimy, whereas salt water was neat and crisp, and the things that grew in it, the seaweed—why, I knew those. So I joined the YWCA to swim in the tank, but that's boring. There's no place to go, and there's nothing living in it to see.

When I went down to the YWCA for the first time, in 1921, the woman at the desk said, "I'm sorry, but this is Negro Day." And I said, "Oh? Then I can't go in?" And she said, "Well, you wouldn't want to, would you?" I said, "Sure. I came down here to swim." She said, "Well, go ahead." I thought, "Well, I better check this out. I'll ask the swimmers. They might not want me to come in." Down I went to the tank on the lower floor. There were about five young women there, swimming around. I beckoned to them to come to the edge of the pool and said, "The woman upstairs told me that this is Negro Day. Would you mind if I came in?"

And they said, "No, come on in!" So I started back up to pay my fee, then I turned to them: "Oh? Are you guys colorfast? Will I come out with black spots all over?" They thought it was pretty funny. They said, "Oh, no, we're colorfast." I said, "Well, so am I. You won't get white spots." So I went swimming. Negro Day was Saturday. I found out later they emptied the tank and put fresh water in on Sundays.

So my athletics was chopped off. Something like this happens to everybody who migrates from home—like an uprooted plant, you've got to put down roots in altogether different ground. Maybe that plant makes it, maybe it doesn't. If it does, okay. It grows sturdy, but different. Never again was I an athlete. The next really physical thing that I got into was much later in life, when I got into Audubon. I became a hiker and a backpacker, and that fascinated me. Can you imagine taking your bed and everything else on your back and going way out into the mountains? In the 1920s, I never was in the walk of life where people did that sort of thing, so I didn't know where to look for it.

I was very lonely living by myself. I was attached to my mother, you know. I was always getting homesick. I went back to Victoria in 1922, but when I got home I found that the reasons why I left were still there. I remember feeling a little resentful that they had painted the post office boxes a different color. Already my homeland was changing beyond my recognition.

So I came back again to Seattle in 1923. At first I stayed with Harry Dalziel and his wife, Kate Parker [Dalziel]. I knew them very well from Victoria. They had a spare room, I could live with them until I found a job, and everything was going great. Then Kate went away for the weekend and left Harry and me in the apartment. In the middle of the night, I woke up. I knew immediately what was happening. Harry was crawling into bed with me, and it wasn't just because his feet were cold. I put my feet up against the wall and shoved. Plop! He went out on the floor. That cooled him off. But I wasn't finished with him yet. I got up. I got my suitcase out. He saw that I was going to leave in the middle of the night, and he begged me not to. He wouldn't bother me anymore. I told him that when I'm bothered once, I make it impossible for anyone to bother me again. He said, "What shall I tell Kate?" I said, "Tell her I ran away with another guy or something. I don't want her hurt. You can tell any kind of story you'd like, and, if necessary, I'll back you up, but that's your problem." I got my clothes on and my things packed, and off I went.

I wandered down the street in the cold early morning. I remembered having recently met Pinky, a friend from my old neighborhood, clerking in Woolworth's dime store. I knew where she lived, downtown in a little apartment. I went knocking at her door at about two o'clock in the morning, she brought me in out of the storm, and that was it.

Now, I could have been raging mad and told Kate and created a hullabaloo. What good would that have done? She was a dear person. I didn't want her hurt. Harry didn't want her hurt. He wasn't all that bad a person, either. He had no reason to think that I would be willing. He just had this desire that overcame him. People have these desires. They don't create them themselves, they're innate. They're stronger in some people than in others. I think that people who are energetic are probably less developed that way. It takes a lot of energy, the sexual thing. If you're climbing mountains and running races, that takes away from the sexual source of energy. For that reason, I think that athletics is good for boys and girls in their teenage years.

Hardly anybody ever made a pass at me, and that was my only case of sexual harassment. I took care of it. In most situations, you can take care of yourself without destroying the man's wife, his family, or his political career. You have to stop and think: Who else am I affecting besides this character?

WITH NYDIA AT ST. THERESA's

I had a lot of jobs, but I never saved enough money to get into nursing. I realized it was a dream I wasn't going to be able to achieve, and I'd better settle down and do what I could do, which was secretarial work. I finally got a job in a law office, a regular daytime job.

After a couple of years without Nydia, I fetched her and reassumed my role as a married woman. I didn't want to have this poor little illegitimate child who'd pass it on to her grandchildren and to generations to come.

We had our home at St. Theresa's for eight years, up by St. James Cathedral, on Terry and Marion. It was for women only, mostly teachers, bookkeepers, nurses, and secretaries. They didn't have child care in those days, and I had finally talked the Sisters into letting me move in with my daughter. It was an exception.

Until Nydia was a lot older, I never had a housekeeping place. It was much simpler not to have to shop and cook and wash dishes and all that.[6] Irish Catholic girls would come out to be the maids, do all the work. They were young and so full of life, all the time just laughing and having a good time. Within the group of 125 women, there were little cliques. Maybe seven or eight or nine of us hung around together. Nydia, about four years old, was part of our clique. She referred to me as her roommate. I put out a little newspaper, and I'd organize a shindig once in a while. The Sisters would come by special arrangement to stay up late—they never wanted to leave.

I was determined not to lie to my child about where she came from. The custom was to have storks bring children and dump them on the floor. Who ever saw a stork flying through the air with a child? Nydia was so little when she asked, "Mother, where did I come from?" It took a great deal of courage on my part to tell her. I thought, "Well, that's done. I managed it! I got through it!" To my amazement, about three months later she said, "Mother, where did I come from?" I must have answered that question three or four times before she quit asking. It wasn't nearly as important to her as it was to me: How was I going to explain this dreadful thing? I was doing all the suffering. Still, I never heard of anybody else who was trying to get the facts of life out to children.

HOME IN SEATTLE, HOME IN PORT ANGELES

*M*y mother, my brother, Bill, and my sister, Dorothy, followed me over the border in about 1925 and settled in Port Angeles. A lot of people who lived in Port Angeles emigrated from Victoria because of the postwar Depression. My family had little money, and it was summertime. They lived in a tent. My mother left Jacob Hughes. He was no longer able to provide for her. The war took away his living. He probably inched along. I used to buy his medicine and send it to him.

Bill got a job as a journeyman electrician at the Crown Z[7] pulp mill. Later, when the war started, Bill moved over to Seattle to work in the shipyards. At that time he met my friend Jo Erickson, a schoolteacher. He married her, then he went to work at Boeing. Bill was a radical, like the rest of the family—a great union person, a shop steward. He loved youngsters, and Nydia adored him. So that was my brother. We were very close.

And my sister—we were close, too. Dorothy got a job tinting pictures for a photographer. She went to the public dances and met Johnny Gallacci, a second-generation Italian. They were beautiful dancers and got married. Dot lived her life out there in Port Angeles. She was uneducated because she just couldn't cut it at school, and she didn't read very much. She was elected treasurer of the garden club, but she didn't know how to keep books, so her husband did it for her. If you'd go in her house, it looked pretty good, but if you ever opened a drawer, everything would fall out. She sat in her kitchen in the morning. It was like sitting on the highway. Neighbors and people who knew her from all over the town came in for a cup of coffee. She held court, a good listener, cheerful and humorous, and always engaged in some interesting project, making a little clay thing or a lamp shade. Then she'd teach all these people to make one. She had the loveliest, deepest blue eyes. And her hair was red, with the clear pink-and-white skin that often goes with it, and no freckles. But she used a lot of makeup and wore ridiculous high heels. A complex person, Dot was. Dot died a year after Johnny. She was in her seventies, the last person I thought would live that long, she had such a poor start in life.

Once Mom, Bill, and Dorothy came over, I continually thought of Port Angeles as my home port. This ended a long period of loneliness. At St. Theresa's I became part of a group, and I had Nydia with me. When I left Seattle for a visit in Port Angeles, I was "going home." But when I was out there, I came "back home" to Seattle. Two homes. So I became thoroughly rooted in the United States.

I still went back and forth quite a bit between Port Angeles and Victoria to visit my friends. It was during Prohibition. They didn't have Prohibition in Canada, and I always brought a bottle back for somebody.

I had various ways of doing it. One time I tied it around Nydia's waist and told her to hold it up and not let it drop below her skirts. It kept showing, and I'd whisper, "Nydia, pull on that rope." Another time I put the bottle under a bunch of wet diapers on top of my baggage. Nobody in Customs wanted to go through that!

WOLF

Now I'll get to my second husband, Herb Wolf, whom I married in 1928 in Portland. We'd been together quite a while. I don't know why I married him. I liked him, he was a nice guy, he really was: I married two nice guys. Nydia was very fond of him, too.[8] Nydia and Wolf and I lived out in the woods beyond Port Angeles in a place called Tyee / Beaver. He was what they call a timber cruiser.[9] Then the mill shut down. He lost his job. We moved in with his mother, and I didn't like that at all—couldn't get a job in Port Angeles, not enough law offices. I came back to Seattle because that's where I could get work. Then we just drifted apart.

When I got the divorce, I proceeded to have my name changed back to my maiden name, Anderson. Then I thought, "This is crazy. I like the name, and everybody knows me as Wolf." So I just kept using "Wolf," but legally, my name is Anderson.

I have a theory about marriage—just cooked it up lately, and I don't know whether it will hold water or not. Marriage is a kind of ownership for life, and that's just not going to work. Human beings can't own each other like things, like objects. No wonder the marriages all break up. Mating for life—I think it's imposed by our social system. Most animals don't mate for life. Take the chimpanzees. These animals are so much like us. Ninety-eight percent of the genes we share in common. The only reason they can't talk is they don't have the larynx to do it. They really shouldn't be in zoos. Anyway, they don't mate for life, and neither should we.

It's the same with children. In a simpler society, they don't belong to the parents. I noticed that when I was up in Alaska, in an Eskimo village.[10] The children belonged to everybody. If the kids didn't like their natural parents, to hell with them. They moved in next door. The kids all roamed around together, went in each other's houses and didn't knock. They came into my tent when I was gone and left me flowers.

PETITION FOR CITIZENSHIP

$\mathcal{B}$ack in Seattle, in 1929, I finally got a job in a law office that suited me. I would have liked to have been a lawyer, but that cost a bunch of money, which I didn't have. I thought lots of times about it, but what good would that have done? Quit my job and go to school—with a child to support? That's the way life pushes you around. But the struggle to succeed was very valuable. It led into productive activity and independence. You switch around as a child and as a young person, and then you do what you can do. I ended up being Hazel Wolf.

I had put off becoming a citizen for a long time because I didn't think it was important. The lawyer I worked for insisted, so I went down to the Immigration [and Naturalization Service (INS) of the U.S. Department of Justice] to file my petition, and I sat and waited with a lot of people from other lands, most of them Asians. I was like an American applying for citizenship, compared to these people, who didn't speak English and were scared to death—afraid of bureaucrats, of all things! Bureaucrats held no terrors for me.

The INS was shouting at the immigrants: "Sit down there, now" and "Blah blah blah." They treated them like animals, so rudely it infuriated me. It went on and on and on as we waited in line. I got up in the middle of this, and I said, "I came here to apply for citizenship, but after watching you abuse these people, whose only sin is they don't speak English very well, I want to tell you I wouldn't belong to this country if you gave it to me," and I flounced out of the place. It wasn't a very good idea, but that's what I did. That was my first go-round with the INS.

The lawyer I worked for persuaded me to go back, but it wasn't until quite some time later. I was only doing it to please this boss of mine. I was advised not to be so hotheaded, and hopefully they would have forgotten this awful scene. The head of the INS took care of me. Everything was in order. Then came the waiting period.

When my final hearing came up, in 1930, I was in the hospital. I had been in a car accident, and a piece of glass went into my back and punctured my lung, which had filled up with water. I was laid up for quite a while. All the hearing stuff—I didn't go, and I didn't do anything about it, didn't renew my application. I just never went near them.

I did go through channels when I came to this country, got a permit, and it was a good thing. I had legal status in this country as a resident alien, so they couldn't shoot me back to Canada without a lot of trouble. But I wasn't a citizen, so I couldn't vote—what little I cared about elections. I had voted once in Canada. Women voted there before they could in the United States. My mother voted in Canada once because they paid her. She took the two dollars and voted for the other person. Once she had moved to the United States, she took out her citizenship, but she wouldn't vote. She thought you were just putting one bunch of rascals in and another bunch out. She despised all government, from the president on down—or up, whichever way you want to look at it—to the precinct-committee level, nothing but contempt for officials: judges, county coroners, everybody. She was adamant against any form of the military. She wouldn't let my brother join the Boy Scouts.

My mother was radical in an intuitive way. She didn't put out leaflets or talk about it. You could put a label on her philosophy—syndicalist, a classification of people who think that all governments are corrupt, and that the labor unions should simply take over—but she didn't know it by that name. She never voted until Roosevelt, and it took a long time for him to win her over. He was whizzing by on Highway 101 in a motorcade touring the Olympic Peninsula in 1937, to see if it should be made into a national park. My mother was picnicking with some little kids by a roadside stream, the only voter within a million miles. Roosevelt waved his hat right at her. She waved back and voted in the next election, her one vote.

I didn't care about becoming a citizen. I thought the government was no good. Why would I want to be a part of this thing? A real anarchist, I thought the political process was useless. You know, it's easy enough to feel that way, even now.

PART III

Communist: 1931–1948

That was my first experience with the Communist Party—action!
Putting the furniture back, fighting the establishment!

I got a feeling for the power of the people.

*O*n the world stage of fear, hunger, and homelessness caused by the Great
Depression, Hazel Wolf created local dramas in order to survive. The scene
was Seattle, 1931, in the line of unemployed winding down the sidewalk
from the welfare office on 2nd and Jackson, where she waited each Friday
for her check. That year, there were 17,190 names on the relief rolls in
Seattle; a year later, there were almost 30,000 names in a population of
366,000.[1] To the south, on nine acres of a filled-in tideflat, was Seattle's
largest Hooverville, a self-governed city of unemployed men, later the site
of the Kingdome. To the north were the smoky taverns of Skid Road, haunt
of fishermen, loggers, and teamsters, the workers who, for the first hundred years of settlement by European Americans, harvested and shipped
the resources of the Northwest. To the east spread Chinatown, now called
the International District, four blocks of stores marked entirely in Chinese
characters. To the west the waterfront outlined a rough intersection
between this provincial outpost and foreign worlds. No longer isolated,
yet still provincial, Seattle since World War I had been firmly tied in to
the rest of the United States through railroads, highways, ships, radios,
newspapers, and Hollywood films.

In 1931 this Seattle scene had not yet been defaced with a fear of Red Communism. Stalin's Gulag, McCarthy's paranoia, the "Domino Theory," and Reagan's "Evil Empire" were all in the future. Thousands of progressive working- and middle-class citizens, concerned more with unemployment than with Russia or the international Communist movement, joined the Communist Party of the United States of America (CPUSA), hoping to remedy the suffering of the Depression. A few years later, Hazel Wolf remembered, "everyone who worked for eight hours a day and asked for a paycheck was called a Communist."

In Seattle and Washington State, there had been strikes, violence against scabs (workers who cross striking union workers' picket lines), and marches on Olympia, the state capital. Demonstrations had been organized by Communists. The participants were mostly unemployed Americans committed to democratic traditions, rather than revolutionary conspirators.[2]

In 1931, Hazel Wolf was thirty-three years old, ready to try again for an education, a career, and the realization of her childhood dreams for her neighborhood. But the Depression intervened. Women were urged to remain at home and to leave what jobs there were for male breadwinners.[3] A single parent, unevenly educated, and scarcely able to support her child on clerical wages, Hazel Wolf couldn't follow that advice. Rather than a barrier, the Depression provided Hazel with a break, a rent in the social fabric, a curtain torn open to a stage without director, roles, or script.

The Communist Party and the Workers' Alliance played the supporting roles in Hazel's drama. Left and liberal organizations, such as the Washington Commonwealth Federation, founded in 1935, and the Communist Party, were possibly more successful in Depression-era Washington than in any other state. The party grew from 1,137 members in 1936 to 5,016 in 1938. Party members won elections to city councils, to the state legislature, and to the U.S. House of Representatives. In the mid-1930s, the Democratic Party carried the Communist program for social justice and reform to the voters.

In contrast to the long history and ambitious aims of the Communist Party, the Workers' Alliance had been founded in the United States in 1935 with a limited agenda: to organize the unemployed. The Workers' Alliance created strong, neighborhood-based activists in Seattle and nationally until the early 1940s, when war preparations absorbed all available labor. The alliance stayed in close touch with day-to-day problems of the workers and even drew middle-class unemployed and sympathetic liberals into its membership.[4] Eleanor Roosevelt was its honorary president, but Communists actually dominated the organization.[5]

When the New Deal began hiring unemployed workers, in the mid-1930s, the Workers' Alliance continued as their advocate. It became a union for those employed in New Deal programs, such as the Works Progress Administration (WPA),[6] which maintained public parks, built bridges, roads, and public buildings, and initiated arts and education projects. At first the WPA tried to break up the Workers' Alliance unions, but, like the brooms that pursued the sorcerer's apprentice in Walt Disney's *Fantasia*, the Workers' Alliance unions reproduced themselves when attacked. Hazel Wolf, well known as a Seattle activist in the 1930s, scripted, directed, and acted in her own street theater to advance the cause of the unemployed.

7 / Education and a Career

TRAINING FOR SOCIAL WORK

I always did want an education. In grammar school I didn't let anything interfere with my major program, athletics. But underneath it all I was thinking, "Yes, I need an education." Then, as I started out in the workaday world, I felt the lack of it very much, but I kept putting it off and putting it off. I thought, "You can't just drop out and start the university when you've only just graduated from elementary school. You have to go through channels!" And that meant high school, which was awfully hard to visualize. Finally, when I was thirty-three, I enrolled in night school at Broadway High. I went for two years. The second year, Nydia and I were attending the same school. My brother thought that was so ridiculous.

I remember studying American History part 1 and part 2 simultaneously. It was a little difficult, keeping them spread apart right. One of the teachers agreed to give me some lessons in French during the summer. I had already completed courses in Latin and I got credit for my work experience and for the fact that I knew shorthand and typing. When I got all of my credits but eight, they gave me a certificate that would get me into the University of Washington.

Meanwhile, the Depression was closing in. I was working full-time as secretary for the Public Health League of Washington, a doctors' lobby, and doing the school thing at night. But there were 13 million unemployed by 1933. The doctors began dropping their membership in the organization. My job was running out. They let the director go and kept me on for a while longer to write radio talks on medical subjects. Not that I knew anything, but the doctors used too many technical phrases that people didn't understand. I could write them better because I didn't know any jargon. I wrote about rabies and measles and tuberculosis, any disease you could imagine, just looked it all up in books and wrote a little fifteen-minute thing. Then I took it to one of the doctors, who corrected all the mistakes. At the end I would say, "See your family doctor." That was one of the givens.

I could see that they weren't going to be able to keep me going, along with the rent and the telephone, so I started making plans. First, I stopped paying bills—the rent, the groceries, anything I didn't have to pay—and I socked the money away in a savings account in the name of Helen Wilcox. She had been director of the doctors' lobby. I had been her secretary. We were very good friends. Then, when the job petered out, I applied for welfare. I had no money, of course, no job—I was unemployed. And I had a daughter. And so in 1933 they put me on relief.[7] I stayed on for a decent interval, and then I came to the welfare people and told them that my friend, Helen Wilcox, had agreed to pay my tuition at the University of Washington. But that's all she would do. She wasn't going to feed or clothe me or give me medical care, only pay my tuition. The welfare people thought that was a wonderful opportunity for me. They let me into the university on the condition that I transfer eight of my university credits to complete high school. So I waited until I got eight credits at a C grade and I transferred them back into my high school record, which did two things: it got me a high school diploma, and it pushed my university grade point average up to 3.5.

There were a few jobs. I'd have found a job, but I wanted to go to the university.

Nydia and I moved up to the University District in June 1934, into a tiny little house north of campus. We didn't have any bath, so I used to take my showers at the university gymnasium on my way to class. I was going to the university, and she was going to Roosevelt High School, eleventh grade. She was fifteen years old, so I could go to meetings anytime I felt like it, and she stayed home and did her homework. She was a very responsible, very gentle, peaceful sort of person—still is. I had a lot of respect for her. I found out early on that she had a little steel rod up her spine, so, despite her gentleness, I avoided controversies—I didn't think I would come out on top.

She took care of me. She saw that I took an umbrella and she watched the expenses and didn't ask for a lot of things. We were on welfare, but she never felt ashamed, and she didn't let any opportunities slip by. One time they gave out clothing and I didn't want any. She said, "Why don't you get some? We can use it for rags if nothing else." That was Nydia.[8] Now she's the center, the matriarch of the family. I'm not. All her children look to her, and I look to her. She's very understanding, very compassionate, and she never unloads her problems on anybody. I'm sure she's had some, but she protects everybody from that sort of thing.

All that worked. Once I got in the university, I applied for a scholarship. Scholarships were based on need and academic qualifications. I had the neediest résumé possible. I was on welfare—you can't get any needier than that—and I had very good grades, both at the high school and for the time I was at the university. So I'm launched. The money I salted away paid for the first quarter. The rest of the time I got scholarships, which also entitled me to a job on campus, in the office of one of the sociology profs. Among the students there were few adults, so I associated with all these kids for two years, just shed my years. I never recovered them.

In those days, the university regulations weren't so sticky. They let me declare my major, sociology, right off the reel. I took thirty-two credits in it, although I was only there two years. They let me take advanced economics without some of the prerequisites. My minor was psychology. You see, I was going to be a social worker[9] because I'm a do-gooder by nature. I just can't help meddling in other people's business.

In the process of amassing these thirty-two credits in sociology, I got a big idea. Here I am on welfare, on the receiving end of social work, and I'm learning all this theory at the university. There was something missing, and that was the administration. So I went to the zone office [welfare office, or Department of Social and Health Services] and said, "Look, I'm getting all this theory at the university. I would like you to give me some kind of project here at the office so I'll learn about the administrative part of it." They were delighted to have me as a volunteer. I was their one rehabilitation case.

Every day for an hour or two I worked on a project, and I got to know all the social workers. When I was waiting in line on Friday to get my voucher, they said, "Oh, you don't need to stand out there on Friday, Mrs. Wolf. We'll give it to you when you come inside." And I said, "Oh no. That's part of my education." I looked forward to those Fridays. I stood outside to get my voucher with the rest of the great unwashed.

I remember—and this is etched in my mind—I went up to the zone office one particular morning to stand in line. It was a cold day. The place was crowded inside and there were two small girls out on the porch obviously waiting for their parent. They sat there, thin and pale and shabbily dressed. I bounced up and said, "How are you today?" And they said, "We're all right." A lump came in my throat and I had to choke back my tears. I knew they weren't.

After a while, I found out some things.

First, I learned that at the university, the theory was that social workers help people who are ill adjusted to adjust to a friendly society. That's the theory.

Second, I learned that inside the welfare administration, the theory was to get a perfectly well-adjusted person, a perfectly sane and healthy person, whose only sin was that he didn't have a job, to adapt to living on nothing. And they called that "interpreting the policy of the administration."

And, third, I learned from standing in line on Fridays, when the welfare checks were cut, just what it was all about.

JOINING THE PARTY

I met my first Communist on a Friday. A bunch of us were in line outside the zone office. It was 1934. There was a guy with a petition. Now, this petition dealt with something I'd never heard of: unemployment insurance. To get the money for that, the plan was to do away with the state militia.

I said, "I never heard of unemployment insurance. That's a great idea. But this getting the funds by doing away with the state militia—you'll never get it that way. That's the only thing that holds this silly system together. You won't get the legislature to do it. Who cooked this thing up?"

He said, "The Communist Party."

I said, "I thought they were only in Russia."

"No, they're all over the world," he said.

About that time, a woman came up to relieve him. She had a little more knowledge and told me, "We're just doing this for propaganda, to alert people about the need for unemployment insurance."

I said, "Well, I still don't think you should try to raise the funds by axing the state militia."[10]

So that was my first step into the Communist Party—criticism!

I went to the meeting at her home that night. It happened that she was being evicted. There we were, arriving for a meeting at her place, and the sheriff was taking all the furniture out and putting it on the sidewalk. So we all picked the furniture up off the sidewalk and carried it around to the back door and put it back in. Then he'd bring it out and we'd put it in. And this went on. The heart of the sheriff wasn't in it. He said, "Aw, the hell with it," and he left. Nice guy. We put the furniture all back in place and had our meeting. So that was my first experience with the Communist Party—action! Putting the furniture back, fighting the establishment![11]

When we finally sat down at the meeting, they gave me Karl Marx's *Communist Manifesto*,[12] but there wasn't anything in there that I hadn't already learned from my father, who believed in socialism, and my mother, who was secretary at the iww [Industrial Workers of the World][13] union, which believed that one big union would solve all the problems. I had literally imbibed it with my mother's milk. But this was the first time I'd seen it all in one book, written so logically and so succinctly. The *Manifesto* didn't change my thinking, it simply reinforced it. I joined the party that night.

You see, I grew up class-conscious. I knew we were poor. I knew exactly what class I came from. I got that from my father. And while I don't remember too much about him, I seem to remember all the things he ever spoke to me about. One of them was that the middle class stood as a buffer between the very poor and the very rich, and I didn't like the middle class. I never saw one, but I didn't like them. I had a kind of mythical idea of what they looked like—big, portly people, bankers, with large stomachs, disagreeable-looking people. I never knew I was going to grow up and be one. Even now I speak middle-class language with an accent, because this is not my true world.

I joined [the Communist Party] because I could see that I had a personal interest in belonging to a group like that. I was in a bad way. Dependent on welfare, on their whims. Here was a group I could belong to that would fight for these things—comrades, rallying around and getting people to come and help. I had sense enough to know that you can't do anything much alone in the way of struggle against the establishment.[14]

In those days, the people who made up the Communist Party were largely immigrants, mostly from Eastern Europe, who had not been assimilated. It was not a middle-class party. I was one of the first white-collar workers who joined. The Depression brought a lot of people like me into the party, and we changed it a lot. I used to criticize their leaflets. They were dogmatic. The party would ask me to put them out on the University of Washington campus, and I'd say, "They don't talk that way here." They didn't talk about the "Bloody Capitalists" or the "Running Dogs of Imperialism"—strong wording that came over from Eastern Europe. So I wrote the leaflets for them. As time went on, more and more middle-class people belonged to the party. They spoke our language.[15]

Meanwhile, I was still at the university, going every day to lectures in economics. We had enormous classes of 250 people sitting up in tiers and the professor was down below on a tiny dais, reading a lot of stuff to us. There was no chance for discussion.

An hour or maybe two in the week, we were in small groups. We'd talk about the textbook. It was full of so much nonsense I could hardly swallow it—open the book to any page! I got into a few arguments, but it wasn't much good. I can remember a case study in this book: they were going to start a glove-manufacturing place, so they went to such and such a location, where there were a lot of skilled glove makers, and set their factory up there—which is, of course, a lot of foolishness. They go where labor's cheap and teach them how to make gloves, and that's it.

For an examination in economics, they gave us true / false. I had a wonderful memory and could recall all the garbage they had spilled out in these big lecture sessions and in the textbook. I knew what they thought was true and what they thought was false, because they accepted as gospel what was in that book. I got an A, even though I didn't believe a word of it.

At the same time, I was taking advanced English. I had to write four thousand words on anything—poetry, fiction—anything. I undertook to write a book review of the economics textbook that I'd memorized entirely. I started in and I just tore the book to pieces. The English prof would call us in from time to time to review how we were getting along with our four-thousand-word ordeal, and he got emotionally involved with my dissertation on this textbook. We'd talk and argue about it, and he forgot that he was supposed to check on my English. I finally persuaded him that what I said was correct, that a lot of the stuff in the economics book was nonsense. He said, "I would like to show this to the head of the Economics Department. Would you mind? I won't put your name on it." I said, "Oh, I'd be glad if you did. And I insist you put my name on it! Also, I'd like you to inform them that I got an A on their stupid true / falses." That textbook was superficial. Every country's education system is designed to keep the people who are in power, in power.

Next it was advanced economics. We studied Adam Smith, Malthus, and Ricardo.[16] When it came to Karl Marx, we spent twenty minutes. I told the professor, Dr. Mund, that I didn't think much of his leaving out Karl Marx. He said, "I haven't spent any time on it. When I took over this job, I took over the notes of my predecessor, and I just read them." So I said, "Wouldn't you like something better than that? I know a bunch of Communists. Why don't I get one of them to help you out on this?" He said, "Okay." So I got busy with one of my friends, who made up a lecture on Marxist economics. The professor was delighted to get it, and he switched from his little twenty-minute thing to a really serious paper on Marx. It may be there now if they still inherit their lecture notes from each other. I don't know.

Now, classes like that just couldn't compete with the education I was getting on the streets. By the time that I had thirty-two credits at the university, I decided that no way did I want to be a social worker. No way. I wasn't going to "interpret the policy" for anybody. Instead of looking for a social work career, I threw my efforts into the Workers' Alliance, where I was head of the Grievance Committee. When somebody needed help, I would lead a delegation down to the zone office, and we'd fight for it.

I stood in line to get my welfare check one Friday. A social worker called me in to the office and said to me, "I see on your record that you have thirty-two hours in sociology. Why don't you get a job with the administration in here?"

"As a social worker?" I said.

"Yes."

"Well, I am a social worker," I said. "I'm doing exactly that. The only difference between you and me is that I can do and say as I please, but you are tied in by all these rules and regulations in that manual."

In the Communist Party and the Workers' Alliance, I felt that I was doing real social work. I wasn't on the outside doing social work. I was one of the needy persons working with my peers, you see. Makes a lot of difference.

I understood the plight of the social workers. They were mostly women, compassionate women. But there was no way for the clients to know that, because it was the social worker who said, "No more cod liver oil for your children this time." And they'd have to say it in such a way that the client wouldn't get angry enough to bombard the place. Social workers were the buffers, "interpreting the policy of the administration." That's the jargon they used.

I was on welfare myself. At one point, we lived in a little cottage on a steep hillside, at the top of a big flight of steps. You could enter from above, too. I had a wood stove. The Welfare delivered a bunch of wood. Each piece was four or five feet long, so it had to be cut. It was wet and in a pile at the bottom of the stairs. There was no way I could buck that stuff up there, no way at all! So what did I do? I sold it to the people down at the foot of the stairs, for their fireplace. Then I went and bought some decent wood, all cut up nicely, and had it delivered above to my woodshed.

The social worker came by. She knew that it had been outrageous to bring me this pile of wood. She leveled her chin and said, "How are you getting along with the wood?"

I said, "Oh, wonderfully well."

She said, "Oh, really? How did you manage?"

I said, "I carried it up the stairs—the neighbors have some sawhorses—and I got a cross-cut saw and chopped it up in pieces. It's all hanging out there in the woodshed, and you can see it."

She stared at me.

I said, "Why don't you drop the subject and talk about something else?"

We both roared with laughter. I didn't pretend I wasn't lying. I was describing to her something that was physically impossible for me to do.

After I'd given up the social work thing, I was still going to the university, studying geology or any old subject I could lay my hands on, since I had nothing else to do. But I'd lost interest. I just thought it was a waste of time. I could get along all right without this university business. I decided to go back to my old trade, the one that I knew: legal secretary. I gradually learned to spell . . . well, I had a dictionary, and I could spell well enough to look up the words.

SOCIAL WORKER: THE CIVIL WORKS ADMINISTRATION (CWA)

What really put an end to my university career was that the government instituted a big hiring program with the CWA, the WPA, and all the other New Deal programs, so everybody was taken off welfare and immediately put into a make-work project, given jobs.[17] So that rescued me from the university. I was pretty well educated anyway: self-educated.

My job with the CWA was wonderful. The CWA used the field houses at places like Garfield [High School] and Green Lake and Alki Point to start up orchestras, basketball, rug making, languages, current-events classes, gymnastics, horseshoe throwing—everything you could think of. The deal was to get the community to come in and participate. They hired a lot of teachers, too—gymnastics people, and so forth.

With this big sociology business on my record, they made me an organizer for community activities. I knocked on every door up and down Alki and all the back streets, and I would say, "I'm from the CWA, and we have a project started," and I'd try to get them to invite me in. Mostly they did because it was raining. Then I would look around to see what I could see. I'd say, "Oh, you make hooked rugs?" Then they'd bring out their rugs, or the mats they were weaving, or the knitting, or the painting, or the whittling. I saw the ladies' horticultural projects and the daughters' toe shoes and the boys' frog collections.

I'd get the unemployed men in the house to show me all the things they made in their spare time. Then, you know, little Johnny played the flute, and I was trying to get people together to make an orchestra. One way or the other, I'd get them all to go down to the community center. It was just bulging with people.

After about three months, they shut it down. The whole thing. I was stricken. All those people, so disappointed. This went on all over the nation. Congress had appropriated some millions of dollars, and then the money ran out. I went back on relief, but I was really mad. All those people whom I had gotten doing something, to break the monotony of their lives! A real tragedy. I don't think I've ever forgiven the government for that.

"I GOT ORGANIZING": THE WPA

*T*hen they started the WPA, which was heavily financed. The deal there was to put people to work. The WPA had manual workers making bridges and digging ditches—employing people, but using as little money for physical, material things as possible. I think they were limited to ten per-cent for tools. Instead of buying big bulldozers, they would buy shovels, and in some cases teaspoons, so that the money could go for wages. Workers got union wages, but they worked short hours in order not to compete with the unions. That beautiful Suzzallo Library at the University of Washington was built by the Works Progress Administration. And the bridges, all the way down the coast on Highway 1. Before then, every time you came to a river, you had to take a little ferry to get across.

A huge section of the WPA was dedicated to adult education. That's where I went for my first WPA job. The project was to get unemployed teachers together with unemployed adults and start them learning. They had no textbooks, no guidance at all. You get a bunch of adults together, and what do you teach them? They don't want to listen to ABCs and "Dick and Jane" stories. They want to know about the goings-on in the world, such things as unemployment and social security, which were just com-ing in. I was the researcher. I was assigned, among other things, to look up social security legislation in Germany, England, and the United States. The teachers would take my material, print it up, and bring it into their classes. They would teach in a lot of different places, in halls around town, out in the neighborhoods. Anyplace there was an empty room, they'd turn it into a classroom.

I got organizing. With the Workers' Alliance, I organized the teach-ers on the WPA Adult Education Project in 1935. We had meetings and of course I was secretary. I'm always secretary. Meanwhile, my research turned up an official, non-WPA teachers' union, a charter for Local 200 of the American Federation of Teachers [AFT], a union that was con-nected to the AFL. The state of Washington had destroyed this union by passing a law that no teacher could belong to a union. There was a clause in every teacher's contract that said if you belonged to a union, the con-tract was breached, and you're out—the yellow-dog contract.[18] The teach-ers had to dismantle their union, but a few diehards didn't turn in the charter. They met in darkened rooms for quite a few years, where I found them.

Then came Roosevelt's program, the NLRB [National Labor Relations Board].[19] Among other things, it provided that it was against the law to interfere with people organizing. So the yellow-dog contract was out, and the teachers were free to organize. We contacted this old AFT charter group of the AFL and suggested to them that our Workers' Alliance WPA Adult Education Project union join their union. We all joined, and I became secretary in 1936 of an American Federation of Teachers local. When I was organizing in the WPA, wherever I was, I would try to organize them into a union affiliated with the mainstream union.

Now, the AFT teachers were reluctant to approach the school board as union members. Even though the law had been passed to protect unions, the school board would try to get around it, and the AFT teachers would just sit and squirm. So we WPA union members stood in for them. Some teacher would be fired, or some injustice would be done, and our WPA union would go up against the school board and speak on behalf of the teacher. Eventually, the public school teachers began to come out of their little corners and take over.

So they fired me for organizing. I got fired from the WPA because of organizing to protect our wages and our hours and the kinds of things we wanted to research and teach!

We had a big hullabaloo over that. The Central Committee of the King County Labor Council went up to the WPA administration and said, "We want our secretary back on the job," et cetera. The WPA made a compromise deal: they wouldn't put me back on the job as a research worker, but they'd put me on another project—same wages, on another project. Okay, we accepted that, and I was assigned to the county auditor's office down in the County-City Building. And they didn't have a union. So there I go again—I organized a union. I was secretary of that one, too—the American Federation of Government Employees—in 1936. Now, I don't believe in union activities for the sake of union activities. I was involved, personally involved. I could never have lived in an ivory tower and gone around organizing a bunch of unions. I have to be one of those who benefits by the organizing.

My WPA job in that office was doing typing and filing and a bunch of stuff like that. The county auditor was reassessing taxes on all the real estate. They had a zillion people out in the field doing reassessments and, as a result, hundreds of thousands of properties were put on the tax rolls.

We found out they were charging some little old lady who owned a five-hundred-dollar house more in taxes than they were charging Boeing.

Now I was secretary of two AFL unions, the teachers and the government employees.

I got fired again for organizing on the job. The Central Committee of the King County Labor Council went up to see the WPA administration about firing me. They made a compromise deal: they would take me off the county auditor's job, but they would give me another one at the same wages, in another place. And so they switched me to the University of Washington campus. And when I got this new assignment, in the spring of 1937, I said to the WPA administrator, "Is there a union out there?" He said, "No." I said to him, "Well, how dumb can you be?" I thought it was hilarious, you know, and I was just roaring with laughter.[20]

So I got out there at the university and started organizing.

I worked for a time in the university's payroll department. They didn't have enough employees, so they worked them overtime. But in fact it was against the law to pay for overtime—under the WPA, we were only allowed to work so many hours a week—so the payroll department promised the workers that if they would work overtime with no pay, they would get time off with pay "later on." Well, I just figured there would be no "later on," you know. They'd get ripped off in the end, they'd get ripped off. I saw the game.

I didn't go for it. I told them I was going to go home at four o'clock. And so I got fired. I came back the next day and said, "Okay, you fired me because I refused to break the law. Now, I'm law-abiding, and I'm going to write to Mr. Harry Hopkins [federal administrator for the WPA] and tell him that I got fired because I refused to break his law." I was put back to work.

I started to walk out at four o'clock. Here are the rest of them, still working away. The administrator catches me on the way out.

"Look here," he says, "we're doing a public service. How are we to get the payroll out?"

"There are a lot of unemployed people out there yet," I say. "Hire them."

"We have no money to hire them."

"What if you don't get the payroll out? What if these thousands of people on the university's payroll don't get their checks? *They're* not going to sit still. *They'll* protest. *They'll* see that you get money to hire your workers. But what you're doing—that's no way to run a ball game."

He didn't take my advice. They put me in their special little office because of the demoralizing effect of my going home at four o'clock while the rest were all staying there for nothing. So I'm in this little office by myself and four o'clock comes. I'm just supposed to go home quietly, but I never do. I always go into the big offices, where I say good-bye to everybody to get more demoralizing going. The other workers just couldn't get up and go out with me. They just didn't have what it takes to fight it. And they never got their compensation, their time off with pay. It was a cruel thing to do to those people. Anyway, I didn't get suckered in on that one.

One of the things I'm most proud of is the organizing I did with William Pennock for the Washington Old Age Pension Union.[21] The senior citizens of that day didn't have any income—not a penny—and no pensions. Bill was a young man, an organizer, and he had a real feeling for older people. He started the pension union, and it wasn't like these senior centers where the men sit around and play checkers and the women knit and look at pretty pictures. He believed in action. It was a grassroots business. Bill started to organize pension unions in every neighborhood and community, all around the state. I wasn't a senior citizen by a long shot, but I organized a bunch of them, too. I went around making speeches, and I specialized in taxes. I'd studied the unfair tax system we had, the sales tax, and how the big burden fell on the poor and elderly, so I would go to the Washington Old Age Pension Union meetings in small communities and explain the pension tax issues.

The pension union launched an initiative to the state legislature: everybody who was over sixty-five and was hard up would get twenty dollars a month. We gathered all the signatures, carried on a campaign, and passed this thing, and it was the first government-funded pension program in the United States, the first time the term "senior citizen" was used. The Communists made that one happen: John Caughlan[22] wrote it, and Bill Pennock organized it and saw it through.

When it was passed, the Washington State Pension Fund also gave old people the right to have hearings when they were denied a pension and to bring their own counsel, someone who did not have to be a lawyer. I often represented people at hearings in the welfare building. Many pensioners were semiliterate, and they didn't know much about law. They'd be nervous and not know how to act. I made the presentation for them and answered the questions the way they should be answered.

8 / Politics as Theater

THE FEDERAL THEATER PROJECT

*F*inally, I found a WPA job that I really wanted. I went to the director of the Federal Theater Project and interviewed for a job. He really wanted me as his secretary. But when I went back to the WPA administrator and said I had found a spot, oh no, no way could I have it.

I demanded to be put on that job. I told them, "The WPA has been organized to preserve people's skills. I do shorthand. The Federal Theater Project wants somebody who does shorthand. If the WPA insists on putting me in jobs where I don't exercise that skill, I will lose it, and when the Depression is all over, I will not be able to resume my proper place as a legal secretary." I told them I was going to write Harry Hopkins about how the Seattle WPA administration was stripping me of my skills. That did it. A second time I didn't have to write to Harry Hopkins. They put me to work in late 1937 for Mr. Connor, director of the Federal Theater Project in Seattle.

I organized a union on that project, of course. But this time it was different, because the Federal Theater—that was the most wonderful thing! For example, the play *Power*. *Power* was banned in most cities because it was advocating government ownership of the utilities. Too "communistic." But because we had Seattle City Light, which was publicly owned, the Federal Theater Project in Seattle embraced the play, and the mayor went to the opening.

That play was so funny! Here's this pathetic consumer, and he wants to buy some potatoes. The guy says they cost two dollars a sack. Well, that's too much, and he goes to another store, where he only gets charged a dollar and a half. Okay, he buys the potatoes. He makes another couple of purchases like that. Then he gets the light bill: seventeen cents a kilowatt hour. He wants to know what a kilowatt is. Nobody knows, and nobody in the audience knows, either. He finally decides, whether he knows what it is or not, he's just not going to pay that much. He's going to go to another place and buy light, and he looks around and there aren't any other places. All three little power companies have gotten together and formed a big monopoly. Onstage, we see the three of them on the telephone, all talking at once, fixing the price. So our consumer is stuck, no place to go. But he's going to fight them. He picks up his coat and he starts to dance around and he rears back as if he's part of a prizefight. Suddenly he gets a real body blow from this invisible man he's fighting. He falls down flat on his back. The lights go out. And that's what happens to the consumer.

Most of the plays that were put on by the Federal Theater Project had a message that was of concern to the people. For example, President Roosevelt made a speech, his inaugural address, at the beginning of his second term, in 1937. He said, "I see one-third of a nation ill-housed, ill-clad, and ill-nourished." And so the Federal Theater Project had a play called *A Third of the Nation,* about slum houses, how the roof would fall in. That caused a big hullabaloo. There was always humor in those plays. Humor.

Another play they put on was called *Spirochete,* which was attacked as pornographic, because right out loud it talked about venereal disease, syphilis—how it originated, how it was brought from Europe by Columbus and his gang, and how it spread like wildfire, and what effects it had on people who got it: you died. All the moral people were up in arms that the play even mentioned it. Think of the plays they put on today, just filled with all kinds of four-letter words. Yet in the Federal Theater Project plays, there wasn't one obscene word. They were really educational.

Hundreds of thousands of people saw these plays. They'd try them out here in the city and then they'd pack the whole bunch up into buses to Ellensburg, Ephrata, and all the little towns. People saw live theater all over the United States for the first time. And the plays were about things the people were interested in, subjects that hit their lives, not just pure entertainment in a vacuum. They were learning.

MILDRED PAIGE

*W*hen I was a kid in Victoria, we had a stock theater company, and I never missed a Saturday performance by the star Mildred Paige. It was sacred. I adored her, of course—a beautiful woman with a dazzling smile. Now, the leading man, a very handsome young man, was her husband. I didn't fall in love with him. May Neilsson from the basketball league and I would buy peanuts and sit in the front seats. We would do all kinds of things to try to run into our heroine, but when we did, we'd never approach her, just gaze from afar.

When I came to Seattle, in 1921, for a brief moment I had a job down on 1st Avenue in a drugstore, an ice-cream parlor. One of these girlie burlesque theaters was right around the corner. Mildred Paige came in and she was crying. She was in the burlesque show! Her handsome husband had abandoned her. Her actor friends were all around her, consoling her. I gave her my all. I served my heroine some ice cream.

I couldn't imagine her in one of those burlesque shows, so I bought a ticket and went in. When she came onstage, I felt better. She wasn't naked—nothing vulgar about it. She sang simple songs, and she still looked dazzling: the immaculate Mildred Paige I had known.

When the WPA switched me over to the Federal Theater Project, I was working next door to the theater where they did rehearsals. I heard her before I saw her. It was the same lovely voice. I would have known it anyplace. If she spoke now, I would know her voice. So I went into the theater and got acquainted with Mildred Paige. I told her how I admired her when I was a kid. We had this little thing in common.

One of the hazards of working on a WPA project was that they were always changing their rules, firing people en masse. All the single men would get fired, or all the single women, or all the mothers who had children. The whole New Deal recovery program was beset—underfunded, red-baited, and sniped at. We'd all been laid off and put back on again and laid off and put back on again.[23] It was a very precarious place to work, I'll tell you.

On one of these sweeps, Mildred Paige was let go with a lot of other single women. We had a union on the project by that time. We went to the administration and just raised holy hell. So did Mr. O'Connor, the director. He was losing one of his star actors. He backed us up.

When you got fired from a WPA project, you got a pink slip. The number of this particular form was 402. So I wrote a play for a rally protesting the layoffs and I entitled it *402*. We had all these good actors, and there was a big audience. When the title of the play was announced, to my amazement they all burst into laughter. We all had one, you see—we all had a 402 in our pocket.

We got Mildred back. Special preference. Mr. O'Connor was a big shot.

PLAYWRIGHT

I wrote so many plays, things that I don't have copies of. I'd write 'em, put 'em on, and tear 'em up. Just one-night stands. When they were cutting relief and we were having big rallies, I wrote a play about welfare. In the play, people get laid off, and they go to the city. They get the runaround. Then they go to the county. They get the runaround. They go to the state and they get the runaround—the theme was this merry-go-round—and I wrote a poem to finish the play. The poem was based around a Supreme Court decision,[24] which the county commissioners were using as an excuse for cutting welfare. I had the chorus inject this all the way through, like a chant: "If you don't know what to say, quote the Supreme Court decision." It really was funny.

When we staged the play at the protest rally, we put [actors playing] welfare people on one side and county commissioners on the other, and they chanted, back and forth, " . . . quote the Supreme Court decision." Five or six hundred people attended the rally. The next day, they all trooped up to the county commissioners' office for a big protest. One county commissioner at that time, an oily type of guy named Tom Smith, said, "Well, I just can't do anything now . . . let me quote the Supreme Court decision." And the whole bunch of us just roared with laughter. Just roared! He was amazed. He stopped and waited until the laughter subsided. Then he said it again, " . . . quote the Supreme Court decision," and off we went again. Finally he threw his hands up and left. He couldn't get through.

That's the thing about the Federal Theater plays: they were true to life and they were funny. The humor took us one step back from life as it was, just a little bit of distance. It kept people from feeling so sorry for themselves, you know. That's a saving grace, to be able to laugh at yourself.

MY MOTHER'S LEGACY

*W*hile I was working at the Federal Theater Project, I got a call that my mother was dying—a massive heart attack. She was sixty-six years old. She was near death when I went over to Port Angeles. The doctor came up. I remember he said to her, "Now, I want you to get better. I don't want you to climb out on the roof anymore." She lived just a few days, but I couldn't stay. If you were off a WPA job more than three days, you got fired. So I had to say good-bye to her, knowing I wouldn't see her again. I was always bitter about that. You couldn't decently see your mother die— one of the chalk marks I have against the establishment.

She had it harder to survive than I ever did. Ill equipped educationally, she had no skills, she had no label. She couldn't teach or be a secretary. She didn't retire from anything. But she wasn't a pessimistic, gloomy person by a long shot. My brother took care of her. They lived together in Port Angeles. She nursed a woman for a while. Anybody with ordinary strength could go out and nurse a sick person. It was quite a different world.

She had nothing to will. The legacy she left us didn't need a will. I was really close to my brother and sister. If she'd written that into a will, it wouldn't have worked, now would it have? She also left a bunch of jam and jellies. Every time I went over to Port Angeles after her death, I'd rob my mother's estate of these preserves. Bit by bit, I got them all.

STREET THEATER

$\mathcal{I}$ got kicked out of the Federal Theater Project—out of the whole WPA—in 1938 for being an alien.[25] Mr. O'Connor tried to exert influence in Washington, D.C., to keep me on, but they were getting arbitrary at that point and winding down the whole program.

Then I was on the street. I went to work for the Workers' Alliance, because it was the only place I had to turn to. They had this big old building at 94 Main Street, down there on the Skid Road, and I was chair of the Grievance Committee, Local 1, not far from what they called a Hooverville, a whole city built up out of cardboard and corrugated iron and bits of this and that, with its own police, little educational things, and a fire department.[26] A lot of the homeless lived there, quite a number of women and some children, but mostly men. Our headquarters was a hangout for these people, the active ones.

We organized on a neighborhood basis. People paid dues. Even unemployed people could always raise up ten-cent dues to pay our rent, which was probably about ten dollars a month. The people would come to our offices with a bunch of grievances. We'd form committees and figure out how to help them. We had monthly meetings and statewide conventions. Thursdays, I would go to Communist Party meetings and see a lot of the same people. Maybe we'd get some help or advice.

One big issue at that time was the way they treated single women. The theory was that everybody on the WPA or on welfare who had good health was supposed to be looking for work. Welfare paid a very little bit of money for rent, fuel, food, and funny clothing that was made in WPA shops by day workers. If a single woman applied for welfare, they would give her a voucher for two weeks' rent. And at the end of two weeks, they wouldn't give her another voucher, on the theory that she would have found work and could pay her rent. Well, there was no work. Consequently, the landlord would be faced with this tenant who had no money and with the choice of letting the person live there for nothing or evicting her.

Once she got evicted, she had to go and find another place and then Welfare would give her another two-week voucher. This was a hardship—

not only having to move but also having to give the employment office a new address every two weeks. They're gonna take a dim view of your stability. You're supposed to live in one place, for heaven's sakes. It was an imposition on the landlords, too, because, contrary to popular belief, landlords are not a heartless class of people. A lot of them were compassionate and they were reluctant to throw a woman out.

Once I was out of the WPA, I had no income, so I applied for relief. I was boarding with friends, Ed and Helen Hill, a family on Eastlake [Avenue]. They were behind me. They didn't charge me rent, but it was an imposition on them. I didn't want to sponge off this family.

So I took one of those cheap little rooms down on 1st Avenue and got a voucher for two weeks. And at the end of two weeks I told the landlady that I wouldn't have any more money for her. I said, "You better evict me." The way to evict people was just to lock the door, you know, and she was reluctant to do that.

I told her that she should lock the door and under no circumstances let me come back in, and not to worry about me. I'd be back one of these days with a voucher for my rent. Otherwise, she was going to have to take care of me for the rest of my life. Well, that was an appalling prospect to her, too, so, very reluctantly, when I left that morning, she locked the door, and I couldn't get back in.

So then I'm a case.

Up at the Workers' Alliance, we got busy fighting this case of my being locked out. We got up a committee, went down to the county commissioners' . . . and nothing happened. So, okay, I'll have to go seek a place to sleep that night. I went up 3rd Avenue to the YWCA. On the way up there, I passed a real estate office with pictures in the windows—all kinds of pretty houses. The excitement's gone and all my buddies are gone and I'm on the street, you know, hoping I can get a place to sleep and feeling a little bit sorry for myself. The sign said BUY YOUR OWN HOME, and that struck me as so damn funny. What a good suggestion! I was more than ready to go out and buy one of those homes! I just stood there laughing.

At the Y I told them my sad story and they gave me a room for the night, but you could only stay at the Y two nights. The women up in the dormitory thought my situation was terrible. All day long the next day, the Grievance Committee of the Workers' Alliance ran around putting pressure on the zone office and then on the county commissioners. Meanwhile, those women in the y dormitory started phoning the zone office: "Give Mrs. Wolf her rent." And they put pressure on the y, too: "Let Mrs. Wolf stay at the y." All the people who belonged to the Workers' Alliance were just pouring telephone calls in on the county commissioners: "Give Mrs. Wolf her rent!"

The welfare workers in the zone office wanted me to win. They felt terrible about making these women go from place to place every two weeks. The battle raged all day long. Then the y started putting pressure on the zone office. With all the publicity I was bringing them, they were going to have all the homeless women in the world coming to the y.

A hectic day. We wound up at the county commissioners' office for a big rally and they said they would pay my rent. Then they said to me, "Go on home." I said, "Not until you call my landlady and tell her that you guarantee the rent." They didn't want to do that and I didn't want to get caught in some bureaucratic crunch with delay and delay and delay. So finally they called her. And down in the zone office, when the supervisor announced to the social workers, "Mrs. Wolf gets her rent," they all cheered, because once they decided to pay mine, they had to pay all of them. It established a precedent—unless, of course, I kept it a secret. But the Workers' Alliance put out a leaflet that heralded the news: "Now you can all go get your rent."

I wouldn't have left my comfortable home on Eastlake to live in that crummy old place if it hadn't been for everybody. When you take a case, you have to pick a stalwart person who can stand up, who won't crumble under you. There's nothing more discouraging for a grievance committee than to find out that the person you're trying to fight for has given up the fight.[27]

ACTOR

I guess I got this idea of being an actor from the Federal Theater Project. There was a young man who cared for his aged aunt. When he got married, he left the aunt stranded. When she applied for relief, they wouldn't give it to her, because she had this nephew who was supposed to support her.

Well, she had no intention of making her nephew support her and he had no intention of letting his aunt starve, either. I told him, "You stick to your guns. You have a right to fall in love. You have a right to marry. And you don't have to support your aunt. She's entitled to a pension and relief and all the rest."

So I went down to the zone office and pretended I was a lady. I had a hat and gloves, and off I went. I asked to see the superintendent—it was the same office where I picked up my own relief check. They didn't recognize me in my hat and gloves. Anyway, I took that risk.

I told them I was Mrs. Foss of the Foss Tug Boat Company, a very well-known company. Every time I see a Foss tugboat I have a laugh about this. I said, "There is a dear old lady whom I have known for a long time and I've taken her on. I take her things to eat and call on her. I went there the other day and she was starving."

They said, "She has a nephew that's supposed to support her."

I said, "I didn't come here to talk about the nephew, I came to talk about Mrs. Sanford. I came to talk about her and her need. Why, I can't go on supporting this woman indefinitely. I don't think it's right. I think you should give her a food allowance and her rent."

We went back and forth and they kept throwing this nephew at me, and I kept throwing him back. On and on, and finally they agreed to take her the emergency food voucher that day, I was so insistent. After all, they weren't going to send the FBI to find out if this woman, Mrs. Foss, really existed. It just never dawned on them that anybody would be so outrageous as to pose as a famous person.

I went back to the Workers' Alliance office and took off my camouflage, hung up my hat and gloves, and I was so happy, pretty darn glad. You know, you have to be creative.

In the Workers' Alliance, I was with like-minded people. I became a social worker after all, but I didn't have to worry about that manual. We were all in the same boat. Nobody was coming from the outside. So that's how I got launched in fighting the establishment. Before, I was fighting my own little individual battles. Now my course was set in a broader basis. And through my experience in the thirties, with the unemployed and with the wpa, my confidence in the people developed. I got a feeling for the power of the people.

9 / The Party

LIVING IN SIN

Nydia was just about ready to become twenty-one years old when I applied again for citizenship. She had been illegally entered [into the United States] simply because nobody realized that a four-year-old child should be registered just like an adult. The ins wanted her to give proof of entry, and records, signed by everybody, going back to 1923. They had quizzed her a lot about my politics.

Because I had gotten involved in the Communist Party, I knew I would be denied [citizenship]. But if I did get it before Nydia was twenty-one, then she would become a citizen with me. So, for that reason, I tried again in 1939. I got turned down on August 14, 1939, on the grounds that I had failed to establish good moral character.[28] It was because I was living with a person I wasn't married to. I don't have anything against marriage. I just didn't like to be married. It was too confining. Nowadays everybody lives in sin, but in those days they didn't.

One of the immigration people warned me ahead of time: "Don't deny it. You'll be perjuring yourself, because they have the goods on you." They were just poised to pounce on me if I lied about it. At the hearing, when they asked if I'd ever lived under a different name, that was my chance to say yes. I pulled the rug out from under them, so they had to drop it and go on to something more ignominious. They were just looking for excuses to turn me down.

The Communists didn't like their people to live in sin, any more than the government did. My brother, Bill, was married in secret so his wife wouldn't lose her job as a teacher in the Seattle Public Schools. In those days, teachers couldn't be married, so they had three options. One was to live in sin. Another was to give up all ideas of having a family life and to devote themselves to teaching. And the third was to keep their marriage a secret. It took World War II to break through the moral barrier that teachers were confronted with. My brother and Jo Erickson went down to Astoria, on the Columbia River, to get married, and I went with them as a witness. It was kept secret even from relatives and close friends. They lived a long way from where she taught school, so they weren't likely to be found out.[29] The Communist Party didn't know about Bill and Jo's secret marriage. All they knew was that my brother was living in sin. So they gossiped, and they put pressure on me to talk Bill out of it. He wasn't a Communist, but he was my brother and he knew everybody.

The sense of family was very strong in the party. I remember thinking, "What good people these are!" You knew them all. They had so much in common politically. What greater bond can you have with people than sharing a religious or political belief? You admire them. They're so intelligent, and they think like you do.

They were mostly poor people. There were some wealthy ones, but they couldn't have a very high profile. It's wonderful to be poor, the only way you can be really free. Now, I don't mean dire poverty, where you're scrambling for something to eat every minute. But if you haven't much to lose materially, then you're pretty free to do as you like, nothing to protect. We had nothing, no stake in society.

"SOLIDARITY FOREVER"

*W*e were always meeting. You don't know what it is to go to meetings until you belong to the Communist Party. We met as a study group at somebody's house. The units were called branches, not cells—that must have been an FBI invention—and they were based on neighborhoods. There were seminars . . . and educationals . . . and fund-raisers. You kept seeing the same people all the time. The marriages were almost tribal. You never married outside the Communist Party because that's where all your friends were. And children, lots of children.

We didn't have cards—"card-carrying Communist," another invention by the FBI. People had assumed names if membership in the party would jeopardize their career in some way. If you were a university professor, you would be known as John Smith to all the party people and you would be protected by meeting only with your unit and not going to party conventions or conferences. All during the thirties, Communists were harassed. The FBI had dossiers and spies all around, which didn't come out in the open until the fifties.

You were always trying to recruit members, people who thought the system was no good. They saw unemployment, starvation, racism, and all these bad things. You'd try to bring them a step farther, to the point where they could see that under a socialist society there would be equality, and then they'd become members of the Communist Party. There was great rejoicing when a new person showed up for the first time. I had a wider field than a lot of people from which to bring recruits into the party. I kept reaching out in the Workers' Alliance, and before that, I'd be meeting people on my WPA jobs and in whatever union I was organizing.

We didn't attract a certain type of ego-tripping person. Those were the people who flunked out. They crumbled under pressure. Most of the people who betrayed the party, who later showed up at the hearings naming names, were egotists. They were popular at last, whereas Communist Party members were out doing things and they weren't in it for themselves.

And it was fun. I wouldn't be in the environmental movement if it weren't fun, and I wouldn't have been in the Communist Party if it hadn't been fun. I remember one time everybody dressed up. I came as a Norwegian and I had a little hat on and a lace collar. Lots of dancing and singing. One time we went up to Lake Washington for a picnic. Darkness took over, and we couldn't find each other. Somebody got the bright idea of singing "Wave Scarlet Banner." Everybody heard it and came toward us, so we got together and had our picnic. We knew all those songs: "Solidarity Forever," "The Four Insurgent Generals." We were a singing bunch.

At the educationals you learned all this boring Marxist stuff, which I already knew. I was not much on theory. I couldn't stand it, hardly. Pamphlets would come out, and you'd have to study them. They taught that ultimately the capitalist system would outgrow its usefulness and be succeeded by a socialist system. But the party never said that we would *create* a revolution. It wasn't going to be created by anybody. It said that a revolutionary situation would *develop* out of existing circumstances. When people were thoroughly disillusioned by the governing powers and in a revolutionary mood, an informed Communist Party would assume leadership because it knew where it was going. Nobody talked about overthrowing the government. Meanwhile, we did all kinds of good things for people.

I was never very high up in the hierarchy. I liked to be on the front line. I was chairman of my unit, so of course when I was chairman, it was going to be different. All the other units were closed, for party members only. I was out there in the ghetto on Yesler and 23rd—those buildings are still there—and I was the only person who had an open Communist headquarters. The rent was negligible, but we couldn't pay our light bill. So we had a guy in the City Light, real high up, and he'd go through the cards every month—"Oh, here they come again"—and he'd take our card and put it way in the back of the box. We never did pay.

I was a pretty devout Communist. We met on Thursday. It was the holy day, like Sunday is to Christians and Saturday is to Seventh Day Adventists. Thursday, all over the world, Communists were meeting. At my unit, the educational would be some boring thing on Marx or Lenin. Afterward we'd have our beans and bread and coffee—like a mission, you know, you've got to stay and listen to the sermon before you can eat! Everybody was invited. Our meetings were filled with people, mostly blacks. Maybe we were going to have a little demonstration someplace and we'd get our unit to come with us. Or maybe Welfare cut down on cod liver oil for somebody's sick children—okay, we'd get cod liver oil for this family from the Welfare and then they'd have to give it to all the families. Everything we did was fighting for individual rights that had been destroyed for one reason or another. Winning those rights would set a precedent for other people who were in the same boat.

Plenty of people were Communists. I think there were maybe 15 or 20 actual members in my unit, and I remember at one point there were 4,500 in the state of Washington, a bunch. We had city, state, and national gatherings. A lot of people who weren't members supported what we were doing. We always said anybody that worked eight hours and went up and asked for their pay was a Communist. Anyone who believed in community was a Communist. Anyone who told the person sitting next to her what she was earning was a Communist. I always used to do that, even though employers don't want to let that information get out. It was kind of a conspiracy and I would break through it as a matter of course. Then people could measure what they were getting against what I was getting and what responsibilities they had against what I had. They never got jealous of me because I never got those kind of wages.

I DIDN'T ALWAYS AGREE

Some people left the party because of ideological differences, but not me. We had over half a million members at one time, and they'd flake off if they didn't like this or that policy. When the Russians made a pact with Hitler in the summer of 1939, a lot of people took it really seriously. Intellectuals, you know, they have a terrible time, but I wasn't even interested. I was a member of the Communist Party of the United States of America working on problems here.

I didn't always agree with the Communist Party, however. For example, Communists would show up when the workers were on strike, and I'd never go, because I thought the party, given its bad reputation in the press, discredited the strike by being there. I went on our own mild demonstrations, where we were confronted with scowling policemen, but never once did they draw their revolvers. For another example, Communists had the theory that the Negroes were a nation, which I thought was ridiculous. The blacks are Americans. They have been here for generations. Now, Stalin wrote a book that I used to study. He had a good head on him for theory. He defined a nation: a common territory, a common economy, and a common this, and a common that. The blacks in this country didn't fulfill that definition. They were scattered all over the United States, and they didn't have a different language. I'd bring this up, but I wasn't going into open warfare with the Communist Party over it. I wasn't organizing blacks for anything except to get some more food!

I thought the Communist Party made a tactical mistake getting in the Democratic Party—one party trying to infiltrate another and dominate it. I went along a little way, but not very far. I helped the Democratic precinct committeeman organize to get a bunch of people to the caucus. Then I just got out of it. When the crunch came, in the fifties, one of the first things the Democratic Party did was purge itself of Communists and anyone who had spoken to a Communist. They purged all the progressive elements. That set the party back I don't know how much. Finally, I didn't agree with imitating everything that Russia did. The language, the hierarchy, and some of the methods—they had a lot of ideas that didn't apply to the American scene. It should have been a more American party than it was, more like the IWW. And the Comintern [the International Arm of the Communist Party, in Moscow]! I think of that whenever I see a common tern. It's got kind of a red bill. There are all sorts of terns. One good tern deserves another, I suppose. If we get socialism in this country, it's going to be a very different kind from what they had in Russia or China or any other part of the world. It's going to be an American socialism that grows out of our democratic way of life.

The head of the Washington State Communist Party was a fellow named Max [Maurice] Raport, from Russia.[30] In his view, decisions were made in Russia, and then you carried them out, come hell or high water. If you deviated, it was terrible. I liked him. He was a brilliant man, a great person for strategy, except he had this authoritarian quirk. I didn't think any red-blooded American should stand for that sort of thing, so I had run-ins with that guy. He would have liked to have me thrown out— I would have fought back, too—but he didn't want a fight. I think he liked me.

And they could not bar me from the Communist Party for being an alien![31] They said the ruling [barring aliens from party membership] was to protect the aliens. I didn't care what silly rulings they made upstairs. I had the right to belong to the Communist Party. My unit had a discussion about it and I convinced them that it was unconstitutional, it was undemocratic, and I wouldn't go along with it. I'm going to protect myself. I don't need any political party to protect me by doing unethical things. Maybe the party was really trying to protect itself, not the aliens. I don't know and I couldn't care less. I don't call on the Democratic Party to protect me by keeping me out of it.

I didn't agree with the party on many things, but that didn't make me anti-Communist. I agreed with them on a whole bunch of other things, and when I came up against something I didn't agree with, I was very outspoken about it, which is what everybody should be. In the Communist Party, I learned organizational tactics. Organizing means getting people together collectively to carry out a task. I learned that if you want to get a job done, the first thing you do is decide whether it's a worthwhile job. Then you get help, and you don't waste any time. Organizing was instinctive with me, but through the party it became conscious. And you don't necessarily have to be the leader—this is something else I learned in the Communist Party. You need to be the organizer. If somebody comes along with exceptional ability and takes over the leadership, then great, that relieves you to do something else, or just to help out a bit. So I wasn't a theorist. I was an *activist.*

I'd say the situation for women in the Communist Party was a little better than it was in the trade union movement, or any other movement except the women's organizations, but, you know, I never was interested in women's issues as such.[32] If something came up in front of me, I'd stop everything and take care of it. The men talked about women's equality— a lot of talk, and not too much action. Concerning women's issues, if I needed to, I would quote Karl Marx: "You can't run a revolution with half the proletariat in the kitchen." Of course, he never said that. I fixed up Marx to suit myself and I got away with it. Scoop [Herbert Phillips][33] knew I did, but he couldn't prove it. He would say, "You're making this up, now, aren't you?" Then I would start to laugh. Our arguments were always a lot of fun, just lots of fun.

We Communists left a heritage for future radical movements and I don't regret a moment of it. It was the most tremendously rich, creative period of American history. As well as the working class, the Depression

bit deep, deep into the middle class. They were educated, they were artic-
ulate, they were desperate, and they joined the Communist Party. They
were shoved into a position where they had to be creative—they had to
be! They were out of work. They were losing their homes.

10 / Premonitions

THE FBI CAME

The Depression was never solved. It was going great guns when the war
broke out in Europe in 1939. People were either drafted into the army or
they got jobs—jobs were running around all over the place. So one after
the other, they went one way or the other until by 1940 the Workers'
Alliance just melted away. There's been nothing like it ever since.

A food broker—that must have been my first job in 1941 after the
Workers' Alliance. It was a small enterprise, one proprietor. He told me
he wanted a bookkeeper who was also an expert secretary. I had always
been a secretary, but I was a little dubious about this bookkeeping business. It was double entry, which I didn't know. He said, "Ah, there's nothing to it." I told him if I didn't get a trial balance at the end of the month,
he'd better get himself a bookkeeper. I took the books home, consulted
all my bookkeeping friends, and read up on it. I copied everything the bookkeeper before me did and tried to follow her reasoning. She was excellent. I spent hours and hours at night poring over these books, and the
upshot of it was, I got a trial balance. At the end of the year, I urged him
to have an auditor come in. I wish I could remember his name, because
he had quite an influence on me. He taught me all kinds of gimmicks that
I've followed ever since, things that I've never seen duplicated—shortcuts
and simplifications.

In 1942 my employer took in a partner and they went into making crates, a very special kind that the armed forces needed to land on beaches in the Pacific War. The crate makers had a silent partner who was a crate inspector for the government. I noticed that flimflam crates would go by. The less they lived up to specifications, the greater their profit would be. Also, the inspector was able to swing contracts their way. I left, outraged. I should have reported it to the *PI* [*Seattle Post-Intelligencer*].

Meanwhile, I volunteered with Travelers' Aid [Society][34] and the YMCA, which were very active during the war. Most days when I got through with my job and had had a bite to eat, I went down to the King Street Station and took care of the people who came off the train. They came to work in the shipyards or for Boeing, but they didn't have any place to stay, so they'd come to the Traveler's Aid desk and I would tell them where to go. Just real busy. I also volunteered for the Office of Price Administration. I gave out ration cards for sugar, coffee, gasoline, and shoes.

In 1943, after the crate makers, I went to the unemployment office, and they begged me to take a job with the air force. They were training bombardiers out at Boeing Field, a long ways from town and poorly paid. I was to be in a barracks with the staff of a lieutenant. They had soldiers in this office, but for continuity they had to have a civilian who wasn't going to be shipped off. So, as a great patriotic gesture, I took this low-paying job. When I got there I found out, to my chagrin, that there really wasn't much work to do. The bookkeeping business consisted of following a manual that was created with the same mentality as the income-tax return: "You enter the figure here on line 2 and then another figure on line 3, and if it's greater than line 2, you do it on line 5." Anybody could follow this dumb manual. I was just doing one little routine, completely in isolation from any other system. If that kind of bookkeeping still permeates the whole government, I can see how difficult it would be to investigate what's really going on.

I was frozen in this job. A lot of people were frozen, shipyard workers and everyone else. You took one of those jobs and you stayed there for the duration, but I had a lot of fun while I was there. Every morning the men would come in and we'd all scramble to divide among us the ten minutes' work there was. Then I read and studied, French or something.

After a month or two, the lieutenant called me in and said that I had failed to clear [a routine security check]. The FBI demanded that I be fired.

I said, "Really? When can I go? Can I go home now?" I was all unfrozen through the work of the FBI!

He said, "You get two weeks' notice."

I said, "I could be blowing the place up in two weeks."

He said if I was in such a hurry, they'd fix up my papers right away. So I went chasing right over to the personnel office and I got out of there by noon. I felt like writing the FBI and saying, "Thanks. You got me out of that one." All during the war, people were weeded out of their jobs for being Communists.

By that time, I was a pretty good bookkeeper. It was easy to get work—they were hollering for people. In 1944 I went to the unemployment office and they offered me a job with the Shoreline School District. The pay was very low and I had a long trip out there. The "in" thing to do was to work for the shipyard and make big money, so they were having difficulties filling the position and that appealed to me.

While I was there, the FBI came, two of them, and closeted themselves with the superintendent, Mr. Howard, and told him the horrible stuff. Furthermore, they told him I had been secretary of the Teachers' Union, which is anathema to all superintendents of school districts. When they left, Mr. Howard said, "They told me you belonged to the Communist Party and the Teachers' Union, and they told me that I should fire you. I told them: 'If there were more good Americans like Mrs. Wolf, this country would be better off. Get lost.'"

We had coffee breaks, one in the morning and one in the afternoon, but you weren't allowed to smoke in the school building. The teachers would go down to the basement, the furnace room, and smoke. I didn't want to do that—the kids might see me—so I'd go across the street to a cafe and get a cup of coffee and smoke a cigarette.

Mr. Howard called me in and said I'd have to stop. I told him it was illegal to smoke on the grounds, which is why I went across the street, and I wasn't about to give up my coffee break. Secretaries had long been struggling to get coffee breaks.

He said, "If you're going over there smoking, all the teachers will be going over there smoking."

I said, "I can't be pushed around like that. I'm going to have my coffee and smoke cigarettes."

He said, "Okay, then, you can't work for the Shoreline School District."

At recess that day I went into the teachers' room and said, "I've been fired because I have a cigarette with my coffee across the street in that little cafe." They were outraged.

Mr. Howard called me in: "It is not right for you to spread it around that you were fired. You have not been fired. You have been told that you don't smoke cigarettes across the street."

I said, "I'm glad to hear that I haven't been fired, because I like it here."

He said, "But you can't stay here if you smoke cigarettes across the street."

I said, "Oh, then I am fired."

"No," he said, "You're choosing it."

I said, "Now let's get this straight. Am I fired or am I not fired?"

We had a big argument. He smoked, too, so I asked him, "Where does this illegal smoking start, just as you leave the schoolground, or when you get a mile away, or when you get into your own home? Where does this business of fooling the kids start? If you went up to the top of Mount Rainier to have your cigarette, some kid from this school could climb up there and catch you. I just can't understand your thinking."

"Well," he said, "it's the taxpayers."

I said, "Oh, you mean the taxpayers don't smoke, and they don't want anyone else to? You're kidding! Most taxpayers smoke, so I'm not going to have a minority of nonsmoking taxpayers push me around. I'll go with the majority."

Then he said, "Well, it's the law."

I said, "It's a foolish law, an abridgment of our freedom, and I'm not going to connive with you to uphold it."

That's the way the argument went, back and forth. We liked each other. He was a good guy, but he had to fire me.

That's when I went to work for Caughlan & Hatten. I called them Coughin' & Hackin'. Their law offices were in Smith Tower, downtown at the corner of Yesler and 2nd. On the street level of Smith Tower, the Communist Party had a bookstore, the Frontier Bookstore. When I went into the store, the manager was bemoaning the fact that the books were in a shambles. Now, I love bookkeeping, I just love bookkeeping, and I was already pretty good at it. I was between jobs, so I said I'd set up their books. I was in there for a little time every day. John Caughlan came into the store, and we got talking. Our paths had crossed during the Depression, especially in the Washington Old Age Pension Union, and we were friends. It turned out he needed a secretary. It was during the period when the war ended, in 1945, because I remember looking out the window and seeing all the celebrations in the streets.

So now I was working in the law offices of civil rights attorneys. They were poor and I was poor. We dedicated a lot of our time to the defense of people who were being deprived of their seamen's papers or their jobs or who were on trial. It was a natural thing for me. If I hadn't had that special place in their office, I suppose I could've gotten a job, because I was a secretary and I didn't have to have a long string of credentials and résumés with me. Professional people in the party had a heck of a time getting a job. They'd drop the résumé off, give names for recommendations, and they'd be betrayed. The employer would ask, "Why did you leave that job?" And they couldn't say, "I got fired because I'm a Communist." Imagine having a job interview with that in your background! But the FBI could hardly have kept up with me. I'd have just gone around the next day and gotten another job, because my talent for typing and shorthand was so low on the scale. And if I had gotten kicked out of every office in Seattle, I could have gone over to Tacoma.[35]

TUBERCULOSIS

It wasn't too long after going to work for John Caughlan that I came down with tuberculosis and went to Firlands Sanatorium. It was two years before I got back to work. The secretary in the office next to John's had been released from Firlands. When I came down with TB, she thought I had caught it from her, and she was devastated. I had quite a time reassuring her that I had contracted the disease from Harry Hughes, my stepbrother. I just made that up to quiet her.

Knowing I had tuberculosis, knowing I was going to the sanatorium—that really got to me. Nydia and her two young children drove me to Firlands and left me. I felt so alone. I went into a room to wait for a nurse to give me a shower and wash my hair and everything. They handed me a card. It was from this same woman who thought she infected me. Feeling really sorry for myself, I opened it. It had a tiny little chain inside, very tiny, like a little necklace, secured at the top and the bottom. At the top there was a head of hair, and at the bottom a neck. You could move the chain around and make funny profiles—long noses, pug noses, little mouths—and that fascinated me. I had to wait a long time, and I played with the chain all the while. I forgot all about the fact that I had tuberculosis and was scheduled for this long, terrible ordeal. When the nurse came in, that was it: I lost my great dread.

I thought it was kind of significant that the card came from this particular young woman. She helped bridge the gap between the real world and the world of sickness. Funny little things like that come up in life and comfort you, and it's always other people who do it. I've had that happen time and time again. I'll be thinking about myself, and you shouldn't do that, you should always be thinking about the outside. Of course, there's nobody closer to you than yourself—it's hard to keep away from it. And that's what this little card did for me. It took me away from myself.

TB is like an ulcer on the lung. I had what they call a shadow. It covered a fairly large area, but it was shallow. Apparently I had a lot of resistance. I'd been ailing a long time, going from doctor to doctor, before an X ray found me out. They had no effective cure then. They'd put you in bed just to stay there. I was nine months in a bed at Firlands Sanatorium.

You know, some people are born great and some have it thrust upon them: I stopped smoking. I used to smoke OPS, Other People's, but I got too sick to eat or smoke. I thought, "This is my chance. I know I'll start eating again, but I don't have to start smoking again." I was able to tell that to Mr. Howard.

The theory was that the lung should be kept perfectly quiet. The treatment consisted of immobilizing people, keeping them isolated from their families and even telephones. If they could have stopped you breathing, I think they would have done it. They had no heat in our place. All the windows were constantly open. "Fresh air is what you need to cure TB," even if you expended all your feeble energy to keep warm. So you lay there under a ton of blankets with several hot water bottles, trying to keep warm while you breathed this freezing air. If any friends came to visit you, they went home with double pneumonia.

At Firlands, laughing was taboo. It would wreck your lungs. We all had cubicles, two people to a cubicle. They had no doors, but there were panels around them and a passage between the rows about eight or nine feet wide. One evening, the young woman in the cubicle across from mine said she had a bottle, just for something funny to say. Nobody could see her. I couldn't even see her. But the whole floor was listening, because the partitions only went a little bit above your head. It was after dinner, at the time when the nurses didn't come busting back and forth very often.

I said, "Oh, how about my coming over and having a party?"

She said, "That would be great."

I actually did get out of bed and go over to her place, knowing that I couldn't be seen when the nurse went by. So that was the beginning of the great party. First we had a drink. We'd talk and we'd laugh and act silly. Then we had another drink. We began to get quarrelsome. Then she downright threw me out.

"Get out of here!" she shouted.

I said, "What? In this rain? I don't have an umbrella."

Of course, the whole floor was in an uproar. She finally got rid of me and I came back to bed. In the morning, when the nurses came clattering in with bedpans and washbasins and made a big hullabaloo to wake everybody up, all of a sudden I heard her groan, "Oh, my head." She had a hangover! Everybody just howled.

I read quite a bit about the history of treatments for TB. That's why I didn't go for this business of never laughing, and never getting up and walking around. So I did both. I laughed my way out of the sanatorium. One of the most joyous Christmases I ever spent in my life was at Firlands.

For one thing, the place was ablaze with decorations and comings and goings. I didn't often have visitors from my family, because it was too hard for them to get there and they had to stay overnight. My daughter lived in Port Angeles with her family, my sister and her husband lived in Port Angeles, my brother lived in Seattle, and they all had their families. They were the last people I expected to see. But they all got together and gave up their own Christmases to make the trip way out there in the country. They all marched in on me, and I was so surprised, so pleased. I know my lungs went in and out, in and out, in and out—probably set me back years!

Nine months of leisure. I never did get caught up on my work all the time I was there. I learned to make gloves, I wrote letters, I wrote book reviews for left-wing newspapers, and I had to do my fingernails! I read a lot. I got interested in freemasonry. They had a mobile library, and the librarian brought me out a whole bunch of books until I exhausted the subject. Then I started reading about the South Pacific Islands. I read my way through various subjects that way. Oh, and I made the mistake of reading Thomas Mann's *The Magic Mountain.* It was too graphic, a horrible book to read when you are yourself in a TB sanatorium with people dying all around you. Three people preceded me out of the probationary ward and three people came in behind me, and of that group I was the only one who survived. I was caught early, before it got too big a hold on me.

I wasn't discharged. I left. I wasn't going to stay there any longer than I had to, and I had tested negative for a couple of months. They wanted me to stay and finish up my cure. I was one of the few people who was getting better, and they wanted to keep their percentage up. But I disregarded their advice and went to live in an apartment in Seattle. Before drugs, you were never cured of TB, your case was just arrested, and you were wedded to that thermometer. I'd take my temperature, and if it went up I'd just about die with worry. The next morning it would be down. I went through that for about two weeks. Then I took the thermometer and broke it in two. I think at that point I broke the hold that TB had over me psychologically.

I went back to visit at Firlands for a long, long time, until all those whom I knew had either died or left. There was one patient, David, who loved music. He died there. Once I was up and walking about, I would bring him records, Beethoven's Fifth, Tchaikovsky's Fifth, and others. He looked at me kind of wistfully and said, "Couldn't you bring a real fifth one of these times?" Then I had an idea that I would get him a bowl of goldfish. I climbed over a fence on a day that was not a visiting day and showed up like an apparition beside his bed, carrying this bowl of goldfish. He almost fell out of bed. Then I beat it back over the fence again. And, you know, they took it away from him. I tried to introduce a little sanity in the sanatorium.

THE SPY TRIAL OF LIEUTENANT REDIN

From my bed in Seattle, I resumed keeping the books for the Frontier Bookstore. I can remember doing a mailing for Hugh DeLacy's campaign in 1946,[36] all from my bed. I spent the winter that way and the summer in a tent at my sister's place in Port Angeles. By the time I went back to work for Caughlan & Hatten, the hysteria had started.

Churchill came to this country, to Fulton, Missouri, on March 5, 1946, right after the war was over, and made the big speech—with Truman right next to him—in which he talked about the Iron Curtain falling between Russia and the West. He was a dyed-in-the-wool anti-Communist strong-man for the British Empire. Remember, he had said, "I'm not going to preside over the dissolution of the Empire." Russian socialism was a threat to the capitalist system. The Russian Revolution took that whole big area out of capitalist exploitation.

Now, when the British army went over to Dunkirk to invade and they were thrust back, the people took all their boats, little and big, and went over there and rescued the army. It's one of the most amazing events in history. Churchill inspired that, I'll give him his due. No one's totally an abomination—even the devil's got his points. But Churchill's speech is what triggered it off in this country. Up to 1946, the Red Army was blessed by General MacArthur. He said thank you to the Red Army for holding

Hitler at Leningrad [St. Petersburg] to the tune of 100,000 deaths, and the Russians held Hitler at Stalingrad [Moscow], too. The fighting practically exterminated the whole damn population, but they held, and that was what broke Hitler: the resistance of the Russian people. Everything else was just a mopping-up exercise on the part of the other allies. Now, suddenly, it was turned the other way. After 1946, Truman took up the anti-Communist line, and it permeated the government right on down through the media, and the people became hysterical. Overnight, they all hated Russia. I wouldn't have believed that the American people could be so brainwashed if I hadn't seen it myself.

The spy trial of Lieutenant Redin, in 1946, was the beginning of the Cold War persecutions here in Seattle. I took a big interest in that trial. His name was Nick, his wife was Galena, and their little girl, Ireska, was born here. He was a representative of the Soviet government sent to Seattle during the war to oversee the shipping of U.S. supplies to Vladivostok under the Lend-Lease agreement.[37] Nick wanted to learn fluent English, so I had him as a student and got paid.

I'm the only person I ever knew who got money from Moscow— "Moscow gold." Communists were always accused of getting "Moscow gold." As a matter of fact, we sent money there! Dues.

I liked that family so much! He wanted to learn idioms like "jalopy," and he'd always make up a class-conscious sentence. I'd say, "Use 'agreement'," and he'd say, "The workers came to an agreement." He was not a Communist. I said, "I hope you're not concerned that I'm a Communist." He said, "Oh, no, I'm not prejudiced against Communists."

Then he was arrested as a spy. It was a poorly contrived frame-up on the part of the government. Caughlan & Hatten represented him. Nydia was a character witness.[38] The family was so personable that they became popular through the trial. The whole phony thing was thoroughly exposed, and the verdict came down unanimously: not guilty. The jury had trouble with one juror. She had been retired from the telephone company, and she was afraid they would take her pension away from her if she voted to acquit. At this point, jurors weren't biased, but they could be intimidated.[39]

PATRIOTIC CITIZEN

$\mathcal{T}$he whole thing is the haves against the have-nots, isn't it? The right is for the money-owning class and the left always tends to the welfare of the general people, the less privileged people. The class lines are there. I could see what was coming—a big anti-Communist move on the part of the government. It still wasn't a crime in 1947 to be a Communist, so I went down and filed for citizenship while there was still time.

In order to testify for citizenship, you have to take an oath. I didn't take it. I told the judge that I was an atheist, and taking an oath on the Bible wouldn't keep me from lying. The judge wanted to know how he could believe me. I said, "Well, you've got to take your chances with me, just like you do with people who take an oath on the Bible. It's no different. My mother taught me not to tell lies, and I don't tell them very often."

I thought the roof was going to fall in on me for that, but it didn't. Then again, I never took an oath, really. I didn't like to do it, but the lawyers and other people advised me to say that I hadn't been a member [of the Communist Party]. They didn't want to take on a big case.

The INS could have gotten me for perjury. They thought about it, but the statute of limitations ran out. They only had so much money, and they went after bigger fry.

I got turned down. It was in the newspaper on the front page.

Mrs. Hazel Anna Wolf, a Canadian citizen accused of Communist sympathies, yesterday was denied American citizenship by Federal District Judge John C. Bowen. She has been a resident of the United States for twenty-four years. Attorney John Caughlan, for whom Mrs. Wolf works as a stenographer, represented her at the hearing. Judge Bowen said Mrs. Wolf had failed, as required by law, to satisfy the court as to her devotion to the principles of the United States Constitution. . . .

The court, in announcing the decision, took judicial cognizance of testimony by two former business associates of Mrs. Wolf that she had spoken to them "admiringly" of the program of a "foreign nation." The judge added: "She is disclosed by the evidence to have written one or more book reviews on Russia for one local newspaper called *The New World.* She seems in this review to have been seeking an opportunity to show up the advantages of life elsewhere than in the United States." Judge Bowen also noted that Mrs. Wolf had made no showing of religious affiliation, thereby leading him to weigh the value of her testimony under oath.

During the hearing on her petition for citizenship, Mrs. Wolf denied membership in the Communist Party and sympathy with it. On the matter of Communism itself, Mrs. Wolf rejected in a low voice all of [naturalization examiner Raymond S.] Sullivan's attempts to connect her with the Reds. "Are you prepared to say," Sullivan asked, "that you have never been an active Communist Party member?" "I am."

Speaking of the Seattle businessmen who testified against Mrs. Wolf earlier in the hearing, Sullivan demanded: "Whom are we to believe— American businessmen with no motive to falsify, or the petitioner, who has a motive, a very strong reason, not to tell the truth?"

Before announcing his decision, Judge Bowen pointed out that the decision was not to be interpreted as a ruling by the court that membership in the Communist Party was, in itself, sufficient grounds on which to deny American citizenship.[40]

Yeah, that was Bowen—Bonehead.

That's right. I had reviewed a book about how the Russian people defeated Hitler at Stalingrad. I remember that dumb judge asking me if I read Russian writers, and I said, "Yes, I do." I mentioned all these pre-Soviet writers whom I had been reading. He'd never heard of Dostoyevski. He said, "What did you say?" I said it again. It's a wonder I pronounced it.

Just then, President Truman, who was soon to issue the executive order[41] that started the witch-hunt, sent me a citation for my volunteer work during the war.

On behalf of the grateful people of the United States, I thank you for your selfless service in your country's need as a volunteer worker for the OFFICE OF PRICE ADMINISTRATION. With your help, our Nation has been able to protect its economy against the impact of total war and to assure its consumers fair prices and a fair distribution of needed goods. As a patriotic

citizen, you have demonstrated your loyalty and devotion in a period of great national danger. Your community and your country will not forget your contribution to victory over our enemies and look to you now for leadership and example in the continuing fight against inflation.
Harry Truman, 1946

Patriotic citizen! Who was he kidding?

PART IV

Fighting Back:
1949–1976

If you said, "Yes, I did belong to the Communist Party,"
then you were deportable. If you said, "No," then they got you
for perjury, whether you'd perjured yourself or not.

I was just there, powerless and strong,
someone who wouldn't chicken out.

*H*azel Wolf was born in Victoria, British Columbia, only about 120 miles north of Seattle, the city where she lived her entire adult life. What was her nationality? Her mother was a U.S. citizen by birth who married a Scottish immigrant to Canada. Did Hazel's mother thereby lose her U.S. citizenship? Was Hazel born Canadian or American? After emigrating from Canada to the United States, she secured a green card but did not become a citizen. She then married a U.S. citizen, Herb Wolf. Did Hazel acquire or regain U.S. citizenship when she married an American? Or was she Canadian and hence a "deportable alien"? These became the crucial questions in Hazel Wolf's deportation case.

In 1948, three years before Senator Joe McCarthy began a national witch-hunt against Communists and left-wing sympathizers, McCarthyism began in the Northwest with the Canwell hearings. Albert Canwell, a Washington State senator from Spokane, succeeded in establishing a joint committee of the Washington State Legislature to investigate "un-American" activities in the Washington Old Age Pension Union (which had just successfully passed an initiative supporting the pension system), the Seattle Labor School, and the Seattle Repertory Playhouse as well as among allegedly left-wing faculty members at the University of Washington. Wielding the investigative power of the state legislature, Canwell provided a preview of Senator Joe McCarthy's tactics.

In 1949, two years before Senator McCarthy began his accusations, Seattle newspapers referred to Hazel Wolf as a "Red." "Red" was becoming the code word that combined "Communist" with "foreign enemy." With the outbreak of the Korean War, in 1950, and the accession of McCarthy, in 1951, headlines in national newspapers made this inflammatory language ordinary—HORDES OF REDS STORM UN POSITIONS, REDS OPEN MAJOR OFFENSIVE, REDS TORTURE 2 U.S. FLYERS INTO FALSE CONFESSION[1]—and helped to create a public that supported annihilation of "Red aliens" both abroad and at home. Although McCarthy was censured by the U.S. Senate on December 2, 1954, anti-Communism severely poisoned the cultural and political environment for decades afterward and still lingers today. Attacks by the Immigration and Naturalization Service (INS) on aliens as "foreign-born subversives" helped to spread the xenophobic atmosphere in which McCarthy flourished.[2]

Between 1949 and 1963, Wolf's deportation case went through six stages: stage one (May 1949–November 1952) began with INS administrative proceedings. During the second stage (November 1952–December 1963), her lawyers took the INS's deportation order to federal court on appeal. In the third stage (March 10, 1955–March 5, 1956), her lawyers and friends tried to get the U.S. Congress to pass special legislation prohibiting her deportation. In the fourth and fifth stages (June 1957–October 1958 and June–October 1960, respectively), her supporters put pressure on Canada and Great Britain, respectively, to reject her as a deportee. In the sixth and final stage (October 1960–December 1963), her case went back to INS administrative hearings.[3] Imprisonment, loss of employment, and harassment extending for ten to fifteen years is what the foreign-born routinely endured in this period.

11 / The INS Hearings

ARRESTED

So in 1949 I got thrown in the slammer.[4] I was working in the law offices of Caughlan & Hatten. Harry Bridges[5] was on trial, and I was in the process of tying up the bundle of transcripts to mail to him when two INS characters came into our offices at the New World Life Building at 10:30 in the morning on May 31 and showed me their badges. I pushed the intercom button and told Barry [Hatten] that people had come in to arrest me. He came charging out of the inner office, where he had a client, and said, "I'll be right over to see you." I said to the INS, "You'll have to wait. I need to wrap up this package and call United Parcel to come and get it." I was just trembling, but you can't tie knots with hands going like that. So I got my hands right still in order to wrap that damn package. Then I telephoned the parcel service and said, "It's on my desk. I'm leaving the office and I don't know when I'm coming back." It made us all chuckle when I said that. By then I was myself and it was just a fun thing. I went off with those two guys.

They took me to a special jail run by Immigration and put me in a cell with two young women from Vancouver, British Columbia. One was a waitress and one was a student nurse. They fastened on me: "What are you in here for?" I said, "I've been accused of trying to overthrow the government by force and violence." I thought they'd laugh, but they didn't. They said, "The goddamn government ought to be overthrown!" They'd never heard of such a noble crime. I was an instant hero. In this cell there was a little library, and on the shelf there was a book that I thought was hilarious: *How to Be a Successful Woman*. I said to the girls, "*Now* they tell me."

Pretty soon after I was arrested, the press came up to my cell. I didn't want to talk to them, because I didn't know what to say, but they came right into my room where I was in prison. I told them: "You can't come in here! A man's home is his castle. Now, this is my home for the time being and I want you to get out of here!" So the guards kicked them out. When they came by a little later, I still wasn't prepared to make a statement, but I blurted: "The American people will see to it that I'm not deported." The papers were full of it.

At first the press treated me like I was some kind of criminal. They referred to me as "the Wolf Woman." A bit later, the headlines came out "Red secretary" or just "woman."[6] But, very quickly, I learned to deal with the press. I found out the reporters only take assignments that are given to them. If their editors don't like the way it's written up, they change the facts, leave things out, put things in. So I learned not to blame the reporters, to treat them well. Gradually, that changed their attitude, and eventually the press was on my side. I remember one of the later headlines, MRS. WOLF'S DEPORTATION ORDER APPEALED[7]—by that time I was Mrs. Wolf.

> In a statement given when she was released from Immigration custody, Mrs. Wolf said: "I have been in the United States twenty-four years. I have been active in trade union and Progressive Party affairs. I don't know why they picked me up at this time. I believe they are trying to intimidate everyone they can, particularly those fighting for civil liberties. I think this method of intimidation will not succeed, either with me or with the American people in general."[8]

BUGGED

*A*ctually, I only spent half a day in jail, just one meal: corn soup. They don't let you have knives and forks, just spoons. I was released at three o'clock that afternoon—didn't even get a chance to finish my jigsaw puzzle. My friends bailed me out, five hundred dollars, which was raised immediately. The theory behind bail is it's supposed to keep you from jumping the country, when that's exactly what they wanted me to do: leave the country. Just try to see the logic of that! The government went after me because they thought I was working-class and a damn good organizer. They rounded everybody up. I would have been offended if they'd skipped over me in all this business.

I didn't waste any time when I was in jail. The two girls told me they had come over the border from Vancouver with a couple of American sailors and registered at a hotel. They hadn't been in their room five minutes before the police came, sent the sailors back to their ship, and put the two girls in the King County Jail. The hotel manager just rented their room out to somebody else.

The girls clammed up because they didn't want their parents or their school to find out. Finally, they realized they would probably sit there the rest of their lives, so they gave their names and addresses. King County turned them over to Immigration for deportation. That's where I ran into them.

They'd had a hearing, but they thought the examiners seemed to know everything already. I took the girls over to the far side of the room and whispered, "This cell is bugged," and I showed them the little hole in the floorboard, which I recognized from pictures of Harry Bridges's hotel room. I told them, "In the morning, I'll see Travelers' Aid about your case, then I'll bring you some shampoo and face cream—and some cigarettes. Throw all of the cigarettes, lit, down that hole. Now, this is a brick building and it won't burn down, but you'll ruin that machine down there bugging you."

I came back to the jail the next morning, loaded with goodies and a plan. The jailer said, "Mrs. Wolf, there's no prison in the world that lets a released prisoner go back and visit friends." I could see why. I had already connived with them about destroying the bug in their cell.

I told the jailer, "You come along, if you want to, but I've got to do something for those girls. They're very young, not even twenty years old. They've done this thing, it's true, but I don't think it should destroy them. You're just going to dump them in Vancouver without any consideration for what's in store for them, whereas I want to put them in touch with Travelers' Aid." So he took me to their cell. I set it all up: the jailer let our Travelers' Aid take them to Vancouver, while Travelers' Aid in Vancouver handled it with their parents and even went to the hospital to intercede for the student nurse so she could continue at school. The Travelers' Aid told me that they'd been wanting to get involved in Immigration cases for a long time.

"ARE YOU NOW OR HAVE YOU EVER BEEN . . ."

My first hearing was in a tiny little room at Immigration six months later, on November 9, 1949. Everybody and his dog showed up. The examiner ran the hearing. There was a long table with the Immigration attorneys and my attorneys seated on both sides, and I came in late—not too late, but later than most people. Of course, I should have pushed my way to the front of the room and sat down in the prisoners' dock, but I didn't. I just stood modestly in the back of the room with the crowd. The poor old examiner was just overwhelmed with all the people breathing down his neck. He said in exasperation, "Everybody who doesn't have a seat, leave the room now." We all went out into the hallway. The next thing I hear is "Where's Hazel?" They tell him, "She's out in the hall." "What's she doing out there? Hazel, you're wanted." I came in, and the examiner said something about my being late. I said, "I was here, but you told the people who didn't have a seat to get out of the room." Everybody roared with laughter.

The examiner didn't think it was funny, but he couldn't help but laugh. I saw this same examiner several times at my hearings. I got to know all of them. I remember that hearing because I almost missed it and because of my smart-aleck one-liner, but I didn't play any more tricks after that first one in the crowded hearing room.

I was charged with conspiring to overthrow the government by force and violence. They never did try any of the Communists on overt acts. It had to do with their ideas, not with whether they'd actually poisoned the wells. It was just a big battle of books is what it was.

I was charged with being a Communist during a time when the party was legal and membership was not a deportable offense. Now, under the constitution of the United States, I couldn't be tried for something that *was not* a crime when I did it. It's called the ex post facto law. However, like the U.S. flag over the bed I was born in, the U.S. Constitution didn't cover me. I was not a citizen and I was not protected by the constitution and the laws of criminal procedure. In my case, the INS thought nothing of trying to deport me for my membership in the Communist Party thirteen years prior to my arrest, when membership was not a deportable ground. I can only charitably assume that the illiterate INS didn't know what the Latin phrase "ex post facto" meant.

Deportation is a civil thing, so all I got were administrative hearings, no trial. If I hadn't taken the precaution of getting a residency card, a green card, back in 1921, when I came here, they would have deported me immediately upon my arrest, as an illegal alien. That card was the only thing that held me here.

I never answered any questions until the final hearing. If I answered their questions and said I *wasn't* a Communist, then they would get me for perjury. They had all kinds of stool pigeons—witnesses—to back them up and swear they saw me at such and such a meeting on such and such an evening where the Communists were planning to overthrow the government by force and violence. They'd even cite the exact time of day they supposedly saw me, and whom I was sitting next to. If I answered their questions and said I *was* a Communist, then I would be immediately deported on my own say-so. Either way, I'd be in trouble. That's why so many people in these political trials took the Fifth Amendment.[9]

There were so many hearings at Immigration, and at every one our attorneys, usually Barry Hatten or John Caughlan, would pick out something they thought was not regular and object to it. We threw up all kinds of these technical roadblocks. The hearings were transcribed by secretaries, not by court reporters. Our lawyers claimed that these secretaries were incompetent, that you couldn't depend on notes that were taken by people who were not certified court reporters, and that therefore I wasn't being given a fair hearing. Some of these objections went up to the federal district courts. We were charging them with violation of my rights, or we charged them with conflict of interest.

To [Presiding Examiner] Ross' question as to whether she wanted to be sworn [in], Mrs. Wolf responded: "Not at this time, on advice of Mr. Caughlan."[10]

Caughlan protested in a formal letter yesterday announcing that he had received oral notice Monday of the hearing Monday. He termed the short notice an "outrageous violation" of his client's rights.[11]

Judge Bowen overruled the contention of Attorney John Caughlan that

Paul N. Ross, Immigration Service Inspector conducting the deportation hearing, was "acting both as prosecutor and judge" in the case.[12]

STOOLIES

They determined that I was a Communist by way of all these stool pigeons, some of whom might have known and some of whom didn't know I was a Communist. They were all just being paid. "Pigeon," in prison terms, is somebody who sings. "Stool," because they sit on a perch—a stool—in court, just like a decoy, not the real thing. That's a stool pigeon, a stoolie, somebody who squeals on somebody else in court.

They had two kinds of witnesses. The first kind had never even laid eyes on me. They were flown in to prove that the Communist Party was trying to overthrow the government by force and violence. They were what we referred to sneeringly as "the stable," and they traveled all around like a circus. It cost the government a bundle, too—they came in from Hawaii or Florida with their quotes from Marx, Engels, Lenin, or any other book of radical theories.[13]

I remember sitting in one of those hearings, with a stoolie testifying some nonsense such as "When the revolution breaks out, the Communists will come rushing out of their cells, firing their .38s as they come." I leaned over and said, "John, they won't win, will they, not with .38s." He said, "Will you shut up!"

The second kind of witness was the local. At my first hearing it was "Army" Armstrong, Katherine Fogg, Clifford Smith, and Ward Warren,[14] former members of the party all equally endowed with indelible stool-pigeon memory concerning microscopic events long gone. They came in and swore that I was a Communist. So that linked me up with this guy who said being a Communist meant you were trying to overthrow the government by force and violence. Those were the techniques the FBI and the Immigration Service used.

It's my theory that the government had some kind of hold on the stoolies. When people were on WPA, they all had to sign oaths that they weren't Communists. I didn't sign it. I don't like to lie unless I have to. I'm not going to lie to keep a job, that's for damn sure. I'm not above telling a lie, but it has to be a very holy cause. And it has to be something that doesn't get anybody in trouble, or it has to be something that will keep somebody from getting in trouble. So I didn't sign it. I stalled and stalled and pretty soon they forgot about it. But most of the stoolies had been on WPA and had signed. Then the FBI had them. They said, "You're going to talk, or we're going to get you up for perjury because we know you were a Communist when you signed the WPA oath." The FBI had a feel for phonies: "This person is vulnerable, we could pay him twenty-five dollars a day and he'd lie off the top of his head for a week." With a little flattery, a little blackmail, and a little coercion, weak people will give in.

Another way they got them is when people grew disgruntled with the party. To sound me out, the government sent people, friends of mine who had turned, to see if I was one of them. For instance, I had a row with the head of the [Washington State] Communist Party, Max Raport. A real row. I liked the guy, but we had a difference of opinion. He hollered at me and I went out and slammed the door. I wasn't going to listen to his abuse. A guy heard about the row and approached me. I didn't trust this person. In fact, I had been accusing him of being a stool pigeon, unreliable, but he wanted to have lunch with me, so I had lunch with him. He probed to find out what my attitude was toward Maurice Raport. The minute he started that, I knew I was talking to the enemy. So I said, "Ah, he's sure got a short fuse, that guy has. He'd blow his top at me, but you know, he's a fine person. He's one of the best leaders that we've ever had, and I admire him very much." That was my way of saying, "Get lost, brother." He was seeing if I was eligible to become a stool pigeon, and he found out that I wasn't. My lunch guy was later denounced as a stoolie.

A lot of rumors go around. When persecution and the heat are on like that, people have a tendency to distrust each other. The right-wingers see a Red under every bed, and the Reds, under pressure, see a spy under every bed. I remember one person coming to me saying that such-and-such a woman was a spy. I cut him off right there: "What did you make a statement like that for? How do you know?" He tried to push it: "She was seen in a government car." I asked, "What kind of government car? The Department of Interior? Department of Agriculture? State Department? Police?

Parks?" Well, he didn't know what kind of a government car. "Government car" was a buzz word, you see, supposed to scare the hell out of me. The woman in question, Jean Gundlach, was secretary to the regional director of the ILWU [International Longshoremen's and Warehousemen's Union]. I said, "Is she still his secretary?" This rumor guy was a Longshoremen's board member, and he said, "Oh no, he let her go." I said, "I think she's still there, and if she is, then obviously her boss, the president, doesn't believe all these rumors about her and she's not a spy. Let's find out."

I called her up and said, "Hi, Jean. I haven't heard from you in a long time. How are you getting along? I just wondered about you." We talk and talk, then we hang up, and I say, "Now, if I hear one word from anybody about that woman being a spy, I'll know where it came from and you'll hear from me."

It was bad here in this country, but it must have been terrible in Germany, just terrible, where people were so afraid of each other. After the war, I ran into a German at the Hoh River Campground, in the Olympic National Park. He joined my two grandsons and me overnight and we walked out of the park together. He told me he was in the Hitler Youth, that all the young people were in it. It was as if kids here were forced to join the Boy Scouts. I said, "How did you feel about the persecution of the Jews?" He said, "Well, it was kind of a dreamy sort of thing, because there were no Jews in the neighborhood or anywhere near where I lived. We didn't know much about what was going on, but I can tell you this— if you did live in a neighborhood where there were Jews, you would keep quiet, because troops were marching around and banging on doors in the middle of the night." We had nothing like that. Our people were not being tortured. Police weren't banging on doors in the middle of the night. We at least went through the motions of a trial for being a Communist, and frequently those accused got acquitted.

On the other hand, jurors were mostly terrorized. There were very few juries that had the courage to go against the government, because reprisals would be taken. There was blacklisting, and the Americans of Japanese descent were sent to camps. A lot of the elements of terror were present here during the McCarthy period [1951–54].

I recall a stoolie at one of my hearings saying he saw me at a fraction meeting in the Workers' Alliance building. "Fraction" is a kind of technical term. It's where the Communists in an organization meet to plan their strategy. I chuckled to myself because I had never been in that building. I hadn't even belonged to the Workers' Alliance—let alone attended a fraction meeting—until they moved to another building. The examiner said, "Well, where were you, if you weren't at that fraction meeting?" And I wasn't able to prove where I was. This was an administrative hearing, not covered by criminal procedure and rules of evidence, so it was practically impossible to impeach their lies.

During those early hearings, these characters who said they saw me sitting in a Communist meeting were lying. I don't say that I didn't sit in Communist meetings, but I never saw *those* people in Communist meetings. One of the four locals who testified against me I didn't know at all. The others I had seen in the Workers' Alliance. Communists couldn't really name each other as such—only the members of their own neighborhood group. You might only suppose who was a member from the company they kept and the projects they worked on. So all the people who said I was a Communist had to make it up. I was one, but none of them really knew that I belonged to the party. There weren't any decent informers.

In the 1930s, I was the only Communist who had an open Communist meeting. I was chairman of my particular neighborhood group, which was out there in the ghetto, mostly blacks. When the crunch came with the McCarthy hearings and the Canwell hearings, the government had informers running out of their ears. But there wasn't one person in all that community who came down to our meeting on Thursdays who was ever an informer. I'm sure they were approached. They all knew I was a Communist, but nobody came up and said so during the hearings.

During the Second World War, I had written a letter to an American soldier in Europe. At the hearing, they read the end of that letter, in which I wrote: "It's time they opened a second front. If they don't do it pretty soon, I'm going to go over there and open it myself. Now, I hope the FBI never gets this letter." When I heard that, I burst out laughing and said, "Wow, they got the letter after all, didn't they!" I was supposed to be terrified and I wasn't. I thought it was hilarious. The whole deportation case was hilarious. That soldier was being surveilled because of our friendship. Imagine going through his mail, stealing the letter, and turning it over to the FBI. Like a vicious bunch of hazardous waste that's put out into a stream, the poison permeated everyplace.

I had as one of my character witnesses Nora McCoy. She was a very, very firm Catholic. Even the Pope didn't terrify Nora McCoy. She was very active, an executive officer in the Washington Old Age Pension Union, a senior citizen, well respected. She testified that in her judgment, Mrs. Wolf was attached to the principles of the constitution and the good order and happiness of the United States, which was exactly the requirement for citizenship.

> The three witnesses, Mrs. Catherine Clark and Mrs. Nora M. McCoy, Seattle, and Mrs. Alpha Hart, Tacoma, all testified that in their judgment Mrs. Wolf is attached to the principles of the constitution and the good order and happiness of the United States.[15]
>
> A former Communist, Paul Crouch, yesterday testified it was clear, in Communist Party literature, that the party believes in the overthrow of the United States government. In all Communist literature, examples of which Crouch identified to be introduced as evidence at the hearing, the "overthrow of capitalism by armed force" is a theme, Crouch said. Communists consider the United States THE capitalist country, Crouch continued, "so it is evident" the overthrow of the United States is advocated.[16]
>
> An admitted former Communist yesterday said he had seen Mrs. Hazel Anna Wolf, fifty-one years old, at closed meetings of the Communist Party. The witness, Ward Warren, Seattle longshoreman, said Mrs. Wolf was a member of the Communist Party in 1938 and 1939.[17]

EXPELLED

> Clifford H. Smith of 4428 Garson St., the first witness for the government, told the hearing that he knew Mrs. Wolf in 1937 or 1938. He said he was present at a Communist meeting when Mrs. Wolf was expelled from the Communist Party because of her participation in another organization.[18]

The stoolie got it wrong. I wasn't expelled, I was suspended. It wasn't the thirties, it was the forties. I'd never laid eyes on that guy, Clifford Smith. He must have been making it up out of whole cloth.

I did have more than one disagreement with the Communist Party, but this incident was too much for them. It was around election time in 1948. The Washington Old Age Pension Union put out a leaflet inviting all the political parties to present their issues. Now, the Pension Union was pretty well owned by the Communists, so they didn't expect the Democrats to come, nor did they expect the Republicans to come, and that night, of course, they didn't come, but a candidate for some revolutionary outfit did. Mabel Conrad, who was president of the Pension Union at the time, was too timid to chair the meeting and asked me if I would do it. The Communists didn't show up and didn't show up. I held the crowd just as long as I could, you know. I didn't want to let the audience all just go home. Finally I said to this revolutionary outfit, "You people like to come up and talk?" That's where I committed the big sin. I was suspended for letting these revolutionaries speak when the Communists didn't show up at their own meeting, and yet it was supposed to be a meeting at which everyone could speak. It makes no sense, and I would do it again that same way. I'd do my whole life the same way.

Some little local committee suspended me—it wasn't done at an open meeting. Then I was just informed. They wanted to control me pretty tightly, but I know what's right and wrong. No political party's going to tell me.

I left town for Port Angeles to lick my wounds. Also, John [Caughlan] and Barry [Hatten] broke up their law partnership and I didn't want to make a choice,[19] so I got an apartment out there on the Peninsula and went to work for a doctor, keeping his books. He fired me when he saw my name in the papers connected with the Communist Party.

I was about to quit that doctor anyway because in September 1952 came the arrests of the seven Communists: Heinie Huff, Bill Pennock, Johnny Daschbach, Terry Pettus, Paul Bowen, Karly Larsen, and Barbara Hartle—she later turned stool pigeon.[20] When I heard about the arrests, I said, "Oh my gosh, I'd better get back to Seattle." John Caughlan said, "What you could do best is organize the typing of the transcript every day for the lawyers to work with." So I undertook the job of mobilizing a bunch of typists. We had two shifts on rented typewriters. Every day they'd hand us a transcript and we'd type like crazy. Then we had people who collated and put them in binders. Secretaries volunteered from all over the city, so many I can't tell you how many. I came back and I did all this for the Communist Party, for these people who had suspended me so unjustly.[21]

I was living with Helga and Herbert Phillips at the time. Herbert Phillips was a Communist and a professor of philosophy at the University of Washington. He got called before the Canwell hearings in 1948, and then the university fired him. Scoop, as we called him, then got a job as a laborer. He had learned how to handle a wheelbarrow when he was a young kid on a farm. Then he got a job packing furniture in a factory, and later on he actually made furniture. When he was of retirement age, he went to California. Helga was one of the most brilliant women I've ever come across. You'd just mention any book or idea, and she'd discuss it with you.

About the time of the Smith Act trial, when they had Communist meetings at the Phillips' house, I would stay upstairs. I was ousted, you see. Helga came upstairs from a meeting one time and said, "Do you know you got fired out of the Communist Party today for nonpayment of dues?" I said, "What? For nonpayment of dues! But I'm suspended." She said, "I paid your dues." I was astounded: "You mean, I'm back in now?" So now I'm back in!

I didn't see how the revolution was ever going to get anywhere.

12 / The Washington Committee for the Protection of the Foreign Born

BY TRIAL AND ERROR

The day after my arrest and release from jail, in May 1949, I got a dollar in the mail with a note pinned to it: "This is for your defense." Now, that was a significant donation, and it was from a guy I'd never heard of, Lyle Mercer. He became the president of the Washington Committee for the Protection of the Foreign Born [WCPFB], which took up the defense of the aliens arrested in Washington and Oregon. John Caughlan's father, a retired Methodist clergyman, was later president of the WCPFB.

All of my friends and a bunch of people I didn't know joined the Washington Committee for the Protection of the Foreign Born. Eighteen of us were the victims of deportation orders, and so we all worked together educating the public, getting out the pamphlets, and raising money for attorneys' out-of-pocket expenses—court filing fees, transcriptions of testimony, and all that. God knows, they didn't get much more. They all served pro bono. We had to raise a lot of money because these cases went to the U.S. Supreme Court.

We put on events, had birthday parties—even charged two dollars for a potluck dinner. And we staged plays at left-wing fund-raisers for the defense. I wrote a comedy, *By Trial and Error,* for a rally in a big hall someplace downtown. It was performed one time in Seattle and one time in Chicago, and maybe in other places—the script was passed around. The people who came were sympathetic, and that play was hilarious, as far as they were concerned. It was based on a hard core of truth. See, you're accused by a bureaucracy, the INS. The bureaucracy sets up the hearings, brings the charges, and makes all the rules. They appoint one of their own as judge, so the group that indicts you also tries you. They also appoint the appeals judges. It's all the same people. Now, in an ordinary case of law, you don't get tried by your accuser. The courts are independent. But this was Immigration! So in *By Trial and Error* I set it up like musical chairs. I had only a few characters sitting at a long table. They'd carry on the hearings for a little bit, then they'd all get up and change chairs and change roles, going right along with the procedures, then change their chairs again to play all the parts—examiner, witness, prosecuting attorney, and stenographer—it was all the same people! Later the appeals judge comes in with a big hat and a cloak over his face, gives his verdict—"Deport!"—and throws back his cloak, and in the end it's the same old guy, the examiner.

In another scene, the counsel for the aliens asks a female stoolie how much she gets paid. "Twenty dollars," she says. "And how much do the men get?" "Twenty-five dollars." "How much does a Filipino get?" "Fifteen dollars." Then the aliens all stand up and chorus: "Why don't you stoolies organize?" That really was true about their unequal wages.[22]

IN IT TOGETHER

$\mathcal{T}$here was never any question but that we [arrestees] were all in it together. We were from all over. Tora Rystad from Norway. Cecil Jay, England. Jim Crane, Ireland. William Mackie, Finland. Boris Sassieff from a tiny country near Georgia, in Russia. George Lukman, Yugoslavia. And many more. I was working long hours for John Caughlan, and then we'd all meet after work at the committee [WCPFB].

There were other committees in other states, wherever there were deportation cases involving foreign-born people. There was a lot of communication among these state committees—a natural development. The headquarters for the American Committee for the Protection of the Foreign Born [ACPFB] were back East, and the head of it was Abner Greene, someone we depended on for his judgment, a very caring person, born and bred in New York City—he had that accent.[23] He was a lawyer, but if he got any payment, it wasn't much. Couple times a year, he'd swing around the states to encourage us. He'd say, "We're going to win all these cases." That's more than one of our attorneys could say, who told me in confidence, "In the end, you'll get deported."

Abner Greene was arrested and put in prison because he wouldn't turn over the books and records of the ACPFB to the [U.S. House of Representatives] Un-American Activities Committee. The family did not want to tell their eleven-year-old son that his father was in jail, so they shipped the boy out here to some relatives and asked me to keep an eye on him. Every once in a while we'd go on a picnic or something, but the boy was homesick, just sick, separated from his family, so I urged them to tell him the truth and let him come home. It was a real shocking experience for that boy.

We had a chairman, but no dues, no structure. We had meetings. We discussed the court cases and the strategies. The committee played a tremendously important part, got bigger and bigger as time went on. More and more people joined. There were hundreds of thousands of Americans who opposed this McCarthy business.

I edited our newsletter, the *Northern Light,* which means that I wrote it.[24] It contained information on events and on the progress of all of our cases, both in Washington and nationally.

Galvan Case Decision a Blow to Constitutional Rights

On May 24 the U.S. Supreme Court handed down a decision in the Galvan case which in effect upholds as constitutional the right of Congress to make past membership in the Communist Party a ground for deportation of non-citizens regardless of the remoteness of the past membership.[25]

People's Programs Presents Reading of 'Salt of the Earth' for WCPFB

On May 22 at the Finnish Hall the great movie "Salt of the Earth" depicting the strike of the Mine-Mill and Smelter workers at Bayard, New Mexico, was presented as a reading by six members of Peoples' Programs. The reading was preceded by an exceptional dinner of Mexican dishes.

Two birthday parties were held by WCPFB in honor of birthdays of Hazel Wolf and George Luckman, both of whom the Committee is defending.

"Crack O' Dawn" distributors were out recently with WCPFB leaflets on the Alcantra case, handing them to Longshoremen at the pay office and dispatching hall.[26]

I included some little literary things:

> The statue of Liberty
> Now torchless & pale
> Still holds up her hand
> —She's asking for bail![27]

Pilgrims Land on Plymouth Rock with no Visas!

Undoubtedly, the Immigration Dept. must consider the day of the landing of the Pilgrims as black indeed, since no officials were on hand to challenge their entry. A belated attempt to expunge this dismal failure from their record would appear to be the only reason for their recent arrest for deportation on May 17 of Fred Williams, active member of Local 208, UAW–CIO. Mr. Williams was born in Plymouth [Pennsylvania] forty-eight years ago and has a birth certificate to prove it! Mr. Williams, however, has a different theory. He states: "My arrest exposes the whole operation of the Justice Department—releasing phony information in order to whip up hysteria. It is obvious that the move is not against me, but against the trade union movement. This frame-up is designed to aid the big corporations and the unscrupulous politicians who use scare and terror tactics in an attempt to silence the people . . . they won't get away with it."[28]

Jeremiah, chapter 7

If ye oppress not the stranger [foreign-born] and the fatherless, and the widow, and shed not innocent blood in this place, neither walk after other gods to your hurt; then will I cause you to dwell in this place, in the land that I gave to your fathers, for ever and ever.[29]

Shakespeare on Deportations

Romeo and Juliet, Act III, Scene 2

Juliet (on learning that a decree of banishment had been given to Romeo): . . . "Romeo is banishèd"—To speak that word / Is father, mother, Tybalt, Romeo, Juliet / All slain, all dead? "Romeo is banishèd!" / There is no end, no limit, measure, bound, / In that word's death; no words can that woe sound.

Act III, Scene 3

Romeo (on learning of the decree): Ha, banishment? Be merciful, say "death"; / For exile has more terror in his look, / Much more than death. Do not say "banishment.". . . the damned use that word in hell. Howling attends it; / How hast thou the heart / . . . To mangle me with that word "banishèd"?[30]

I agreed with Romeo. It would be a bad trip.

Marion Kinney loomed large in my life after I was arrested. I was the first one arrested, and she was the one who raised money to bail me out. I don't think she was impelled by deep love for me. I could have been a horrible person, and she would have done it if I had been unjustly arrested. She didn't head up the [Washington] Committee for the Protection of the Foreign Born, but she was the person who did the work, organized it, raised the funds, and kept the thing going. She was a tremendous organizer. The friendship became more emotionally involved as we worked together, and it has endured to this day. I never go more than a month without calling her.[31]

I met Marion Kinney after the war. For a long time, she was in charge of the Frontier Bookstore, aka the People's Bookstore, maintained by the Communist Party largely for the sale of Leninist and Marxist literature and other way-out leftist books. On first meeting Marion, you get the impression that she is a very endearing and unsophisticated young child, but don't let that fool you. I don't mean to say she's not endearing and unsophisticated. She's something else. When I was working for John Caughlan, she came into the office to sell me some tickets. Well, I had a real ironclad resistance to all ticket sellers because I was approached three times a day, at least, to buy tickets, and I never bought a ticket. She made this pitch, and I was overwhelmed with pity. Poor little Marion! How can she ever sell enough tickets? She couldn't persuade anybody. So I bought one to something at the Moore Theater. I went, and who was the master of ceremonies in this big theater, jammed to the rafters with people? Marion Kinney, making a real militant pitch to the audience.

Marion was a Communist. There was a time during the McCarthy period when the Communist Party probably panicked unduly. They thought all the chief executive members ought to go into hiding. She was chosen to go away, just leave, hide up someplace, so she couldn't be arrested. But Marion didn't leave, and didn't leave. She "just couldn't get away right now." She'd "leave next week." Everyone finally forgot about it. Of course, she wasn't arrested. She kept the Communist bookstore going all during the McCarthy period. They never raided it. What would have been the use? They'd only have gotten a bunch of books.

Marion got a job in a restaurant as a waitress. The FBI put the pressure on the restaurant, and they fired her. So for a while she drove a cab.

Incidentally, when the FBI decided to arrest those who went into hiding, they knew exactly where each one of them was. William Pennock was one of them. The day he was to testify, I walked with him as far as the courthouse steps. He told me that he was afraid they would ask him questions, and he wouldn't answer them right, and then he'd lose his credibility with his constituents, who were all these thousands and thousands of senior citizens.

During the trial, he worked at a paying job, he was in court all day, and he spent all night working in the offices of the Washington Old Age Pension Union. He was just worn to a frazzle. He took pills to put him to sleep and he took pills to wake him up—the pills were in his pockets all the time. So one particular night, he just ate a bunch of pills, the ones that put him to sleep, and he didn't wake up.[32]

He had one of the biggest funeral processions ever held in Seattle. It was miles long. I was in there organizing for it. I worked with John Caughlan's first wife, who knew all the rituals for funerals. We set up the casket with guards at either end, who changed at intervals. John Caughlan led the ceremony at the grave site, quoting from Lenin. Sarah Jackson sang—she was a gifted black actor and singer whom I knew through the Federal Theater Project—and then the people spoke. It didn't take anything to get the crowd out, just the fact that Bill had died. Especially the older people poured out for a hero's funeral—in the middle of the Smith Act trial of the McCarthy period!

His grave is in the Lake View Cemetery, where all the Seattle pioneers are buried. The monument says that he was a person of the people. I don't get much pleasure out of cemeteries, but I went there recently to see if I could find his grave. I wanted to see that monument.

THE FINNISH OLD LADY

During the witch-hunt, there was a lot of intimidation. They wouldn't give insurance to Communists, and the oil companies wouldn't give me credit cards, but I managed to get one by finagling around while I was in Los Angeles on a visit. The FBI played Cops and Robbers, though they didn't monkey with me much directly. They had a technique: go in pairs. One was a tough guy who would threaten, and the other was a soft-spoken guy who would say, "No, don't be so hard on this person."

There was an old Finnish lady in Kirkland. She had some kind of radical background—probably went all the way back to Finland. She was chopping wood when the FBI went out there to harass her. When she found out who they were, she turned on them, shook her finger like an angry god on a potato vine, and said, "Do your parents know what kind of shameful work you're doing?" She just roasted the hell out of them. All the time she had the ax. They went flying out of there and never came back. Nobody's going to attack an old lady who stands up for her rights.

ERNESTO, CHRIS, AND THE
FILIPINO CANNERY WORKERS

After I was arrested, the INS grabbed a bunch more people in Washington and Oregon, including the entire leadership of the Filipino cannery workers' union. I can remember the Filipinos. Ernesto Mangaoang, the business agent for Local 37. Chris Mensalvis, the president, with an American-born wife and two children. Ponce Torres, Raymon Tancioco, Joe Prudencio, all with wives and children. And Casimaro Absolor, who was totally blind.

The Filipino cannery union had always been under the control of crooked people. Once a year, the companies would load the Filipinos into steerage in the hold of a boat in Seattle and dump them at the canneries in Alaska, where there was nothing—no food, no entertainment—and unspeakable conditions. The union leaders would assign their friends to go up on the first boatload to set up the gambling establishments. Since there was no other recreation for the workers, they'd come back to Seattle at the end of the summer with no money at all. It seems that the Mafia controlled the Filipino union. The union would get the cannery workers to gamble but the money was actually owed back to the Mafia. The canneries were in on it, too: they would subtract money from the workers' wages to pay their gambling debts. That's how the white company owners and the thug Filipinos in the union worked hand-in-glove to fleece the workers. In the decades prior to the Second World War, some people tried to reform the union, and they were murdered. After the war, Ernesto, Chris, and Ponce became officers in the International Longshoremen's and Warehousemen's Union Local 37. They finally broke up this racket, put a halt to the gambling, and organized the workers for better conditions.

Carlos Bulosan, a well-known Filipino writer, was a friend of mine. In his book *America Is in the Heart,*[33] he describes the conditions under which the Filipino workers lived. The worse their conditions were, the less it cost to feed and transport them, and the bigger the profits for the industry. So when the union got into the hands of people who were really concerned about the workers, the workers got contracts, and everything changed. They were flown up to Alaska and they got decent food, showers. I don't suppose it was a Garden of Eden, but it was a different world. The owners were faced with strikes they couldn't afford in the middle of the season.

Now, they wanted to get rid of the new leadership in the union, so they used the big Red Scare. At the end of the season, when the Filipinos came back to Seattle and the West Coast, the INS would hold them for deportation without a hearing.

The Filipinos might have been accused as Communists, I don't remember. They went after everybody. In the 1950s, if you even looked sideways to the left, you were dubbed a Communist and they were out to get you. I'm not bitter. I don't know who makes these decisions, I never have. If I did, I'd go give 'em a piece of my mind, which I can hardly spare.

The WCPFB took care of the Filipinos, bailed them out of jail, and took their cases. I remember one of them, Joe Alvarez, was in prison with no bail. He had never heard of us, but we had heard of him. Marion and I went around raising the five hundred dollars, got the order, and went to the Immigration Station to release him. He was just amazed to be free!

The WCPFB lawyers contended that the Filipinos were not subject to deportation, one, because they hadn't left the country, they'd simply gone to Alaska—you couldn't say Alaska was a foreign country, even though

Nellie Frayne Anderson with the infant Hazel Anna Cummings Anderson in christening dress, May 4, 1898.

Dorothy (Dot) Anderson Hughes, 1905.

Bill (Sonny) Anderson Hughes, Victoria, B.C., 1922.

Eighth-grade class of "Old Man Campbell,"
North Woods School, Victoria, B.C., 1913.

Jacob Hughes, 1915 *(left);* Nellie Frayne Anderson at the beach,
Esquimalt Lagoon, 1913 *(right).*

Nellie and Dot, 1913.

Diving from the bridge at The Gorge, Victoria, B.C., 1915.

Hazel Anderson ("Leo") Hughes, 1912. "I look scared to death here,
but a lot of kids are trying to make me laugh."

Willetta and Bugs, 1913.

Playing in canoes under the bridge at The Gorge, 1910.

Hazel Anderson ("Leo") Hughes, 1910.

Klondike play, 1916. "The play is about the Gold Rush. In Act I, the miners count their gold dust. The robber, Audrey, is coming around the tent."

Hazel Anderson ("Leo") Hughes, 1916.

Hazel Anderson ("Leo") Hughes, Cadboro Bay, 1916.

Harry Parker, 1916.

Ella Dalziel, 1916.

Ted Dalziel and Hazel Anderson ("Leo") Hughes, 1916.

Hazel ("Leo") and Nydia Dalziel, 1920: "I left Ted while we were in San Francisco, where he worked in the shipyards as a journeyman electrician."

The basketball team, with Nydia as mascot, 1921.
Hazel ("Leo") Dalziel is in the front row, center.

Hazel ("Leo") Dalziel, immigrant to Seattle, about 1922.

Nellie Frayne Anderson Hughes, 1938, just before her death, at age 66.

Hazel Wolf recovering from tuberculosis, 1947.

Hazel Wolf (right), legal secretary, Seattle, 1948.

Hazel Wolf, legal secretary, Caughlan and Hatten, Seattle, 1948.
Photo courtesy of Goldie Caughlan.

Bill Anderson Hughes and his wife, Jo Hughes, 1945.

Seattle's Hooverville, 1937.
Photo courtesy of the Museum of History and Industry, Seattle.

HAZEL ANNA WOLF of Seattle faces deportation to England where she never has been.

Seattle Woman Ordered Shipped To British Isles

The Oregonian, February 13, 1961.

Hazel Wolf at the time of the Immigration and
Naturalization hearings, Seattle, about 1953.

Marion Kinney, executive director, Washington Committee
for the Protection of the Foreign Born, 1965.

MANGAOANG VICTORY

--FIRST CRACK IN WALTER-McCARRAN ACT.

When the US Supreme Court upheld the lower court decision in the case of Mangaoang vs. Boyd of the Immigration Dept. on Nov. 14th, it dealt the first setback to the oppressive Walter-McCarran Act. The winning of the case represents another great achievement in the long fight of ILWU #37 for union security, and it represents the removal of a dangerous threat to the security of 46,000 Filipinos who settled in this country prior to 1934.

Before this decision 46,000 Filipinos under the Walter-McCarran Act could be deported for even a minor breach of the laws committed in the past or that might be committed in the future.

Before this decision any member of ILWU #37 who showed a fighting union spirit in the never-ending struggle against the Salmon Industry for a decent living, could be deported as a "subversive".

Before this decision the very lives of some 12 ILWU members, or former members, were at stake. Those men, if sent to the Philippine Islands faced possible execution! Their families faced poverty and the tragedy of separation. These men, whom the Supreme Court has declared "undeportable" are Ernesto Mangaoang, Business Agent of Local #37, Chris Mensalvos, President, who has an American born wife and two children; Ponce Torres, who has a young daughter; Ramon Tancioco, who has a wife and two little ones; Joe Prudencio who has a wife, a son and a daughter; Casimoro Absolor, who is totally blind; and other members of the local in Portland: Pedro Cabornay and Joe Raymundo.

Credit for this victory should be taken by the Washington Committee for Protection of Foreign Born, the ILWU #37 Defense Committee, and to the many supporters, financial and otherwise, of both those committees. The attorneys who guided this far-reaching case to its splendid conclusion are Siegfried Hesse, John Caughlan and C.T. Hatten.

"YOU CANT DO THAT TO ME" cries John Boyd to US Supreme Ct.

When the US Supreme Court upheld the contention of Ernesto Mangaoang that he was not deportable, John P. Boyd, Immigration Director, was, to put it mildly, "fit to be tied". He displayed his petulance in a childish refusal to return Ernesto's bail even though he had been ordered by the court to do so as far back as August 3rd. The bondsman has been forced to seek legal help to get his $5000.00.

* * *

Leaders of the Cannery Workers' and Farm Laborers' Union (FTA-CIO, Local 7) turn over $312.75 collected from members working in Briston Bay, Alaska, to the Caughlan Defense Committee. Standing, from left: Pablo Sorio, Pauline Paet, Pete Quitoriano, Balbine Tacazon. Seated, from left: Hazel Wolf, committee secretary; John Caughlan, who represented the union for many years; and Ernesto Mangaoang, chairman of the union's Defense Committee. Photo originally published in *The New World*, August 19, 1948.

Eugene V. Dennett is sworn in at the Canwell hearings, 1948.
Photo courtesy of the Museum of History and Industry, Seattle.

H. C. "Army" Armstrong at the Canwell hearings witness table, 1948.
Photo courtesy of the Museum of History and Industry, Seattle.

Merritt Smith and Marion Kinney, 1972.

William Mackie, Hazel Wolf, and Hamish McKay, about 1976.

Hazel Wolf, about 1965.

Seattle Audubon Society Field Day, Boise Cascade Wenas Public
Campground, Yakima County, Washington, May 28-30, 1966.
From left: Beatrice Buzzette, Hazel Wolf, Emily Haig.

Helen Engle at Hazel Wolf's 90th birthday party, March 10, 1988.

Hazel Wolf testifies before the Washington state legislature, Olympia, 1970s.
Photo courtesy of Isabel Egglin.

(Facing page, top) Hazel Wolf and her attorney, John Caughlan, prepare for her deportation hearings at the Immigration and Naturalization Service, November 1949. Photo courtesy of the *Seattle Times*.

(Facing page, bottom) Bernice DeLorme and Hazel Wolf, Indian-Conservationist Conference, Daybreak Star Indian Cultural Center, Seattle, 1979.

(Above) Governor Booth Gardner, Tom Hubbard, Ken Weiner, Robert Redford, and Hazel Wolf aboard the *Golden Delicious* on Seattle's Duwamish River, 1988.

(Left) Hazel Wolf, Tumwater Canyon, Washington, 1978.
(Right) Hazel Wolf, Point Reyes Bird Observatory, California, 1965.

Hazel Wolf, 1994. Photo by Fred Felleman.

Hazel Wolf with nurse, X-ray machine, and infant respirator at Fernando Vélez Paiz Children's Hospital, Managua, Nicaragua, 1989. St. Mark's Episcopal Cathedral and celebrants at Wolf's 90th birthday party raised the funds for the equipment.

President Daniel Ortega of Nicaragua signs Hazel Wolf's speech at the Fourth Biennial Congress on the Fate and Hope of the Earth, Managua, 1989.

Sandinista war veterans outside Managua, Nicaragua,
on their way to vote, February 1990.

Audubon Society demonstration on the steps of the U.S. Capitol, 1996.
Hazel Wolf is in the middle of the front row.

Hazel Wolf and students, Decatur Middle School,
Decatur, Alabama, January 1992.

Hazel Wolf holds the diploma for the honorary doctorate conferred on her by
Seattle University, June 1997. The document read in part, "Hazel Wolf is one of
the most remarkable, spirited women living in the United States today."

Hazel Wolf with Jesse Jackson Jr. at her 90th birthday party, March 10, 1988.

Hiking buddies at Washington Governor Mike Lowry's birthday party and declaration of Hazel Wolf Day, March 21, 1996. From left: Hazel Wolf, Ruths B and C (Boyle and Cameron), Gladys Squires.

Joe De La Cruz, Hazel Wolf, and granddaughter Ann Levick Sargent
at Hazel Wolf's 100th birthday party, March 14, 1998.

Hazel Wolf, 1993. Photo courtesy of Bernadette Mertens.

it was a U.S. territory, not a state, in the 1950s. And two, they weren't deportable because they'd never *entered* the country—ninety percent of them came between 1898 and 1946, when the Philippine Islands were owned by the United States as a colony. They weren't citizens, but they weren't aliens, either. They were nationals who didn't have to go through immigration. They could go back and forth as freely as citizens. So they couldn't be deported, and the Supreme Court of the United States upheld that—a big side victory that isn't discussed very much.

I had quite a little bit to do with the members of Local 37. John [Caughlan] and then Barry [Hatten] had been their lawyer long before the deportation cases. When John was charged with perjury, in 1948,[34] and I was his fund-raiser, the cannery union raised a lot of money for us. They gave me a check to show their gratitude for what John and the other lawyers had done for them. There's a picture of John, Ernesto, some other cannery union members, and myself on the occasion of handing this check over. I'm grinning like the cat that swallowed the canary.

The Filipinos were all friends of mine. I was in and out of their cannery workers' headquarters, which was at the corner of 2nd Avenue South and Washington Street. I wrote their leaflets and brochures and I went to their dances. I went to their homes and had dinner with them. They had a special delicacy, just for me—squid, a most unsavory-looking business. I took a bite, and it felt like my mouth was full of butterflies. I swallowed it, and the butterflies went to my stomach. They were all looking at me. "Ah," I said, "that's good." They said, "Here, eat some more!"

THE ANNIE HOBSON FAMILY

I traveled a bit on the other deportation cases. Not a lot, because, you know, I had to work eight hours a day. I went with Jessica Mitford[35] to Detroit to support Annie Hobson's family. Annie Hobson was from England, but she lived in Seattle. She had a daughter who was more or less inadvertently born in Canada. Annie had spent about three weeks of her life there, given birth, and then come with her daughter back to this country. Her daughter married a Communist in Detroit, and they produced two children. The government arrested the daughter's husband as a Communist. He had a Purple Heart from the war, but they took away his disability pension and put him in jail.

The INS brought proceedings against Annie's daughter, who was to be deported to Canada. Then they brought proceedings in Seattle against Annie Hobson, who was to be sent to England. I don't know what was supposed to happen to her two teenage grandchildren. That's how the INS held the family together.

Now, these two children were very gifted. Every year, the American Legion or some such hoopla people like that had a contest for children to write an essay on why they liked America. The boy won it, much to the dismay of the American Legion. And that wasn't all. When the daughter was old enough to enter the contest, she won it, too.

These cases went on for sometimes twenty years, because our lawyers fought them tooth and nail. The courts were our weapon, but we seldom won anything through the courts. We just fought for time, or until the climate changed, or we died.[36] Eventually, Annie's son-in-law was released from jail. They had to drop the deportation order against the granddaughter and the mother. But Annie Hobson died before they got around to her. Annie went to her reward without a blessing from the Immigration. She eluded them.[37]

THE WOLF CASE

I was in the papers a lot, but I wasn't participating in all those court cases. I had a life of my own to lead. It was the lawyers' battle. There was a network of firms all over the country, all of them pro bono, because nobody had any money. There was the Hazel Wolf case, this abstract thing, and there was my personal life—get up every morning, have breakfast, go to work, come home at night. Two different things. I forgot about it half the time, but once in a while I had to dip in and show up at some hearing, or in court. I'd be there for a while and then go back into my own life again.

There was tremendous sympathy for me in Canada, in the women's movement there, and in the trade-union movement. The *Vancouver Sun* wrote to John [Caughlan] in 1953 and said, "Anytime she wants to come back, we've got a job for her and a place to live." Everybody said, "Why don't you go?" The job was better than anything I'd had here. I said, "I can't. I've got this case, the Wolf case. So thank them. If I actually get deported, then we'll talk about this job." I had a responsibility to the people who were fighting for civil liberties in this country, for freedom from persecution, for freedom of speech, freedom of everything. I wasn't taking any offers from Canada or anybody else.

The Washington Committee [for the Protection of the Foreign Born] and the lawyers worked really closely together, but after I went back to work for John, all the strategy was his. I didn't realize it until I read a draft of this chapter. I thought, "My gosh, that guy's creative." I used to say all the time, "I work for John Caughlan," and he'd say, "No, I work for Hazel Wolf." We'd argue about it, but now I see, he really did work for me.[38]

In all the litigation, I was the plaintiff, suing for my rights, and the defendant was the U.S. Attorney General. I lived through quite a few attorneys general in all those years. They came and went. I worked in San Francisco for a while in 1954, so sometimes I went up to the federal appeals court and attended my own case. There I met Mr. Rose, the government attorney against me. He told me that he had made a special trip back to New York to try to get them to dismiss my case. There were a few bad spots, but in general I got along with the staff at Immigration very well. I knew that they didn't start this thing.

The local INS officials could have said, "I'll resign before I'll arrest an innocent person on this trumped-up charge. I don't like the law. It's not just, and rather than be party to it, I'll resign." But what would they have gained by that? If the whole Board of Appeals had resigned, that would have been something else again. But if some obscure examiner resigned, nobody would have even noticed that he was gone. So what did they do instead? They dragged their feet, and they were friendly to us. And they let us know in various ways that they didn't like what was going on.

I had to go down there to the Immigration Station every Tuesday at four o'clock in the afternoon and report. What a nuisance. You know,

I'm working, and here I've got to leave my job, get a cab, and go down there. So on one particular day, when it was late and I was busy, I told John Caughlan, "I'm not going down there. Period."

He was upset. "You've got to go. That's one of the conditions for your release on bail."

I said, "I can't help it. I'm not going down there anymore. You call them up and tell them that they know where I am. If they want me, they can come and get me."

John called them up. "I have a very stubborn client. She says that she's not ever going to come down there again."

They said, "Oh well, tell her to send us a postcard every Tuesday and report once a month instead."

I used to go on a lot of hikes, and I'd time them so that I could send my postcard to the INS from Hungry Horse Dam or someplace like that. The man I had to report to once a month was a former Interior Department naturalist who had been wounded in the war. I'd bring my wilderness pictures, and he'd bring his. We had so much in common. Then he'd say, "Oh, by the way, sign this"—he always had my files with him. They were all done up in wide canvas strips, and the piles were so big he'd have to use both arms to carry them. I was walking behind him one day, and I said, "This file of mine is getting heavier and heavier. Pretty soon it'll weigh as much as I do. When that day comes, why don't we call the whole deal off?"

13 / To the Brink

THE FBI AND THE INS

$\mathcal{I}$ just assumed that the FBI bugged my telephone at John Caughlan's office—be foolish if I hadn't. I loved to get on the phone and make nasty remarks about the FBI. One time I was talking about cake recipes. I said,

"Hey, remember, this phone's bugged. Let the FBI wives get their own damn cake recipes." I took any chance I got to show what contempt I had for them. I used the name Wolf, but Anderson was still my legal name. The FBI never found out the simple fact that they were persecuting someone with an assumed name.

I didn't take any chances with my relatives. As a child, I was very close to all my mother's people, to my Aunt Sally and my four cousins. When I came here in the early 1920s to live permanently, I was in and out of their house all the time. But when I joined the Communist Party, I called my cousin Lois and I told her, "I'm not ever going to call you again, or ever visit you, or ever mention your name or anyone in your family to anybody, and hopefully the FBI will never run you down as a connection of mine." I knew that eventually the government would come around and try to pick me off. I knew because I was a student of Karl Marx, because I was working-class, and because I'm not stupid. But I didn't want to worry that family. If I actually got deported, then I'd contact them: "Here's the end of it. See you later." And, you know, it worked. The FBI in all their glory never caught up with them.

I couldn't protect my immediate family, however. My brother and sister and Nydia and their families were outraged at what the government was trying to do to me. They didn't try to avoid me because I was contaminated. My mother had welded a common political philosophy among us. I imagine it was the FBI, but it could have been the immigration department, that sent people to question Nydia's neighbors out in Port Angeles. A long time later, Nydia's neighbor told her what she had said to the agents: "Yes, I've met her mother. We've had coffee together, but the conversation was strictly about the kids and the neighborhood. She didn't try to organize anything in Port Angeles."

At no time was I able to go across the border into Canada, because they would nail me there, and I wouldn't be able to come back in. But in 1953 I wanted to go. I had a foster sister, Jean, who lived in the interior of British Columbia with her three children, and I wanted to see them. So I got a driver's license under an assumed name. I actually took the test, and I was very careful not to drive too well. I was just learning, you see. I got a library card made out in that name. I had a letter addressed to me, written on an envelope and sent through the mail to that name. I tried to get a phony birth certificate, but that didn't work. Now, no one of these documents was sufficient, but I thought the combined bunch would work. And if it didn't work, I knew how to get back into the country because I knew where I could climb over a fence and get in. You have to take risks in this world.

I visited Jean—spent a very nice time up there on their homestead. Coming back in, I thought I'd come by way of Victoria on the ferry that comes to Port Angeles. As I came through U.S. Customs in Canada, the officer scolded me for being "so American" and only bringing my driver's license and my library card—no passport, no birth certificate, no nothing. He just thought I was stupid and he felt sorry for me, so he stamped my entry card. When we got off at Port Angeles, Nydia was at the bottom of the gangplank waiting for me. There was a second customs officer at the top, where Nydia could just see him. I noticed that as the officer was given the entry card, he'd turn away from the traveler and put the card in a pile, working in a kind of rhythm. So when he came to me, I gave him the card, and while he was turned away from me, I thumbed my nose at him. Nydia was nearly fainting down there at the bottom of the gangplank.

Then, in 1954, the immigration department decided to round everybody up—we were all floating around on bail, you see. They started with Ernesto Mangaoang. He had a room with a fiery guy, a Filipino named Matthias. Immigration banged on their door at 2:00 A.M. Matthias went to the door but didn't open it. He yelled, "Who's out there?" And they said, "It's the immigration department, and we want Ernesto Mangaoang." Matthias shouted, "I'm standing here with my revolver. You try to get in this door, and I'll just shoot you full of holes." That's more than Immigration had bargained for. They retreated to their car and held a consultation. Ernesto phoned John [Caughlan], who told him, "Go with them. Don't start a shooting war over it. Tell Matthias to cool it." In the meantime, John got on the telephone with all the other deportees. We all scrambled. It was 2:00 A.M., but I got in my car and drove through all the back roads to Tacoma—I didn't want any traffic cop saying, "Yes, I saw that license number." I moved in with a friend of mine, put my car in her garage and shut the door so they couldn't find me, and stayed with her until I got the all-clear. I don't know if they intended to work every-body over or not, but there was no use sitting around like a duck wait-ing to find out.[39]

"TELL MRS. W. NOT TO WORRY"

*O*n March 5, 1956, the Senate Judiciary Committee finally tabled S.B. 1425, which would have made my deportation illegal. Here's a little "if only" story that involved Supreme Court Justice William O. Douglas.

He had a vacation place out by the Makah Indian Reservation, on the tip of the Olympic Peninsula. Augie Slater was a guide who lived up there and would take Justice Douglas out on hunting parties up into the moun-tain wilderness every summer. I'd known Augie a long time. I know a lot of people out there. He may even have been a Communist.

So I was ordered deported, again and again and again, by the District Court. That's old hat. Then we'd appealed. It went to the Circuit Court, and we'd appealed from that to the U.S. Supreme Court. So, okay, we were back at the District Court level one summer. Augie worried they'd turn me down at District and Circuit Courts, then it would go to the Supreme Court, which wasn't in session over the summer. He knew that William O. Douglas had the jurisdiction out here for emergencies. But Augie got antsy, wrote to William O., and told him all about my case: "Be sure to watch for it, don't let them deport her." William O. wrote a postcard to Augie: "Tell Mrs. W. not to worry." It was signed "Bill." One of the short-est Supreme Court decisions that was ever handed down.

But the case never got to him. A year later, on April 22, 1957, it did get to the U.S. Supreme Court when the court was in session. For the second time they denied the petition for writ of certiorari and there was nothing between me and Canada. I was supposed to go to Canada because I was born there. The Canadians were obliged by treaty to take any nationals who were deported, but if they could have figured out any way to refuse to take me, they'd have done it. They, and a lot of other nations, were very much opposed to the witch-hunting that was going on here.

WOMAN WITHOUT A COUNTRY

Marion Kinney and the wcpfb got up a letter-writing campaign to the Canadian press and legislators.[40] It was all over the papers there.[41] The Canadian legislators wrote feisty protest letters to our attorney general. They were really on my side: "In view of Mrs. Wolf's record, it is stupid to carry on a persecution of this kind. Because she held certain opinions twenty years ago, she doesn't necessarily hold them today."

> Three Canadian legislators have protested to Attorney General Herbert Brownell against the deportation to Canada of Mrs. Hazel Anna Wolf of Seattle, the Canadian Press reported today from Victoria.[42]

Meanwhile, John Caughlan was nosing around in the law books and coming up with new grounds for a court case. "She may not be an alien at all," he told the press. He tried to prove that my mother never lost her citizenship when she married a [Scottish immigrant to Canada]. Therefore I was a U.S. citizen, always had been.[43]

Okay, the Supreme Court didn't buy that one, either. They turned me down a third time, on June 30, 1958, but now John was onto citizenship issues and he found a defining case: a woman had crossed from Canada to be a prostitute in the U.S.—wanted a better life, like everybody else who has come here. Of course, anybody who comes here with narcotics or for prostitution is deportable. But she'd married an American citizen, and when they came to deport her, her lawyer said, "She's not Canadian. She lost her citizenship through her marriage, which took place before 1932." Before 1932, Canadian women lost their citizenship when they married foreigners. We informed Immigration that I wasn't a Canadian citizen, because I'd married Herb Wolf, a U.S. citizen, in 1928. The Canadians were tickled to death to get out from underneath it. In the fall of 1958, the Canadians informed the American government, "We are not going to take her. She is not a Canadian citizen." Here I'd been all those years, a woman without a country![44]

Mrs. Hazel Anna Wolf, sixty, whom the United States has been trying to expel since 1949, will not be accepted for deportation by her native Canada, John Caughlan, her attorney, said today. Caughlan said he has been informed that under a Canadian law in effect up to 1932, Mrs. Wolf lost her Canadian citizenship December 30, 1928, when she was married to Herbert Dunning Wolf, an American citizen, in Portland, Oregon. The government has been trying to deport Mrs. Wolf on grounds of Communist Party membership. She has lived in the United States since 1922. She was born in Victoria, British Columbia.[45]

I thought it was all over. I'd review the status of all the Seattle cases in the *Northern Light,* and I'd put myself in with "undeportables," those whose countries of origin had refused to accept them. We undeportables lived under a kind of house arrest provided for in the [1952] Walter-McCarran Act, but we seemed out of danger of deportation. Boris Sassieff, one of the other undeportables, and I were called down to Immigration to read our testimony and to initial every page. I'm writing on the corner of each page, "H.A.W. . . . . H.A.W." I nudge Boris. "Look what I'm writing here—*HAW, HAW, HAW.*" He says, "Look what I'm writing—*BS, BS, BS.*"

A BIG LIE

*T*he INS had to sit back and lick their wounds for a while. After about a year and a half, they finally came up with a better idea. They would say I had received citizenship through my father, who was a British subject. So in early 1960, the INS applied for travel papers to deport me to England, and England complied.

The immigration service then decided to deport her to England, on the theory that her father, born in Gibraltar, was a citizen of the British Commonwealth. She has never been to England, and as far as she knows neither had her father, George Anderson. His father, William Anderson, from

Scotland, was a member of the 176th Highland Regiment, which manned the fort at Gibraltar. The mother was also from Scotland, and the entire family eventually immigrated to the United States [sic].

"I don't really know what I'm charged with. If it was to advocate the overthrow of this country by force and violence, then I'm not guilty," said Wolf.[46]

The deportation was scheduled for June 12, 1960. John and the wcpfb lawyers immediately filed papers for a stay of deportation, to give me time to defend myself in court on the grounds that to deport a person to a place she didn't come from, or to which she had no ties, was "cruel and unusual punishment," prohibited in the constitution.[47] The judge in Seattle—it must have been Bowen[48] again—turned down the stay, since, he said, the constitution doesn't cover aliens. That was May 31, 1960. We had twelve days to do all these appeals to the 9th Circuit Court in San Francisco, but we were all ready to go. Our attorneys were also all ready to go in Washington, D.C., to the Supreme Court if it became necessary.

John was really upset. He told the papers, "I feel it is an outrageous action on the part of our government to deport a longtime resident who has committed no offense whatsoever. This is banishment. I always thought that went out with the rack and the thumbscrew. If carried out, her deportation will establish a precedent for all the other 'undeportables.' If they can send her to England, they can send her to Outer Mongolia. This is an attempt to find a convenient dumping ground for exiles."[49] As a judge said later, "According to this argument, in cases where no country in the world would receive a deportatable alien, he could be put on a raft and shoved into the ocean beyond the three-mile limit."[50]

I had twelve days to assemble 150 pounds of my worldly goods. John P. Boyd, who was still the ins district director for Seattle, took the precaution of warning Washington State Senator Magnuson: "The subject has been identified with Communist-front organizations continuously since the institution of the deportation proceedings in 1949 to the present time. In view of this fact it is quite possible that you will receive other letters from members of subversive and front organizations protesting the subject's deportation to England."[51] Unfortunately, neither Senator Magnuson nor Senator Jackson, who received a slew of letters on my behalf, and who had plenty of power in the U.S. Senate at that time, lifted a finger. They had made their reputations as anti-Communists, Cold Warriors.

In this emergency, I wrote to Mrs. Franklin D. Roosevelt. She didn't look into it. Instead, she sent me back a form letter. "Dear Mrs. Wolf: On receipt of your letter I wrote the Attorney General and I am forwarding the reply, which explains the position taken in regard to your deportation. Very sincerely yours, (signed) Eleanor Roosevelt." William P. Rogers, the attorney general under President Eisenhower in 1961, had sent her a rehash of one of Commissioner Swing's[52] reports on me. I wasn't surprised—would have dropped dead if she had looked into it. When asked to go against their class interests, the ruling class is not going to stand up to it. They were hysterical. I'll be glad to see them get hysterical again one of these days. And I don't condemn Mrs. Roosevelt because she made this one error. I just can't be bothered wasting my time and energy on this trivia. That's why I've lived so long. Nevertheless, this letter from Mrs. Roosevelt—I never forgave her.

John and I went over to see the British consul here in Seattle—a stuffed shirt if there ever was one. John was very gentlemanly. They talked. The guy was solid.

"We will not rescind the travel papers, blah, blah, blah . . . but no special provision will be made for you in England" is what he said.

So finally John said, "Well, I realized that the British Empire was falling to pieces, but I didn't know they were that desperate for citizens."

The consul stood up. "Sir!" he said. An underling lounging by the door winked at me, and I winked back.

At some point during these frantic days before the deportation date [June 12, 1960], Marion [Kinney] "got busy." She told me that she was working a split-shift at a cafe, and on her way home she was thinking about my coming deportation to England. She called from her home phone to one of the liberal newspapers in London and got them started on it. They got everybody in England excited about the deportation of this poor woman.

So a reporter called from London and asked me, "What would you do if you got deported over here to England?" I said, "I don't know a single person in England. I'm a legal secretary. I know nothing about British legal procedure, and I couldn't possibly qualify for a job. My only recourse would be the dole. And furthermore, because I speak English with an accent, people would think that I'm an American and probably throw rocks at me." That's how my case got all over the British newspapers. Even France wrote about it, and Finland.[53]

With all of the publicity going on, John wrote to some attorneys in London about my imminent departure to England. They were so outraged that they took it to the Parliament. Any member of Parliament [MP] can ask a secretary a question from the floor, so they set up a committee of the Labor MPs to ask the question to the foreign secretary. "Why did you issue travel papers to this woman who's been in the United States for forty-odd years and whose relatives are there?" The foreign secretary answered, "Because the U.S. government assured us that she didn't have any roots and no relatives there—only a daughter from whom she has been estranged for many years." Supposedly, I didn't even know where Nydia lived. And that was what the American government told the British government.

Now, the British lawyers were mad at me and John for selling them a bill of goods! So we got busy and got affidavits from every damn relative I had. Nydia sent a letter to support my case. My brother and his wife, my sister, her husband, and even my grandson, Dal—I had relatives crawling out my ears, all just from my immediate family. Well, that put a damper on everything. The U.S. government was caught in a big lie.

So the British hedged.[54] Imagine! One government lying to another over a stupid little deportation, but it's true! Our government was so discredited in the eyes of the British government and the Canadian government! That, and the dying down of the McCarthy hysteria, was what really killed the Wolf case.

I went to England many years later, but I had to pay my fare both ways. A bitter blow—I could have had at least one way paid if I had gone when I had the chance.

THE CLOSEST SHAVE

The INS didn't stop trying to deport me to England. The case was still going in the San Francisco Court of Appeals. I had planned a camping trip with my friend Lorraine from Bellingham. She called and said, "Well, I guess the camping trip is off." I said, "No, it isn't. I'm not going to change my plans just because they've scheduled another deportation." One reporter asked me, "So what are you going to do next?" I told him, and the headline came out: MRS. WOLF TO CAMP WHILE JUDGES PONDER.[55] Lorraine and I were looking over the magnificent scene at the north rim of the Grand Canyon, and I said, "Those poor old judges—pondering while we're out here at this beautiful place."

For the first time, they pondered in my favor. On June 8, 1960, the 9th Circuit [Court] granted me a stay of deportation and sent my case back down to the District Court for a consideration of the constitutional issues. So, okay, I may be covered by the U.S. Constitution. It was a major victory.

A few months later, in the late fall of 1960, I had to show up at the Federal District Court in Seattle. The courtroom was crowded. I had been ordered to pack 150 pounds of my belongings ready to go. Will the judge stay the deportation to consider constitutional issues, or will he order them to grab me by the collar right there in court and take me out? I prepared for both eventualities, my car all packed with gear and my little nephew Bobby—Bill and Jo's boy—with me, ready to go camping out at Kalaloch, on the Pacific Ocean, and my suitcases packed, too, in case I was deported. And I dressed for both occasions—a suit on in court, but my slacks out in the car with the camping gear.

Bobby and I were sitting in the back row of benches in the courtroom waiting for this judge to make up his mind about whether the constitution covered me. Judges always start backward, you see, and you don't know until the last minute whether they are going to say yes or no. So this judge started with history—blah, blah, blah, all the way down. Bobby was asking, "What's he saying?" I said, "I don't know, he's backing into it." And the judge talked some more and some more, and finally I leaned over to Bobby: "Ah, I think he's going to be with us. Yeah, I think we're going camping, kid." That was the closest shave.[56]

14 / This Is My Home

EVERYBODY LIED

The case had been going on and on. So here's Immigration in a bad way. They had to fight out the constitutional issue—whether aliens are covered— and it would have to go all the way back up to the U.S. Supreme Court. That would take a couple of years, maybe longer. They got a black eye from the bunch of lies they told the British government. The lie made it into the international press, so even if the INS won on the constitutional issue, it was very unlikely they would get another set of travel papers out of the British, who just didn't want to hear any more about the Wolf case. While the INS was winning all the battles, we were slowly but surely winning the war.[57]

Now the INS approached us: how about they make a motion to move the whole thing out of the courts, back to the administrative level? Due to certain changes in law and certain precedents from other cases, blah, blah, blah, in which deportation was canceled because the person was a Communist but not in any meaningful way, I might be entitled, blah, blah, blah, at the administrative level. That was great with us. If we didn't like what they did at the administrative level, we'd start through the courts again, and I'd be eighty years old and still fighting this case. I could outlive Immigration. Commissioner Swing had already retired.

Of course Immigration never intended to hold any hearings. They just wanted to sweep it under the rug so that they could win. They didn't call the hearings, and they didn't call the hearings. My attorneys didn't want to have the hearings, either, because they were busy people and there was no money in it for them. They were saying, "Let sleeping dogs lie." I was saying, "Yeah, they are dogs, and they are asleep. But they'll wake up again, and they're still dogs. I don't want a deportation order hanging over my head for the rest of my life, when all they have to do is dust it off. There's no statute of limitations. Bad times could come and they'll start all over again. They could send me to Hollywood—worse fate than England or Canada. Furthermore, I want to apply and become a citizen, and I can't as long as I have this order on me."

In 1963, we finally pressured the INS into a hearing. The government didn't bother with the imported experts—this business of proving that the Communists were trying to blow things up. They were just going to rely on two local people, and neither wanted to testify against me.

The first, Eugene Dennett,[58] was shamefaced. In an executive session he had said under oath that I was a Communist, so he had to keep on saying that or he'd have been in deep trouble. In these executive sessions, called by congressional committees, the FBI threw a lot of names at informers and asked, "Is this person a Communist?" And the stoolie'd say, "Yes, yes, yes," all the way down the line, people they didn't even know.

It kind of pays to be nice to people. I was the one friendly, smiling face Eugene Dennett ever saw once the rumor got around that he was giving testimony in the executive sessions. I knew him real well. John contacted him and said, "Well, can you make just a little bit of a Communist out of her? You know, not a very important Communist?" Yeah, he could do that. I said to John later, "I almost got mad at that guy. He made me so inconsequential that I was only trusted to carry messages in sealed envelopes."

The other stool pigeon that was used against me in the hearings was Harold Brockway. Harold had a drinking problem. He was unstable. When all the shouting was over and the New Deal came to an end, he had a job lined up in Arabia, but first he had to sign an oath that he had never belonged to the Communist Party. He signed it, which was perjury, and he got called into an executive session with the House Un-American Activities Committee or one of those outfits. He swore under oath that I was a Communist, to avoid being charged with perjury. He thought that would be the end of it, but they put the squeeze on him: "You stool against Hazel, we won't put you in jail." I was the only one he stooled against, to my knowledge.

Now, we were very good friends in the old days. He was president of the Workers' Alliance, and I was chair of the Grievance Committee. Everybody thought he was a Communist, but I didn't *know* that he was, because I never saw him at anything but Workers' Alliance activities. He didn't *know* I was a Communist, either. He testified that I was, but he had to make up phony evidence that he saw me sitting in a Communist meeting or paying my dues.

When they subpoenaed him to testify against me, it just shattered the guy. Me, of all people. John referred him to another lawyer friend of ours, who advised him that if he tried to get out from under it and testified that I wasn't a Communist, they'd have him for perjury. And if he refused to testify, they would have him for contempt of court. So Harold could take his choice. Either way, he'd go to the clink.

For my first character witness, I asked Marion Kinney. Now, Marion was a known Communist, and John objected: "Who ever heard of a Communist being tried for being a Communist getting a Communist to testify as a character witness?" I said, "She's one of my best friends. She can really testify as to what kind of person I am, and she's going to be one of my character witnesses."

And I had an old man, Merritt Smith, from the Skid Road, a really dirty old guy who had food down the front of his clothes and bought his stuff two or three sizes too big for him. He drifted into the office one time and told me that the FBI was following him and he heard voices in his head. He wanted to help, so I had him join the bank of typists I'd set up for the Smith Act trial. He was a terrible typist, but you could read it, and he was very loyal to the job—typed all the way through. I undertook to be his friend. I got him into a church downtown and they put him on a committee to go see sick people. I got him a volunteer job in the WCPFB, in an office where there were a lot of old guys folding and mimeographing and sending out things. They were busy all the time.

Then I would have lunch with him once a month. I'm no martyr, you know. I enjoyed my lunches with him. He was well read. He had gone through law school, but he had never taken the bar. He read everything about the Supreme Court, and he got me doing it. He wrote all kinds of letters to congressmen on [behalf of] my case. He was really a great person—just lacked a few important marbles, that's all.

Anytime, day or night, that he heard voices or thought that people were following him, he was to call me and I would come. He was always saying, "You've done so much for me, and I can't do anything for you." I said to John, "Here's a chance for Merritt Smith to do something for me." John was appalled: "You don't want that guy. He looks so terrible." I said, "I don't care what he looks like. This is my case. I know people."

Just as I was leaving that morning for the hearing, my niece, Donna, my sister Dorothy's daughter, called on me. I said, "Oh Donna, I've got a hearing today." She said, "I want to testify." I said, "No, you keep out of this. I don't want my family involved." She insisted. Okay, so Donna came.

It was that same room at INS again. The examiner was sent up from California. In the morning, as usual, I wasn't going to testify, but as the hearing got started, John made some objections, and the examiner upheld him—three times! In the whole history of my case, the court had never upheld an objection of ours or failed to grant an objection to the other side. I said to John at the first recess, "I think this guy is listening. Let's put on a case. I don't mind testifying before him."

The hearing was well along when Harold Brockway was called, and then, before he really got started, another recess was declared. Everybody cleared out of the hearing room, and I encountered him in the hallway. There was nobody around and I can see him now—he's coming up on the one side of the hallway, and I'm going down.

He says, "Leo, what am I going to do?"

I tell him, "If you say I wasn't a Communist when you've sworn on oath that I was, you'll go to jail for perjury. If you refuse to testify, you'll go to jail for contempt, and, Harold, I do not want to see you go to jail. So you go ahead and stool on me just as much as you like. And don't worry about it, kid, because, let me tell you, I'm not ever going to be deported. I'm as safe as if I were in God's pocket, so just go ahead."

He breaks into a sob, and I pat him on the shoulder. We walk down the hall together.

So with my permission he testified that I was a Communist. But he told them all kinds of funny stuff. He made me into a great big Communist—a really important one—which was, of course, the wrong tack, from John's point of view.

Donna testified to all the glorious things I had done for her, her sister, her mother and father, my daughter, and my grandchildren. To have heard her talk, you'd have thought I was the mainstay of the entire family. I thought, "God, what a wonderful person she's describing." I was just enchanted.

Merritt showed up looking like a banker. He must have gone down to the Goodwill and got a fresh suit of clothes that morning after breakfast. His hair was in place and, as I said, he was an educated man, and he talked about the lunches he had with me over the years. He knew my political ideas from A to Z—that I was a good liberal, had believed in Truman's Fair Deal, and at no time had I ever even hinted I wanted to overthrow the government by force or violence. He was a marvelous witness.

When Marion [Kinney] testified, there was a little hassle. In cross-examination, the prosecutor asked her if she ever went under an assumed name, and with some confusion she admitted that she did. The prosecutor didn't give her a chance to explain. Of course, she had been forced to use an assumed name so the FBI wouldn't convince her employers to fire her. She would use her maiden name or her previous married name when she hired on to a new job, but it made her look kind of devious. Prosecutors are skilled that way.

When it came to examining me, the prosecutor held a box. He'd ask me a bunch of questions, and then he'd pull something from this little box of goodies.

"Did you ever own stock in the Frontier Bookstore?"

Oh no, I'd never owned any stock in the Frontier Bookstore, that was ridiculous.

"Well, do you recognize this?"

And out of his box he pulled a stock certificate made out to Hazel Wolf. I said that I guessed I had owned stock in the Frontier Bookstore. I'd never received any dividends, I could tell him that, but I rather thought it was a device to pry a ten-dollar donation out of me, and I'd completely forgotten that I'd received a certificate. The prosecutor actually thought he had caught me with this phony stock.

Next he pulled a letter out of the box—and this was kind of touchy—a plea for funds for the Hazel Wolf case, signed by three women.

He said, "Do you know these three women?"

I responded, "Before we go any further in this, I want you to understand I'm not saying whether I know anybody or I don't know them. I'm going to clam up, for the simple reason that if I say that I know them, they're going to be tarred as Communists, and they'll be hounded and harassed, and I'm not going to have that happen to any of my friends, or anybody that signs anything or is associated with me in any way. So just don't ask that kind of question."

The prosecutor said to the examiner, "I would like you to direct the witness to answer that question."

The examiner stood up. "I direct you to answer that question."

I said, "What will happen to me if I don't?"

And he said, "You will have refused to answer, and then you'll find out."

I said, "Okay, I'm not answering."

And then I waited for him to lower the boom on me, but he said to the prosecutor, "Go on with your next question."

I almost fell off my chair.

They could have cited me until they were blue in the face and I would not have answered that question. The examiner could then have taken my refusal before a federal judge and I would have been in contempt, but a little spell in the pokey isn't going to hurt anybody. I'd have had a newspaper started in no time.

Finally, the examiner asked me if I had ever been a member of the party, and I didn't know what to answer on that one. John and I went into a huddle. We weighed it back and forth, pros and cons, and finally decided I would say that I had been. I could say that I wasn't now, but I didn't know exactly when I had left.[59] I thought that no matter what I said, the prosecutor would come up with some kind of stool-pigeon evidence that had me in the party later than I remembered.

After the huddle, the examiner asked again, "Were you a member of the Communist Party?"

I hesitated.

He said under his breath, and sort of half-angry, "I can't hand down a decision in your favor if you won't answer that question."

I answered the question. I told him that I had been.

He said, "Are you now?" and I said, "No." He didn't ask me when I left. That closed the testimony.

We waited for the examiner to speak. First he evaluated each witness. He didn't believe a word that Harold said, the one who made me the big-shot Communist.[60] The only one left was Eugene, who said that I was a nothing.[61] Then he handed down a decision dismissing the deportation order. The reason wasn't cruel and unusual punishment. And it wasn't due process. And it wasn't that I had lived here more than forty years, and worked for unions and the unemployed, and had all my family here. And it wasn't that my mother was a citizen. It was based on a recent administrative decision in which it was said that certain aliens who were members of the Communist Party *did not really know what they were doing!*[62]

Everybody on the witness stand lied. They thought they knew all about me—they didn't. I wasn't perfect like my niece said. I wasn't a big-shot Communist, and I wasn't a nothing, but I was through with the Wolf case. I wasn't going to be deported. I was just going to live my life.

THE PETITION FOR CITIZENSHIP

*M*any years later, after the case had been won but I still wasn't a citizen, I went down to Immigration to see if it was safe for me to go on a canoe trip to the Canadian Boundary Waters area, and it wasn't. The fella said, "Yeah, don't go there. You're still on the blacklist. They might not let you back in at the border. . . . But Mr. Tuttle's here, and he'd probably like to see you."

Mr. Tuttle was the prosecutor for the very first hearing I ever had on the administrative level. I went in to speak with him.

"You know, I feel sorry about this thing. I was your first case. It's too bad you had to lose your very first case."

He laughed and urged me to file again for citizenship, but I said, "Oh no, you'll just have a bunch of stool pigeons who will testify against me. I don't want to go through that again."

But I did.

Unfortunately, when I filed my petition and went to the hearing, I ran into one of these rotten apples. Right away, I knew the examiner was not in my camp because he said, "You know, you are entitled to have an attorney." I said, "Why do I need an attorney when I'm simply filing a petition for citizenship?" He said, "Well, I'm just letting you know." I said, "Let's get started." I didn't know if he wanted to pick on me or was just doing what came natural, but I knew my goose was cooked.

The first political question he asked me was, did I believe in revolutions? I said that, yes, I believed in the one in 1776—didn't he? That's the way it went all morning. I was just baiting him and having a good time. Then, at quarter to twelve, I looked at my watch, sprang to my feet, and said, "Oh, it's lunchtime. Let's knock off, shall we?" I stood up, and so did the secretary who was taking notes. This poor guy—I annoyed him no end.

During lunch I got a call from one of the INS officials. Down I went to Immigration. They said, "You know, that judge is going to rule against you. Withdraw your petition, then come back in a couple of years. He'll be long gone, and you'll get your papers."

I petitioned to remove my petition. I suppose the guy wet himself because he had no place to go with his big denial of my citizenship.

Two years went by. I filed my petition again in 1974. Then came my hearing. The young man asked me some questions about my mother and father, where they came from, when I came to this country—just routine questions. Then he asked me one political question.

"Do you regret being a member of the Communist Party?"

I said, "No, no. There are three reasons why I don't regret being a Communist. One is that I did more good for people while I was in the Communist Party than I have ever after. Two is that your life follows a path. When you come to a fork in the road, just take it. I came to a point in my life where I became a Communist, and that path just flowed right on till here I am today, and I like where I am today. And three is that I guess I could have saved myself a lot of trouble by not joining, but then I wouldn't have met a nice guy like you."

He was just laughing. He said, "You made my day" and recommended me for citizenship.

Nydia and my granddaughter Ann and I went up to the ceremony and there were a bunch of people up there, mostly Asians, a few Canadians and Scandinavians. I remember Judge Vorhees. Instead of saying, "Oh, you lucky people, you've come to this wonderful country from your miserable country," he said, "I welcome you with your diverse cultures, which will enrich the lives of all of us." He went on like that. I was just spellbound listening. They called my name, I went up, and Immigration handed me the roll of my papers. The guy said out of the corner of his mouth, "Well, you finally made it, Mrs. Wolf." And I said, "Yes, thanks to the immigration department."

There's just one more thing I'll add. Ann and Nydia and I went over to a pub to make a toast. Now, when you apply for citizenship, you have to forswear your allegiance to your former sovereign and then you swear your allegiance to the new bunch. I raised my glass, and I said, "To hell with Queen Elizabeth, and to hell with Richard Nixon, too." I didn't say to hell with the American government—I'd formed an attachment to it. But I still don't think of myself as an American. I'm an internationalist. I have U.S. citizenship in order to be secure and not be moved around and discriminated against. Strictly a legality. I don't feel any particular loyalty to this country. In fact, I think it's a pain in the neck.

I have no adherence to any religion, political party, nation, or color. Nothing. I learned it from my father and from my life. I am a citizen of the world. And I have great feelings of patriotism for the people of the world. I have nothing to do with the ruling class. I'm a citizen of the oppressed working people and that's the vast majority. Still, there's that little poem: "Breathes there a man with soul so dead / Who never to himself has said, / This is my home, my native land, / This is my native land."[63]

I remember when I was arrested, the press wanted a statement from me. I said that the American people would not let me be deported. I only half believed it. But when I got through, I did believe it. I just have a tremendous faith in the people—if they have the facts. I think it is safe to say that because of the successful defense of the foreign-born in the 1950s, resulting in considerable erosion of the Walter-McCarran Act, all foreign-born are more secure.[64] And it was the people, thousands of people, who kept these deportations from happening.

I grew up in poverty. I'm a person of the streets, but I had some very good people. I was loved. My mother was always there. She worked hard all day, and when she came home she played with us after dinner. Anytime she could, she gave us her undivided attention. I couldn't spell it out in so many words, but I felt secure. So I didn't feel personally attacked by the government. I saw it as part of the big picture. I was just there, powerless and strong, someone who wouldn't chicken out. Somebody always stops the nonsense, all through history.

COMING OUT AS A COMMUNIST

In 1976, after I became a citizen and was going full-tilt in the environmental movement, I came out as a former Communist. Emmett Watson, the dean of Seattle newspaper columnists, wanted to write about me. I had lunch with him and his assistant, Carol Barnard, who became a good friend of mine. We talked and I answered all his questions, but my membership in the party wasn't discussed. I didn't even think about it.

After the interview, he looked in the archives at his newspaper, the *Seattle Post-Intelligencer,* and he found the whole mess, article after article about my deportation case.

He called me up that same afternoon and said, "If I don't say something about it, somebody will write a letter to the editor saying, 'Watson's covering up.' If I do say something about it, it might be embarrassing to you. So what do you want me to do?"

I said, "Anything you find out about me, put in your column. I couldn't care less what you put in about my past. I'm not ashamed of it."

He said, "How do you want to handle it?"

I said, "Listen, Emmett, you're getting paid to write that column. You handle it. It's your baby."

So it came out in a Sunday column. That's where it first surfaced. He did a nice job of pulling the teeth from it. He made it sound like the Communist Party was a gentle little program.

For quite a few months now I've had this thing about Hazel Wolf, meaning a case of heroine-worship. Hazel is a lovely wisp of a lady who is secretary of the Seattle Audubon Society, also vice president of the Federation of Western Outdoor Clubs. Hazel knows every bird in the book, and some that probably aren't recorded.

The weekly *Argus* once named Hazel "Conservationist of the Year," but I don't remember which year. It doesn't matter, really, since Hazel would qualify for almost any year you can name.

To know Hazel you have to get a glimpse of her lifestyle. She isn't always in when you call, since she frequently goes off to climb a mountain or run a few rapids. She is an expert swimmer, a confirmed, busy backpacker, and skilled at handling a canoe. "Of course, Hazel is slowing down a bit, but not much," says her friend Grace Patrick. "She's still ready to tackle almost anything. She's only seventy-eight." But I managed to catch Hazel for lunch a few days ago. This was a few days before she went snowshoeing at Leavenworth. "This spring," she said, "I'll fly to the Arctic Circle to camp in the North Slope of the Brooks Range. I want to see some caribou and grizzlies and wolves and any number of nesting birds."

Hazel has a quick, intelligent mind, and enjoys saying outrageously funny things. I mentioned that some gray whales had recently been sighted in Puget Sound, and of course Hazel knew all about that. When an Everett reporter called Hazel to ask how far south the gray whales migrated, she told him: "Well, they went as far as Olympia, got one whiff of the Legislature, turned around, and headed north."

By now you must have gathered that Hazel's life is full of the joyous things. She grew up in Victoria, came to Seattle in 1923. For many long years, from 1949 to the early sixties, the U.S. Government tried to have Hazel deported. She had once belonged to the Communist Party, and thus was considered a menace to Our Way of Life. By the time Hazel won her right to stay here, the Party, not unlike the whooping crane, had become almost extinct. Today we have radicals, revolutionaries, and terrorists who make the old-line ex-Communists seem like reformers in the PTA. Anyway, Hazel is too busy to fret about the past. There are birds, animals, trees—even humans—to be protected, for the Audubon Society, once derisively called "bird-watchers," has broadened its concerns to include all creatures in the ecological system.[65]

As I became more of a media person, giving interviews, I didn't neglect my past with the Communist Party. Now I make sure that gets into every article written about me, and I think that's important. People have to weigh my membership in the party against what they already know about me. They might think, "The party can't be that bad, if Hazel thinks it's great. Here's somebody who is in the public eye and who is not trying to cover up the fact that she was a Communist." And I'm not saying that I left the Communists because I thought they were bad or wrong. Nor am I pretending that they were perfect, either, because they weren't. They had a lot of shortcomings. But in the overall picture, they did a great job.

Emmett wrote about me again in 1985. By this time, we could joke.

"Do they give you a bad time about that Communist thing?" I asked her. Hazel's eyes twinkled. "Oh, yes," she said, "but not much. Sometimes they red-bait me, but they're always sorry when they do it, because I might shake my finger at them and tell them, 'Better not fool around with this old Communist.'"[66]

Not too long ago I was able to tell the courts not to fool around with me, too. I was a character witness in a political trial of a Mexican and an El Salvadoran accused of breaking immigration laws. The Mexican was Miguel Orozco, who had married John Caughlan's stepdaughter. They had had two children.

It was a scandal in the early 1990s the way Immigration was deporting refugees back to their countries, where they were sure to be persecuted. The public was getting outraged. So Immigration responded with a cooling-off measure. Anybody from El Salvador who left there for persecution reasons and came to this country before September 19, 1992, could stay— everybody else goes back. In response, citizens formed organizations designed to help refugees, and University Baptist Church was the leader of them. Through this church John's son-in-law, Miguel Orozco, helped refugees. Next thing you know, Miguel and a man from El Salvador were charged with having falsified refugees' papers to make it look like they came to this country before the deadline. If he had been found guilty, he would have been deported back to Mexico. Conceivably, his family would have joined him there. But the fellow from El Salvador would have gone back for certain persecution. His wife and child were here, too.[67]

This cruelty, it's a part of our system. In some areas, the INS is good. In other areas, they're beating up people at the border.

I'd known Miguel and his family for ten years, so they thought I'd be a great character witness at his trial—I could testify that he'd never told a lie and all that. The lawyer on the case wanted to brief me on how to say what an honest guy he was.

When I went to the law offices, I told the lawyer, "There's something about me you should know. I wouldn't want it to crop up in the middle of the trial and embarrass you. I was a member of the Communist Party. As a character witness, the prosecutor might try to discredit me with the jury by revealing this. Now, I don't care if they reveal it or not, but I want you to consider that maybe I should not be a character witness."

The lawyer said, "Ah, don't worry, they always try to get character witnesses off the stand as fast as they can."

I said, "Okay. It's your choice."

I went up to the federal courthouse, all dressed up, looking my most saintly. They said to me, after they'd sworn me in, "Give your full name, spell your last name, and tell your age." I said, "Hazel Wolf, W-o-l-f." And then I said, very coyly, "Now, you're not going to believe this, but I'm ninety-six years old." The judge, whom I know—I had lunch with her, actually; she must have been astonished to see me walk in there—and everybody else just tittered, because I was so kind of childlike, boasting about my age and how young I looked.

They asked me about Miguel. Was he honest? Then the immigration prosecuting attorney did cross-examine me. I knew damn well she would—she wouldn't think of missing a chance to discredit me. But she asked the wrong question.

"Is it true, Mrs. Wolf," she said, "that you were deported?"

I looked at her kind of strangely, and I said, "Deported? No, no. I'm still here."

Everybody tittered. But before she had time to catch her breath, I said, "However, there is a little core of truth in what you're saying. Would you like me to explain it?"

If she'd had any sense, she'd have said no. Even if she had, I would have insisted that our attorney get me back on the stand to explain. Anyway, she said yes.

So I turned to the jury—and I know how to turn to the jury when I really want them to hear—and I said, "During the McCarthy period, I was accused of being a member of the Communist Party and of conspiring to overthrow the government by force and violence."

I looked the least violent person they'd seen in a long time. And I'm smiling all the time, like I think it's a big joke—not too much, just enough. Then I continued.

"After fourteen years of litigation, the deportation order was canceled."

I knew they bought it, and it was the truth, too. So that was a blow at her trying to discredit me with the jury.

She wasn't satisfied. She was going to take another shot at me, so she said, "Well, Mrs. Wolf, you must be quite bitter, isn't that true, with the immigration department?"

I said, "Bitter? Oh no, no, no. This was a political case. Decisions are not made at the local level. They are made upstairs someplace in Washington, D.C. I have no idea who makes the decisions, whether it's men or women, or whether it's a committee. How can I be bitter at people whom I don't even know exist? The only contact I've had with the immigration department has been locally, and they've been very kind to me, right from the very beginning—treated me with respect, helpful when I got my papers, and certainly I'm not bitter."

She got me down off the stand.

At the break, I went over to the prosecutor and said, "Hey, what do you mean by trying to deport me?"

She said, "Well, I sure messed that up."

I said, "You sure did. But I came over here for a special purpose. I want you to know that I really was sincere when I said I wasn't bitter. I'm not bitter at you, I'm not bitter at anyone in Immigration. I really feel beholden to them, that I have my citizenship today. I just want you to know that."

Not many people are so open about their past in the Communist Party as I am. My coming out publicly and saying I was formerly a member of the Communist Party, and that I was not an anti-Communist, was a big, bold step on my part, but I would never reveal that fact about somebody else. A lot of people don't want to be known as having been members. I see people all the time who were in the Communist Party. They pop up in the peace movement, in senior citizens' organizations, and in unions. I don't know if they're still members or not, but I don't ask them, "Are you a member of the Communist Party?" It's an impertinent question.

PART V

Environmentalist: 1964–2000

Organize, organize, organize.

Fight on all fronts, all the time.

Everything's connected.
I just make the connections as I go along.

*A*fter fourteen years of persecution, the Immigration and Naturalization Service had nothing to show for its efforts; after fourteen years of resistance, Hazel Wolf had been transformed from a naturally talented grassroots activist into a seasoned leader, aware of her power as a member of a community to withstand the mighty U.S. government and even to change it. Her victory proved her methods: organization, persistence, and humor. What lucky organization would she light on next? She chose the Seattle Audubon Society. "Mrs. Wolf" first appears on the Seattle Audubon Society membership list in 1959, but it wasn't until 1964 that Wolf really got hooked.

In 1962, Rachel Carson's *Silent Spring* initiated a momentous change in national attitudes toward the environment. In 1964, the National Audubon Society (NAS) started its first large-scale membership campaign, doubling its membership to sixty thousand by 1968. In 1969, Hazel Wolf started organizing Audubon chapters, got up steam during the 1970s environmental decade, and continued unabated in the 1980s and 1990s, her last prize the Victoria, British Columbia, Audubon Society chapter, founded in 1997. What a fortunate conjunction of history, National Audubon objectives, and local talent!

While kicking up grassroots activity in the Northwest, Wolf kept close ties with NAS in the East, just as in the 1950s she had tied her campaign for local victims of deportation to the American Committee for the Protection of the Foreign Born. As she did back then, she shuttled between national and local headquarters.

Audubon was particularly well positioned to reap the benefits of Earth Day 1970, when environmentalism emerged as a mass social movement. Wolf helped gather Audubon people who wanted to fight for the environment and avoid the divisive political movements of the early 1970s. Yet for several decades the environmental movement split left and right, working class and middle class, and people of color and whites. The disenfranchised criticized wilderness preservation as part of the affluent lifestyle, and the privileged rejected any negative analysis of capitalism. Wolf jumped into the demilitarized zone between the two sides to knit the connections. Around the fringes of articles, editorials, speeches, letters, and congressional testimony, she maintained the framework of social justice and civil rights for environmental issues without ever pushing or arguing for it. For example, she brought to the attention of her colleagues the plight of strawberry pickers sprayed with pesticides in California and of unemployed loggers on the Olympic Peninsula. At ease in New York and Washington, D.C., Wolf kept her friends whether or not they approved of her resolutions. By the year 2000, Audubon and the Big Ten environmental organizations (the Sierra Club, the Wilderness Coalition, Friends of the Earth, Greenpeace, and the rest) had adopted language of connection with the poor and underprivileged, had attempted to diversify their boards, and had funded environmental justice programs for poor, urban constituents. In the long run, Wolf's unifying perspective prevailed.

15 / In the City, in the Wilderness with Audubon

THE BROWN CREEPER

In 1964, after all this deportation business was over, I was somewhat at loose ends. One of my hiking friends, Irene Urquhart, belonged to the Audubon Society, and she was always trying to get me to join it. Cost a dollar. I put her off and I put her off. I didn't want to belong to that bunch of bird-watchers. Finally, to get her off my back, I gave her a dollar.

Then, of course, she insisted that I go on a field trip, to Lincoln Park [in West Seattle]. A lot of big trees there. Everybody was looking up at a Doug fir. They handed me a pair of binoculars, and there was a bird, a little brown bird the same color as the tree, going up the trunk, pick-pick-pick as it went. When it got to the first lateral bough, it would dive down to the bottom of the next tree and go up and up and up, eating and eating—something I couldn't see, it was so small—and then down again to the bottom of another tree. I was told this was a brown creeper and that it always went up the tree, never down, and that it made its nest under pieces of loose bark on the tree trunks. I saw that little brown creeper, and I *knew* that bird. It worked hard for a living, and so did I. It had a lifestyle, always up the tree, just like I had a lifestyle—get up in the morning, eat breakfast, catch a bus and go to work, eat lunch and go back to work, come home at night. I related to that bird.

By the way, there's another bird, the nuthatch, that comes down the tree. I don't know if they ever collide.[1]

I reasoned that if this little brown creeper did such interesting things, other birds must similarly have little paths that they follow, little lifestyles, and I began to observe them. Of course, the more you know about any living creature, the more intimately you like it. Before, I had a general com-passion for all of nature. Now I began to have it on an individual basis, a sort of love connected to it.

SECRETARY OF SEATTLE AUDUBON

*T*hen Irene gave me another little shove by bullying me into attending a membership meeting of the Seattle Audubon Society. There was a big has-sle on the floor about the constitution and by-laws. Feelings ran high, loud speeches were made, and birds were not even thought of. All my life I'd been in a law office, and earlier I'd been mixed up in labor unions and the Communist Party, so I'd drawn up quite a few constitutions and by-laws. I said to the Audubon Society president, "Give me a copy of your docu-ments, and I'll make a draft for you." They were filled with contradictions and clauses that didn't belong there. I cleaned the whole thing up and a few days later handed it back to the president. The next day she called me and said, "I know you were in the Communist Party and Communists are good organizers. I'd like you to come to the board meetings." I decided to go.

They had just rented their first office space, in the Joshua Green Building downtown, so I volunteered to head up the committee buying supplies. Now, I wouldn't think of stocking an office without consulting with some-body else, so I scrounged around, got three or four people, and had them up to my place. The president of Audubon showed up to this little com-mittee to buy office supplies! After bunches of cups of coffee and sand-wiches, we cooked up a list. By that time, I became known to a few people in Audubon, so sometime before I retired at age sixty-seven from John Caughlan's office, the nominating committee asked me if I would accept the position of secretary. I'd learned enough about the Audubon program to realize it was a good one, so I said yes. With no one else nominated, I was elected—unanimously. That was in 1965, and they have not been able to dislodge me from that position in all these thirty-five years. Nobody ever ran against me. Whether they were afraid to run, or whether they thought they might win and be stuck with the job, I don't know. Every year I tell the nominating committee, "If you don't nominate me, then

I'll get a friend to put me up for president from the floor, and because of name familiarity, I'll be elected. Now, you might as well settle for secretary, or you'll have me as president."

Just before I came in, the "bird-watchers" in the Audubon Society suffered a stunning defeat from which they never recovered. The issue was whether to remain a little bird-watching club or to affiliate with the National Audubon Society. The president, Dr. Claude Heckman, managed this transition in 1962.[2] He may have done some hanky-panky, flooded a certain meeting with his people—I made a career out of not knowing how he did it. The people who lost still managed to kick Dr. Heckman out, they were so mad. The minute they affiliated, Seattle Audubon Society began to broaden politically and numerically. New people came into Seattle Audubon through the National Audubon membership drives, and they were reading the national magazine, which was much more political in those days, so the "bird-watchers" receded until you could just barely see them on the horizon.

Then came Rachel Carson's *Silent Spring,* in 1962. DDT was getting in the food chain, and, sure enough, the eagles were laying eggs with such soft shells that they broke them with their claws and created omelets. Pelicans were suffering the same way. We got a bumper sticker in our Audubon magazine—BAN DDT. Then Audubon began to extend its concern to all wildlife. Then they found that in order to protect wildlife, they had to protect habitats. So we took on clear-cutting, polluted air, polluted water, soil erosion, and, inch by bloody inch, nuclear power and war. We found ourselves covering the whole world, yes, and it extends from our little community into the state, into the nation, and pretty soon to the universe, and now they're leaving a lot of clutter up there on the moon. It's just like John Muir said—"When we try to pick out anything by itself, we find it hitched to everything else in the universe."[3]

"NOTHING GLAMOROUS ABOUT IT"

First of all, I got on the publications and newsletter committees. You can't keep me away from a newsletter. Then, having organized the buying of supplies, I was persuaded by the president to be the office manager, and through that I got very deeply involved in Audubon. The office was a tiny little place about the size of a postage stamp, with a desk, a supply cabinet, a showcase for all the literature, and one table. The mailing list of between four hundred and five hundred members was kept on metal stencils called Address-O-Graphs. The newsletter, *The Warbler,* was done by stencils and ground out on the mimeograph machine. Everything was done by hand.

I could see that they had an inefficient system for organizing volunteers. I set it up so that there were six people staffing the office, one for each day of the week: Ella Miller, Della Patch, Dudley Doe, Mildred Melanie, Amy McQuay, and Debbie Dewey. There was almost no turnover—either they left the country or died. Each of these volunteers had his or her own little kingdom independent of me, of each other, and of the board. For instance, Della, who came in on Mondays, was a retired science teacher who took charge of the slide program with the garden clubs and the schools. It was a thriving program in those days. And Dudley took care of the membership list—he kept the Address-O-Graph plates up-to-date. That was a full-time job for a whole day, Tuesdays. I pulled together all the loose ends on Thursdays. We took care of mail, we kept up connections with government agencies and the National Audubon Society, and we sent out welcome letters and questionnaires to new members. That's where we got a good many of our volunteers. I went on field trips looking for birds—members would identify birds over the phone, which was the main reason why people called Audubon. Throughout all of this, I learned how to handle volunteers. You can't *tell* them to do anything.

I convened annual volunteer meetings. Came the day for our big meeting, and we would go over the manual I had put together and update it. We all liked each other and we put up with each other's idiosyncrasies. Now, I've been given a lot of recognition and awards for my work in the environmental movement, but it all comes down to the organizing skills I learned in the thirties—that is, getting everyone involved—and the office skills I practiced as a legal secretary. Nothing glamorous about it, but we put Seattle Audubon on the map.

Publishing is a big business, and the board was always reluctant to plunge into it. They feared financial disaster and so they stuck with a lit-tle pamphlet, *Birds of Seattle,* then a little larger pamphlet, *Birds of King County,* and then a very small edition of *Birds of Puget Sound.* I had a real fight on my hands to get the board to publish Earl Larrison's *Washington Wildflowers.*[4] I had to maneuver. The board set up a committee for the sole purpose of sabotaging the book. I insisted on being on the commit-tee. I told them, "I didn't come here to disrupt your task. I'm not going to open my mouth the whole time you're discussing. I'm just going to file a minority report in favor of publication." Because of my minority report, the board voted to publish the book. It was a howling success— went through two printings, and I'm currently trying to get them to go into a third. The same thing happened with Robert Pyle's *Watching Wash-ington Butterflies.*[5] The board didn't think these books would sell, but in the heyday of our publishing we sold forty-eight thousand dollars of mer-chandise a year.

Volunteers did all the wrapping, all the mailing, all the invoicing. We'd hold a big mailing party to send out publicity to all the schools in the states of Washington and Oregon, to all the libraries, and to every name we could lay our hands on. We put out six or seven thousand pieces of mail, all the envelopes written by hand. We approached all the retail outfits. We also found an agent who went around in a car, selling books at the retail stores. And the books sold like wildfire. When you put on a promotion like that, they sell.

BIRDING BINGE

The day I retired as John Caughlan's secretary, on February 19, 1965, I had my ski outfit on and I brought my snowshoes to the office. At five o'clock I went straight to the bus depot and out to Ellensburg, where an Audubon friend, Ruth Boyle, and I went out on a trip. I felt like a kid out of school on vacation. For a long time I had been frustrated in Seattle, separated from nature. Joining the Audubon Society started me on a career of getting out of the city, or just going to the parks and looking at birds, which I could afford to do with a bus token. Pretty soon Ruth and I got acquainted with Ruth Anderson, Ruth Cameron, and Gladys Squires, and we found that we all liked trips. Ruth Anderson, Ruth Boyle, and Ruth Cameron—I called them Ruths A, B, and C.

I went on a binge with these friends, camping all over the United States, looking at birds, or anything else that came up.[6] We avoided all cities—covered almost the entire United States. Now, that's a lot of trips. Sometimes we'd be gone for six weeks. In those days you didn't go to camping sites. You just stopped at the side of the road or trail, pitched your tent, made dinner, and went to sleep. It was that simple. Now it's all regulated.

I was always a water person, so I liked to run rivers, too—the Grand Canyon of the Colorado, the Rogue, the North Platte, the Grande Ronde River in Oregon, and many others. In 1967, when Ruth Boyle and I arrived at Ely, Minnesota, to begin our trip into the Boundary Waters Canoe Wilderness Area,[7] we had just a little pile of gear—raincoats, a change of clothing if we got wet, food. We brought only pitted prunes, and we seriously thought about cutting the handles off our toothbrushes.

"Is that all you've got?" is what they said when we rented the canoe. They asked, "Only you two women?"

I said, "Do you think we need more women?"

Then they asked, "Do you know how to paddle?"

They made us go out on the water while they watched to see if we could paddle. They didn't want to let us go into this dangerous wilderness.

All we had was a compass and a map. We camped wherever we found a place, and we portaged eighteen times. Ruth carried the canoe, her shoulder pads on, her head inside it. I led, carrying the gear. The portages had been established in the ice age by animals following the receding glaciers, making paths around waterfalls and rapids. They were followed by the pre-Columbian Indians, who went the same way. They used little stones to make their fireplaces. Later, the traders, the French Canadians carrying their big three-hundred-pound packs, camped in the same places. Then along came Ruth and Hazel. We used the same Indian stones and the same paths that the animals had started for us, worn deep like little trenches.

We didn't see many other people out in the wilderness for ten days and it was just great. We saw wildlife—moose and loons. We'd hear the bullfrogs. *Whoomp! Whoomp!* No matter how quietly we paddled up to them, they could hear us and stop their *whoomp*ing. Most of the people I talk about are long gone, but Ruth is still living. When I hear of a good movie, I call her up and we go to it. She's a strong woman, very religious, and pretty solemn, so she doesn't always see my jokes.

I've been on many other trips—hiking, rafting rivers, visiting every wildlife refuge in England, Scotland, and Wales, just for starters. In 1983, I organized a fund-raising trip to Costa Rica for Seattle Audubon Society and then went on it. That's when I met Dr. Alexander Skutch, at his home, Finca los Cusingos, near one of the Organization for Tropical Studies field stations.[8] I saw Wedgwood-blue butterflies with seven-inch wingspreads, orchids in the trees, and all kinds of birds that made a tremendous racket— saltators, brush finches, many colorful tanagers, honeycreepers, hummingbirds, manakins, nightingale thrushes, and toucans. I was out walking with Dr. Skutch, and I said, "Oh, listen to that olive-sided flycatcher." In all this hullaballoo, it stood out like a sore thumb, and I could recognize it. He said, "You have a fantastic ear." I said, "Many of our Washington birds end up here in the winter. They're the only calls that are going to make sense to me in all this chaos." I also saw big waves of Swainson's and broad-winged hawks, pewees, vireos, orioles, and many varieties of warblers. And they were precious, more precious to me than the most gorgeous birds down there.

Why do we go out and sleep in silly places with rocks and pinecones? Because we yearn for reunion with nature. We're all children of nature. I think it's in everybody. People sleep in the park across my street in the summertime. There's all kinds of wild things to enjoy here in the city, now that I don't go out on these big trips. I had a wasps' nest as big as a basketball up there in the corner of my awning. I watched it all summer. And there are squirrels that go across that cable outside my window. Every once in a while they're running along it like it was Interstate 5.

QUIET AND FACTUAL LIKE EMILY HAIG

At my first Seattle Audubon membership meeting, Emily Haig stood up and gave a long, detailed report on some lobbying she'd done in

Olympia. I watched her and thought, "I want to know that woman," and, although she was quite a bit older than I was, I set about deliberately to become acquainted with her. I succeeded, and wound up living in her home from 1969 to 1979. It was a great big ten-room house on Capitol Hill and she'd fixed the upstairs into an apartment, where I lived. It was a very delightful ten years. She taught me everything that she possibly could.[9]

She was a stalwart, a conservationist well known on the West Coast who had received citations from the National Audubon Society and from the governor of the state of Washington. She was chairwoman of the Conservation Committee of the Seattle Audubon Society. When the committee decided that it wanted somebody to testify on behalf of a certain issue, she would persuade me to do it and help me get my testimony ready. Then she would be free to testify at the same hearing for one of the other organizations she belonged to, like the Sierra Club. So we'd hit them twice.

When she could no longer drive, I would take her to Sierra Club board meetings, and I'd listen. She introduced me to the Olympic Parks Associates[10] and promoted my nomination as secretary. I'm still on the board. I went to North Cascades Conservation Council[11] meetings with her and became secretary. And when the Washington Environmental Council[12] was set up, she made sure that I was one of the people in on the ground floor.

Emily was a kindly person. She had her own little domain, but she was never autocratic. She didn't have to have her fingers in everything. She got a lot of people involved and let them realize their own potential without interfering. She was also very conservative, a Republican who thought Mr. Nixon had been put upon during the Watergate hearings in 1973 and 1974. The minute I found out how she felt about him, I just didn't talk about Watergate. Nobody was going to change her mind.

Governor Evans, a Republican whom she adored, appointed her to a commission on the state parks in 1978. He put her in there with a bunch of rednecks to evaluate the plan he'd drawn up. Now, she didn't like that plan, while all of the other people on the commission were for it a hundred percent. The governor wanted a unanimous decision. I remember her anguish. She actually paced the floor because of her love for Governor Evans.

I said, "Emily, I know you're not going to vote *for* that plan. You could *abstain,* but I think you should vote *against* it and hand in a minority report. The governor will understand."

She did it, and the whole thing blew up because of her minority report.

As I got better educated in the issues, I testified frequently at hearings, sometimes before a legislative committee, sometimes before an agency. I testified many times before congressional committees in Washington, D.C., too. I always made people laugh, and I didn't get stirred up over things. I don't hate the developers, and I don't hate the timber barons and the oil tycoons. I look on them as institutions, as bureaucracies. How can you hate a bureaucracy? You might deplore what it does, but you don't hate it the way you might someone who does some bad thing to you. And when you start going up against a big institution, you talk to the individuals, and you find out they're really nice people.

By watching Emily Haig, I learned you have to make compromises in relation to people that you're working with. You can't be really mad at a person, way deep down. You can be angry at a situation, an abstraction, but not at a person. Anger is a consumer passion—it eats you up. Sometimes I've looked like I was mad at someone, but I was putting on an act for some purpose. Under the influence of Emily Haig, I developed a kind of quiet and factual way of giving testimony or participating in meetings, and I always add something funny.

I still don't say much at Seattle Audubon board meetings. I just wait. Pretty soon somebody gives my opinion, so I don't have to say anything. If everybody's finished and they haven't said something I think they should have said, then I'll speak. And that doesn't happen very often.

I don't take on issues that aren't going to work. For example, in 1997 I couldn't get Audubon to endorse the destruction of the mountain goats in Olympic National Park. They wallow, destroy the plant life, eat right down to the roots, and cause mudslides. They are an introduced species. A board member said he liked his children to be able to see those goats. I told him to tell his children to look down and see the Flett's violets— found only in Olympic National Park—before the goats chewed them to extinction. I lost the vote and went home to lick my wounds. So, okay, I got my thoughts organized with facts and figures, the whole argument, and sent every board member a report. At the end of it I said, "This is the last time I'll approach you on this subject," and then I put an asterisk, and way down at the bottom of the last page I wrote, "But don't count on it." This time, it went through.

HOW TO MANAGE THE TIMBER INDUSTRY

*O*ne of my very first field trips with Seattle Audubon took us out to prime timberland owned by the Boise Cascade Company in the sunny desert interior of Washington State. Chasing birds, we ran across a small campground that Boise had established for its employees. I wrote a letter addressed to the Boise Cascade Timber Corporation, Yakima, Washington: "We saw seventy species of birds when we were here for a weekend. Would you please put up a sign, 'Protect Our Wildlife' at the campground?'" The letter made it to a vice president who was a bird-watcher. He was happy to put up the sign. Next Memorial Day weekend, we arrived for a campout, and there it was: MEMBERS OF SEATTLE AUDUBON SOCIETY SAW SEVENTY SPECIES OF BIRDS IN THIS AREA IN SEPTEMBER 1964. PLEASE PROTECT THE WILDLIFE. The vice president and his family and other Boise [Cascade Company] people came to the campout, brought us apples, and made speeches at our campfire. You see, there are lots of ways that environmentalists and the timber industry can work together. We made it an annual event—the Memorial Day campout at Wenas Creek.[13] Some three hundred members come every year from around the state. It's a big family thing. We have field trips—over the years, we have identified two hundred and fifteen species of birds—children's activities, campfire programs, and singing. Audubon members from the eastern and western parts of the state get to know each other.[14]

One year we arrived at Wenas to find that someone had started to clear the brush and cut down snags, which would have destroyed the value of the place as a wildlife refuge. We complained to the Boise Cascade Company—not in an angry way, just pointing out to them that if they went in there with all this housekeeping and interfered with the ecology, they'd defeat their purpose of keeping it as a wildlife refuge. Boise met with a committee from Seattle Audubon and asked for a set of standards for preservation of the area. We got our heads together and made some recommendations. One was that they move the logging road completely out of the area, let it go back to nature, and prohibit motorcyclists from using the entrance road. Another recommendation was that they fence in the campground, to keep the cattle from trampling and eating up the underbrush. Another was that they provide corrals for horses. People had tied their horses to trees, and the horses had gone around and around and stripped the bark, eventually killing the trees. Boise followed every one of our suggestions, spent thousands of dollars. Eventually they established a wildlife refuge, and we gave them an award to show our appreciation. In May 1999, we celebrated our thirty-fourth anniversary at the Wenas Creek campout.

I think the turning point for the Seattle Audubon Society and my role in it was when we agreed to host the sixty-fifth annual National Audubon Society convention in May 1970, only a few weeks after the first Earth Day, April 22, 1970. The Seattle board was afraid to take it on. I said, " Okay, *I'll* be chairman." It was two years' work getting that thing going, lining it all up. A thousand people had to be taken care of—housing, programs, banquets, and speakers. I reserved the Opera House, the entire suite of rooms at the Seattle Center, and five hundred rooms at the Washington Plaza Hotel—which had not yet been built! I had committees in charge of decorations, hospitality, publicity, and finances, and a chairman for each one.

We got tremendous publicity because I went to see the editor of the *Seattle Times* and the AP and UPI news services and chatted with them one on one. The *Times* ran a front-page spread, in color, of bird cartoons, and all kinds of bird stories throughout the paper. I visited the Seattle Art Museum, and they put up their famous Japanese work called *Crows* [Edo period, ca. 1650], as well as bird paintings by Kenneth Callahan and other Northwest artists. They had special days and special shows just for Audubon. I also got the National Park Service to install a premier exhibit at Seattle Center of black-and-white photographs taken in parks all over the nation. We got articles in all of the neighborhood papers. Governor Evans declared May, the month of the convention, Washington State Bird Month, and he held a ceremony in Olympia, to which we all went trooping down.

Dr. Elvis Stahr, the newly elected national president, made the keynote address and accepted a deed from Seattle Audubon, making National Audubon owner of a muddy little lot in the Nisqually Delta[15] so it would have standing in court if needed in a future lawsuit. It was the most beautiful convention that had ever taken place—everybody said that. But then, it was at the Seattle Center in late spring, when all the rhododendrons were out, and we took the national board to breakfast in the Space Needle. It was perfect weather. "Very unusual," we assured the visiting Audubon members, because we didn't want any of the thousand people to settle in Seattle.

After the convention, our membership jumped up to eighteen hundred in no time, and we cleared thirteen thousand dollars from our two post-convention field trips into Canada and into Alaska. It was quite a transformation. Boise Cascade gave every person at that convention a cellophane bag with a fir seedling, little roots and everything. Now they're planted all over the United States—in Florida, Texas, and Tennessee. People still come up to me at National Audubon conventions to tell me, "My Washington State tree is growing." I found out later that those treelets came from Pennsylvania, but Boise Cascade got a lot of PR out of it. Of course, that didn't stop us from suing them and testifying against them at hearings whenever we needed to. No hard feelings. If they do something that is laudable, we give them credit. And if they do something that's not so good, we tell them about that, too. You never know in this rickety old world when you're going to need an ally. You don't want to alienate somebody just because you're having a big fight with them. I remember sitting down at a banquet next to the Boise vice president and saying, "Oh, hi, John. How are you coming along with the destruction of our national forests?"

PUTTING THE BEE ON

So I got organizing. Seattle Audubon had jurisdiction over the entire state of Washington minus the areas around Spokane and Olympia, which already had Audubon societies. National sent me the list of these members scattered all over the state. I started with Tacoma, where there were twenty members. We never saw the whites of their eyes at our meetings—why not get them started on a chapter of their own? I sent out a mimeographed letter to them and asked three questions. Would they like a chapter of their own? If so, would they like to become involved in forming one? And did they know anyone in the area who would like to be a member of the Audubon Society? I got responses back from fifteen, and none of them knew each other.

One of them, Helen Engle, I recognized because she bought a lot of our books. I phoned her up and asked her if we could have a meeting at her house.

"Oh, yes, I'd love to."

I said, "I'll invite the nineteen others, and you invite any friends that you have. Would you mind fixing some coffee? I'll bring the cookies."

Well, she'd do both coffee and cookies. I always offer, but I never have to bring the cookies.

About ten of the original twenty came to Helen's. I waited while people talked a bit, so I could get a feel for the different individuals. Somebody always stands out. Then I started twisting arms.

"Now, if you want a chapter, you have to have some kind of officers." Putting the bee on the one who stood out, who happened to be Helen, I said, "How about being chairman? This is only temporary. After you have your first meeting and get some more people in as members, you hold elections."

Poor Helen said yes.

I got the secretary by saying, "By the way, I think we ought to be taking some notes on this meeting. Would you mind taking some notes?" And I gave someone near me paper and a pencil. A treasurer wasn't hard to get—anybody will be treasurer. People always like to edit newsletters, so there was no problem there. I waited to get the conservation chairman—probably the most important position in the local Audubon societies—until I could identify somebody who was a little more political. Then we set a date for the next meeting. From that original Tacoma ten, it's grown to two thousand, and Helen Engle, its first president, is now on the board of the National Audubon Society.

Helen Engle is a special friend of mine, but we don't have much time together.[16] We meet at conferences, and that's the worst place to try to nail down a friend. I think that I made a big difference in her life. She had seven children, and she just went to PTA meeting after PTA meeting. I came along and diverted her from that fruitless pursuit. With her ability to mobilize people and to get them engaged, she did a fantastic job of organizing the chapter. She has a good grasp of the issues, is a fine speaker—what I call a warm and fuzzy speaker, very personal—just altogether an outstanding person. Helen was appointed to the National Audubon board because she had worked so effectively on the Nisqually Delta, among other things.

It wasn't so easy in Olympia. There was an Olympia Audubon Society already in existence, but they just wouldn't affiliate with the National. The chairman was a one-man organization. I kept bugging him to get with it. He kept saying, "Well, you come down and explain it to everybody." So I made two trips to Olympia to address the meeting about all the advantages of being part of the National Audubon Society. The provision of all address labels, the regional and national conferences, the national magazine in the hands of all members, national support and publicity for local initiatives, congressional lobbying, and of course the jump in membership—all would come with affiliation. By the time I made it back home, he'd called to say they'd had another meeting and decided that they weren't ready for affiliation yet. This went on and on. I thought, "They're never going to be ready for it." I got in touch with the one-man organization, and I said, "I'm going to come down there and organize another chapter. You can help me, and your chapter will be affiliated with the National, or, if you don't feel like it, never mind. We won't solicit your members or take your name." So I went down and organized the Black Hills Audubon Society, affiliated with National. Within a year, the one-man organization had invited Black Hills to meet with his group, whose membership all went into the Black Hills society. He was conservation chairman for several years.

The new chapters always jelled. Sometimes they wavered, and it looked like they weren't going to make it, but then they'd get new leadership and off they'd go. I went down to Aberdeen and got a chapter started there on the Washington coast. First thing they did was launch out on a very impractical lawsuit against the Army Corps of Engineers, raising hackles on all sides. One of their members lost his job because of it, and their chapter disappeared into the woodwork. I waited a little while and tried again, but the newspaperman who invited me to come down wouldn't join the organization—it would have destroyed his credibility as an objective reporter for the area. Very depressing. Two failures in one spot.

Then I was asked to speak at a women's weekend retreat down on the Longview Peninsula. I invited the women who were there from Aberdeen to have breakfast with me, a group of eight, none of whom had ever heard of Audubon. I told them about hearings coming up on the marine sanctuary for Bowerman Basin,[17] and they all promised to go. I said, "How about starting an Audubon chapter down there? I'll help you, if you'd like to do that." They said, "Yeah, that would be great." Right next door was the Black Hills Audubon Society. They helped. Now, every year, I receive the newsletter of the Grays Harbor Audubon Society, as they're called, advertising their big Bowerman Basin Festival for the return of the birds, millions of birds. It's their last resting place this side of the Copper River, Alaska. I attended the festival once, way out on the isthmus, when the birds flew in a huge *whoosh* just over my head and then landed to feed.

I watch the newsletters of these chapters to see if some of the original organizers are still officers or committee chairs, and I write to them. Of twenty-six Audubon chapters in Washington State, I helped start twenty-one. We turned a bunch of bird-watchers into an effective environmental lobby. We went from a couple of hundred to five thousand members in Seattle, and somewhere around eighteen thousand in the state. In 1975, I founded the annual meeting of the Washington State Council of Audubon Chapters so all these new groups could get together. On my way home from a speech at a school or community center, I might stop at what looks like the main bar or restaurant in town, start talking with the owners and the clientele, and find out who the birders are. When I get home I write to them, call a meeting, get the gang going. Organize, organize, organize.

A group of scientists visiting from the Soviet Union in early 1989 wanted to start an Audubon chapter. They found out about my reputation for organizing, so they trooped into my tiny little living room, along with several translators, to get my help. One of them claimed the government wouldn't tolerate any organizations that it didn't control. I told them, "Surely the government wouldn't mind a half a dozen people walking around looking at birds in Leningrad." They said, "There aren't any birds in Leningrad." I told them that I had seen many birds in the parks of Leningrad on trips there in 1986 and 1987. The Leningrad Audubon Society came out of that meeting.

I'm always getting new members for the Audubon Society. It's the birds—everybody loves birds. I was getting out of a cab one day, and suddenly the cab driver said, "Do you accept Jesus as your personal savior?" I said, "No, do you?" He proceeded to give me a hard sell. I listened patiently. After a while I said, "I've been hearing what you're saying, and I know you want me to join you, but now I want you to listen to what I have to say. I'm an environmentalist, and I want you to join me in the Seattle Audubon Society. I'll join your organization if you'll join my organization. Now that's fair, isn't it?" We had a big laugh over it.

On a radio talk show in Port Angeles, one caller identified himself as Larry, and he said, "I know you, Hazel!" I knew lots of kids out there in Port Angeles. I know their grandchildren. I didn't know him, but I pretended that I did. I said, "Oh, hi, Larry! What are you doing out there?" And he started into his right-wing fundamentalism, on and on. I could see he was using the radio program as a platform for his agenda. Finally I said, "Larry, that's very interesting. I never heard any of this before, so I don't know what to say to you. I'll tell you what—why don't you join the Audubon Society so that we can talk more about it?" We just laughed and got on with the program.

I couldn't persuade Studs Terkel to join the Audubon Society when he came out to interview me for his book *Coming of Age*.[18] But he insisted I receive fifty dollars and sign a contract stating that I was paid for the interview. He had to protect himself against some future lawsuit. After arguing, I finally took the fifty dollars and used it to buy a membership in the National Audubon Society for Mrs. Terkel. In 1997 I signed up eighty-eight new members for Seattle Audubon, mostly people I'd met at hearings or my speeches, and that helped us get a thousand dollars from the National for the most new members recruited by any chapter.[19] Like the song about Joe Hill told us:

And standing there as big as life,
And smiling with his eyes,
Joe says, "What they forgot to kill
Went on to organize. . . ."[20]

INCLUDING STARLINGS

*I*n 1979, eight of us flew to Fairbanks, in Alaska, then took a bush plane to Kaktovik, an Eskimo village on Barter Island, in the Beaufort Sea, up by the Arctic Ocean. The northern coast of Alaska is largely marshland, no place to camp. So from there we took another bush plane about fifty miles inland to the William O. Douglas Arctic National Wildlife Refuge that we're right now fighting so hard to keep. The bush plane took just two people at a time. One sat by the pilot, the other by the baggage. Now, I'm scared to death of planes, but I have to go in the damn things all the time anyway. This time, I wasn't a bit frightened going in, because the plane closely followed the contours of the earth. I looked out and, wow, I could see bison, and wolves . . . I saw four grizzlies. It was the tundra! There were birch trees running along the ground like vines, no stand-ups.

They let us off on the north slope of the Brooks Range, on the shore of a frozen lake, Schraeder Lake, that was beginning to thaw a little around the edges. The fish were just climbing up the banks. It takes hundreds of years to replace the tundra once it's been damaged, so we moved our tents around every day or so. With twenty-four-hour daylight, we could read, take pictures, go on hikes—the sun was always shining in this gorgeous country. We noticed that the polar squirrels all went to bed at nine o'clock, but we didn't have sense enough to do that, just wallowing in all this perpetual daylight. Some loons had their nest on the bank of the lake. Of course we didn't go anywhere near it, but we watched. The two birds left the nest, and a raven came and ate all their eggs. Were we pissed! That's the only word I can use. The male flew away and the female stayed. The next day, I remained in camp while everybody went for a hike. I heard a loon call from far off. The female answered the call, and pretty soon the male came in. Then I saw them do a nuptial dance. He started about a hundred yards away from her. Then he'd dive and swim toward her underwater, and when he'd met her, they'd put their heads next to each other and come up out of the water together. Then he'd turn around and fly just on top of the water all the way back to his starting point. When he reached it, he hit the water with his foot and his wing. The couple started to build another nest. I'll bet they learned this time not to leave the nest together. Birds learn by trial and error—it's not all instinct. They have to be taught by their parents and by experience, just like humans.

Watching animals was all old hat on the plane coming out from the north slope, so I was perfectly miserable sitting on the baggage, hanging on to the plane, hoping nobody would lean and make it tip over. When we finally landed, I said to my friend, who sat by the pilot, "I get so mad at myself. Why couldn't I enjoy that trip?" She said, "You had nothing to worry about, Hazel. That pilot was going to sleep. I had to keep waking him up."

I was pretty interested in birds this whole time. One of my hiking friends, Ruth Anderson, was what they call an avid bird-watcher. She'd looked every bird in North America in the eye. She knew them by their names and calls. On trips with her, she would sight the birds and tell their names, and I would write them down. In that way, I collected more than five hundred birds for my lifelist. I also knew a lot of birds on my own and I knew lots of bird calls. I picked it up. And I read. A bird never passes that I don't see, even in the city—a crow, a robin. I'll be sitting in a board meeting and I'll hear the geese, see a gull. I don't stop and look at it, but I'm aware of it. It's part of the air that I'm used to.

And I like all of them, including starlings. How can people say they like birds and hate any one of them? I don't understand. Just because they eat our orchards is no reason to dislike them. Some people hate them because they get into other birds' nests, but we all eat each other for lunch, not just starlings. Starlings aren't selfish. When they find some food, they call all of their fellow starlings to share it. If something happens to the parent birds, the community feeds the orphans until they can forage for themselves. Starlings are just black. If they had pretty green and red feathers, maybe humans wouldn't pick on them. When spring is on the way, their beaks begin to turn yellow in streaks. I always look for that as a harbinger of warm weather.

There are two kinds of chickadees—black-capped and chestnut-backed. I wonder if the black-capped chickadees look down on the chestnut-backed chickadees. Maybe one black-capped would say to the other, "I have no prejudices against the chestnut-backed chickadee, I just wouldn't want my sister to marry one." I knew a member of the Audubon Society who hated sparrows, so he shot them. And some people don't like cowbirds because they lay their eggs in other birds' nests. I think cowbirds have a real feel for family values. By nature they have to follow the cattle. The cattle like them because they eat the bugs off their backs. The cowbirds have to move when the cattle move. To ensure that they'll have descendants, they look around for a place to lay their eggs, and they put them in other birds' nests. That demonstrates strong family values. We should love them for that.

When I was a child, I didn't know one bird from another, one tree from another. But on my trips, after I retired, I learned all kinds of things about animals and their environments. Then I'd use that information in the speeches I was making for Audubon and other organizations. Also, I never burned out, because I would leave the city and go to very, very remote places. When you do that, especially if you are staying overnight, you have all kinds of problems to solve. Where is a dry place? Is it going to rain? Does this thing leak? Can I get this fire going? You're involved with these minute-to-minute problems that you just have to solve, and you forget all the important situations that you left behind in the city. After struggling outdoors for two or three days, you come back to the city world, and it looks nice and fresh. Your mind is completely rested with solving different kinds of problems and you can go back to work again. It really doesn't matter whether you go on a camping trip for several days or whether you're limited to visiting the city parks. You don't go to a park to see all the other people. You go to see what's there. You need to know the names of birds, trees, and flowers so you can recognize them when you see them. Those identifications are very refreshing to your mind. You can't struggle with two things at once, you know—worrying about your personal problems, and trying to see what the birds are doing.

KAYAKING

$\mathcal{I}$ like the kayak better than any other mode of transportation. With half your body below the waterline, you feel part of the water, safe and secure. Kayaking exercises your back and all your muscles, but it's not a strain. It feels just like dancing.

In the 1980s, I did two kayaking trips to Baja, Mexico. Eight of us flew down to La Paz, on the east side of the peninsula, about one hundred miles before you get to the very tip. The organizer of the trip, Ron Yarnell, had hired a fishing boat. With the tents and kayaks folded up in big canvas bags, he took us about twenty miles out from the Bay of La Paz, to an island called Espíritu Santo. It was uninhabited because it had no water. We had to bring our own beer. The beaches were snowy white sand. Behind them were lagoons with hundreds of birds. We paddled from beach to beach to beach, the length of this island, about fifteen miles. At night the fishermen would come to catch the shrimp feeding on the surface of the water. We'd paddle out and get a bag for about twenty-five cents.

The second time, we went through the same routine at a different island, but when we got back to La Paz, I went with Ron in his pickup truck—I was in that truck just the other day—to Scammons Lagoon, on the west side of Baja California, about halfway down to the point. A small bay within the forty-mile-wide lagoon is where the gray whales give birth to their young in the winter. The lagoon was just filled with these gray whales and their young, who were really having fun sliding over their parents' backs. While we were there, the whales were slowly moving out of the lagoon on their long trip north for the summer. They could have banged their tails or bumped us from underneath, but they never touched us in our kayaks. I paddled right up to them and looked them in one eye and paddled around to look in the other eye. They, on the other hand, could see both my eyes with one of theirs. We just looked at each other. It was a real thrill to get that close to such magnificent animals.

One time Jo Anne Heron and I took our kayaks on the tourist steamer that runs up the Inside Passage along Canada to Alaska. Within the fjords, enormous glaciers break off and calve into the sea. Our boat kept a respectful distance because there'd be a tremendous splash created by pieces of glacier as big as a building breaking off into the water. When the tourists found out we were going to get off the steamer to go way up the inlet to Glacier Bay National Park, in Alaska, they just about had a fit, and they begged us not to go, but of course we were going. So they got out their cameras—*click-click-click.* And they let us off.

The whole area was filled with icebergs, so beautiful, all floating loose in the water. Some looked like swans. We didn't go close to the huge ones, because if you were nearby when the time came for them to keel over, they would finish you off. We pushed our way carefully through the smaller icebergs until we got to the park at the end of the inlet. The glaciers up there are receding. In other words, there's not enough precipitation to replace what melts off into the inlet, so two hundred years ago the glaciers were maybe twenty miles longer than they are today. We banked our kayaks and hiked inland on the glacier. There was no life up there—none. The rocks were completely bare. The water was milky, no fish in it. We saw one gull come up the inlet, turn around, and go back again. Occasionally we saw a seal sitting on a big iceberg, but only to enjoy the sun. We slept on rocks, knowing that last year they had been covered with ice. Then we paddled all the way back out of the inlet. On our way back, we decided to find out where life started. On a cliff we saw the first sign—a little green streak at the water's edge. Farther on we saw bits of lichen, a very primitive form of life, both the kind that grows on the rock and the kind that grows curling in the air. And then we saw, in a little curved-out place, a tuft of grass, then brush, bushes, and trees as we paddled toward the sea.

My last kayak trip was in August 1997. The Chevron Corporation gave me an award, and for the presentation they wanted a videotape of me in a kayak. We went out on a Sunday to the slough that comes into the [Washington Park] Arboretum from Lake Washington, not far from where I live on Capitol Hill. I'm kayaking up and down, water lilies on either side of me, and suddenly a great blue heron came to see all of the proceedings. The video people burst into flames, they were so excited. I must have paddled twenty miles, never got outside the slough, back and forth behind this great blue heron, who, amazed at what was going on, looked and looked at me, and then went back to what it was doing—catching fish. This took hours in that boiling sun, doing it again, doing it again, doing it over again, all day long. I decided I'll never be a movie actor. They had no respect for my then ninety-nine years. They were giving me a two-thousand-dollar award, and they were ready to take my life in exchange.

16 / Playing Politics

COLUMBIA RIVER SONG

I've run into some ambitious people who glory in the fact that they're president. You can tell their ego is titillated. I like to see the organization I'm with do what I think is right, but I don't make a big career out of it. I was president only once in my life, from 1978 to 1980, and that was because of the emergency at Federation of Western Outdoor Clubs [FWOC]. With the help of other people who believed in the federation, we breathed new life into it.[21]

By accident, my interest in the Columbia Basin Project began at that time.[22] The federation had just secured a new editor for their newsletter, *Outdoors West*, but only by twisting his arm unmercifully. We all vowed to help him out. I volunteered four thousand words on the proposed five-hundred-thousand-acre Columbia Basin Project. I didn't know beans about it, but I knew I could hear a speaker on the subject from the Bureau of Land Management [BLM], which is responsible for the project, at an upcoming state conference of Audubon chapters. I thought I could just sit there, take a bunch of notes, and whip out a definitive article.

Alas, the speaker never mentioned the project directly. He spoke in detail about the great mitigation, or trade-off, of one species for another when, after irrigation, the water table would rise and create marshes—deer would be gone, but how many more ducks there would be—and similar bureaucratic bemusements. I dozed gently through it all, but when I awakened, I realized that I was stuck with a four-thousand-word article on a subject about which I knew nothing except that the BLM guys were a bunch of phonies who weren't talking.

I wanted to keep my promise to the editor of *Outdoors West,* so as a first step I sent away for a copy of the 1975 environmental impact statement, which was at least six inches thick. It took me three months to reduce it to seventeen pages. I found out that the project started way back during the Depression with the Grand Coulee Dam, which had multiple purposes—to provide employment, to build a dam that would produce hydroelectric energy, to provide flood control, and to provide water, ultimately for a million acres of irrigated desert, but they started with half a million. As was characteristic of the times, no consideration was given to Indians, fish, wildlife, flora, or aesthetic values. In 1942, the turbines began to turn, electricity started going all over the place, and water started squirting out on the desert.

I happened to be up there in 1952, and I took a picture of a man harvesting peas. It was the first year that the high plateau had ever produced crops, and he was growing for seed, not for market.

Time rolled on and Congress decided to go ahead and irrigate the second half-million acres on the east side of the Columbia River—that is, to siphon water out of the river a second time. Congress made the appropriation and the work started in 1976, first on the extra pumps, but they got bogged down and didn't have funds to complete the second Bacon Siphons[23] and the thousands of miles of canals that were to transport the water up onto the east high plateau, as it's called. After the next recession, neither Congress nor Washington State was of a mind to make any more appropriations.

So, okay, I got the basics. I began to go around to public agencies like the U.S. Fish and Wildlife down in Olympia, the Department of Ecology in Lacey, the Washington State Department of Game,[24] and the [federal] Bureau of Reclamation, which invited me on a two-day tour with the project manager, Jim Cole. We saw the area to be inundated, a combination of dryland farming and scrub, which is sagebrush desert and grassland. We came upon a beetle, a great big brown fellow about half an inch long, that at the slightest touch stood on its head and gave out a little shoot of liquid.[25] No doubt this was at one time a survival strategy of considerable value. I thought sadly that standing on its head so cleverly, for whatever reason, would be of no help when the waters came. All the bugs would be gone, and the flowers, and the hawks and the falcons—all the things that made that place their home were going to lose it. I wondered who could be benefiting from all this destruction.

I spent two days in Wilson Creek with Harvey and Catherine Bohnet, who were dryland farmers. They farmed about nine hundred acres of wheat, barley, and rapeseed—you have to have a big acreage to make a living at it. I learned all about the dryland farmers, who love the land and love to farm, mom-and-pop operations that didn't want their land inundated by the Columbia Basin Project—sixty percent of them said so in a survey. They use very little chemical fertilizer because they plow in the stubble and leave some of the fields fallow to rejuvenate. The land is used in cycles, and the crops are rotated to defeat pests.

In irrigation farming, which was proposed by the Columbia Basin Project, the farmers pour on massive doses of chemically based fertilizer, pesticides, and herbicides. Every year—the land never has a rest. Eventually it's done for, and the only service it provides is to hold up a plant that actually grows with just water and chemicals. The chemicals finally poison the soil and leach all kinds of bad things into the rivers. *Now* I had no trouble identifying the proponents of the project—the chemical companies, the farm-machinery manufacturers, the banks, insurance companies, chambers of commerce—and politicians, for the usual pork-barrel reasons.

The naturally watered and fertile lands in the state would be forced out of the farming business by agriculture dependent on federal subsidies and elaborate technologies. The original 1942 irrigation project mandated small farms. Later, people could apply for a hundred and sixty acres, or, if there was a spouse, they could get twice that much. Soon they found that it wasn't profitable on very little capital to maintain one of those little farms. So what did they do? In order to get out from under a bad deal, they leased their land to somebody else. That somebody else happened to be agribusiness—absentee landlords who happen to be big corporations that can afford the chemicals and the machines.

All this amateur research gave birth to the article I finally wrote for *Outdoors West,* published in 1977 and titled "Roll On, Columbia." I'll quote from the opening sentence.

> With progress defined in terms of greater exploitation of the land and ever-increasing generation of power, Woody Guthrie wrote his Columbia River song. He said: "Your power is turning the darkness to dawn," and he described the Dam as "the biggest thing built by the hands of man, to run the great factories and water the land."[26]

In my article, I questioned whether Woody would have written the song as he did, had he known that this great irrigation project, as well as others throughout the West, could result in the destruction of the soil through the use of massive doses of fertilizer, pesticides, and herbicides, the monocrop, and the burning of the stubble, finally leading to the desertification of the region, which is what happened in the Palouse country of Washington and in parts of the Sacramento Valley [California], so I'm told. And this is not something that just happened in modern times. Whole civilizations have disappeared in North Africa and East Asia because of irrigation.[27]

"The Columbia River no longer rolls on," I wrote. "Harnessed, it creeps and seeps along on its placid passage to the sea."

Ralph Nader pointed out long ago that if we continue to abuse nature, nature will turn against us with a ferocity that will make any other form of violence seem like child's play. In the end, the river will have the last word.

TESTIFYING

I started a lone crusade against the Columbia Basin Project but soon discovered three other crusaders. Dr. Norman K. Whittlesey, a respected agricultural economist at Washington State University, pointed out that the government and the farmers would be paying about three dollars per acre for irrigation, but the cost of replacing the lost and used electricity would be a hundred and seventy-one dollars per acre each year, or about a hundred million dollars annually.[28] This conclusion was strengthened by the findings of Dr. Glen Petry, an economist from Washington State University, and by Dr. Martin Marks, an economist from the University of Washington, who figured benefits to the costs at twenty-five cents for a dollar invested.[29]

My crusade started with getting all of the Audubon chapters to oppose the Columbia Basin Project. I drew the National Audubon Society in on it, but they only gave me lip service. They had other irrigation projects they felt were more menacing than this one way out in the Pacific Northwest.

Plenty of people were ambivalent about completing the project. The public utility districts did not want energy in the form of water taken from the river and pumped up onto the plateau. They wanted to keep the water behind the dam going through the turbines, not only at Grand Coulee but all the way down the river, to create energy. The dryland farmers, barge people, commercial fishermen, sports people, recreation people, the salmon, and the environmentalists also all wanted the water in the river.

By this time, I was president of the Federation of Western Outdoor Clubs and responsible for the 1978 annual conference program, so I geared part of the program to the Columbia Basin Project–East High Plateau, as the project was now called. As panelists, I invited dryland farmers, led by my friend Catherine Bohnet. I also invited the Colville Indians, whose land and whole way of life had been expropriated by the Grand Coulee Dam. The federation had no trouble passing my resolution against the project.

Then I was invited by the National Audubon Society to present at a big conference in Washington, D.C., on rivers. At that same time, in 1979, the U.S. Senate Subcommittee on Appropriations was in session considering the funding for completion of the Columbia Basin Project. I was determined that I was going to appear before that subcommittee and tell my story.

First I wrote and told them I was coming. Would they please put me on the agenda someplace? I had a little speech to make. They wrote back, "Sorry. There is no room left on the agenda."

That didn't bother me. I went anyway. The Senate Subcommittee on Appropriations sat up high in front of the room on benches in a semicircle, the chairman in the middle, and some poor unfortunate guy at one end, a senator whose name I forget.

I go up to him, show him the letters, and say, "I came anyway, all the way from Seattle, and now I've got to testify about the Columbia Basin Project."

"No way," he says.

I say, "I can't take no for an answer. You go up and talk to the chairman and see if he won't make a place for me."

He trots up and talks to the chairman, comes back. "No way."

I say, "Look, I've *got* to talk to this committee. When I get back, what am I going to say to the people who paid my way to come here? I'm from way up in the Pacific Northwest, and I've just *got* to testify."

He says, "Well, you're pretty persistent. Come back tomorrow at two o'clock and talk to me again."

I say, "Okay, I'll come back. But in the meantime, would you lend me five dollars? I have only two dollars and fifty cents, and I have to get a cab and I'm not sure if that's going to be enough. If I don't come back tomorrow, you get rid of me for five bucks. But if I do come back, you get your five dollars back."

He thought that was pretty funny, so he lent me the five dollars.

The next day, promptly at two o'clock, I'm down there in the audience, holding my five dollars up to public view, and I beckon to my friend, the senator in the end seat, to come over to me. Everybody could see this. He came over.

I said, "Here's your five dollars. They're all going to think you're taking a bribe, won't they!"

That set the audience off.

He says, "Well, I've thought this over, and we've talked it over, and if you will guarantee to limit your talk to five minutes, you can go on."

I say, "Okay, I'll guarantee to limit my talk to five minutes. But remember this about me—my word isn't worth a damn!"

It comes my turn to speak. I say everything I wanted to in the five minutes. To back it up, I hand up to the chairman a copy of Dr. Petry's economic analysis.

The next day, I'm wheeling around the corridors of Congress, lobbying on all kinds of things. Somebody comes up to me and says, "Oh, hi, Mrs. Wolf."

I say, "Do I know you?"

He says, "My God, I'm the senator who got you before that committee."

I say, "Oh, I didn't recognize you out of your seat at the end of that row of benches."

He says, "Well, I'm telling you this—I'll never forget you!"

The subcommittee didn't take my advice. In 1979, the U.S. Congress went ahead with the appropriation to complete the irrigation technology, but with an awkward twist. Congress would complete the second Bacon Siphon and tunnels, but Washington State would have to find the money to send the water through them, thus throwing the ball into the court of the state legislature and leaving a lot of ditches, tunnels, canals, and engineering feats hooked up to the Grand Coulee Dam. So there it was, like an unfinished freeway that sits twisting up in the air.

The BLM was out looking for money to send the water gushing through. In 1983, spurred on by Tub Hanson, who represented the Grand Coulee District, the Washington State Senate passed the necessary legislation, but, alas, the whole thing got bogged down in a subcommittee of the State House when the three economists arrived to point out that the cost-benefit [ratio] was one dollar to twenty-five cents, and they spelled it out for them: the economy would realize twenty-five cents for every dollar it gave to construction of the project. That scared the wadding out of the House committee.

The Bureau of Reclamation, reeling from this setback, gathered support from those who sought to benefit from the project and made another attempt in 1984 to get the state funds. This time the bill sailed through the Senate, but the House merely allocated a hundred thousand dollars to study the project. Much time passed. I kept inquiring through contacts in Washington, D.C., and Olympia about what happened to the hundred thousand dollars. I learned that they did not intend to study the project itself, but to review a new draft environmental impact statement [DEIS] put out by the Bureau of Reclamation. That's the last I heard of the hundred thousand dollars, which seemed to have drifted into outer space.

I visited the manager of the project at the bureau, Jim Cole, and asked him, "When are you going to get your environmental impact statement out?"

He said, "I'm having a hard time getting the money to do it."

I said, "Jim, you're not ever going to irrigate those five hundred thousand acres. Don't you know that way deep down?"

He grinned.

I'd been fighting him not as a person but as the project manager, and we'd become good friends. I like those people. And I know they like me, too. I asked him how his boy was getting on, and he said that he had a job with the Fish and Wildlife Department. I said, "You better yank him out of there, Jim, because they're going to brainwash that kid, and he's going to fight you and your phony old projects."

Meanwhile, the dryland farmers made applications for exemption. They brought lawsuits. They tried to get a bill passed through the state legislature. It all failed, but they kept on fighting. I lost track of Catherine Bohnet until one day she called me and said, "We got our farm exempted, and it's a precedent-setting decision, which means that other farmers can, too. This could knock a hole in the project because together we occupy a lot of the land."

The Bureau of Reclamation held more hearings, so I rounded up the whole Conservation Committee of the Seattle Audubon Society to testify. By then I had the Sierra Club, the Washington Environmental Council, Friends of the Earth, and the Washington State Council of Audubon Chapters all turning out for testimony at the state legislature and the Bureau hearings on the DEIS.

The bureau next tried to sell their project to Audubon Societies and other organizations. Whenever I'd hear they were going to make a presentation at a chapter, I'd show up, too. And there they'd be with all their beautiful charts. And there I'd be with all my facts and figures. And I'd say, "Okay, Jim. I'm here again to pull the rug out from under you guys!" Fight on all fronts, all the time.

I sent them a copy of my *Outdoors West* article. One of them called me from the bureau office in Ephrata and said, "We just want you to know,

Hazel, how much we liked your article." I said, "Oh, no. That's devastating. I really must have missed the bus if you guys like it!"

This story has a happy ending. In 1989, Governor Booth Gardner got into the act and directed state agencies to submit comments on the DEIS. The Departments of Ecology, Transportation, Fish and Wildlife, and Energy all came down on the project. The final blow came from the federal General Accounting Office, which emphasized the outrageous cost-benefit analysis.

In the face of so much opposition, the bureau tried an end run by starting with a mere seventy thousand acres rather than the whole package. Everyone was awaiting the environmental impact statement on this reduced venture when Dan Beard, the new director of the Bureau of Land Management, publicly announced in 1994 that the Columbia Basin Project had been shelved. Dan Beard was later on the staff of the National Audubon Society.

What is it that impels government bureaucracies to continue with a project, no matter how impractical, how damaging, how expensive, and how contrary to common sense? Is it that if they do not keep increasing projects, they would be reduced to the mere maintenance of those in place? Is it a form of empire building?

A RUN FOR THE PRESIDENCY

By 1983, I realized that a lot of our troubles stemmed from the Reagan administration,[30] so I decided to get involved by running for president of the United States of America. I also wanted to get opposition to the Columbia Basin Project into the Washington State Democratic platform for the election year of 1984. I had to start at the bottom. I had to get myself elected as Democratic precinct committeeperson for my neighborhood.

At the precinct caucus that year, there was no one to lead as committeeperson, and only three people showed up from this great big precinct of three hundred and seventy-five Democratic voters. So we three made all the decisions for everybody else. It wasn't democratic! We could have passed a resolution to overturn the government! I figured out how to get myself on the ballot as committeeperson, but how was I to get those three hundred and seventy-five people from this crazy precinct of mine to show up and vote for me? How was I going to doorbell for the Democratic candidates? Just four blocks, and the people all locked up in apartments.

I had the phone numbers of all three hundred and seventy-five, so I just kept calling and calling until I got one person to let me into each building. Then I made three hundred and seventy-five packages of the Democratic campaign literature and wrote my name as precinct committeeperson on the top. My contacts let me into each apartment building, and I put the literature out. It was a tremendous job. I don't ever want to have to go through that again!

I got a hundred percent of the vote—nobody filed against me. So now I was a regular guy. Anybody who filed against me in the next election wouldn't have a chance. I ran into two people at the polling booth. I convinced them to help by telling them that unless we got a big turnout at the caucus meeting, I would pass resolutions to overturn the government. The next year, they all came over to my place to plan our blitz of the neighborhood. We did it in half an hour—no time at all!

As a result of all our efforts, plenty of people came to the caucus meeting. There was no problem with my resolution on the Columbia Basin Project. All I had to do was tell them what the score was, and my precinct caucus was up in arms against it. I was elected from the caucus to the district convention.

At the 43rd District convention, anyone who wanted to be a delegate to the legislative convention got up there to file. There were twenty-eight positions to fill, and sixty-eight people filed, each of whom had one minute to say why they should be elected. Most of the nominees were old-line Democrats. In their sixty seconds they said what big Democrats they were, been in there for *x* number of years, known party workhorses. I'm W, the last one to speak. Nobody knew me, and I didn't know that much about the Democratic Party. In my sixty seconds, I told them I was from the Audubon Society and that I had been bird-watching for a good many years, but I thought there were some birds in Washington, D.C., that needed careful watching. That made them laugh. Then I said that I had nothing to offer, that I wasn't even a hardcore Democrat, because I voted for a Republican for governor when Dixie Lee Ray ran as the Democrat.[31] That got another big laugh, since by that time everybody hated her, and most Democrats voted for the Republican, too. As I sat down, people were still chuckling. Here I am, a bird-watcher and a no-good Democrat, but when the votes were counted, would you believe I came in third? I went around asking people, "Why did you vote for me? Was it because of my pretty blue skirt? My white hair? My jokes?" They'd just laugh and say, "I don't know, I just like your style," or "You're just a special person." They'd never heard of me, but they have since.

I was opposed at this district convention by the corporate farmers from the southeast part of the state in favor of the Columbia Basin Project. They approached me in the rest room with their facts and figures. I said, "Let's discuss this at the Resolutions Committee meeting." That meeting went on and on. Before we even got to my resolution, people started going home, among them these corporate farmers with all their facts and figures. I stayed, so at some ungodly hour, my resolution opposing the Columbia Basin Project went sailing through.

In the next round, the legislative convention, I told another joke. In my sixty seconds, I said that I thought everybody had misunderstood Reagan when they said he didn't care for people. He really did—from conception to birth. That cracked them up. They voted for me again, and I got to follow my resolution up to the state level, where the corporate farmers once again found me in the rest room and tried to talk me out of it with all their facts and figures. I asked the chair of the state convention to recognize me when my resolution came up. He said, "We've heard enough from you. We have two thousand people in this place, and they all have a right to be heard." There were five microphones for people who spoke from the floor, so I got someone to staff each microphone, and when they got recognized, they were to turn the microphone over to me.

When my resolution against the Columbia Basin Project came up, people were milling around eating hot dogs or pulling little caucuses, in no shape to listen to the corporate farmers' bunch of facts and figures.

In contrast, I made one of the shortest speeches of my life. I said, "I'm opposed to this Columbia Basin Project. My precinct opposed it, and so have three economists, who have concluded that the cost-benefit [ratio] of the Columbia Basin Project is one dollar to twenty-five cents. Now, who pays the difference? We do, the ratepayers and the taxpayers, and so I urge you to vote against the project." There wasn't a dissenting vote. The Washington State Democratic Party was on record opposing the Columbia Basin Project and I had met one of my objectives in going into politics.

But in my other objective, to become president of the United States of America, I was blocked.[32] I couldn't go to the national Democratic convention in 1984 because the delegates were not elected, they were chosen. It's easy to see that I would have won in an open election at the state convention, provided they gave me sixty seconds to speak. Right there is a big bottleneck that keeps democracy stunted.

They talk about grassroots democracy—it never sprouts, it's trampled. If people knew about caucuses, knew where they were, knew what was involved, this would be a different country. Decisions about who gets to run and what the party platforms are going to be would not be made in smoke-filled rooms—or rest rooms. But they are. The process is concealed from preschool, kindergarten, elementary school, high school, college, and graduate students—from the American people. The grassroots never gets above ground. But that's where I stay, at the grassroots, working in organizations.

So my involvement in politics stays at the precinct level—or at the national level, whenever I get a photo opportunity to promote my causes. When Robert Redford campaigned for the Dukakis campaign,[33] I was cast by the national media as his latest flame, and there was something to that. I was invited to be part of his national tour when it hit Seattle. We sailed on the *Golden Delicious,* a yacht owned by one of the governor's friends, on the Duwamish River, heavily polluted with industrial chemicals. Unlike the time with the *Newington,*[34] I was on board and talked with my crush. Redford was making statements for the press. Flashbulbs were popping all over the place. Then he came up and put his arm around me for all the pictures, which they broadcast nationally. Now I, too, am a matinee idol, as well as his girlfriend.

17 / *Building Coalitions*

ONE VOTE FOR THE INDIANS

As a youngster in Victoria, when we played Cowboys and Indians, I was always an Indian. I had that natural affinity. As I learned more about modern Indians, I began to see their side of things.

While president of the Federation of Western Outdoor Clubs, in 1978, I began my career of coalition building. My first one was with the Indians, but it took me a little while to figure it out.

One tribe, the Quileutes, live adjacent to Olympic National Park, which takes up almost the entire Olympic Peninsula. Their residences were on a floodplain. When their population increased, they were especially interested in getting their people out of that plain. They applied to the National Park Service for parkland at a higher elevation with more room.

The National Park Service opposed Indian expansion into the Olympic National Park. Officers from the Park Service came to a board meeting of the Olympic Park Associates, the citizens' organization that bird-dogs Olympic National Park, to ask us to join them in their opposition. I had just joined that board.

"The park is sacred," the officers told us then. "Nothing must touch the park."

Now, I spend a lot of time at board meetings for various environmental organizations. Usually I sit and listen. I wouldn't give them my opinion if they asked. When something concrete comes up, then I approach individuals, but I don't make speeches at a policy-making meeting. I don't see any point in antagonizing good people. I want to be friends with everybody and I won't break with them until it's absolutely necessary. So after the National Park Service spoke, a vote was taken, and instead of saying anything, I simply abstained.

When I got home, I was thoroughly ashamed of myself. That was a time when I should have spoken up, and didn't. I wanted to be friends with everybody, you see.

One of the board members was vociferously anti-Indian. He approached the *Seattle Post-Intelligencer* and they quoted him as saying, "The Olympic Park Associates has gone on record as opposed to granting additional land to the greedy and aggressive Quileute Indians." The chair of Olympic Park Associates wrote a letter to the editor of the *PI,* apologizing for the phrase "greedy and aggressive," and she also called a board meeting during which the chair and the anti-Indian guy continually lambasted each other. Finally somebody made a motion, and I was able to speak.

I sure did speak. I said, "We have taken the land away from the Indians at the point of a gun. It wasn't given to us by the Indians. We took it. And I don't care if they get back the whole damn park, let alone this miserable little four hundred acres that they are asking for. This has been gnawing at me ever since we took the vote last time. I want it known loud and clear how I feel about the opposition we've taken to the Quileute Indians, who haven't anyplace to build their houses."

I felt good! I insulted all my friends. If that's the way it's going to be, that's the way it's going to be. I'm not going to trade off a whole Indian tribe for a few friends.

The board voted anyway, affirming their opposition to the Indians. I cast the only vote against it and then asked that my name be put in the minutes as the one in opposition. In the car on the way home, we were talking and laughing about it all. I could see they still loved me.

This racism—it'll come up anyplace. I sat through it the first time because I was new on the board and I didn't know just how to handle it. And when I don't know what to do, I do nothing.

Finally Congress stepped in. After the National Park Service and the Olympic Park Associates had alienated every tribe from here to New England, Congress gave that plateau to the Indians. And the National Park Service purists wanted to save the land, keep it pristine! You know, you must never compromise your principles for some sentimental ideal like that.

MAKING FRIENDS WITH INDIANS

In the 1960s, Indians were very militant. They changed tactics in the seventies, got into lawsuits and began to win.[35] Some of us at Seattle Audubon became aware of the fact that most of the litigation the Indians were engaged in had to do with protection of the environment. So in 1978, as president of the Federation of Western Outdoor Clubs, I decided we would invite a panel of Native Americans to our forty-sixth annual convention to discuss with us the many issues we knew we must have in common. My problem was, I didn't know any Indians—not a one.

I went through the American Friends Service Committee, the Quakers, and they suggested I contact Joe De La Cruz, the tribal chairman of the Quinaults.

When I called, Joe exclaimed, "This is a miracle. I was just leaving to attend a meeting in Seattle, and one of the items on our agenda is, how can we get in touch with the environmentalists?"

It was an idea whose time had come. Everything's connected. I just make the connections as I go along.

Joe furnished us with four speakers for our panel—Joe from the Quinaults, Russell Jim of the Yakamas, Mel Tonasket from the Colvilles, and Rudey Ryser, who represented a number of tribes in Puget Sound. This was the first time a lot of us had come within shouting distance of a Native American. I remember Russell Jim from the Yakama [Nation] had long braids, which, he told me, are what connected him with the earth. The talks were exciting, followed by lots of questions.

At the break, we sat in the sun out on the grass together and came up with the idea of holding a conference of Native Americans and environmentalists to study more in depth what we had in common. That's the kind of coalition I had in mind—one that agrees on common things and avoids the controversial ones.

Meanwhile, the editor of *Outdoors West* sponsored five anti-Indian motions in the Resolutions Committee of the forty-sixth annual convention: fishing in the mouth of such and such river with double bait—let's condemn them for that!—and other nitpicking little things. The chairman of the Resolutions Committee conducted the meeting. I was president of the organization, but I sat as an ordinary rank-and-file guy down in the audience at committee meetings.

When they came to the first of the motions, I got up and said, "This is one of a series of five resolutions, all of them against Indians. For one thing, I think they're racist. And for another, they're nitpicking. I think that if we're trying to form a coalition with Indians and still we pass five anti-Indian resolutions, they're going to say, 'Well, the white man's done it again.' So I move that this one, and all the other ones, be stricken."

The anti-Indian editor and one other person got up and made fiery speeches. The chairman of the Resolutions Committee permitted all kinds of manipulations, amendments, and points of order by these two people. This went on and on, and I could see that confusion was spreading through the audience.

Finally I said, "I think this thing should be put to a vote now. I would like you to do that, Mr. Chairman."

He said, "Well, I'm not going to do it."

I said, "Okay. Then I will." So I walked up and I reached out my hand and took the mike from him.

The chairman sat down, grumbling audibly, "If you want to run this committee, you can."

I said, "Well, it's simple. All those in favor of deleting these resolutions, say 'aye.'" Everybody said aye. "Contrary?" Two contraries.

The chairman was slumped down in a front seat, eating cookies. Now, this man was a professor at Stanford or some horrible place. And who was I? I don't even have a B.S.! But I wanted him to come back and finish his job. So I looked down at him and said, "Dan, quit eating those cookies now, and come back here and finish your job," as if I was speaking to an unruly grandchild. That was a tense and electric moment, and I've never ceased to be grateful to him for stepping back up onstage and continuing the meeting. I wrote and told him so afterward.

The editor of *Outdoors West* who had sponsored the resolutions was so mad that he resigned. Well, good riddance. He gave two reasons for his resignation, both of which I thought were valid. One was "Hazel's very high-handed procedure at the convention," and the other was "I want to write an article about Indians for *Outdoors West* and I know she won't print it." That's how I became editor, which I've been doing for the past twenty years.

There's just times when you have to step in and do things like that. It would have caused irreparable damage if any of those resolutions had passed. Indian people are very sensitive. They've been kicked around for so long that they suspect the white man. You've got to prove that you're their friend. And the least little thing off-balance could have destroyed the beginnings of our coalition.

After the FWOC convention, the American Friends Service Committee gave five thousand dollars to the conference idea. We hired a full-time staff person, Bernice Delorme, a member of the Chippewas, who made the contacts with the tribes. Since we were sponsored by the Quakers, the Indians were happy to set up meetings with us. The Quakers are the only organization they trust, you know—William Penn never broke a treaty.

In 1979, Bernice and I set out in my old Chevy to visit some fifteen of the tribes in Washington State and three in British Columbia. It took us all summer. I told the Indians where I was coming from, what our concerns were, and I asked about their concerns and their reaction to the proposed conference. I realized later that my being an elder didn't hurt our reception at the reservations. I would get all the environmentalists living near the reservation to meet with me, too, separately—people from the Sierra Club, Audubon, Friends of the Earth, the Federation of Western Outdoor Clubs, the Oregon Wilderness Coalition, and the Washington Environmental Council. So I was building in two directions. To organize the conference, we set up an eight-person steering committee—four Native Americans, and four representatives of environmental organizations.

The conference was held September 28–30, 1979, in the Daybreak Star Indian Cultural Center in Seattle. Ten tribes sent delegates, including two from British Columbia and the Nez Perce from Idaho. Representatives of seventeen environmental groups came as well—Bernie Whitebear of

United Indians of All Tribes, Joan Thomas from the Washington Environmental Council, Frank Bennett of the Lower Elwha Tribal Council, and many others, more than two hundred people talking about the Endangered Species Act, native fish and mammals, wetlands and estuaries, and birds.[36]

We were all very excited. Nothing like this had ever happened before. After three days together sharing ideas and entertainment, friendships were formed and alliances established that have endured to this day. We never had to have another conference!

THE INTERTRIBAL CONSERVATIONIST COALITION

*I*mmediately following the conference, we teamed up on opposing the construction of the Northern Tier Pipeline to transport Alaska oil from Port Angeles, on the Olympic Peninsula, all the way to the Mississippi.[37] The pipeline would have cut through a lot of sacred lands protected by the American Indian Religious Act, something I'd never heard of before. The Makahs, the Quileutes, the Hohs, the Quinaults—fifteen tribes and as many environmental organizations, including the National Audubon Society and the Sierra Club, joined in a lawsuit to stop construction. Before it came to a trial, Governor Spellman[38] vetoed the harebrained proposal.

Next the Lummis—Kurt Russell and Cha-das-ska-dum-which-ta-lum[39]—contacted me. The IRS had put a retroactive tax on the Indians' commercial catch, which they couldn't pay. Then the IRS took their boats and held them in escrow for the back taxes. The Lummis fought back with a bill submitted to the U.S. Congress. It went sailing through the Senate but got bogged down in a committee of the House. They couldn't budge it. That's when they called me. So Seattle Audubon passed a resolution directed at our lobbyist in Washington, D.C., to get that bill out of committee. We were only one of many outfits that put the pressure on Washington, D.C., and we sprung it out. The bill then passed in the House, and the poor IRS had to give the Indians back their boats and money. Trying to screw the Indians again—it's that simple. The IRS had wanted to clear out the competition so that white fishermen would get the catch.

If it hadn't been for that conference, we never would have known there was an IRS fight, and they never would have known we gave a damn.

The Boldt case[40] was our most famous collaboration. The Indians were trying to get back the rights to their traditional fishing grounds, promised in the original treaties, but there were no fish to bargain over. The "aggressive Indians" had been blamed for the decline in the fishery resource. Little attention had been paid to environmental sources of degradation, such as logging, road building, stream channelization, dams, and agribusiness. The State of Washington was partially to blame because it hadn't adequately enforced environmental laws—the Shoreline Management Act, the Forest Practices Act, the Hydraulic Act, and others—which was its obligation under Indian treaties. It was an environmental problem, not an Indian problem, so I decided to file an amicus curiae [friend of the court] brief to the Federal District Court that was hearing phase two of the Boldt case. I got the Federation of Western Outdoor Clubs behind it, but I wanted a coalition.[41]

A pro bono guy, Charles Ehlert, agreed to write it. He and I went to a board meeting of the Sierra Club in Seattle and made our pitch. They were delighted to go in with us on the amicus brief, and they voted unanimously. The head honchos at the Sierra Club stepped right over their heads and refused to let them. I went to San Francisco to talk to the head people, and I came back empty-handed. Then I realized that the Sierra Club was already in the Federation [of Western Outdoor Clubs] as a member club, so I filed on behalf of the federation. Our brief, filed with the court in 1979, helped to refocus attention on serious environmental questions of concern not just to Indians but to the entire community. The Boldt judgment ultimately came down on the side of Indian and environmental rights.

I support all efforts toward preserving the rights of Indian peoples. As an immigrant to this land, as we all are, I look back on the past injustice with both horror and compassion. But I have no sense of guilt for these crimes committed by my ancestors. One does not pick one's ancestors. However, I do feel responsible for doing everything possible to repair the damage done by them to the native peoples.

I'm not working on issues with any of the Native Americans right now.

If something came up, I'd tell them to call the Audubon Society in their area if they hadn't already. Bernie Whitebear, Russell Jim—they're all friends who invite me places. I'm waiting for Joe De La Cruz to take me to lunch and get back the coat he left at my apartment after a powwow.

When I went visiting all the tribes that summer, I looked up the Jamestown S'Klallams. I found out the tribal chairman was a young man in college at the University of Washington. I hunted him down in a basement apartment. He couldn't come to the conference, because he was spending all his spare time trying to get his tribe recognized by the federal government. In order to do that, he had to locate people all over the United States and prove that they belonged to the tribe. That was his life's work. It was 1979, more than twenty years ago.

Unbeknownst to me, my granddaughter, Ann Sargent, volunteered a while back as a paralegal to the executive director of the Jamestown S'Klallams, out there where she lives, in Sequim, on the Olympic Peninsula. It was Ron Allen, that same young man I'd looked up years ago. He had finally won recognition for his tribe from the federal government. Money came in, so he hired my granddaughter as his secretary. I go out to Sequim every once in a while to play bingo at the tribe's Seven Cedars Casino near where Ann works. At my last visit, I won ten dollars and seventy-five cents in a kind of slot machine.

CONNECTIONS

Now I'm trying to make other connections—with the labor movement, for starters. A key person in the movement to bring labor and environmentalists together is Ron Judd, chairman of the King County Labor Council. He realizes more than anybody else the need for allies, so he sent out invitations to a conference in 1994. He worked like a dog.

I went to the meeting. The environmentalists turned out, but labor didn't and I know why. The labor movement was very strong after the organizing campaign that took place during the Depression of the thirties. But it was destroyed by the McCarthy era, reduced from thirty-five percent to thirteen percent of the labor force because, along with the

Communists, they cleaned out all the progressives from the union leadership. They were replaced for forty years by compromisers, do-nothing bureaucrats. With the elections in the AFL–CIO in October 1996, the progressives came back in. The fact that they have a woman as vice president and a Latino as treasurer indicates a big shift.

Their "new" policy is to organize the unorganized. Traditionally, organized environmentalists are middle-class white people—professional people like nurses and teachers. They're not pro-union, but they're not anti-union, either. But both labor and environmentalists need allies. I invited Ron Judd to give a talk on labor and the environment for the FWOC annual conference in 1998. I got him to write an article for *Outdoors West,* too.

Most organizations I'm part of are relatively conservative, so I'm always building coalitions toward the left. I know when I can't do something—I wouldn't take a position on the United Nations, for instance. But I did take a position on peace.[42] Environmentalists were hard put to say why they shouldn't join the nuclear freeze campaign in the 1980s. What's the use of saving all this wilderness, and what's the use of having all this clean air, if nuclear bombs are going to be thrown around? That should be our first priority—keeping the bombs out of circulation. Otherwise, we're just spinning our wheels. National security can no longer be defined in terms of military security, only in terms of environmental security.

So I got on the board of the local freeze campaign in order to start building the coalition. Then I sent around a petition and got about three hundred names on it. All the Washington State Audubon chapters came out for the freeze campaign, and somebody from every chapter signed the petition. I also got signatures in Oregon, California, and Alaska. When we sent the petition back to the National Audubon Society, the board voted it down. Instead, they decided to hold a conference where all kinds of important people would tell us what the *results* of a nuclear war would be. The brochure[43] invited people to come to a hotel in Washington, D.C., with a registration fee of a hundred and forty dollars. It cost about seven hundred dollars, all told. Carl Sagan was one of the important people who was going to be there.

I thought, "Boy, this is really going to be grassroots, isn't it!" I wrote the conference organizer, a friend of mine, a letter: "Dear Chapin, I sure love this grassroots event that you're setting up at a hundred and forty dollars registration fee plus hotel. I'm sorry you've got a bunch of dimwits back there among the rich people in the East who don't know what the results of a nuclear war would be, and who can afford to go to your conference. I don't have to spend all that money to find out. I wish you luck."

We have to work to keep the nuclear mushroom from coming up. The demise of the so-called Evil Empire lifted a lot of the threat, but bombs are still stockpiled and represent an ever-present danger. Nuclear war seems like lightning or earthquakes—uncontrollable. But we have the power to stop it, if we will. And that consists of organizing, organizing, organizing.

BROTHERHOOD

A while back, the Federation of Western Outdoor Clubs board came under the control of avid hikers. FWOC was immersed in trails—trails here, trails there, and lawsuits about trails. They wanted the Pacific Crest Trail to go through grizzly country in Oregon, but they should keep out of it. The grizzlies just need to eat up a couple of people. Then the United States will send a big army to kill the grizzlies. If the Pacific Crest Trail has to loop all the way around the state of Oregon to avoid grizzly country, I'm all for it. Otherwise, no trail.

It's just talk now, so I keep quiet. But if the trailblazers start making a concrete effort to get their corridor, then I will get Audubon and a lot of other organizations to express dismay. They should stay away from grizzlies. I'm not opinionated. I'm just always right.

Hiking is not my number-one priority. I'm a kind of heretic. In fact, I wouldn't care if nobody ever went into the wilderness, including myself, much as I like to. There are some places we just don't belong. Mount Rainier is an example, according to the Native Americans. It was the place "up there" where they never went. Only "civilized" white people climb mountains for the sake of getting to the top. Native Americans had a practical reason for not climbing Mount Rainier, too—it was very hazardous, and they might fall down and break their neck. They had better sense than to risk their lives just for the hell of it. Sacred means that you don't go there, not that you hike there en masse to get in touch with nature.

One of the big reasons for everyone wanting to save wild places is so they can commune in solitude with nature. That annoys me very much. I wouldn't put my little finger out to save wilderness for meditation. If everybody adhered to that, the wilderness would be so crowded there would be no privacy. You'd have to come back to the city to commune with nature. Everybody's up there on the mountaintops.

Here's how the environmentalists defeat themselves. A recent article in *Audubon* magazine tells about Florida's Sacahatchy Strand, describes the swamp and how remote it is—"It's too wild to be wholly known or even surveyed." The magazine shouldn't publish articles like that. Now everybody in the environmental movement will be making a beeline for the place. They will want to get that spiritual experience.

And who will stop them? There is only one way for workers to stop corporations from cutting the labor force, and that's by organizing in unions. Sacahatchy Strand and Mount Rainier can't organize to stop from being violated, to stop from being destroyed. That's where we come in.

Nature can just take its course without human interference for holy or unholy reasons. I'm concerned to save things for their own sake. And I am concerned about the practical reasons, too. I'm not overlooking the fact that there's beauty and it's inspirational. But the main fact is that we protect nature out of practical need, our survival.

Nature is everything. Everything is nature—the stars, you and me, mice and everything, including the big bang. A little over a hundred years ago, Frederick Engels wrote that we don't rule nature like a conqueror over foreign people, but with flesh, blood, and brain, we belong to nature and exist in its midst. We have the advantage over other living things by being able to understand nature's laws. Otherwise, we're just one of the species.[44] Through the countless centuries of evolution, our species, Homo sapiens, has had a tough row to hoe to survive. We don't have much going for us. We have very little hair, and this is mostly in patches, and some lose a lot from the top of their heads rather soon in life. We have almost nothing to protect us from the rain, snow, or sun—no feathers, scales, wool, fur, or even fuzz. In fact, we're almost naked. And we are physically handicapped compared to other animals. For example, we can't run very fast to overtake something to eat other than plants. We can't see very well nor for great distances, as eagles, owls, hawks, and many mammals can, nor are we able to see on both sides at once, gnat-eyed, like horses and frogs. We have hardly any sense of smell. Our hearing is defective. We cannot climb trees, like monkeys. We cannot slither along skillfully, like snakes. We are indifferent swimmers, and we cannot fly, of course. So, in summation, we are a sorry species.

And how was it possible for humans to hunt the abundantly endowed and superior animals? The answer is simple—we ganged up on them. And we are not the only animals that gang up for survival. It's characteristic of horses, sheep, wolves, deer, starlings, bees, ants, and many others. "Gregarious" is the term used to describe this trait in mammals. It comes in the gene package. One human could not kill a lion or overtake a deer, but many humans hunting together could, just as many wolves acting together can bring down a moose. We had to develop our gregariousness in order to survive. This has been explained to my satisfaction in Teilhard de Chardin's *The Phenomenon of Man*.[45]

In human beings, "gregariousness" is another word for "brotherhood." It is so ingrained that one of the greatest punishments devised by humans, outside of death, is solitary confinement. We can hardly withstand it. Wherefore I'd say that brotherhood is in our genes. I am sorry to have to use such a sexist word, but "sisterhood" is just as sexist if used in a general sense. The only word I can think of is "siblinghood," which should be kept restricted by law for use only by sociologists. So I am back to the warm, fuzzy word of "brotherhood."

That human beings have a profound longing for brotherhood is nowhere more evident than in the teachings of the great religions of the world. The holy books of Buddhism, Judaism, Confucianism, Islam, and the practices of many indigenous peoples call for brotherhood. Christ said, "Love thy neighbor as thyself." Unfortunately, many of these religions have a poor track record. But if you examine the religions—not the people who belong to them, but the sacred books that are supposed to guide them— they all contain a golden core of brotherhood. This has been explained to my satisfaction in Dr. Alexander Skutch's *Golden Core of Religion*.[46]

Dr. Skutch, having studied all these religions, was himself a pacifist and a vegetarian as a matter of principle. Like Albert Einstein, he believed in reverence for all life. Dr. Skutch didn't even kill mosquitoes. I share some of those beliefs, but I'm not going to let any mosquitoes buzz around and bite me, you know. I'll certainly destroy a bees' nest if they're going to sting all my friends. Still, I don't like to kill anything. Like spiders—if I find them, I very carefully catch them so I don't injure them, and I put them outside. The same with bees. I learned how to release animals that get caught, but I don't carry it to extremes. Dr. Skutch killed green snakes because they raided the nests of birds he was studying on his farm in Costa Rica, but he had to go to a lot of trouble to justify these killings. I don't have these troubles, because I'm not a mystic or a religious person. I just make up my rules as I go along.

No species in the whole living world has ever destroyed its habitat knowingly, willfully. They might do it unwittingly, or as a consequence of being unable to adapt, but not deliberately. I think this is a law that holds good for all of creation, including humans. This need for brotherhood, for keeping together and working together, is in our genes, and it's in our culture, and I think that these two things will come together to save our habitat. It'll be a long and stormy road and I don't know how we're going to do it. I can't see that far into the future. I just go along from day to day. But I see the awareness growing in people in all walks of life.

Now, this gregariousness is not going to save us just because it's in our genes. We have to activate it. And that means get out to meetings. As a child, I thought meetings were so romantic, exciting, and important. I wondered if I would ever go to one when I grew up. I must have had a premonition that I was going to spend the latter half of my life in meetings. I still like them.

SECRETARY POWER

I've risen as high as I expect to rise in the environmental movement—secretary of Seattle Audubon Society for thirty-five years. I like to be secretary. I feel at home taking minutes. I've been secretary in practically every organization I've joined. My mother was a secretary. My granddaughter is a secretary. We make a long line of secretaries. Because I've been Audubon secretary for so many years, I've saved the board all kinds of time. I say, "Oh, that was done. Now, how about this instead?" We don't have to reinvent the wheel. And nobody wants my job. When you're dealing with a volunteer movement, there's nobody lining up just panting to get your position.

I've found that as secretary I can freewheel around, like edit the paper or start a campaign—things I wouldn't have time to do as president. During the time I was secretary for the Audubon Society, I was also the office manager, doing the job that they now pay staff to do. I was also on the newsletter committee, on publications, in charge of exhibits, and I worked on membership drives, so I traveled around. And then, being secretary for many organizations puts me on their executive committee. So from any position—secretary, treasurer, vice president, or president— you can be a leader, but secretary gives you the most freedom, as I found out.

It's common knowledge that, as secretaries, women in almost any enterprise do all the work. Men hold the top positions and get all the credit. The Audubon Society was run by men and the work was done by women. At a convention in the early 1980s, I noticed that in the general sessions every moderator was a man, every panelist was a man. They did squeeze in a woman once, at the tail end. They called her up from the audience to represent the League of Conservation Voters. She had five minutes to tell us how to vote in an upcoming election. Then she went back into the great unwashed. Oh, yes, and they let Helen Engle of Tahoma Audubon pick the card out of the bowl when they were drawing for door prizes. Since then, things have changed, but only somewhat.

I'm convinced about the importance of women in the environmental movement, whatever their official positions have been. Whenever I can, I give my speech about it. I list many, many women activists to give my audience lots of ammunition.

You know the true story of creation—God created man, and then she stood back and looked at him. She said, "I know I can do better than that," and she did—Eve. She is my role model. If it hadn't been for Eve, with her initiative and courage, we'd still be sitting in that damn garden wondering what the apple tastes like, wouldn't we? Who wants to sit in a garden for eternity? She got us out into the real world.

LIKE THE WOLVES

 𝒰nseating President Reagan was quite an inspiration to me in the 1980s. To bolster my campaign, I went down to the Urban League to help register voters. About sixty of us showed up and there were a lot of my old comrades—hadn't seen them for ages. I teamed up with another woman and went down to the unemployment office. We asked the manager, "Can we put up a little voter registration table?" I was right back there at the zone office, now called Employment Services, but this time I was a lady, coming in from the outside to register voters. It was great to be back among my own people, despite the fact that I was an environmentalist and got my name in the paper and wore funny clothes and wasn't hungry. I felt that I was home. Short years ago, I was standing in that line.

It's a matter of adaptation. Most of the time I'm ladylike because the situation demands it. If I go to a welfare office where many people are uneducated, I adapt to their way of talking so that we can communicate without a barrier. I don't dress up fancy, but I don't go ragged either—kind of halfway in between.

I learned how to adapt when I was a child. We lived in a rough neighborhood. I was tough and I swore and did all kinds of bad things. When she was not so hard up, my mother would send me to the school at St. Anne's Convent. After four or five months, my mother couldn't pay my tuition and I would return to public school, so I learned how easy it is to change your language and your image to meet conditions. I don't say you have to go all out. You can retain some of your own. Just give a little, just blend in with the scenery, like the wolves. I'm like the wolves in having this capacity to become part of the picture wherever I go.

Very few people have encountered wolves. I'm one of the fortunate ones. A bunch of us were hiking in Denali National Park in Alaska in 1970 when we came across a wolf eating a young goat, a kid. When the wolf saw us, it ran way up a steep bank and perched up on the ridge, limned against the sky looking down on us, then disappeared. When we came back later, there was the half-eaten animal. The wolf had not returned to its kill. Several days later, it still hadn't come back, so terrified is the wolf of people.

Another time, I was kayaking up near Glacier Bay National Park with a friend. On our way home, we stopped at a big raft moored in an inlet. It was a ranger station. They invited us to stay overnight, so instead of camping on the beach we slept on their raft, where we woke up early in the morning to the most beautiful music I had ever heard. It was a whole chorus of wolves up on the other side of the inlet, an orchestra with all the instruments in tune.

The third time, I was driving in the Yukon and there was a wolf running across the road in front of my car. I stopped, got out, and chased it, just for the hell of it. It ran through the woods. I went tearing after it. Felt like a kid—felt like running. And suddenly it melted. It just wasn't there anymore, though it probably could see me. It didn't outrun me, it just outmelted me.

I have an identity with wolves and an instinct for camouflage. It's sort of a survival technique, isn't it? I'm sure that I bring some element of camouflage to every conversation I have. I don't know what is the real me. Every once in a while I do know, but it has to be something really terrific to jar me out of my camouflage and make me let fly with what I really think. And I still wouldn't say it, if it would ruffle people's feathers. If there's something closer to the bone, my guess is it would come out of my allegiance to the working class, what they suffer and why, and what's their due in the world. I want to keep in touch with my people, who are not really the middle-class folk I run around with. They're friends, but they're not my childhood people where I came from.

LIKE THE SPARROWS

*S*parrows are streetwise, and so am I. Like the sparrows, I stay poor. It's better for my health. I can't afford rich food. I don't buy bacon. I don't buy canned stuff, frozen stuff, packaged foods, never anything dried— that's all expensive. I buy fresh vegetables, fresh fruit. And I buy everything in season. Now the season's on for grapes. They're coming from Chile. I don't buy any meat after reading in John Robbins's book[47] about how brutally the animals are treated. Besides, I don't have much time to fool around cooking things. Did I say yet that I hate to cook? But I do eat an apple a day. I can't afford medical examinations. I can't buy pills. I can't get sick, because I have no insurance. I go to the beauty school and get my permanent waves for fifteen dollars with a senior citizens' discount— that includes haircut, wave set, and the whole bit.

I might be put in jail if I tell this story about how I got my wages upped. When I was a legal secretary working for John Caughlan, he did a big portion of his work pro bono. Consequently, he and his family starved, and I starved, because he couldn't afford to pay me very much. A couple of years before my retirement, I began worrying about this, knowing that my pension would be determined by how much I had earned in wages. So I persuaded an unscrupulous friend of mine, a secondhand-store owner, to put me on his payroll with a big salary. I'd take the check and cash it and give it back to him. This went on for two years. He paid my social security and withholding tax to the government, in return for which I did a little bookkeeping for him. So when I retired I had a substantial salary, which accounts for the fact that I can live on my pension. I don't know what the crime is, but the statute of limitations has not run out, so I may be making a big mistake in spreading this all over the world.

There are only two things on my conscience, should I have to meet that guy at the pearly gates. One is this unscrupulous act with the secondhand dealer. And the other is my travel bank account. It's not in my name. It's pretty high, by the way, because of the awards I've received. I have a CD [certificate of deposit]. It just rolls over. They have to cart me off in a wooden box before I'll take anything out of this bank account for something other than travel. I can go anyplace I want. I went to Nicaragua. I went to Brock Evans's wedding in Washington, D.C. I flew twice to England, many times to Baja California, and every year to the National Audubon Society Convention.

I get eight hundred and twenty-two dollars per month from Social

Security. And because of my poverty I get a rent subsidy, so my rent is only two hundred and nine dollars—up a little bit since last year, but my pension went up, too. I enjoyed the benefit of the raise in my pension for quite a few months before the rent went up. So now I'm really ahead. Oh, incidentally, after I was interviewed by the HUD [Housing and Urban Development] people, and I furnished all the stuff they wanted to see— the rent subsidy is based on your income—they told me my rent would now be two hundred and nineteen dollars. The guy called me up a day later and said, "Hazel, I really made a big mistake on your rent. It's only two hundred and nine dollars." So that gives me another ten dollars to give away. If you look at my checkbook—ten dollars, ten dollars—I give everybody ten dollars. I don't make any big donations to anybody, including the Audubon Society—just small ones, in keeping with my lowly position, mostly to environmental causes. But I also belong to the Southern Poverty Law Center, the United Farm Workers, and Amnesty International. I belong to a lot of things.

It costs me about a hundred dollars a month to eat. My family sees that I'm dressed well. Ann always buys me beautiful dresses. I wear things that I made myself when I was working and had more time. So living costs me practically nothing. Food, clothing, shelter—what else is there in life? The rest of the money, what good is it to me? I don't want anything.

I have a little arthritis in both thumbs. It doesn't hurt, and there's no swelling that's noticeable, but I've lost the muscular power. I can cut my fingernails, but I really can't cut my toenails. They're too tough. So I get them cut for free through the Country Doctor [Clinic, in Seattle], where I'm on the board.

The people who work there—technicians, doctors, chemists, registered nurses—all work for peanuts. I love to go. It's free for seniors. I go for this toenail business. Now, the people who come there are poor people. One is a man who's mentally impaired in some way. I see him go up the steps, then he stops and turns around and turns around and turns around. I know his name, Robert. So when I see him on the street I say, "Hi, Robert. I met you at the toenail place." I'd say fifty percent of the people there are African American, and there are some Spanish-speaking people. And I feel good. I'm with my people. We're all seated in a semicircle of chairs, our feet in warm water in a pan, and here are these white professional women and men, like little Jesuses, washing the feet of the poor people.

Poverty, if not carried beyond the point that threatens survival, can be a friend. One of my greatest advantages is that I was born poor, and I stayed poor. I long ago came to the conclusion that only the poor are really independent.

PART VI

One Neighborhood: 1984–2000

El pueblo unido jamás será vencido.
The people united will never be defeated.

We need to get back to our original home, you know.

*I*n 1979 the revolutionary Sandinistas of Nicaragua attempted to cut one small Central American country loose from the global system of free trade. They planned an economy that would benefit the people rather than international corporations and wealthy middle-class owners. They were nationalists who intended that their land of luscious rain forest, mountains, and valleys would also be a beneficiary of their rule. Under the Sandinistas in the 1980s, Nicaragua connected stewardship for the land with democratic socialism for the people.

In 1984, with a flash of recognition, Hazel Wolf saw the significance of revolutionary Nicaragua. It was something like love at first sight. In Nicaragua she experienced a vision of the future, a synthesis of her past as working-class organizer and her present as environmental organizer: people and land part of one living community within a modern economy. Wolf traveled to Nicaragua five times in the decade between 1984 and 1994, each time returning to the United States to enunciate the vision—sometimes four and five times a week—for audiences that ranged from conservative business organizations to schoolchildren, universities, and church groups. She was a regional and national harbinger of the

Nicaraguan revolution. The U.S. Congress and chief executive, meanwhile, alternately provided and withheld support for the Contras,[1] a guerrilla force in the mountains of Nicaragua that opposed the revolution.

Like thousands of North American and European visitors, Wolf was entranced by the Nicaraguans' openness and their determination to provide health care for their people and conservation practices for their land. Although she was not blind to the continuing poverty of the people and the ineptitude of the bureaucracy, she and her Nicaraguan friends were deceived about the regime's ability to survive.

Hazel Wolf returned from her trips to Central America with a new, global perspective on her work. She saw that the struggle of the world's indigenous peoples against logging and drilling parallels the struggle of North American poor and minority populations against pollution. People of low income, a large percentage of whom are people of color, suffer disproportionately from polluted air, water, and soil because dumps, incinerators, nuclear-waste facilities, and factories are located in their neighborhoods. The same economics that force cultures and species into extinction force disenfranchised minorities into unemployment, drugs, and early death. In the 1980s, in order to combat this situation, called "environmental racism," poor and minority communities began to build the environmental justice movement. Wolf saw in this movement the potential for an environmental coalition that could have a democratizing influence similar to that of trade unionism in the 1930s and of civil rights in the 1960s.

18 / Nicaragua: My Second Country

REVOLUTIONARY SOCIETY

It's a huge cathedral, destroyed in the 1972 Managua earthquake. The shell is still there, but it's empty inside—I've been in it. One of the towers is broken off. The other one still has a bell. The enormous arched entrance of the church faces a great plaza that accommodates three hundred and fifty thousand people. They call it the Plaza de la Revolución. That's where the Sandinistas held their last rally before the February 1990 election.

We could only drive our cars to within a mile and a half of the place, then we had to walk in the boiling sun. It was an incredible scene. We pushed our way through until we were right in the middle and stayed the afternoon. There were bullhorns and a lot of loud music. The people know all kinds of revolutionary songs—not just one line and then peter out, but the whole song, song after song. We were waiting for Daniel Ortega, the Sandinista candidate for president of Nicaragua.

Over the entrance to the church there was a balcony. Somehow or other, hundreds of people got up there and on up into the towers. One person was on top with a flag. The bell started to toll.[2] It was beautiful—the roar of the crowd, and in the background this bell. The day had been cloudy earlier, with a little spatter of rain. So there was the rainbow, right over the top of the church. Was that a promise?

Daniel Ortega was a simple person. He didn't dress up with a three-piece suit and tie. He wore jeans. Apparently he didn't have a bodyguard. If he did, it wouldn't have done him much good, because he arrived on the back of a flatbed truck. He had no reservations about mixing with the people—just pushed his way with his truck through that enormous crowd inch by inch by inch and the people surging around, surging around. They rushed up to get pictures of him holding their babies. As he spoke, the crowd lunged toward the truck. Marion Kinney, who came with me on this trip, almost got trampled. It was kind of scary there for a minute.

I stood four hours in the boiling sun at that big rally. I got so tired that I just sat down in the dirt with all those feet—other people sat down, too. Vendors of food and soft drinks pushed their way through the crowd, their baskets on top of their heads. A young teenager came up and gave me a baseball cap with Daniel's picture on it. I gave it to my grandson, Pete, when I got home.

My interest in Nicaragua began six years earlier, in 1984, when I was dragged kicking and screaming to the University of Washington to hear a panel[3] of people who had spent a couple of years there. One of them was a silvaculturalist who told us how the new government had stopped all logging in the tropical rain forests and set them aside as national parks. I learned that efforts to restore the pine forests were handicapped by right-wing antigovernment snipers murdering the field workers. Their refor-estation methods read like a Sierra Club management plan, idealistic and seldom used in the United States. Another speaker, an entomologist and adviser to the Nicaraguan government, discussed the poisonous pesticides sold to Third World countries by chemical corporations, which have been prohibited from marketing them at home. Finally, the author Nick Allen[4] told us how Nicaraguan farmers use trapping and other biological alter-natives instead of pesticides. According to these people who had been there, Nicaragua was doing exactly what we're trying to get this bloody coun-try to do. I was impressed, so I signed a mailing list. Then everything about Nicaragua started showing up in my mail.

That's how I got an invitation for an environmentalist tour of Nica-ragua in 1985. It intrigued me for two reasons—one, to go to Nicaragua and see all these wonders for myself, and, two, to go with Dave Brower.[5] His organization, Earth Island Institute, made the arrangements for the trip.

I met Dave Brower during a break at a conference in Seattle. I heard him say, "They always have beer and wine at these things, which I loathe. What I'd like is a martini." I said, "If that's what you want, come with me." I led him out of the building and across the street to a bar for the first of many martinis that I shared with Dave Brower. Naturally, I thought a trip to Nicaragua with Dave Brower would be fun. Besides, I have my savings salted away especially for trips, and trips only. There were eight of us, guests of the Association of Biologists and Ecologists of Nicaragua [ABEN].[6]

It was a grueling itinerary. You got up at the crack of dawn, and didn't get to bed till who knows what time. I was the only one who didn't get diarrhea, and I drank everything, too—I'm not careful. I've never got-ten sick—not in Mexico, nor in crazy places camping all the way down

Baja, nor in Costa Rica. It was a group of twenty-two people in Costa Rica, and I was the only one who didn't get sick. I think it's because I drink so much beer.

Diarrhea was one of the things that killed little children in Nicaragua. Now the children are better fed. Before the revolution, all the fields were planted in export crops—tobacco, coffee, bananas—because that's where the profits were. When the dictator, Anastasio Somoza, took off, he left two million acres of the finest arable land. The government appropriated his land and that of his friends and associates. They made state farms out of some of it, and they distributed the rest in small farm holdings to thirty thousand landless peasants. That's the kind of land reform that has to be done throughout all of Latin America. The former landowners were all over here in Miami, drooling to get their land back, but the government gave the new owners legal title. The peasants converted the land to corn, beans, fruit, and rice. That made food available to a lot of people, and the children showed it. None were begging on the streets, which says something to anyone who's been to Latin America.

Before the revolution, the peasants, who had been running up and down the rows of the big plantations like machines, didn't know how to farm. The new government set up farmers' schools to teach them. We visited one that was using methane gas generated from a sewage treatment plant to run turbines. These in turn produced energy for electricity and small machines. The farmers were to go home to their villages and introduce these simple techniques, solving the sewage problem and producing energy at the same time. France and other European nations had donated models for the manufacture of farm machinery, such as seeders, cultivators, and hand plows—all painted bright red and blue. Where do you suppose these farmers got all the metal for new production? Scrap iron. Nothing was wasted. A windmill, gleaming in the sunlight with its yellow paint, was made of scrap iron, and the large wheel to which the blades were attached was a used automobile tire rim. They had no money for nuclear plants. They didn't have coal or oil, so they were forced to use alternate forms of energy—wind, solar, and small hydros on creeks, which didn't do a lot of damage by inundating thousands and thousands of acres.

A small reservoir would be created, but it didn't preclude the fish from feeding and spawning. These little dams furnished enough electricity for a farm village to run its equipment.

I visited a government dairy farm. They grew their own fodder. They used organic fertilizer, naturally, from all the cows right there. They never used chemical pesticides, just rotated the crop to disturb the pests, or let the land lie fallow for a couple of years—all the modern methods.

Our bus took us all over the country. We saw intelligent reforestation—not huge tree plantations like Weyerhaeuser's, with row after row of Douglas fir, but diversified forests. They were saving the soil with windbreaks—eucalyptus and other kinds of trees planted in five rows. But the war against the Contras took forty percent of their budget, so most of these efforts were crippled.

All of the conservation methods I saw in Nicaragua are common knowledge—methods we have been trying to get our government to put into effect, with little success, and that was the difference. When I got there, I felt for the first time in my life that I was in a country with a government that had the interest of the ordinary people in mind and not just the corporations who want two cars in every garage and pressure to buy a third. In Nicaragua, they actually took the land into account.

We were invited to speak on UN World Environment Day as honored guests of students at the National University in Managua. I told the students to speak in short sentences, and with our good interpreters I felt I was really talking to them. In my speech I said that the U.S. government was based on a revolution two hundred years ago, when we threw off the British. In the course of that revolution, we lost almost every battle, but we won the war. I said that they had a similar problem. Maybe they would lose quite a few battles, but they, too, would win the war. Boy, did that ever get applause! Then I said that one thing I admired about their country was their beautiful trees, which they had because of their long rainy season—it takes a lot of rain to make such beautiful trees. I told them that where I came from we, too, had lots of rain and beautiful trees, and everybody who's born up there in the Northwest of the U.S.A. has webbed feet, like a duck. And I put my hands up, fingers spread out, to illustrate. So we laughed together about that. The students told me, "We place our confidence in the judgment of the great majority of the United States people," and urged us to spread information about Nicaragua to our people when we returned.

It was a most profound experience. I came home with a mission. I had stacks of mail, but I started lining up speeches right away. I always closed my speeches with the hope that the strong confidence the Nicaraguan students expressed in the good judgment of the American people was not misplaced.

"WHEREAS, ALAS, WE DEPLORE . . ."

I suppose it was all those speeches that got me an invitation from the Association of Biologists and Ecologists of Nicaragua to attend as U.S. observer the Primera Conferencia Centroamericana de Acción Ambiental, the First Central American Conference on Environmental Action, in May 1987 in Managua. It was sponsored by the Environmental Project on Central America, UNESCO [United Nations Educational, Scientific, and Cultural Organizations], the ministry of the interior of Holland, the Royal Norwegian Ministry of Development, and other international bodies. Guatemala, Honduras, Costa Rica, Nicaragua, El Salvador, and Panama, as well as Mexico, sent a total of a hundred and eighty delegates, at a time when all those governments except for Nicaragua were under the thumb of the United States.

I called Global Tomorrow, a prestigious coalition of the big environmental organizations in Washington, D.C., and offered to represent them officially, so I had their letter and off I went on my second visit to Nicaragua. I didn't know one word of Spanish, and I had to go through customs and immigration twice each time, going and coming. The way you do it, if you can't speak Spanish, is to look pathetic. They just rush you right through to save time—never even look at your baggage.

At the conference, I found out about the environmental problems in all of Central America. The region's history of unequal resource distribution has brought on widespread poverty and environmental destruction, problems that have led to social upheavals in recent decades. Central

America's position as an isthmus, separating two oceans and joining two continents, guards wilderness treasures as yet unknown to science as a result of the union of flora and fauna from both land masses. We learned that Central America's rain forests are being destroyed at the rate of four thousand square kilometers each year, resulting in the loss of genetic and cultural diversity. Pesticide contamination is a serious ecological and health problem for all of the countries, as well as for the United States, since Central American agricultural products contaminated with pesticides such as DDT are returned to U.S. consumers. Pressure from the conference contributed to Nicaraguan President Ortega's decision in June 1987 to halt logging of thirty-two hundred square kilometers of virgin tropical rain forest at the border with Costa Rica.

It was stressed at the conference that military conflicts have diverted funds from environmental programs. It was a time when most Central American countries had dictators—shooting people in the street whenever they popped up. Several representatives to the conference said they didn't feel safe going home.

We had interpreters. They weren't professional, but I got a pretty good idea of what was going on. I looked at the program, and to my horror there wasn't one woman moderator, just a couple on a panel toward the end. I was pretty outraged. I'm no feminist, but I am very quick to resent discrimination when it happens to me personally, or to the next-door neighbor. Here they had these marvelous women, many of them scientists, and not one of them was speaking.

I got some of the women together and said, "We've got to turn this thing around. Let's cook up a resolution." I wrote it in English and one of them translated it into Spanish. Then I said, "Here's the game plan. First I'll go around and get some of the men to endorse the resolution. That will help get us on the program immediately. I'll read it in English to the conference, and María Luisa, you read it in Spanish." María Luisa Robleto, whom I knew from my first trip, was the head of Movimiento Ambiente Nicaragua, the environmental movement in Nicaragua. She would only do it if I first explained that I'd asked her to. Otherwise, she said, it would look like she was pushing herself forward. I went around and tapped various guys for their signature. Every one of them said, "I think that's great. Wish I'd thought of it." I knew then that they weren't mean—they had just overlooked the women. It's customary to overlook women. With all these signatures collected ahead, the resolution would pass with flying colors. María Luisa and I approached the fellow in charge of the program with our request to address the conference right at the end of the current session. What could he do, say no? It was so much fun.

At the very next break in the sessions, I was introduced at the podium as the U.S. observer and I read our resolution to the one hundred and eighty delegates and twenty international observers. My first "whereas" buttered them up—commended them on the wonderful program, the breadth of the speakers—and congratulated them for having attracted so many talented women delegates. I read it with feeling, feigning solemnity, frowning in fake seriousness, so that it was funny.

Then I lowered the boom on them: "Whereas, alas, we deplore"—and that started them laughing—"that there are no women speakers or monitors in the whole program. . . ." Then I gave them the final "whereas"— "that with any big conference, all of the nitty-gritty work is done by women and this one is no exception." The "therefores" read that we would like the women, who did so much of the work to make this conference a success, to be publicly named and acknowledged at the end, and that in future conferences there be women speakers and monitors.

I was grinning by that time and the audience was all laughing. I said that I had asked María Luisa to read the resolution in Spanish. She got up, a little scared, and read it dead seriously, just like Moses coming down from Mount Sinai with the Ten Commandments, which was a contrast to my mock pomposity—very funny in itself. I got back to the podium, and with the same big grin I said, "All in favor, say *sí*," a mixture of Spanish and English. With a roar of laughter, they said *sí*. And I said, "Na, na, na, no—*sí!*" And I cupped my hand to my ear. So they screamed, "*Sí*," and the roof almost fell in. I said "Oposición? No oposición. Resolución pass. Adiós." And I got down off the platform. I wouldn't let them vote against it—that's democracy in action! We sent the resolution around for the delegates' signatures. All one hundred and eighty signed. I ran this resolution over a bunch of macho people like a steamroller. After that, everybody knew me. All one hundred and eighty must have come up to me in the breaks between sessions.

I didn't expect the results to be quite so astonishing. The next day, they struck one of the monitors off the program, and who was put in his place but María Luisa. At the end of the conference, they had all the women stand up and be counted—who did this, who did that. Furthermore, in the resolutions, which were all on environmental issues, they included a special one on the role of women. Then they gave me an award for my work on behalf of women. And I've never even belonged to a women's organization! It's just incidental. But when I see something in front of my nose, I will stop whatever I'm doing and try to take care of it.[7]

After the conference, I went with the other U.S. observer, Dr. Bert Pfeiffer, to help deliver medical supplies to a hospital in Rivas, about sixty miles outside of Managua. The day I got back home, I made a speech to the 43rd District Democrats about Nicaragua, but it took me a week to get through the stack of mail on my kitchen table.

MY FIVE-MINUTE SPEECH

*N*ext I was invited as a delegate to the Fourth Biennial Congress on the Fate and Hope of the Earth, set for the spring of 1989 in Managua. The first two of these biennial congresses were held in the United States, the third in Canada, and this fourth one in Nicaragua. I think holding it there was symbolic—a shift in perspective to a very controversial nation of the Third World. The Association of Biologists and Ecologists of Nicaragua was expecting five hundred people; two thousand showed up, representing sixty-seven nations. It gave the Nicaraguans a tremendous boost that their tiny little nation would attract all those people and from so many countries.

I added a little plus to it by putting the squeeze on the National Audubon Society to appoint me their official delegate. I was the only official representative from an environmental organization in the United States.

The Sierra Club, Greenpeace, Friends of the Earth, and other groups all thought it was too controversial. I was to report back to the National Audubon Society with suggestions for how it could help the environmental program of Nicaragua.

I decided to enroll in Spanish classes at Seattle Central Community College so I could participate in the conference, but I couldn't find time to study. So I arrived in Managua two weeks ahead of time, in March 1989, to go to Spanish language school. María Luisa Robleto invited me to live with her family in the barrio.

My community college Spanish, you see, just wouldn't come in the right places. On my way to Managua, for example, I had to spend a night in Mexico City. When I got to the hotel, the concierge let me in my room, turned on all the lights, and disappeared. Well, okay, I'm fine. I took a shower and did all the things that I wanted to do. When I was ready to turn the lights out, I spent twenty minutes going over every inch of that room looking for a switch. I even got up on the writing desk to see if there was some gimmick up there in the ceiling, but those two bright lights were caged in heavy wire. I couldn't possibly call the office. I knew how to say "light" but not "turn off." I had to leave the damn things on all night, blaring down on me.

In Managua, I studied intensely from 9 A.M. to 1 P.M., but my teacher and I had an awful time getting ideas across to each other, searching in *diccionarios,* just laughing and having a good time. After lunch we went on field trips to cattle ranches, farms, and beaches. One time we attended a ribbon-cutting ceremony at a women's center opening in Metagalpa, a fairly good-sized town about a couple hours' drive from Managua. The ceremony was performed by Doris Tijerino, one of the great national heroines, a guerrilla fighter who was captured before the revolution, imprisoned, tortured, and raped. When she was released, she was pregnant. They were willing for her to have an abortion, but she said, "No, I won't kill the child. The child is innocent." Now he was fifteen years old, her pride and joy. Doris was head of the national police. I ran into women in very high places in Nicaragua. Imagine a woman as the head of the FBI or the CIA—this is what's coming for us. When I was introduced to her—the Nicaraguans are very affectionate—she leaned over and kissed me on the cheek. I said, "Well, this is the first time I have ever been kissed by a cop."

The local conference organizers, María Luisa Robleto and Juan José Monteil, president of ABEN, were desperate to get the Fourth Biennial Congress on the Fate and Hope of the Earth into the media. Because of my age and my history in Nicaragua, and because I was staying at the home of María Luisa, I was real handy—they exploited me shamelessly. I talked over the radio, and they arranged two television appearances, one on Mother's Day, during which a pop star sang a special Mother's Day song dedicated to me—mother of my one child. The newspaper known as *La Barracada* interviewed me and put my picture on the front page. The article said, more or less, "Here's Hazel Wolf, young at ninety-one. Her fight to save the earth began with the birds." Any publicity for the conference mentioned Dave Brower, known there as the head of the environmental movement of the United States, and Hazel Wolf. You'd think we were the only two people attending.

There were about a hundred and twenty-five from U.S. peace and environmental groups, and many more hundreds from all over the world. I was surprised at the number of NGOs [nongovernmental organizations] that had been organized by indigenous people representing ancient cultures. But, alas, there were no coalitions. I tried to organize one at the hotel. Only about thirty-five people turned up. We suggested that the organizers of the next conference build into the program time for representatives from different nations to get together and find their common issues. The [fourth biennial] congress proposed setting up several global institutions—for example, an international economic order, which would allow Third World countries access to the economic, scientific, and technical means for development. Another was a world environmental tribunal that would enact laws prohibiting environmentally damaging practices and hold those who caused ecological damage responsible. In addition, the congress called on the United States to cease threats, hostile acts, and coercive economic measures against Nicaragua.

Women were well represented as speakers, as moderators, and in all the important places. You know, it's old hat here—everyone is raising the question of women—but when I raised it in Latin America, it had a much greater significance. Much of the workforce in those agricultural countries is women, and they are discriminated against terribly. They kept mentioning it throughout the conference. A lot of the women at the conference were from Africa, and they are really militant, those African women, so beautiful and strong. They wear earrings and little braids in their hair. There I was with my pale skin, but I hung out with them. We weren't on a first-name basis because I couldn't pronounce their names.

Just before the conference began, María Luisa Robleto told me that they would like me to make a little speech, but she was vague about when I was to make it and what it was to be about. Five minutes, she said. I think José Monteil, who planned the sessions, began to feel that I was an asset that he had overlooked—that maybe I should have been on the printed program, although they never did get the final program out.

I was trying to write the damn speech by hand, filling up pages and getting nowhere. I couldn't look at them to get them in order. I've lived my whole life by a typewriter—never looked at the keys. I was determined to wind it up in Spanish. I wrote the Spanish part, but I knew it was haywire, so I took it to the school, got the grammar all straightened out. About two days into the conference, I still didn't have my speech in order and they might have called on me at any time. I had to have a typewriter.

That afternoon I was wandering around our meeting place, the Centro de Convenciones Olaf Palme—a huge and beautiful conference center donated by the government of Sweden—looking bewildered, when a woman came up to me and said, "Can I help you?" She spoke English! I said, "I'm desperately in need of a typewriter." "Come with me," she said. Well, who do you suppose she was? María DeSoto, the director of the conference center, and the sister of Miguel DeSoto, the foreign minister of Nicaragua. That's how I got into those august hands.

She was just snap, snap, snap—took me into her office, had them bring me coffee, and then led me to a typewriter. It was real high-tech and I had difficulty with it. Nevertheless, I fixed my speech somewhat so that I could read it. I brought it back to María DeSoto and practiced reading it to her. And at the end she said, "That gives me chicken pimples." I said, "No, goose bumps." She said, "No, chicken pimples!" I had written "on the tenth anniversary of the revolution," and she inserted a correction—"on the tenth anniversary of the triumph of the revolution." Then she said, "This is untidy-looking. Let me have it retyped for you. I hope you don't mind if we put it on our letterhead, because we'd like to have a copy signed by you for our archives." She disappeared with my precious speech. I thought, "Gee, maybe I've got some kind of dynamite here."

Now I felt real good. They could call on me any time. Well, nothing happened. I had it in my briefcase every day. Friday was the last day. The whole thing ended at around five o'clock, but at a closing ceremony that evening, no less than President Ortega was coming to make a major address. I felt pretty miserable, so after dinner I went to a bar with a friend and had a rum and Coca-Cola.

When we arrived at the assembly, the place was packed and I couldn't find an empty seat except in the two front rows, where ribbons reserved the seats for the embassy people. In the second row was an empty seat near the aisle. I got under the ribbon and sat there. A young usher came over to me and grumbled in Spanish to get me to leave. I came back at him with the most atrocious Spanish that I could muster—pronounced my H's, put the accent on the wrong syllables—and it went something like this: "Habla no espanyol, me diplomat." Three times he grumbled at me, and three times I put on the same little act. He saw that he had only two options. One was to leave this stubborn, ignorant, stupid old lady where she was, and the other was to pick her up bodily and carry her out screaming. Just then I saw María DeSoto. I whoo-whooed at her and she waved back, so she knew where I was.

Safely in my seat, I chatted for a little while with the ambassador from Norway on my left and the ambassador from Sweden on my right. Then I said, "Could you point out for me the delegation from the United States?" I knew very well there wasn't one.[8] We all started to laugh. "You won't find them here," they said. I said, "Wasn't one of them kicked out, a real wicked person tied up with the CIA?" Then they knew how I stood, and to my amazement they started in telling me what they thought of the American government's policy on Nicaragua.

The next thing I knew, Daniel came in from the back—everybody calls him Daniel—and walked down to the stage. The people all left their seats and went dashing down the aisles after him. You couldn't see him, there were so many cameras taking pictures.

When that was over, I heard them say "Hazel Wolf." I thought, "Did I hear right?" I couldn't believe it and I just stayed in my seat.

María DeSoto came running up. "Hazel, they're calling you!"

I got out of my seat, clutching my little bag with my speech in it. I passed Ortega, bowed and smiled at him, and climbed up on the stage. I put my hands on the podium, and I looked down on those two thousand people, and I never felt calmer in my whole life. I felt like they were one person, and they were all my friends—you know, I was speaking to one big person. I very meticulously took out my speech and started reading it.

President Ortega, and other friends: It has been a great honor to be here and to represent the National Audubon Society of the United States, an organization of over half a million members devoted to education and environmental protection. Founded in 1906 with the sole purpose of saving an endangered species of bird, the snowy egret, from being hunted to extinction for its beautiful breeding-season feathers, it has since broadened its interest to include all aspects of environmental preservation. We carry out our objectives through education, research, and political action to influence government policy at all levels. We work from the grassroots base of more than five hundred autonomous community organizations. Almost all work is done by volunteers.

This next paragraph I copied word for word out of the letter appointing me as representative of the National Audubon Society.

While the National Society has taken no stated position on the war in Central America, it does support a change in the United States' definition of national security to include an emphasis on environmental security and supports a $600 million shift in foreign-aid funding from military assistance to development assistance, particularly in the area of sustainable agriculture, conservation of energy, and protection of natural resources.

That's where the first applause came—when I read the official position, which I think is pretty wimpish. I read on.

I have been requested by my organization to learn at this Fourth Biennial Congress on the Fate and Hope of the Earth what U.S. citizens can do to promote peace and environmental security. I have learned from this congress that we should demand of our government that it should cease giving aid to the Contras, . . .

Big applause.

. . . to military dictators of Central America, and to other oppressive governments throughout the world, that aid should be restricted to projects of benefit to the people and to the environment.

More big applause.

I believe the majority of the people of the United States will understand the wisdom of such a change in U.S. foreign policy if they are acquainted with the realities revealed at this congress and will work together with indigenous people and the nongovernmental organizations of the Third World and the technically developed world.

More applause.

I believe that women of all countries should demand and receive justice and equal rights in order to add their voices to the struggle for the rights of all people for a safe environment and for peace, because without their participation it can't be done.

Lots of applause for this reference to women—I had to wait until they simmered down. Then I ended it.

This is the message I hope to carry to my homeland to the best of my ability. Since my visits to Nicaragua in 1985 and 1987, I've learned to speak a little Spanish. Therefore, . . .

And I read in Spanish.

. . . saludo al pueblo de Nicaragua, y agradezco su hospitalidad.

"I greet the people of Nicaragua, and I am grateful for their hospitality."

Con la celebración del décimo aniversario del triunfo de la revolución, estoy convencida que el pueblo seguirá adelante para alcanzar la paz y una mejor vida porque . . .

"With the celebration of the tenth anniversary of the triumph of the revolution, I am convinced that the people will go forward to achieve peace and a better life because . . ." Then I used that famous Latin American slogan, quickening my speed and giving it the rhythm they give it.

. . . el pueblo unido jamás será vencido.

"The people united will never be defeated."

That phrase—it's historic. From me, it was secondhand. I've never been in a revolution, never had anyone in my family killed. But people in the audience knew what it meant to fight the Contras, to suffer the loss of seventy thousand people. So when I came out with this Latin American slogan, they went out of their minds. I was amazed. The president jumped up, everyone stood up, and they clapped and clapped and clapped. And that just practically destroyed me. I thought I better get down off the podium and go back to my seat.

Then Daniel made his speech—it was an hour and a quarter long. Very interesting. After he finished, the people mobbed him again. María DeSoto dragged me through the crowd to meet him. He said something nice about my speech, and I said, "I think my speech was better than yours." He said, "Yeah?" I said, "Yeah! Mine was *corto*." That's when he embraced me. Then everybody was taking pictures. The African delegates got me and him in the middle and his arm around all of us. So Robert Redford is out the window. I've dumped him and taken on Daniel instead.

The next day, the conference was televised—it went on all day long—and the two things that they featured were Ortega's speech and the Spanish part of my speech. Every place I went for the next few days—"Ah, I saw you on television." One of the delegates told me that he got in a cab with his conference badge on, and the cab driver said, "Oh, you're from that congress. That old woman from the United States—when she got up and said, 'The people united will never be defeated,' that lifted me up, that lifted me up."

And that was the significance to that poor little bedraggled nation that was struggling for independence against overwhelming odds. To have two thousand people from all over the world, sixty-seven nations, hold their conference in Nicaragua—it was a real morale boost to those people. I heard that over and over again. My little speech defying my own government in public contributed to it. That's the story.

The tumult and the shouting dies; / The Captains and the Kings depart.[9]

I always think of that after a big conference.

When I got back, I was far from well. I got diarrhea, which I'd never gotten before in Latin America, and an awful cold. And I had two stacks of mail, each a foot high, and I spent three days just throwing away what I wasn't going to read.

THE 1990 ELECTIONS

I was thoroughly involved now with Nicaragua—my second country. I would have liked to stay there, but I didn't speak the language. I was of no use to them. I could do my best service to Nicaragua right here in my own country. I had the Kiwanis Club and a Presbyterian church all lined up for speeches even before I left for Nicaragua. I spoke to a bunch of hard-core Republicans up in Bothell, and I wasn't going to make my joke about Dan Quayle,[10] but I did. Why should I pull punches for those guys? Afterward, they came up to me and said they felt they were hearing the other side for the first time. They just couldn't imagine that I would stand up there with all my white hair and tell them lies.

I was very much concerned with the 1990 Nicaraguan elections because I knew that the Bush administration, under the false assumption that money can do anything, was pouring millions into the parties opposing the revolutionary Sandinistas. If the Sandinista Party won, the United States would say that the election was fraudulent, so I wanted to observe the electoral process before, during, and after the election. Then I could come back and tell the truth I'd gained through my own experience in an area where there was a lot of misinformation—a small thing that I could do.

The Sandinista government knew that the elections were going to be fair, so they welcomed people from all over to come and see. There was a team from the Central American countries, the OAS [Organization of American States]. Jimmy Carter took a delegation. The United Nations had a team. In order to become an official election observer, you had to get an okay from the Supreme Electoral Council of Nicaragua, which Carter and the others had received. I wasn't part of all that. I decided to just enroll in the Spanish-language school in Managua at the time of the elections.

Meanwhile, at 8:00 every morning I went to Spanish class at Seattle Central Community College. I could say almost anything I wanted to in my own way with my limited vocabulary, but I hadn't yet studied the future or the past tense. The reporters on the college newspaper, the *City Collegian,* found out I was enrolled, interviewed me, and put the article on the front page with a picture. I was really in now with the *City Collegian.* When I told them I was going to Nicaragua to observe the elections, they wanted me to get a press card and fax dispatches back to them at the college so they could scoop the *Seattle P.-I.* [*Post-Intelligencer*] and the *Seattle Times.* I enrolled in Journalism 104, attended one class, wrote a few more articles—all proof that I was on the staff of the *City Collegian*—and I got my press card. Now if Jimmy Carter had a press conference, I could go to it, or any press conference held anyplace. Also, I would have access to polling stations. Then I heard that the Supreme Electoral Council of Nicaragua had designated the students in the Spanish-language school I would be attending as official election observers. Sooner or later, I do the things I think about doing.

When Marion Kinney and I left Seattle in February 1990, we had an extra suitcase and a huge carton filled with medical supplies for the Rivia Hospital and the women's clinic on the outskirts of Managua. In my suitcase I had all kinds of little gifts and packages—beans for this person, packets of spices for that one, and letters I was supposed to deliver. On the way, we spent the night in Mexico City with my friend Homero Aridjis, a poet and quite a famous one.[11] He had asked me to bring him some canned smoked salmon, a certain brand obtainable only in Ballard, the Scandinavian neighborhood in Seattle, and he paid me back with two big bottles of tequila. My suitcase was crammed full.

When we arrived in Managua, there were campaign rallies all over. I managed to get on television, dancing in the streets at one of the rallies. I think they chose me because of my white hair. They don't have many old people in Nicaragua. They die young. Over half of the people are under fifteen. Sixteen-year-olds can vote. The Sandinista Party also featured me in a front-page write-up in *La Barracada*. After a few days I wrote a dispatch for the *City Collegian*, faxed it to them, and they published it—on-the-spot reporting. Fortunately, I didn't say what I thought the outcome of the election would be. Everybody thought that the Sandinistas were going to win, including UNO, the United Nicaraguan Opposition. We drove out in the countryside the day before the final rally in the church plaza. A ragtag bunch of people, about two hundred *campesinos*, came marching down the highway. We got off the road to let them go by. I got out of the van and waved my scarf—red and black, the Sandinistas' colors. The marchers raised their hands with fingers outspread to indicate five. This gesture was a Sandinista symbol, as five was the number the Sandinistas had been assigned on the ballot. Coming from Estelí, about a hundred miles from Managua, they were all war veterans and war victims, in wheelchairs and on crutches and with people pushing them in carts. They had made one overnight stop and had one more before they'd get to Managua for the rally the next day. Marching in that brilliant sun, having such a good time.

On election day, we observers from the school started out in a bus very early, but people were already lined up for blocks. At first I thought they should have more polling booths. Later I learned that over ninety percent of the people voted. Now, in my 43rd District Democratic precinct, I have three hundred and fifty people and if they all came out to vote they would be lined up around the blocks, too. Instead, on elections they trickle in all day long, with less than fifty percent voting. We really don't have democratic elections in this country. It's a facade.

At the first voting booth, I went up to the window and took a picture. I was armed with my international press credentials hanging on a long pink ribbon around my neck. Also around my neck was an official observer's card, a little wood panel, so I could go into the voting booth. Each party had a number. The UNO coalition was number one, the Sandinistas were number five, and there were several other parties, each with a number, among them the Communists—quite distinct from the Sandinistas, by the way. The people just marked an X by the number. That's how they voted. To keep people from voting twice, they had to stick their thumb in ink that wouldn't come off for seventy-two hours. On election days, everybody in Nicaragua has a blue thumb.

We must have stopped at twenty places. The people were patient and serious, not like at the rallies where we had such great fun. When the results were in, I tell you, everybody was just stricken with grief. People were crying. That night I brought out the bottles of tequila. You would have thought that people from UNO, the coalition, would have been dancing in the streets, but there wasn't a peep out of them, either.

The next day, the Sandinistas held a spontaneous rally, even more fun than the first one. The only organizing for this one consisted of announcements over the radio and the television. We were all laughing, playing games, having a good time. Five or six fellows would get their arms around each other and make a circle. Then people climbed up on top of them and made a circle of arms, and then some more climbed up, and finally there would be one at the top who waved the flag. The crowd cheered throughout. Half the time these mountains would all collapse. The crowd cheered at that, too. All this time, food was going around, everybody munching, singing songs. So spontaneous. I don't know what it was about. Maybe it was a victory for Daniel, for democracy, for the peaceful transition from one party to another.

After all that enthusiasm, why did the people vote against the Sandinistas? Unskilled workers, hungry, war weary, they knew that the United States had endorsed Violeta Chamorro[12] and had thrown millions into her campaign. The Pope had blessed her. They thought that if they voted for her, the United States would lift the embargo, UNO would disarm the Contras so that the men could come home to their communities, and the World Bank would give the new government a bunch of money to get their economy going. If they had voted for the Sandinistas, they might have faced an invasion, because they learned from Panama and Grenada that if the United States doesn't like a government, they just go in there and topple it.[13]

I flew home after the election. I had been in boiling heat for days, I had lost about five pounds, and I was really tired. Sure enough, it was raining when I got to Seattle and the kitchen table was covered with mail a foot high. I started opening letters and working on regaining those pounds.

LAST VISIT

*O*nce more, in 1994, I embarked for Nicaragua, this time as part of a five-woman delegation from St. Mark's Cathedral. I have strong ties there through my effort to raise funds for medical supplies for Nicaragua.[14] The purpose of my fifth trip was to deliver books, toys, clothing, medical supplies, and an infant respirator to Somoto, in the northwestern district, where a coalition of churches called NEHAP [Nicaraguan Episcopal Health Assistance Project] has a sister relationship with a whole parish. We took duffel bags full of medical supplies with us—antibiotics, bandages, and all kinds of medicines.

But the main reason I wanted to make one more trip to Nicaragua was to check on my friends and my "family"—María Luisa Robleto, her husband, and their children. They were strong Sandinistas and had all lost their jobs under the new UNO government. I found they had landed on their feet pretty well. A daughter, who was fired from the university, took over the management of the family farm in Estelí. A son, who was a medical doctor in the army, became employed at one of the hospitals. A friend, Lorenzo Cardenal, had been director of the national parks under the Sandinista government. An UNO person was appointed in his place. However, since Lorenzo was the only person who knew anything about managing parks, they kept him on as deputy director. He became so disillusioned with the way things were handled that he resigned and is now head of an environmental organization. María Luisa Robleto herself, formerly head of ABEN, the environmental movement in Nicaragua, left to attend the university at Santiago, Chile.

While I was in Managua, a transportation strike broke out. First the buses, then the taxis. Once the cabs joined, the strikers set up road blocks against private cars. These were broken up by the police, with several lives lost. It was uncomfortable to be confronted at intersections by soldiers with rifles, and to find them stationed all over the place. Our police in Seattle modestly keep their revolvers hidden, but these soldiers carried rifles in plain sight and looked so grim that you had the feeling they would blaze away at you just for being you.

In Somoto, I was supposed to take pictures of "our" machines, for the people at St. Mark's who'd raised the funds.[15] The hospital put out the red carpet. I took my pictures, then they took me into the intensive care ward to see the ninetieth-birthday-party respirator and take a picture of that. The hospital director and I were all dressed in white, with gloves and great gauzy covers over our shoes and over our heads. There were all the little babies in cribs. Most of them had diarrhea. While I was feeling sad about them, the director said, "You know, we need another infant respirator." I heard myself saying, "When I get back, you'll get one almost immediately."[16]

I was absolutely done in by the time I got home. Lost five pounds again, but I was the only one of the five who didn't get sick, despite the fact that

I drank water that was no doubt polluted, and ate fruit from roadside stands while everybody screamed at me. Before we left Seattle, I had submitted to one shot, for hepatitis, at a doctor's urging, but that was it. I don't like shots and pills, and apparently I have a pretty good immune system. As soon as I spent a few hours recycling the ninety percent junk in the mile-high stack of mail, I took off for Port Angeles, where I could just relax and work on regaining the lost pounds.

I learned on my last trip that Nicaragua was going downhill badly. Every month I get *La Barracada*, and it tells me all the sorrowful news. There's unemployment and inflation, and all the kinds of violence, homelessness, drugs, and drunkenness that go with them. And that's the job the United States did on Nicaragua.

19 / Global to Local: More Connections

WITH INDIGENOUS PEOPLES

One thing that improved under the UNO government of Nicaragua was the treatment of the indigenous peoples,[17] the Ramas and the Miskito, who live on the Atlantic Coast. The Sandinistas had at first forced them to be part of Nicaragua instead of recognizing their local autonomy, and so many of them joined the Contras. Later the Sandinistas recognized their mistake and established the right of indigenous people "to preserve and develop their cultural identity within the framework of national unity, to choose their own form of social organizations, and to administer local affairs in conformity with their traditions"—that's from the Nicaraguan constitution, which is still in place. So they finally got it straight that indigenous peoples have the right to live peacefully on their lands, without the threat of clear-cutting and irrigation farming.

Sarah James, from the Gwitch'n people in Alaska, is one of the indigenous people I met at the Fourth Biennial Conference. Her main battle is to keep gas and oil exploration out of the Arctic National Wildlife Refuge.[18] That's one of Audubon's main battles, too, so we started working together— phone calls back and forth, donations from Audubon to the Gwitch'n. I bring her case up all the time in my speeches on women and the global environmental movement, and I write letters to my congressmen.

I met Wangari Maathai[19] at a National Audubon convention, and we struck it off right away. I talk with her on the telephone from time to time. We both spoke in Orlando, Florida, at the national convention of the Junior League. Wangari heads the National Council of Women of Kenya and the Green Belt Movement. In the villages of Kenya, they had cut down the trees for firewood and the wells had dried up. Wangari launched a campaign to plant ten million trees, and most of those were planted by women. For that achievement she was awarded ten thousand dollars by the United Nations.

Wangari then organized women against a high-rise development in the middle of Nairobi's Uhuru Park. At a 1992 demonstration with poor, rural women, the police came and beat them up, beat Wangari into unconsciousness. From her hospital bed, Wangari continued the struggle. I found out about it from Amnesty International, so I phoned up the head of the Junior League and together we put on a big campaign, sent letters out to everybody with exactly whom they should write to. Wangari recovered enough to attend the 1992 Earth Summit in Rio, where she helped organize the women. But she still had to face a charge of treason when she returned to Kenya. Her international friends tried to persuade her not to go back, but no way—she was going back to fight the charge. She's a really strong woman. So her friends put on a campaign to raise money for a security guard for her. I sent a check. I'm only one among thousands, globally, who have stood by her. She figures prominently in my talks and letters.

I had an adventure with another indigenous group, the Lacandones of Mexico. The Lacandones are survivors of the once powerful Mayan people who have lived for centuries in an old-growth rain forest on the southern border of Mexico and Guatemala. They speak their own language and they live a simple life in the rain forest. The Mexican government, trying to solve the problems of its overpopulated cities, encouraged unemployed workers to migrate to the rain forest, cut the trees, and start farming. The Lacandones naturally were outraged. My friends, the Lummi Indians from up near Bellingham, wanted to bring some of the Lacandone people to the United States and expose the Mexican government's policy. I helped my friends Kurt Russell and Cha-das-ska-dum-which-ta-lum raise the money. Then I arranged to have the Lacandones on the agenda of the Audubon Society's national convention in Tucson, Arizona, where they would be able to talk to a thousand people from all over the United States.

After a lot of shenanigans trying to get the Lacandones out of the country without the Mexican authorities knowing why they were leaving, they arrived in Tucson, looked around, saw a few cactus, and said, "Who cut down all the trees?" They couldn't conceive of land without trees. When we told them water for the crops was pumped from underground wells, they didn't believe it.

A whole group of us, including two Lummis and two Lacandones, left the National Audubon convention early to visit the Hopis and some other tribes up in northern Arizona. We talked with the elders of the tribes and enlisted their support for the campaign against the Mexican government's policy. Then we came back to Seattle and held two big fund-raisers for them, one sponsored by Seattle Audubon. In the end, all of us—Lummis, Lacandones, and friends—trooped up to Forks, on the Olympic Peninsula, for a visit with the Quileutes, who brought out the red carpet—salmon roasting on sticks, and dances. The Lacandones and I danced with the rest of the Indians there, feet down flat and a rhythm. You have to practice it. You can't just walk on out there. Because of all the water and trees, the Lacandones felt right at home.[20]

The Quileutes took us out in a whaling canoe with eighteen paddlers. The [Quillayute] River comes down into the ocean there and makes a basin. I thought we'd paddle around it. Sitting up in the prow of the boat, I was looking back at paddlers, but in front of me sat a very important person with a special hat on. He set the pace. To my distress, the canoe slid right out of the estuary and into a narrow inlet, where waves were hitting the rocks and shooting spumes about a mile high—we were within inches of them! We were going out into the ocean, where the waves were huge and continuous. I held on rigidly, really scared. The head paddler leaned over to me and said, "Hazel, I won't let anything happen to you." I thought, "Of course not. They've been doing this for centuries. They're not going to take me out into the Pacific and dump me!" So I relaxed and enjoyed it.

WITH SEATTLE NEIGHBORHOODS

Nowadays the neighborhood includes the whole globe, plus the debris we left on the moon. Neighborhoods used to be held together by the children, I think. The adults were away working. The kids would get out and play in the streets. Through the kids, the adults were apt to get acquainted with each other. Nowadays they get together because of pollution. Nowadays acid rain falls gently from heaven on both the just and the unjust.

I came home from Nicaragua to my Capitol Hill neighborhood in central Seattle. I decided to work with poor and minority people, to engage them in the environmental movement.

The environmental movement consists of a particular segment of the population, almost a hundred percent white. It's isolated from the mainstream of working-class people. Class bias is in our roots. White, well-to-do Audubon people had nothing else for entertainment but to go looking at birds. Not an idea in their heads about threatened species until they went looking for the snowy egret, which was being hunted to extinction for the plumage in women's hats. The same with the Sierra Club. John Muir wanted to save wilderness for the young people who liked to hike— that is, white people with money enough to buy all that fancy equipment, go places. And it continued that way.

In general, environmentalists don't suffer from unemployment, prejudice, and poverty. The well-to-do mean to do well. They could chatter around and say all these things, but they're not impelled to do something about it, because it doesn't really hit their lives, whereas poverty was my life. But now they've got to feel it, because now we're all slowly losing life together through environmental degradation.

The environmental movement thinks it's big, but it isn't. We're a very small percentage of the population. Organized and committed as it is, the movement does not have enough political clout to put through the program of preserving the planet. We have to reach out to the rest of the community, especially people of color and poor people, to find out what their concerns are. It means getting together to see what we have in common.

I started with a friend of mine, Jesse Wineberry, an African American state representative from my district to the Washington State legislature, whose father was deacon of a church. I got Jesse, his father, and Rev. McKinney, minister of Mount Zion Baptist Church, the largest African American Baptist church in Seattle, to send out invitations on their letterhead to a breakfast meeting. Fifteen or twenty showed up for the breakfast, mostly African American men, friends of Rev. McKinney's, and my friends—the head of the Washington Environmental Council, the director of the Church Council of Greater Seattle, the president of Seattle Audubon, and a former president and longtime stalwart, Bob Grant. We figured that one of the things we had in common was Initiative 547, to stop the banks from redlining in the Central District, refusing to lend money to people of color, especially African Americans. We planned to promote Initiative 547 through ads in three black community newspapers.

We had another breakfast. A bunch of people came, but not the same people. Then we had a potluck dinner, and all kinds of different people came. All we did was have facilitators and flip charts and the process and the jargon—talk, talk, talk. I went through this more than once. The facilitator, not the president, runs the meetings. Everybody says something and it all goes up on a big sheet of paper. You turn it over, you fill another sheet, and then put them all up on the wall. At the end of the meeting, you gather them all down and roll them all up. I don't know what the hell they do with the flip charts after that. I told the people at the potluck I was sick and tired of all this talk, and I, for one, was leaving—now! That was the last I heard of that group.

So I made a different approach. Bob Grant and I asked Seattle Audubon to make us a committee of Seattle Audubon. Even though Audubon was still thinking exclusively about wildlife and wet spots, it very kindly supported us throughout the whole endeavor. Bob and I went to see people—Cheryl Chow and Martha Choe on the City Council, other prominent people in the Chinese community, the Filipino community, and the African American community. One on one—that's the way you do it. You'd be surprised at all the running around we did. I remember going to a school where a Japanese woman in the community was the principal. When we set up a steering committee, it was really multicultural.

This one jelled. We called it the Community Coalition for Environmental Justice [CCEJ], and we decided to have a conference to link the neighborhoods and the environmental movement, but the board was going to charge a twenty-five-dollar registration fee. I keep quiet most of the time, but when something like that comes up, I really go after it. I just kept pounding at them. "Who do you want to come to this conference, a bunch of millionaires? Or do you want the people who are involved?" I said it over and over, and I finally won enough of them. I doubt that I'd have gone to the conference myself for that price.

More than two hundred people came to our conference—"What's Actually in Our Backyard?"[21]—on a Saturday in February 1994. A real mix—legislators, people from the neighborhoods, Native American friends of mine, and environmentalists. We presented the research on environmental degradation in poor neighborhoods. We had workshops to find out what would be of interest both to the people in the community and to the environmental movement. We had a session on the Duwamish River, which flows through the southern part of the city. The air and water there are polluted with industrial chemicals. The [mostly Southeast Asian] immigrants living along the river, who have no way of knowing, are eating fish riddled with chemicals. At the end of the conference, the Duwamish neighborhood was identified as one of the key places where we could work together.

CCEJ was just a steering committee for a conference. We had to find a structure, and that wasn't easy. You would see different people at every meeting. We changed presidents about five times. In and out they flowed, like liquid. The board consisted of three African Americans—president, vice president, and secretary. The treasurer was white. One Filipina, one

African American, and three whites were board members at large. Whites were in the minority and there was a lot of discussion about how to keep it that way. We didn't want to be overcome with whites. Nevertheless, the board kept getting whiter all the time. I remember one woman left in a huff, saying, "There aren't enough people of color here." So she took it upon herself to reduce their numbers by one more.

I was concerned about something else, too. There are a number of environmental justice coalitions in the United States, largely in Mississippi, Tennessee, Louisiana, North Carolina, and in the Southwest, and they originated with the people who are affected. Ours originated with Seattle Audubon and the people of color we recruited. We were all, people of color and whites, in the role of do-gooders, coming from our comfortable places to these uncomfortable places, telling these people they've been put upon and spurring them to action. It wouldn't work. I suggested that we set up a series of meetings at somebody's house in the Duwamish community and knock on doors and get the neighborhood to come, get the people involved in the organization. I suggested, also, that we look around to other parts of the city that have been kicked around and go into these areas and knock door to door.

Well! The board wasn't interested in discussing it. They were bogged down with facilitators, but I kept pounding. I made it my objective to get someone from the area whom I knew on the board. I made a motion that she be elected. A woman of color opposed me—she didn't believe in *Robert's Rules of Order*.[22] She believed in consensus, despite the fact that under consensus rule, if one person doesn't agree, then the organization can't do anything. I said, "You've got to take a vote. You can't let one person determine your policy." She stuck it out, and nobody backed me up. She'd been to the university, unfortunately, and learned a bunch of garbage about how to handle organizations—facilitator and flip sheets and the jargon that goes with it. She was full of it. It took from February to June to get a mission statement. I had cooked one up in five minutes when I made the application for the 501(c)(3) [federal nonprofit status] many months earlier.[23]

Here's how we got our 501(c)(3) tax-exempt status. I sent for all the forms, filled them all in, and filed them. Sometimes you just do it—let the chips fall where they want to fall. I did it because I knew that we would never get anywhere without one. Meanwhile, I got so fed up with this bunch that I quit.

They called a general membership meeting in my absence, and to my amazement, they elected new officers, people that I'd never heard of. I found out the name of the new president [an African American union activist], looked his number up in the phone book, and called him up.

"Are you Larry Montgomery, the president of the Community Coalition for Environmental Justice?" Yes, he was. I thought, "There is life in this damn organization yet. Let's get back in there."

Once I was voted onto the board, I heard the treasurer say she had no time for keeping the books. I'm a bookkeeper, so I did it for a while. I opened up a bank account in our name, put all the papers through. We got out a newsletter and some mailings. I guess that was progress, wasn't it?

Because I had gone over their heads and filed the 501(c)(3), one of the new board members made a direct attack on me. She called me all kinds of terrible things, including "undemocratic" and "racist." I just took it. I never said anything. The next time she appeared at a meeting, she was all smiles. She had had dinner with some of her friends, people who just adore me. She had mentioned Hazel Wolf, and they said, "Oh, that wonderful person. How lucky can you get?" So she stopped attacking me. She'd climbed on the bandwagon, you might say.

But by this time, the thing had jelled. I got one of my young friends to join the board. There were enough people for all the jobs, so I just drifted away into something else. I'm still a dues-paying member. I write articles for their newsletter, and I go to their conferences. The latest was on multicultural and environmental education. I liked it. Too bad they didn't have a facilitator to slow it down!

Years ago, during the Depression, when I was working for the Workers' Alliance, I wanted to fight the unjust rent policy for single women. But I had a comfortable place with friends. I never missed a meal, and I had a nice warm bed, even if it was only because of my friends' hospitality. In order to lead that struggle I had to move, move into a flea-bitten place downtown. I was fighting to get my rent among the people who were in the same boat I was in. Now I hear that CCEJ wants to raise funds to hire a community organizer, yet they never held meetings in the Duwamish neighborhood or brought those people onto the board.[24]

WITH PRISONERS

*W*hen she was in elementary school, Nydia had a goldfish bowl with one fish that went round and round, and round and round, twenty-four hours a day. I couldn't tolerate it. I filled the bathtub up and dumped the fish in. I wanted to give it a real treat. It went round and round, and round and round, in the same small circle. It had no concept of freedom! I guess it was free in its little bowl. I stuck it back in. I suppose if I'd left it in the bathtub long enough, it would have found out that this barrier wasn't there, but I had to take a bath.

I don't like anything prisoned up. I don't like zoos, pets tied up, things in cages. When I was a kid, I'd hear somebody had escaped from prison. I'd imagine that I'd get them food, hide them, fancy little daydreams like that. In those days, there were chain gangs that marched through town on their way to work on the roads. I would never look at them. I didn't want to embarrass them.

Freedom—it's human. It permeates all of life. Freedom of the tree to seek the sun.

I've kept up with quite a few prisoners. When I was working for John Caughlan, whenever he'd lose a case, his client would land in jail. If this client had no family, I'd go to see him. Glenn Williams, for example, the author of *From Alcatraz to the White House.*[25] He proves my theory about childhood daydreams. I wanted to be a doctor, cure people, and I ended up helping old people, the unemployed, and immigrants. Glenn Williams wanted to be a big-shot gangster like Al Capone. When he grew up, he just went and became a bank robber. He robbed twenty banks. He was an unruly prisoner, gave them a lot of trouble, and finally wound up at Alcatraz. There he had a change in his thinking, largely due to one of the guards and a priest. He was released from Alcatraz to finish his sentence at McNeil Island,[26] where he met my employer, John Caughlan, who was in prison in 1963 on the trumped-up charge of income tax evasion. When Glenn was finally released, he called on John, so I met him at the office.

Glenn started a little car-washing business in used-car lots in Seattle. He didn't have any money, just some brushes, buckets, and detergent. Business was good, and he needed some help. He was forbidden to hire released prisoners, but they went straight to the place. The word gets around in prisons. They tap on the walls and tell each other things. When they move from one prison to another, they take all the gossip with them, so everything is known by prisoners all over the United States—and the world, even—before the wardens hear about it. I was keeping Glenn's books for free, and I would spend part of my time getting phony social security cards for these guys. It was a weird Christmas party at Glenn's in 1972. We were all sitting around, I was making all these men laugh, and I was the only person there who wasn't an ex-prisoner!

Glenn was nominated for a Jefferson Award[27] and granted a full pardon, which meant he went back to Washington, D.C., for breakfast with President Reagan. I suggested to Glenn, "Why don't you write *From the White House to Alcatraz*? Get the whole bunch of them in there?"

Glenn is still around. We have lunch together every once in a while. I don't ask why my prison friends are in jail. If I did, I might go screaming out of the place. What if the record said, "Very fond of killing elderly people"? The less I know, the better. Dave, a Port Angeles person, is one who was up for murder. I barely knew him, but he was tried and convicted and sent to Walla Walla [site of a state prison], and the papers were full of it. You can't write to prisoners without their consent, but you can send Christmas cards, so I sent him one. He was so pleased—he didn't have a friend in the world. He wrote to me and gave the consent for me to write him. I visited him at Walla Walla.

Then there's the time I helped get Dave Beck[28] out of solitary confinement at McNeil. They'd thrown him in the hole, as they called it, for loaning money to another prisoner. I heard the story—I was part of the grapevine at that time—and told his lawyer, who raised such a fuss that they had to let Mr. Beck out of solitary.

Oddly enough, the prison doctor was a bird-watcher, so I went on his field trips all over McNeil Island. I met some famous prisoners there—Brownie[29] and some others.

I met Ed Browder years ago, when he wrote from NcNeil Island to the Seattle Audubon Society to invite us to an exhibit of the prisoners' art at the Tacoma Mall. He's an artist, and a lot of his paintings depict birds. The warden was permitting him to come over from McNeil Island Federal Penitentiary with the pictures. I called Helen Engle[30] and we went to the exhibit. Well, he wasn't there. The warden had changed his mind, and we had to settle for having lunch with a bank robber. I wrote to say I was sorry we had missed him. He wrote back, I wrote back, he wrote back—we've been corresponding for almost thirty years.

I could see why the warden had changed his mind. Ed faced a twenty-five-year sentence and had every reason to run away. Ed's crime was that he had signed for a loan for a business project. He put up some bonds as security to the bank. Well, that bank was robbed! The police recovered the bonds, which, it turned out, were part of a famous heist in Montreal, so they nabbed Ed and tried to get him to say where he got the bonds. He wasn't talking, for two reasons—he's not that kind of guy, and his life wouldn't have been worth a plugged nickel if he had. If there's anything prisoners hate, it's a squealer. They'd have got him in jail or out. So he didn't talk. The court gave him the big twenty-five-year sentence, thinking it would pry him loose, get him to talk. He still had nine years to go when I met him. For a couple of years, I visited him every six weeks. For Christmas 1991, Ed was in prison in New Mexico, so I sent him *From Alcatraz to the White House.* In his letters, though, he wasn't emotional. He didn't even write "Dear Hazel." It's only lately that he's been saying "Love" at the end—only lately.[31]

I helped Ed file a petition to spring him on time served. It didn't wash. Finally, the statute of limitations ran out on the heist, so I got Emmett Watson, the *Seattle Times* columnist, and all kinds of people to write to the parole officer, and he was out on parole.

The next thing I knew, he had jumped. His wife called me, crying. One of the teachers at McNeil got a call from Ed: "I'm in South America. I want you to know I'm safe, I'm not ever coming back, and give my love to Hazel." The teacher walked right over to the federal building in Seattle, turned on the computer, and up comes Ed! He's in jail in Texas! The dumb bunny. He had flown back to visit his wife. The FBI had picked him up and thrown him back in jail.

He wouldn't write to me first, not in a thousand years. He'd have been too embarrassed. So I wrote him: "Hi, Ed. What do you want me to do to spring you out of the slammer this time?" That broke the ice, and we resumed our correspondence. We've carried it on for a long time. I know a great deal about him—much more than his wife does, as a matter of fact. He was always going to be in trouble.[32]

He finally got out of there on parole, but I didn't hear from him for quite a while. Christmas came, and I didn't get a card. The phone line was disconnected. He wasn't a young man. I thought he had died. Finally, his son told me he was in a Mexican prison. Somebody had hired Ed to deliver a plane from the United States to Mexico and then teach the owner how to fly. On the way, Ed dropped down at Nogales for gas, where they picked him up, framed him for two hundred and fifty kilos of marijuana in the plane, and threw him in the slammer. He wouldn't confess, so they tortured him. Every once in a while the United States and Mexico have a housecleaning by exchanging prisoners, so Ed was exchanged, but he was in terrible condition. They had put electric prods on his genitals, he had to have operations on his ear, and there was a scar on his nose they didn't even bother with. He recovered pretty well.

I'm not too sure he was framed, but for sure he broke his parole. In 1992, Ed was free on parole again. This time he stuck with it. I've visited him a few times, and our correspondence covers quite a lot. We are really very close.[33]

WITH CHILDREN

I speak often with small children—kindergarteners, first and second graders. I can't take them out in the field—we're confined to the classroom—but I get them to relate to nature by telling them anecdotes about how animals eat and play and have fun, just like little human animals do.

First we talk about squirrels, how they gather nuts and then dig holes and hide them. "Oftentimes," I tell them, "the squirrels forget where they hide them." Then I say, "I do that all the time—forget where I put something every once in a while. Don't you?" Yes, they do. I say to the teacher, "Do you ever forget?" Sure. Then I say, "Okay, we're all a bunch of squirrels."

Next I play a trick on them. I tell them eagles have a tremendous wing-spread. If you stretched their wings and turned them sideways, they'd be taller than the tallest basketball player, but they eat hardly anything but dead fish. How disgusting. "Did any of you ever eat dead fish?" Of course not. "Let me have a show of hands of anybody who has eaten dead fish." Not a hand goes up. I say, "So you all eat live fish, do you?" Then they know that I've trapped them.

I tell them about the bushtits, the tiniest of birds, only three and a quarter inches long and a tail as long as its body. "They fly around in little groups, all landing on a bush or tree, eating the eggs of insects, then moving on. They keep in touch with each other by means of light, gentle notes. One day a group of bushtits was passing through where I lived. One struck a plate glass window and fell to the ground. I thought maybe it had just been knocked out, so I put it in a little box and left it in the sun to recover. The whole group of bushtits came back several times. They were looking for their lost companion. The fallen one finally came to, and the next time the group flew over, it joined them, and away they all went. It was clear to me that the group didn't want to leave the neighborhood until they had found their small friend."

I go on to tell the children about the animals I've met on my many trips, how I've seen young hawks chasing each other in the sky, round and round, and gulls just letting the wind take them on the air, not looking for food, just having fun. I tell them about the time I was out walking in the Washington Park Arboretum by a slough that had a very thin coat of ice with holes in it here and there. "A robin flew down, landed on the ice, slid up to a hole and flew up, then flew back down and did it again, five times. It wasn't looking for food. It was having fun sliding on the ice." I tell them, "All young things have fun."

My next anecdote comes from a wildlife refuge in California. "I saw mallard ducks and a red fox playing a game together. The mallards were feeding down by a pond. Up on a hill, a little mound nearby, was the fox. Now, animals are afraid of people, not automobiles, so I just stopped and stayed put inside my car and they didn't pay any attention to me." I illustrate with my hands: "The fox was up here, and the mallards were down there. He jumped down into the middle of them. They all flew up in a terrible flutter. He went back up to his mound. They all came quietly back to feeding by the pond. Several times this game went on. I had to conclude they were having fun. The mallards knew that the fox wasn't hungry, because if he had been, he'd have gotten one the first time he sprung into them, wouldn't he? So they knew he wasn't hungry, and it was fun."

I ask the class to help me with a problem. "I've never figured out how baby spiders have fun. But I bet they do." We all think for a moment. "Oh, I bet I know how they have fun! Spiderwebs are very fragile. Sometimes the webs probably break and hang down in threads. I bet the baby spiders hang on to the ends and use them like bungee cords, bouncing up and down. That's how they have fun." The kids are wild about that. They love that idea of swinging freely in the air.

They like to know that animals are very, very clever and can make things that people can't make. I tell them, "I don't believe any person could ever make a web like a spider, or a bird's nest made of mud, grass, feathers, and moss, all put together so the wind cannot blow it away or the rain get into it. And all they have to work with are their feet and beaks."

Once they have learned how wonderful the creatures are, I ask them to join me in protecting them. I say, "I don't think I would step on even the smallest bug or ant if I could help it, particularly when it wasn't going to bite me."

Sometimes I end my talk to elementary school children with a joke. "The mother was trying to get her son to get up and go to school, and he wouldn't get up. She called him several times. He still didn't get up. She said, 'Come on, now. You've got to get up and go to school.' He said, 'No, I'm not going to school anymore. The teachers hate me, the students hate

me, and they all treat me mean. I'm not going back to school anymore.'
'But son,' the mother said, 'remember, you're the principal.'" Here's the
joke I tell my eighth-graders: "What is dark brown, sweet, and very, very
dangerous?" Answer: "A shark-infested chocolate pudding." That cracks
the kids up, but the teachers just groan.

I like the questions kids ask me. "Do you still have your own teeth?"
"Have you got a boyfriend?" I tell them that I have most of my own teeth
and that I'm still looking for a boyfriend, but I can't find one that can
cook. I ask them to keep their eyes peeled for one that can cook because
they are hard to come by.

They don't lie awake at night thinking about it, but all young people
fear old age. They see old people and think, "That looks pretty bad," and
they know that sooner or later they're going to be that way. I sensed that
was on the minds of the thirty children who wrote me letters from Decatur,
Alabama. Their teacher, Emily Amberson, read about me in 1992 in *USA
Today* and set up the letter-writing project. I decided to fly thirty-five hundred miles to their school and personally answer their questions about
what it was like to be as old as I am.[34]

I said to them, "Now, some of you have asked me how it feels to be in
your nineties. I'll tell you how it feels. I feel like Hazel. I felt like Hazel in
my eighties. I felt like Hazel when I was fifty. As far back as I can remember, I've felt like Hazel. Now, don't you all feel like yourselves?" And they
all did. "Okay, so we all feel like ourselves, no matter where we are, or
what age. But there is a difference when you're ninety. When I was your
age, for beginners, I hated school. Every day in school was a pain in the
neck. All I wanted to do was play basketball, go swimming, climb mountains, slide down the other side, tear around madly in all directions. No
school for me. But there were some things I never wanted to do. One of
them was I never wanted to make a speech in front of a bunch of strangers.
Now I'm in my nineties. I don't want to play basketball. No way! I don't
want to climb mountains. I don't want to do any of those things. The one
thing I like to do is make speeches in front of a bunch of strangers, like I
am doing now. So you do what you want to do when you're fourteen,
and you do what you want to do when you're ninety. But whatever you
do, you've got to have fun."

Then they looked at me with a different eye. They were thinking, "Boy, she's doing what she wants to do. She's having a good time. It must be great to be ninety! It's something to look forward to."

ONE-LINERS

I travel all over the place to give speeches. I've been invited to Iowa, Illinois, Florida, Alabama, Minnesota, and California—to universities, schools, and all kinds of groups. I work on my speeches, polish them all up beforehand, and then read them. I don't stray off the subject, I don't leave out anything, and things are all in their logical order. There ought to be one good laugh on every page. It's only fair to your listeners to let them off the hook every minute or two.

I try to start each speech in a way that's relevant to the audience. When I spoke to the prisoners at Monroe State Reformatory, I gave them a talk that I love to do, "Great Women in My Life." But I had to get a laugh out of them to start with. So I told them about being kissed by a cop in Nicaragua. Those guys started to laugh, and they never stopped. When I came to the podium at the Association of Women Judges, they gave me a standing ovation. I started my speech by saying, "It's about time you stood up for me. Every time you came into a courtroom—and I've been in a good number of courtrooms in my life—I've had to stand up for you." That really got 'em.

When I was in Alabama [Decatur], on Sunday we went to church. I asked Emily Amberson what denomination it was. She said, "We're in the Bible Belt. We're Baptist." I said, "Soft-shell or hard-shell?" That cracked up all her friends who were standing by the church door. She said, "Some of our older people still go in for foot-washing. It's hard-shell."

A few years ago, I was asked to be one of the speakers at a press conference for the RTA, the Regional Transit Authority. It proposes to tax citizens for construction of light rail and bus lanes throughout the Puget Sound area. The opposition came up first, among whom was Norm Wynn, a very important person in the Mountaineers Club. He mentioned in his talk that he gives me rides all the time to meetings and hearings, his point being that he carpools or catches a bus, so there's no need for this Regional Transit Authority and their bonds. When my turn came to testify, I said that I was so sorry to see that Norm Wynn was on the other side of this issue, because now I knew I wouldn't get any rides, he'd be so mad at me. I'd probably have to get a skateboard. Everybody laughed at that. Cynthia Sullivan, a King County councilwoman, said, "Don't worry, Hazel, I'll give you a ride. Just call me up anytime." Then the press conference degenerated into personal comments back and forth. I never said anything of substance at all, just one-liners to get them laughing. I did say that if we keep going the way we are, more and more cars because of all this population coming in, we'll come to a screeching halt. They just can't sit and do nothing. The citizens have been thinking about RTA for some thirty years now, and it's time to put it into effect. But I didn't talk about details of the RTA, because I don't know them. When it was over, the King County Council crowded around me to tell me how funny I was. Now everyone was going to vote for the RTA because they'd remember laughing at my jokes—at least I hope that's the way it works.

My jokes do have something to do with my effectiveness as a political activist. They only rise when I'm there, in the situation. Something always tickles me, makes me giggle. Then I say it, and everybody giggles at it. Then I get in the newspaper.

This one makes me laugh every time I think about it. I went to a hearing on the cleanup of toxic wastes on the Hanford Nuclear Reservation. The people who work on the reservation, in south central Washington, were there testifying, protecting their jobs. After the hearing, some environmentalists cornered one of the Hanford employees. Our people were being really rude to him, and I didn't like that. So I went up to the group to break it up: "What are you guys talking about?" Then I turned to the Hanford employee in a friendly way and said, "You live near the Columbia River?"

"Yeah."

"There are a lot of birds in that area. Do you see many birds there?"

"Yes," he said. "There are a lot of birds. They poop all over my roof. I want to kill them all."

I said, "You know, if I were you, I would get down on my knees every night and thank God that cows don't fly."

That took care of that guy.

"AN ATHEIST FAVORABLY DISPOSED TOWARD RELIGION"

*I*n December 1996 I found myself in Walla Walla, at a Seventh Day Adventist college. The day started in an enormous church, a regular cathedral that held hundreds of people. I was kept out in a little anteroom with the president of the college, who was also the reverend who ran this Seventh Day Adventist church. As the organ got going, we marched in solemnly and took our seats, facing the audience. It was packed, not only with students but with people from the city, too, because they'd advertised it. The first thing on the program was a prelude. The second was another prelude. The third was a prayer. The fourth was Hymn no. 191, "Love Divine." Then a reading from Ecclesiastes, and Hymn no. 565. It ended with a benediction, and we were to be ushered out by a Felix Mendelssohn fugue.

Stuck in with all this holy stuff was "Address: Hazel Wolf: 'Great Women in My Life.'" There I was, in the heart of reaction, to talk about the 104th Republican Congress, my hidden agenda. I was at the pulpit. I faced this huge audience and started my speech. They laughed all the way through the first half—all these great women in my life, beginning with a spider: "Amongst spiders she might be a very handsome creature." And all I really wanted to tell them was what a bunch of creeps they just elected in Washington, D.C. But I didn't want to rub anybody the wrong way— there's no point in that. So I tested the waters. I talked about how my daughter had affected my disposition. "She never liked me to holler at her. When I did, she would say, softly, 'Don't hodder at me, mother.' Then I would return to normal. And I don't think now that I would hodder even at Newt Gingrich if I met him."[35] "Ha, ha, ha!"—the audience went into an uproar. I knew where I was then. So after the laughter had died down, I said, "But don't count on it."

I told them how the 104th Congress was attacking human dignity and destroying environmental laws. I explained that only a very small minority of citizens had voted in the last election, and the new radicals had won by the slimmest of margins, so they had no mandate. Then I told them what to do about it—register to vote, and then get a fistful of voter registration forms and stand out on the street corners anywhere and get other people to register, right up to November, and then get busy and get the voters out, from house to house.

The reason they invited me was because one of the religion professors read in Studs Terkel's book *Coming of Age* [36] that I was an atheist. He'd never run into one, so he wanted me to answer questions about it. So, okay, later that day I go to his class. No prepared speech, just questions.

First they asked me why I was an atheist. I said, "I'm an atheist for the same reason you're Christians. Because my parents were atheists, like your parents were Christians. They weren't Buddhists or Muslims, they were Christians."

Everybody bought that. I went on.

"I don't worry about being an atheist, any more than a lot of Christians worry about being Christians. There are bad Christians in this world, but most Christians are good. There are bad atheists, also, but I want to be a good atheist."

I responded to their questions about what a good atheist was—exercising stewardship over the land, organizing, blah blah blah. I also assured them that I wouldn't try to convert anybody to atheism. I wouldn't lift a finger even to help someone become an atheist, because I have nothing to offer them. Nothing! If people get any comfort from a religious belief or any other kind of belief, I wouldn't want to disturb it—there's a need for comfort in this world.

"And if I'm wrong," I told them at the end, "I've got some insurance. My insurance is that Jesus said to the man, 'If you clothed me when I was naked, fed me when I was hungry, comforted me when I was sick, and visited me when I was in prison, you will find yourself on the right hand of God on judgment day.' Well, I worked for welfare, clothing and feeding children, and I worked for old-age insurance, to comfort the sick. And the only time I was ever at Walla Walla except for today was to visit that prison up on the hill. So maybe I'll be seeing you guys in heaven."

I was never sent to church as a child. In fact, I grew up without prejudice against religion, which is a nice way to grow up—each to his own. But religion performs a very valuable service to a lot of people. It has been the motive for the greatest works of art, drama, painting, and music. It eases the passage through a very difficult world. Most people are trying to be good for one reason or another. I wouldn't want to take people's reason for being good away from them, especially when it connected them with the Catholic Church. I'm exceedingly fond of the Catholic Church. It started in my childhood with the Sisters [at St. Anne's Convent] in kindergarten. So I'm an atheist favorably disposed toward religion.

Traditionally, the Catholic Church always sided with the ruling class and the military against the interests of the people, whereas the church's true role in society was to gang up with the oppressed against the military and the ruling class—that's liberation theology in a nutshell.[37] Among the most corrupt of the orders were the Jesuits. In fact, they became a household word for shenanigans. But things turn into their opposites. Now the Jesuits are the ones who really have concern for the people, and not for their own. They've attracted all the best elements of the church, as have the Maryknolls. They're men, but I'm a member of their auxiliary. Their first object is to better the conditions of the people, wherever they are. Converting to Catholicism only comes second.

The Jesuits are behind Seattle University, which bestowed on me an honorary doctorate in June 1997. Seattle University encourages gays and lesbians, they're interracial, and the disciplines in their curriculum all have an environmental core to them. The fact that they would give me an honor when I'm a known atheist is an indication of just how liberal they are.

At the graduation ceremony, when I was invested with this doctorate, I made a funny little speech.[38] Through the whole thing, I had to go slowly and keep pausing to give them a chance to laugh. Almost before I was done, they were giving me a standing ovation. It was a great pleasure to be recognized. All people want to be recognized. It's the people who are not ever recognized who are so unhappy. My cup runneth over, but I have to adjust my halo from time to time.

Archbishop Murphy of the Seattle Catholic Archdiocese, who died a few weeks later, got an honorary Ph.D. with me. The day before, they had a reception for the two of us, and we'd also gotten to know each other at the many events connected to this thing, and I just loved the guy. I knew that he had leukemia, and that his days were numbered. I went to his funeral. St. James Cathedral takes up a whole block. The people were lined up almost all the way around the block, waiting to get into the service. When they opened the doors, people started going in, and we got closer and closer and closer—turned the corner, turned another corner, approaching the main entrance. We were a long way from the entrance when they closed the doors—the place was crammed.

There's a way to get through crowds. It's like going through water. You do it gently. You just take a teeny little step. You don't push anybody. Then you take another teeny little step, and you don't push anybody. I told my friend, "Stay right behind me, now, because I can get through this crowd—get closer than we are now, anyway." Sure enough, we got to the door, and we got into the outer foyer, but not any further. I could see into the cathedral, but I couldn't hear the guy who was talking. I stood there an hour.

WORDS FOR THE CREATOR

If I were the Creator, with all the power that the Christian Creator is supposed to have, and if I couldn't figure out a better universe than the one we've got, I would just quit my job and go on unemployment. This universe, where one thing eats another—I think that it's savage and I've thought that for a long time. I would do a better job. How can I worship a Creator that I feel is morally inferior to me? I just don't believe in the guy. If there is one, I've made a big mistake. And when I meet Him, eyeball to eyeball, before He consigns me to the nether regions, I'll tell Him just what I think of Him.

I don't believe in prayer and I wouldn't pray if I needed to. It's so illogical. Here's this magnificent deity that created us, shaped everything, and mapped it out ahead of time. And He made certain decisions. "I'm going to make a mountain. I'm going to create people. Stars! Come out!" Now, we're praying to get that guy to change his mind? We think he made a wrong decision? I think that's an insult. A mother will pray for her son to come back from war. The Creator might have figured, "I'll lop him off in this war." She prays, and then He changes his mind? He's moved by the mother's grief? This all doesn't make sense to me. What about the other guys? If I believed in prayer and I thought somebody was going to make decisions on the basis of my pleading, I'd say, "Stop the war. Knock off all those munitions people who are getting millions of dollars out of this." Or I'd say, "Let them all come home."

I don't buy that mystic stuff, either, but my friends invite me to a lot of rituals, and I enjoy attending—for example, the white buffalo ceremony. An albino calf was born in Wisconsin. The traditional Indians in the tribe seized upon it as fulfilling a prophecy. I was invited to sit with the elders at the ceremony in Seattle for the white calf. There was drumming and chanting and dancing. The Makahs and the Lummis were the only western tribes represented, but many came from Alaska. They had beautiful costumes and dances—not just teenagers, but little kids and elderly people participating, too. I'll have to admit that most of it was over my head, because I'm not a religious or philosophic type person. Nevertheless, I have a lot of respect for good Native Americans, as I have for good Christians. Maybe I'm missing something, but whether I am or not, I don't know, so it doesn't hurt me.

Now here's a question—what started this whole thing rolling? Most scientists believe that creation started with the Big Bang. I never bought that—not for five minutes. Here's the true story of creation. I didn't make it up, but I tell it.

After delivering a lecture on the solar system, William James[39] was approached by an elder of the Iroquois Nation, who claimed she had a theory superior to the one described by him.

"We don't live on a ball rotating around the sun," she said. "We live on a crust of earth on the back of a giant turtle."

Not wishing to demolish this absurd argument with the massive scientific evidence at his command, James decided to dissuade his opponent gently.

"If your theory is correct, Madam, what does this turtle stand on?"

"You're a very clever man, Mr. James, and that's a good question, but I can answer it. The first turtle stands on the back of a second, far larger turtle."

"But what does the second turtle stand on?" James asked.

The old lady responded patiently, "It's no use, Mr. James. It's turtles all the way down."

And I'm saying, where did the energy come from that created the Big Bang? It's Big Bangs all the way down.

Now here's another question—do we have an evolution that's based on randomness, or is it planned and designed? I feel that it is random, there's no design, and there's no justice. And I don't care. I just don't care! So what! You live here. Whether or not the universe is random doesn't alter anything. My job is to introduce some justice where I can in my small way. It's the job of all people to introduce peace despite all this random business, or lack of it, because we are thinking and feeling beings who can judge and plan for the future. We're part of the web, but we're a qualitative leap above the rest of the animal kingdom because we have in us this gift, a certain freedom of will. It's partly conscious and partly unconscious. We don't have absolute control because, after all, we're basically victims of our environment and our culture, but we have some control, and we have some responsibility. A two-edged sword—we can plan destruction, or we can plan the other way. That's our challenge. Most people are going in the way of trying to improve things, so the randomness doesn't bother me in the slightest bit.

People invent God to explain this human difference, this strange leap. It's natural to invent answers to things we don't understand. When the thunder came, primitive humans knew it was caused by something bigger than they were, so they got Thor, the god of thunder. We found out that thunder is caused by two clouds coming together, so we dumped Thor and went on until we found another blank and put in another kind of a god. We keep casting these gods aside. It's a system of crutches to deal with the basic randomness that is too much for people to bear. I've run into deeply religious people who rely entirely on them. I wouldn't want to knock the crutches out from under them. The shock would be terrible unless they gave up them up willingly by thinking their way out of it. See, I've lived without them all my life, so to me it's old hat.

Well, yes, I do have a crutch. It's my faith in human beings and it's never been knocked out from under me. I can read all the crime columns in the world and I'm not going to let go of that crutch. I have that faith that human beings are headed toward brotherhood. We're pretty young. We've only been able to read and write for three thousand years. We have lots of time unless some natural disaster takes care of the planet, or they blow this thing up with a nuclear bomb, or they keep cutting the trees and polluting the rivers.

"JUST HANG IN THERE"

People need to know that their own interest coincides in the long run with the interest of the general community. City-livers all think they're individuals. That's one reason they're unhappy, lonely, and afraid. When they get into a community activity, they're more contented. They discover they're part of something. I've always felt most comfortable when I'm part of a team, doing things together. I liked to swim, but I always did my best in relays. I don't resent what any member of the team does to bring us forward. Individuals may make a difference by initiating a project. So, okay, they can take a bow for having thought of it. After that, if they don't get some allies, they won't make it. It's a collective process.

I'm not doing some great thing for humanity. I wanted to play basketball, but I was also contributing to women's rights. When the Depression came, I was on welfare, and I got involved in getting a better break for everybody. My own civil liberties were at stake during the McCarthy period, and the same with the environment. Nobody loves more than I do to hike around and see birds. I want clean air and I don't want to drink polluted water. I don't want to see all our forests taken down and our climate altered. I don't like to see all this stuff spewed into the air, changing the climate and jeopardizing my health. All the way through I am fighting for myself, and for everyone.

I'm always scolding young people who get depressed. I've heard "Reagan did us in" or "Bush is a fraud, all is lost." I'd say, "What do you mean, all is lost? We lived through Hoover, didn't we? We lived through Nixon. We lived through things more impossible than Clinton. He's here today and gone tomorrow. We're going to be here forever, we and our ilk. We'll keep struggling together. We lose a few, we gain a lot. Just hang in there. That might be helpful."

"DO NOT STAND AT MY GRAVE AND WEEP"

I never worry about my own personal death, just like I never worry about nuclear war. Like lightning. If it strikes you, you have nothing to worry about. If it doesn't strike you, you have nothing to worry about. You can't fear what you don't know.

Death is a gift. You've lived your life and you're gone to your rest. You're ended. You're not going to be bored, because you're not conscious in this sleep. And since you don't wake up, you won't know if you've dreamed, and you won't be bored by your dreams. So death is a gift, a very precious gift. It's even more precious than birth because you don't ask to be born, you know, and you don't pick your parents. But you can ask to die. When I'm ready to die, I'll just ask. If I feel like it, I'll hand the gift to myself. Maybe I'll die running for a bus. I was born in 1898. I'm going to live till the year 2000, so I can have been in three centuries. Then I'm going.

My granddaughter Ann gave me a lithograph of this poem, "An Indian Memorial," because she knows I like it. It expresses my views on death.

Do not stand at my grave and weep.
I am not there.
I do not sleep.
I am a thousand winds that blow.

I am the diamond glint on snow.
I am the sunlight on ripened grain.
I am the gentle autumn rain.
When you wake in the morning's hush,
I am the swift uplifting rush
of quiet birds in circling flight.
I am the soft starlight at night.
Do not stand at my grave and weep;
I am not there—I do not sleep.

If you shed one tear when I die, I'll never speak to you again. "Never speak to you again"—evidently I don't expect to be dead! I'm going to come up a mushroom, and talk like a mushroom. Or glint on the snow.

Epilogue

Nydia Levick, Hazel Wolf's daughter, starts the story.

Mom had almost recovered from hip replacement surgery in November 1999. It was during the World Trade Organization meeting in Seattle, and she had been asking her friends to break her out of Providence Hospital so that she could lead the demonstrations. For the holidays, I took her to my home in Port Angeles, where we worked on *Outdoors West.* She had recovered enough to walk on her own.

On Tuesday night, January 18, 2000, she couldn't sleep—pain in her lower back. I bundled her into the car and drove down to Port Angeles Hospital. She mumbled, "I've been here long enough" and said out loud, "The trouble with dying is, people cry a lot." Then she asked me, "Nydia, would you mind if I died?" I said, "Mum, if you think that's what you would like to do, then it's okay." Her mind was perfectly clear with her dying.

When the doctor came in, she asked him, "How do you go about dying?" He answered, "Well, that's not my area of expertise. You're going to have to find your own way." She told him one story after another and urged him to join the Audubon Society. The nurse clued me in that I should call the family. The rest of the hospital was full, so my sons and daughters and all my grandchildren just stayed down in the emergency ward, the whole family, the whole night. At 5:30 A.M. her heart actually stopped for a moment.

Ann Sargent, Hazel Wolf's granddaughter, takes up the story.

At about 5:30 A.M. Leo asked for more morphine, but the doctor wouldn't give it to her. Her blood pressure was too low. After a while she said, "Nobody should be in this much pain when they're dying."

I said, "You can have more morphine, Leo, but it will kill you."

She replied, "Would that be such a bad thing?"

I threw it back at her. "What do you say?"

She said, "I don't know. Let me think about it."

After about fifteen minutes she called to me. "I'll take it." When I asked the doctor for more, he said, "Her blood pressure is up. We can give it to her now."

The pain receded and never came back. At 10:00 on the morning of January 19, 2000, we moved her to a nursing home in Sequim. We thought she'd be back at Nydia's the next day. Leo was pleased with the place—big open fields outside the window, sun streaming in.

Then "Hazel" started to show up again. She demanded the door be closed and a sign put up—PLEASE KNOCK. Too many staff were visiting her room. At lunch she said, "Look what they feed me—chicken sandwich with limp lettuce! Let's save it and show it to the doctor." I took the washcloth and wiped her feet, washed her hands.

She was beginning to get fretful about *Outdoors West*. "Ann, how's that going?" When she heard I had finished it, she just beamed.

I was going to sleep the night in the chair. At 10:00 P.M. I went up to her bed. She was all cuddled up warm, her hand by her cheek. I put my hand in her hand. She kissed it. Then she was sleeping, so I went home.

The doctor called two hours later and told me that a little before midnight she had wakened and asked for a cookie. He went to get one, came back, and she had gone, her hands behind her head, as if she were resting in a hammock.

Family Reminiscences

NYDIA LEVICK, HAZEL WOLF'S DAUGHTER

I have only one memory of Victoria, and that's having a tea party in the backyard. They let me use my little peach dishes, which disappeared in one of our moves. But I remember a lot of little things about St. Theresa's [in Seattle]. The Sisters stole my roller skates. I left them out in the lobby for about the umpteenth time, so they disappeared. I saw them on the chapel steps later.

They had Irish gals cleaning our room, and one time they got me all dressed up like a nun, with the black wimple around my head, and the rosary, and a belt, and the whole works. I must have been seven or eight years old. From there I went into the chapel where all the Sisters were praying—and giggling. Sister Superior saw me coming. She frowned at me and I smiled back. I threw them into a tizzy because I did what they did. I bowed in the aisle, I did the rosary, everything. From then on I was a Sister. I had an altar in the chapel, and I was quite serious about it. I had an altar in the bedroom, too, a little red table and chairs and a lace covering. And I had no compunction about stealing for my altar. I said to Sister Barry—Sister Bartholomew—"That's real holy water there, Sister. I go over to the cathedral and help myself." She was Irish—oh boy, was she ever Irish. She said, "That's okay. It'll keep the auld one out."

I didn't pick up Catholicism, though I went to the Catholic elementary school attached to St. Theresa's. I was supposed to practice my piano when they had catechism. I practiced too long and didn't go back to class on time, and the teacher bawled me out. That was the last she saw of me. I quit that school. Nobody in my whole family ever raised their voice to me. My Uncle Bill and I argued, but it was different. That teacher hurt my feelings.

Mom found out I wasn't going to school, so she walked with me in the morning. I stood on the corner and waved good-bye until she was far enough away. Then I turned and ran like heck the other way. I found a streetcar and rode downtown. I loved the waterfront. A man and his wife, who ran a tobacco store and had a big dog, fed me candy bars. I spent a lot of time with them, though they worried about it. I knew what time to go home. I'd wait at a corner with a bunch of people. Then I'd get on the streetcar with them, and the conductor would think I was with these people. I got pretty streetwise, but that didn't mean much in those days. You could wander any place you wanted to. Sexual harassment or getting kidnapped—none of that was ever thought of.

I took a dollar and a half out of Mom's purse, changed out of my school uniform, and put on the only dress I had at that time, a gorgeous yellow silk with black trim. Then I went down to the ferry dock and bought a ticket to go over to my grandmother in Port Angeles, but the ferry didn't leave until midnight. The people there ratted on me, and I got picked up by the truant officer. Mom tried all kinds of stuff to get me to go back to the Catholic school, but I wouldn't because the teacher had bawled me out. So she shipped me back to my grandmother's in Port Angeles. My grandmother lived with my Uncle Bill, and my Aunt Dot lived next door. In fact, I bought the house I've got now because it was a block away from Aunt Dot's. I would stay with my grandmother a lot of the school years. I was really split between two households. I went to fourteen different schools between Seattle and Port Angeles—Washington, Lincoln, Queen of Angels, Roosevelt, Bryant, Broadway . . . I hit 'em all.

I was in the fifth grade, eleven or twelve years old, when we lived at Tyee / Beaver. It was 1929. I can only remember what year it was because of the new car that went into the lake, a 1929 Chrysler. We lived way out with Herb Wolf, way out. It was heavy timber then, and they were in the process of logging it out. Now it's timbered again, second growth. I don't remember when Mom married him. He more or less ignored me. I mean, he was a very quiet person, and I didn't have a lot of conversations with him. He was kind. I'd bum money off him. Spoiled a couple of poker games for him, I know that.

Mom had a house built before she moved us to Beaver. She was a neat freak, still is. I can remember that my bedroom in that house was always just so. My room was pink, with curtains that matched the bedspread. All my dolls sat on a pink chair, and my toys were in a box. I don't remember ever having a toy out. When I had my family, I taught my kids just to throw all their toys under the bed.

Then we moved to Port Angeles, and then to Seattle, right back into St. Theresa's for the second time. Pretty soon I changed my uniform, took some money, and headed back to Port Angeles. Again, the people at the ferry terminal turned me over to the truant officer. He took me to an office and fed me doughnuts and a bottle of pop. Mom came on her lunch hour, and they all talked. They said that St. Theresa's wasn't a good place for a child to be raised because there was no place to play. The upshot of it was that Mom was to find a place to live where there were some kids. My grandmother came over and stayed with me at St. Theresa's until Mom found a house out on Ravenna Boulevard where I would have schoolmates. I went to Bryant School while we were there. Mom was having a hard time making it. She couldn't afford the house and transportation to where she worked.

I knew my way around and took care of myself.

The Depression

I graduated from the eighth grade at Longfellow School in Seattle in 1932. We lived on Fifteenth and Harrison, a nice apartment—that part was great. I don't think I even noticed the Depression particularly, because I never had anything in the first place, so I never went without anything. I can remember that we went to a great big warehouse full of shoes. I got a pair of white shoes. At school a whole bunch of us were standing in a row, and here's a gal with the same kind of shoes I had, so I knew where she'd gotten them. When I was in high school in Port Angeles, my senior year I had a skirt and a top that matched, and I had a smock. That's all the clothes I had, so I had to switch from one to the other all the time.

In 1934, in eleventh grade out at Roosevelt High School, in Seattle, a bunch of us followed along on a parade with the college kids on Armistice Day. The principal came out and said, "You're all expelled! You can never come back!" The kids panicked and ran.

The students who went on the parade were told to bring letters from their parents, promising obedience or some damn thing. Mom wouldn't write anything like that, so I went to school without a letter. I stuck out like a sore thumb because everybody else's parents docilely wrote these letters.

They tried to put pressure on me through my Latin teacher, whom I liked a lot. I was really shook up. They were threatening my Latin teacher's job, and I didn't know how to protect her. Mom said, "That's her problem, not your problem." Finally it came to a screeching halt. They told me not to come to school.

I said, "Now what do I do?"

Mom said, "Go to school."

She gave me a letter about how the law provided that anybody under sixteen had to be in school. They were violating the law by forcing onto the streets a child whose mother worked all day long—I would have no supervision. So I went to school and sat down, and nothing happened.

I wasn't aware of Mom's activities. I was a teenage kid going to high school, and I had my own problems. I remember going to my friend's house in Laurelhurst, the rich district near Roosevelt High School. Her father was an officer in the Crown Zellerbach Corporation. I saw a note from her mother on her bedside table that said, "Don't play with Nydia anymore. Her mother's a Communist."

Meanwhile, my Uncle Bill and my grandmother lost their house in Port Angeles and moved to Yakima. My Uncle Bill worked in the orchards, and my grandmother sorted fruit for a while, but she was too old to do that, so she took care of somebody's kids.

This is hard to believe—my Uncle Bill and my grandmother rode the rails back to Seattle. She said to him, "If you're going to do it, I'm going to do it." She had to have been in her sixties. He lifted her and a big duffel bag onto a ladder of a slowly moving train. Then he caught the ladder at the other end of the car. They both got up to the top and from there went down inside this train. At the freight yard, the cop saw them but didn't kick them off. He said, "You've got to get a different car. If this lumber falls, you're dead." He helped them get back to Port Angeles.

Uncle Bill and my grandmother then moved out to a one-room cabin at Lake Sutherland. I spent my whole last summer before my senior year in 1935 out there. Our cabin was on the side of the lake with no road. My dad contributed ten dollars a month, and Mom contributed ten dollars a month. I got six dollars a month working for a neighbor. So we had twenty-six dollars for three of us to live on. My Uncle Bill didn't work then. He had a bad heart, which we didn't know until a long time later. My Uncle Johnny, Aunt Dot's husband, supplied electricity to that little house. Uncle Bill would take the money and hitchhike into town to buy the groceries. I can remember waiting for him to get back, down to our last potato. We were joking, "Watch that it doesn't overcook."

That particular summer was just a wonderful summer. I ran around in bare feet and I picked blackberries. I'd go up and down the lake in a little dugout canoe, pick up bark, bring it back, and throw it on the fire. I had a gym suit left over from high school and I wore it night and day. If I felt like it, I'd go in swimming. By nighttime, it had to be dry because I was going to sleep in it. My Uncle Bill and I fixed up a boat together. He was a really outstanding person in my life. I can remember my grandmother saying, "Don't hit her, Bill," because we used to argue like mad. We went to baseball games together. He was always going to name his boat the *Nydia D.* We were almost like brother-sister, but it wasn't that. He wasn't a father, either—didn't discipline me in any way.

My life wasn't particularly involved with Mom's. After Roosevelt High School in Seattle, when I was sixteen, I never lived with her again, and during those sixteen years I spent almost half with my grandmother. My grandmother was very patient and very affectionate. I used to sleep with her. She'd be reading in bed, books that I wasn't supposed to read. I'd put my head on her shoulder, and she'd put her arm around me, and I'd read her book anyway—Smith's *Love Stories,* or *Redbook.*

I graduated from Roosevelt High School in Port Angeles in June 1936 at age seventeen, and all of a sudden I had no place to live. My grandmother couldn't afford me anymore. I didn't have a job. Mom was living with a couple of gals. I didn't necessarily marry for that reason, but anyhow it solved everybody's problems.

My husband, Fred Kilmer, and I had a great life. We built a big trailer truck and lived wherever he was cutting wood. For six of our married years, we never had lights and water, right up until the war. He decided to sign up with a Boeing training school in Port Angeles. Then we moved to Seattle, into a defense house out at Lake City. I had two children with him—Juanita, born in Port Angeles, and Dal, in Lake City in a snowstorm. Mom got out there for that one. She was there for all of them.

We moved into several places in the meantime, minus lights and water, always. He got drafted because he changed too many jobs. When he got shipped out in World War II, I moved back to Port Angeles. Been there ever since.

Character Witness

I worked for the county library most of my life, and Lieutenant Redin was the reason I didn't work there between 1946 and 1956. I was called to testify for Nick Redin, and actually I had only met the man maybe twice. I got involved simply because Mom had met his wife, Galena, in a dental office. She needed a buggy, and I had one I didn't need. Mom and Galya came to my house to get this buggy. In return, Galya and Nick asked me and my husband to dinner. Neither one of them spoke very much English, so I can't say that our conversations amounted to very much.

Nick was accused by a shipbuilder of spying about the radar. When they asked me to be a character witness at his trial, I said, "Sure." I had nothing against the people whatsoever.

They asked me a lot of stupid questions at the trial.

"Do you subscribe to a certain newspaper? Can you remember the name of it?"

I said, "Yes, my husband had wanted to get information about the election from that newspaper." He was in the union at Boeing, and the newspaper was probably on the labor side.

I was on the stand for a long time because of this newspaper. The prosecutor said, "This paper is supposed to be anti-Fascist. Can you tell me what Fascism is?"

And I said, "No, I just know that the Italians got it and they don't like it."

Then he said, "And what is Communism, Mrs. Kilmer?"

There I was, trying to think—"Who's got Communism? Where do they have Communism?" But I just went blank. I was still full of the stupid answer I'd given about Fascism.

The judge interrupted. "The answer to that question would take too long."

Finally I said, "I never even paid much attention, because I couldn't vote." I wasn't a citizen at the time.

When I was interviewed in the newspaper about testifying for him, they asked me, "Do you think he is guilty?" I said, "No, he doesn't speak enough English."[1] Very sensible answer, you know. The librarian said that the resultant publicity was not good for a library, so she fired me.

ANN SARGENT, HAZEL WOLF'S GRANDDAUGHTER

We lived in a little tiny house in Port Angeles, the same one my mom lives in now. My grandmother came over every single summer to take us backpacking, my two brothers and me, and that was a big event in my life. We stopped going when she was about eighty-seven.

She was organized, really organized. We had to measure out all our food and weigh it. She'd divide the load, and we would each carry the same amount—eighteen pounds, I remember. We tried to sneak in a candy bar or a sucker, but she always found us out.

She was a hard driver—"Come on, you kids, let's get hiking." She'd stop at a flower and name it, and she'd name the birds and trees. She could name them all. We hiked out on the Olympic Peninsula, out by Neah Bay. Hit all the Indian reservations, of course. She taught me to love the land

and to protect it. We never littered. We always spread our fire out. She never wasted or destroyed anything. When we ran into deer or bear, she told us to stay our distance, that it was their land, don't crowd them.

I was about twelve or thirteen years old when they decided she was a Communist and they were going to throw her out of the country. My father would say that I couldn't go camping with her anymore because it would look bad, we'd be associated with her. I'd tell Leo—she wouldn't let me call her "Grandmother"—and she'd say, "Oh, they'll change their minds. I'm coming over." The night before, he'd say, "You're not going," but I'd pack anyway. She'd come right up to the house whether it made my father uncomfortable or not. He wouldn't say much to her face, and we'd leave for the mountains. Then one summer Leo wasn't even supposed to come out to our house because of this thing. I made it clear to my mom that, with or without permission, summer was coming, it was my week, and I'd be on the bus. I think that's part of her in me, that nothing would've stopped me.

She liked my husband, Roy, even though he is almost everything she was against—timber logger, hunter. She said, "If you ever think, when you're out and you're meeting all these exciting, adventurous people, that you could be better off, you should stay where you are. You have a nice husband."

When my mom and I went with her to Monterey, California, for her Audubon award, my grandmother pulled me aside in the airport bathroom and said, "If you and your mother don't quit doing stuff for me, carrying my suitcase, helping me in and out of the car, walking me through the airport—I've about had it. I need to carry my own purse and my own suitcase, or I won't have any muscle tone, and I'm tired of you telling me what to do."

I said, "Well, Leo, it looks bad when somebody like me, in my forties, is walking through the airport with a hundred-year-old who is carrying her own suitcase. People actually come up to me and say, 'Well, can *I* help her?' So if you let me carry your suitcase in public, I promise I'll give it back to you."

She laughed and said, "All right, you can carry it through the airport, but that's it."

1. "Port Angeles Woman Nervous in Crowded Court Room," *Port Angeles Evening News,* 1946: "The dark-haired 1936 Roosevelt high school graduate considers it unlikely that Nicolai Redin bought any plans. 'It seems to me that in his work there he could have gotten information without having to pay for it,' she laughed. 'Anyway,' she said seriously, 'knowing the difficulties they have with the English language, it's hard for me to believe he could have discussed technical points.' Mrs. Kilmer has been working at the library here, but has resigned now that her husband is due home."

The Hazel Wolf Deportation Case

The Immigration and Naturalization Service arrested Hazel Wolf in 1949 on charges that she was an alien who had belonged to an organization that advocated the forceful overthrow of the United States government. During the first, administrative stage of Wolf's deportation case (May 1949–November 1952), her lawyers tried to stop the hearings and appeals on points of procedure.

In the spring of 1950, after five months of hearings, INS district director John P. Boyd sent the hearings transcript to Washington, D.C., for a decision. The federal INS commissioner ordered Wolf's deportation. In the summer of 1950, that decision was appealed by John Caughlan and other lawyers for the Washington Committee for the Protection of the Foreign Born (WCPFB), the local branch of the organization formed to resist attacks on noncitizens during the McCarthy period. During the appeals hearings in Seattle, the WCPFB lawyers threw up technical roadblocks—for example, a motion to disqualify the hearing examiner, John W. Keane, because of personal bias (as an employee of the INS he couldn't have been impartial). On August 10, 1950, the defense submitted seven motions on technical rulings, none of which was upheld.[1] The appeals hearings that summer inspired the INS to new tactics as well (for example, the use of new stoolies with new "evidence" about Wolf's subversive activities). The appeals hearings dragged on for two years.

In 1952, when President Eisenhower appointed a World War II buddy, J. M. Swing, as commissioner general of the Immigration and Naturalization Service, Hazel Wolf gained a formidable adversary in Washington, D.C. For nearly a decade, Swing did the work of the witch-hunt by ordering the deportation of hundreds of U.S. residents. He was well acquainted with the Hazel Wolf case and personally intervened several times to order her deportation.[2]

The administrative stage of the case ended when the Board of Immigration Appeals, in Washington, D.C., upheld the local decision to deny her appeal. Commissioner General Swing of the INS ordered her deportation and set the date.[3]

Wolf signed her deportation order. In accord with international agreements on deportations, Canada had already issued a letter of consent for her repatriation. She had been given six months before the INS would usher her to the border, but the day after she received the denial of her appeal to the INS, her lawyers in the WCPFB moved the case on appeal into the federal courts, thus beginning the second, litigating phase of her resistance (November 1952–December 1963). From then on, her case was continuously in federal court.

Hazel Wolf's life and court cases were abruptly intercepted by the Seattle Smith Act trial, in 1953. In fact, Wolf's 1947 citizenship trial, the 1948 Canwell hearings, and the first stage of her deportation hearings in 1949–52 could be viewed as a dress rehearsal for the Seattle Smith Act trial. In this trial, the government charged U.S. citizens with subversion instead of limiting itself to the more vulnerable "foreign-born." The Smith Act, named after its sponsor, Congressman Howard W. Smith of Virginia, had been passed in 1940 as a rider to the Alien Registration Act, but arrests and trials didn't begin until the 1950s. The act is still on the books (U.S. Code, Title 18, Section 2385) and prohibits anyone from teaching or advocating the overthrow of the government by force and violence; from publishing, selling, distributing, or printing material that teaches or advocates the overthrow of the government by force and violence; or from organizing the overthrow of the government by force and violence. The framers of the act had the Communist Party in mind. Almost every major U.S. city had its Smith Act trials, beginning with one in New York City in 1948, the Foley Square trial.

As in Hazel Wolf's hearings, the government strategy in the Seattle Smith Act trial was first to expose Communist theory in major works of literature and then to show that this theory was meant to be activated for revolution. The next step was to show that each defendant became part of the Communist conspiracy by joining the party and becoming an active member, teaching and advocating the theory of revolution. The Supreme Court of the United States, in reviewing the 1948 Foley Square case in New York, permitted the government to argue only that the defendants were members of an organization that theoretically advocated revolutionary force and violence. The government was not required to argue that defendants took actions or advocated revolutionary actions. The Smith Act trial defendants received five-year prison sentences. The trials all but destroyed the Communist Party.

While Wolf was busy volunteering for the Smith Act defendants, the quick wit and persistence of her lawyers pulled her back from the brink. The second, litigating stage of her resistance began on November 27, 1952, when Barry Hatten and John Caughlan challenged her deportation order in federal court on the grounds that she had been deprived of "due process" guaranteed in the Constitution under Article V: "No person shall be . . . deprived of life, liberty or property, without due process of law." U.S. District judge William J. Lindberg rejected the Hatten and Caughlan contention that constitutional protections would be relevant in a deportation case. This was the same judge who presided over the Seattle Smith Act trial a few months later, in spring 1953. The next stop for Wolf's case was the 9th Circuit Court of Appeals, in San Francisco, where the appeal was again rejected in 1954. From there, Hatten and Caughlan petitioned the U.S. Supreme Court.

Between 1955 and 1960, the case went up three times to the U.S. Supreme Court. Three times the Supreme Court denied writ of certiorari, meaning the justices refused to review the case because they found it involved no constitutional issues; that is, they decided that the Constitution didn't cover resident aliens. Each time the Supreme Court denied writ of certiorari, Hatten and Caughlan would research a new issue in the case and begin the appeal process all over again at the U.S. District Court in Seattle, whence it would work its way up through the 9th Circuit Court and on up to the U.S. Supreme Court, around and around.

While Hazel Wolf was staying one step ahead of the FBI and the INS,

Caughlan and Hatten were losing the battles in court. On February 28, 1955, the U.S. Supreme Court denied her petition for the first time. Now there was nothing to stop Commissioner General Swing of the INS from carrying out the deportation order.

However, the WCPFB had been scrambling to find a connection to Washington, D.C., to open up a new, political front. On March 10, 1955, just a few days after the Supreme Court denied her petition, the WCPFB persuaded Senator Langer, a Republican from North Dakota who happened to be a friend of the executive secretary of the Democratic Party of Washington State, to introduce a private bill on Wolf's behalf.

During this third, political phase of Wolf's defense (March 10, 1955– March 5, 1956), the WCPFB tackled McCarthyism head-on in the U.S. Congress by pushing for amendments to the 1952 Walter-McCarran Act. The amendments would have prevented the INS from pursuing its antiforeign, anti-Communist tactics. Specifically, the WCPFB advocated for bills that would have exempted from deportation longtime residents such as Hazel Wolf. It also pushed bills that would have enforced the ex post facto law.[4] Letters from church people, lawyers, and WCPFB friends flooded the offices of Washington's Senators Warren Magnuson and Henry Jackson. None of the bills made it through Congress.

At that point, Commissioner General Swing tried to pull a sneak attack. According to Senate conventions, Wolf's deportation was automatically stayed until the Judiciary Committee and Congress considered Senator Langer's bill, S.B. 1425. No action was taken on the bill before the August 1955 recess. Her deportation should have been stayed until Congress convened in January 1956. Knowing that the Judiciary Committee's chairman, Senator Kilgore, was in Europe, and that Senator Langer was on a tour, Swing ordered Wolf deported in October 1955.

On the day she was to report to the INS for her deportation, Wolf's attorney Barry Hatten spent the day trying to convince INS district director John P. Boyd that he couldn't deport Wolf while the bill was pending. According to Hatten, "I'd call Kilgore, who would promise to call Swing, then I'd call Boyd and say, 'She's not going to show up.' He was practically going to kidnap her, put her on a bus, and dump her across the border—we knew they did that kind of thing. It was the nearest we came to them actually grabbing her." Members of the wcpfb hastily located Senator Langer and informed him of the threatened deportation. Senator Langer asserted the Senate's priority in the matter, and Commissioner General Swing agreed to stay the deportation until February 1, 1956, by which time Congress was supposed to act on the bill. Meanwhile, the wcpfb organized a letter-writing campaign to members of the Senate, to the Judiciary Committee, and to Washington State Senators Magnuson and Jackson. "Maggie" and "Scoop," as they were called, respectively, replied with a wave of form letters deferring to the ins.[5]

Commissioner General Swing himself appeared before the Judiciary Committee in early 1956 to testify on Wolf's case. He wrote to the committee, "Despite representation to the contrary, it is indicated that Mrs. Wolf's Communist activities have continued since 1933." He insinuated that she was a foreign agent: "She is divorced and has no one dependent upon her for support. Her only relative in the United States is a married daughter."[6]

Meanwhile, the lawyers were still filing appeals. Readers of the local Seattle papers could follow the outlines of the drama. No sooner was Wolf "safe" one week than she would be bound for Canada the next.[7]

February 1956 was a busy month for Wolf and the wcpfb , both in the U.S. Congress and in the courts:

> Hazel Wolf, after being "deported" by the local newspapers on an average of once a year for the past six years, finally hit the headlines with a "stay" of deportation on February 10. Her attorney, C. T. [Barry] Hatten, filed a motion to reopen her case for the purpose of enabling her to make an application for suspension of deportation. [U.S. District Court] Judge [William J.] Lindberg upheld the immigration department in its denial of her motion, but granted a stay to permit her to appeal to the Circuit Court. The $250 bond was posted and notice of appeal filed.[8]

In the spring of 1957, in the face of yet another deportation crisis, the wcpfb turned its attention to Canada. The fourth, Canadian phase of Hazel Wolf's defense (June 1957–October 1958) followed a familiar pattern: a letter-writing campaign to members of the Canadian Parliament and continuous action in federal court. Her attorney John Caughlan tried to prove that Wolf was not a Canadian but an American, and hence not a deportable alien under the Walter-McCarran Act. His new motion in U.S. District Court alleged that "the government erred in assuming Mrs. Wolf was an alien. Even though Mrs. Wolf was born in Canada she has U.S. citizenship because her mother was a citizen." Caughlan had discovered that from 1855 on, children who were born abroad but who had one parent who was an American citizen were deemed to have U.S. citizenship. According to his motion, it was only after the 1907 Naturalization Law that a woman was deprived of her citizenship by marriage to an alien. Nellie Frayne (U.S. citizen) married George Anderson (Scots immigrant to Canada) in 1894, and their daughter Hazel was born in 1898, at a time when, by law, Caughlan alleged, Nellie Anderson's U.S. citizenship would have conferred U.S. citizenship on her daughter Hazel.

In response, the government relied on an 1898 law that gave citizenship only to children born of American fathers who had married a foreigner. On November 27, 1957, the U.S. District Court rejected Caughlan's contention that Nellie Anderson and her daughter Hazel were U.S. citizens, and he set another deportation date. Caughlan appealed to the Circuit Court and then to the U.S. Supreme Court. In June 1958 the U.S. Supreme Court insisted that Wolf was not a citizen, by refusing for the third and final time to hear her case. The court reasoned that women, before 1922, lost their citizenship by marrying foreigners; therefore, Wolf was not an American through her mother, period. The Cable Act of 1922 allowed women to keep their citizenship after marriage to a foreigner. Sometime after 1923, Nellie Frayne Anderson Hughes had paid a small fee to have her U.S. citizenship restored, whereas her daughter, Hazel Wolf, had neglected to become a citizen.

Between October 14, 1958, and May 13, 1960, there was a lull in activities related to Wolf's case. Then, suddenly, John P. Boyd, INS district director, sent a letter ordering Wolf to report for deportation in thirty days, on June 12, 1960. In his letter, Boyd announced that "the matter was submitted to the local British Consul General with a view to securing authority for the subject's deportation to England inasmuch as she was a British subject at the time of her birth and has never become expatriated of British nationality. The local British Consul General has informed this office that he is now prepared to issue a travel document for use in effecting the subject's deportation to England." Thus the government initiated the fifth, British stage of the Wolf deportation case (June–October 1960) and a frantic letter-writing campaign by the WCPFB to the members of the press and the Parliament of Great Britain.

The goal was to persuade the English not to recognize her as a British subject and hence to reject her as a United States deportee. The WCPFB contacted British lawyers in London and aroused both moral and legal interest in her case: they argued that Mrs. Wolf had no relatives in England, had never been to England, and would not be able to find work there as a sixty-two-year-old legal secretary because she had no knowledge of British law. If deported to England, they claimed, she would soon become a "public charge."

Simultaneously, John Caughlan reopened the court case in U.S. District Court by filing a motion on the unconstitutionality of deporting someone to a country in which she had not been born. The motion was a direct political challenge to the Walter-McCarran Act of 1952, which permitted deportation of an alien to any country that would accept her.

Once again, the strategy of persuading the receiving country to reject Wolf as a U.S. deportee worked, but this time with international repercussions. On June 1, 1960, David Ormsby-Gore, the British foreign affairs minister of state, requested that the U.S. Department of State "reconsider its decision to deport a British subject who has been living in America since 1922." The U.S. State Department had represented to the British that Wolf had no connections in the United States, whereas a flood of letters to the British foreign desk from her relatives in Seattle and Port Angeles attested to the contrary. With the U.S. State Department's lie about Wolf's connections uncovered, the INS retreated.

One week after the British "request to reconsider," the 9th Circuit Court of Appeals in San Francisco ruled in Wolf's favor: constitutional issues might be involved, the court said, if the government tried to deport a noncitizen to a country where she had never lived. On December 20, 1962, Wolf was officially released by the INS "on her own recognizance."

The 9th Circuit Court required a three-judge panel to make a ruling on whether constitutional issues were involved, and it even affirmed the possibility that Wolf's U.S. citizenship derived from her mother. Eventually, the 9th Circuit Court ruled that Wolf's deportation order to Great Britain violated constitutional protections.

In the sixth and final stage (October 1960–December 1963), Wolf's deportation case went back to INS administrative hearings and was dismissed. The case had successfully challenged the constitutionality of the Walter-McCarran Act of 1952, which permitted deportation of aliens to any country that would accept them. Because she had no clear citizenship rights in any country, there was no place to which the INS could deport Hazel Wolf.

1. *Seattle Times,* Aug. 10, 1950: "John W. Keane, hearing examiner, deferred action on a defense motion to disqualify himself as examiner because of 'personal bias.' The motion, along with six others, was submitted by C. T. Hatten, attorney for Mrs. Wolf."

2. Eventually, as reported in the *Seattle Post-Intelligencer* on Feb. 2, 1961, Swing was investigated for corruption by the House Government Operations Committee for flying to Mexico on hunting trips at the taxpayers' expense. He was also investigated by Congress for having Mexican illegal aliens shipped from Texas to Tampico on a boat where conditions were so foul that forty Mexicans leaped over the side of the vessel into Tampico harbor (five of them drowned). Swing also put his daughter on the payroll and hired two generals. Finally, it was Swing who ordered the sudden arrest of William Heikkila in San Francisco and had him whisked off to Finland. Heikkila's father was a Finnish citizen living in Minnesota; his mother, a native of Finland, was a naturalized American citizen. Heikkila lived in the United States but had never been naturalized. For this reason, and because of his activities in the Communist Party during the 1930s, deportation proceedings were instituted against him in 1947. The trials and appeals continued until 1958, but in the end Heikkila remained in the United States. The incident gave the United States a black eye throughout Scandinavia.

3. *Seattle Times,* Nov. 17, 1952: "A warrant for the deportation to Canada of Mrs. Hazel Anna Wolf, former secretary to John Caughlan, Seattle attorney, was issued today. John P. Boyd, district director of Immigration, said the decision of a hearing board in Seattle that Mrs. Wolf should be deported has been upheld by the Board of Immigration Appeals in Washington. A letter was sent to Mrs. Wolf today, Boyd said, ordering her to report to immigration authorities for deportation November 26."

4. After passage of the Walter-McCarran Act, the "foreign-born" could be pros-

ecuted for membership in the Communist Party "after the fact"; that is, they could be prosecuted for having been members at a time in the past when membership had been legal.

5. "Campaign Growing to Stop Hazel Wolf Deportation February First," *The Northern Light* 3:1 (1956), 1:

> When Senator William Langer introduced SB1425 for the relief of Hazel Anna Wolf last March, long-established precedent should have ensured stay of her deportation until Congress acted on the bill. However, only the intervention of Sen. Langer prevented the Immigration from deporting Mrs. Wolf last October, despite the bill. At that time Immigration Commissioner J. M. Swing agreed to postpone the matter "until February 1 if Congress had not passed the bill."
>
> The WCPFB is doing everything possible to acquaint the public with this inhumane and shameful intention of the Immigration. It has and is calling on all of its supporters to write Sen. Magnuson at Washington, D.C., about this case, urging him to advise Commissioner Swing that the people of Washington demand that the February 1 order be canceled.
>
> Copies of letters already sent have been received. The Michigan Foreign Born Committee has written Senator Kilgore, Chairman of the Senate Judiciary Committee, and has pledged Mrs. Wolf its support. Robert W. Kenny, former Attorney General of California, wrote Sen. Kilgore; also California attorneys John W. Porter, Esther Shandler, Leo Gallager, Daniel G. Marshall, Laurence Spencer, Wm. B. Esterman, Al. L. Wirin, and others.

6. J. M. Swing, letter to Sen. Richard L. Neuberger (Oregon), Nov. 12, 1957.

7. "Mrs. Wolf Gets Another Stay of Deportation," *Seattle Times,* Feb. 16, 1956; "Mrs. Wolf Loses Fight on Deportation," *Seattle Times,* Feb. 21, 1956.

8. "Local Cases," *The Northern Light* 3:2 (1956), 2.

Marion Kinney's Story

I dropped everything and started working on the Washington Committee for the Protection of the Foreign Born. Sure, Hazel was a very big reason—they were trying to deport my friend Hazel, and they couldn't do that to me! But it was more than that. We had a number of people who were in danger of being deported. So we had to get busy and do all this work.

We had meetings every month. It was a loose organization, not tight like a dues-paying membership organization, but there were numbers of people who were concerned about this affront to people's liberty and happiness. A lot of the "aliens" had been here a long time. For instance, Boris Sassieff came over here when he was fourteen from a remote place near Georgia, in what had been for a long time the Soviet Union. So, having been here all this time, he considered the United States his country. He worked in the Frontier Bookstore, where I worked, until he died. We stopped them from deporting him. Ha! There were some people who went to jail, but they were the ones who didn't belong to organizations that stuck together and fought.

I was up before the [House] Un-American Activities Committee three times. They didn't get me. If you refused to talk to them and called forth the Fifth Amendment, they still couldn't do anything to you. Taking the Fifth meant that you had done all these bad things, but that they couldn't make you tell, under the constitution. But they still smeared you with the guilt of whatever you were supposed to be guilty of, which was never very clear. You could say a few things to the Un-American Activities Committee, but you had to be very careful to keep within the realm of the Fifth Amendment, because once you'd admitted one thing, they'd question you about the rest. So when I was up there, I managed to say, in one way or another, what I thought of the bloody Un-American Activities Committee without ruining my chances of using the Fifth Amendment. You had to be able to spit at 'em without having them put you in jail.

The FBI never came to see me directly, but they were after me. I just refused to acknowledge that they were. I hated 'em. It was social torture— you were ostracized. Nobody would hire you, that was the main thing. I was working at the Roma Cafe, which was a very good place to work. I got fired because somebody called them up and said I was a Communist. That was 1959. I wrote to congressmen and to the American Civil Liberties Union and complained—I was a free American! They couldn't do that to me! I could join any bloody organization I wanted to that wasn't Murder, Incorporated.

John Caughlan's Story

To those of use who knew Hazel Wolf back in the thirties, forties, and fifties, she was Leo. She says she first met me when she came to the King County Prosecutor's Office to collect my Communist Party dues. That would have to have been in 1938 or 1939, when I was a deputy prosecuting attorney. I don't remember the dues-collection part of our meeting, but I certainly do remember Leo from soon after my return to Seattle. She was a person who put the meaning of "active" into the word "activist," then as now, and I knew all about her well before 1938, before we actually met.

Her political work at that time was with an organization of the unemployed, the Workers' Alliance, and with the Washington Old Age Pension Union. I know that she gave plenty of grief to those who caused the people grief when she was the head of the Workers' Alliance Grievance Committee. Leo and I worked together on many projects in the late 1930s and early 1940s, especially in these two organizations. The Communist Party in the state of Washington was as homegrown and down to earth as was its predecessor in militant action of the 1910s and 1920s, the Industrial Workers of the World, or the Wobblies, as the IWW was affectionately or contemptuously called.

Leo never regarded herself as an intellectual. She joined the Communist Party because it was just what she had been looking for—a place where she, as a woman, could be effective in taking action for what she believed in. The party gave people an opportunity to participate at every level of working people's everyday struggles—in unions, in the Workers' Alliance and the Pension Union, in helping elect legislators who would support their goals, and in challenging the bureaucrats and city, county, and state officials who refused to respond to reasonable demands of ordinary people. The tremendous growth of the Communist Party in this period occurred because people like Leo, in the CIO, the AFL, and hundreds of different organizations, were seen as those who worked for ordinary people's common goals and who got things done.

After a successful bout with tuberculosis in the mid-1940s at Firlands Sanatorium, Leo came to work in our law office in earnest. There she bore out her reputation for being an indefatigable worker for the causes she believed in, and in time our office became virtually a "cause"—one that remained so for nearly thirty years. She displayed her skill for organization and efficiency and quickly but imperceptibly became the office manager in function, if not in title. It was she who saw to it that clients paid their bills, that there was money to operate, that funds were not misspent or wasted, and that cases moved forward. She had confidence in her own good sense and judgment and a strong streak of independence, which, however, never caused my partner, Barry Hatten, or me any problems.

She soon became our "boss" in a different sense because it was during her tenure in our office that the Immigration and Naturalization Service began its Thirty Years' War to deport her. She became not only an indispensable employee, but a client, and, as lawyers sometimes say, the client is boss. Immigration was determined to get this dangerous subversive out of the United States, if possible to Canada, where she was born, or to Gibraltar, where her father was born, or to England, to which both Canada and Gibraltar presumably owed allegiance, or, it sometimes seemed to us, they just wanted to put her in a boat and shove it out to sea if nothing else worked. We, or course, were equally determined to thwart this outrage. Our office became a staging area for legal and political battles with the INS.

Her agenda, and ours, was of course much broader than the Hazel Wolf case. Immigration's deportation proceeding against her was but one of many instituted against present, former, or merely suspected Communists, some nationally and internationally known, like Harry Bridges. We followed the progress of every deportation case anywhere with intense interest. Our office assumed active legal responsibility for the more than twenty or so Seattle deportation and denaturalization cases. We would never have succeeded in stopping the government juggernaut had it not been for the network of strategists, lawyers, and skillful legal workers developed by the American Committee for the Protection of the Foreign Born, headed by Abner Greene in New York and counseled by the unsurpassed legal genius Carol Weiss King.

Equally if not more important in Leo's work with the committee was her genius for fund-raising. The defense of the committee's and our clients was able to continue only because of donated funds or donated work. All of those whom we represented as lawyers, and for whom the state committee assumed responsibility, were working people without resources to pay for transcripts on appeal, transportation for lawyers to travel to the Court of Appeals in San Francisco or to the U.S. Supreme Court in Washington, D.C., or fees to keep their lawyers alive.

We had to find the right approach and the right legal and political strategy for each case. Some were easy. INS would never be able to deport Boris Sassieff or Maurice Raport because they came from Russia, and the Soviet Union refused to accept U.S. political deportees. Leo's case was afforded a variety of legal, political, and personal approaches, and we explored them all.

Hazel once told me—she denies this—that at some stage of her career, when the Communist Party was going through one of its many changes in policy, she said something like, "Well, does this mean we aren't really going to have some sort of revolution where we can throw the crooks out of the courthouse and take it over ourselves?"

Hazel Wolf Tells the Deportation Story of William Mackie and Hamish McKay

The Washington Committee for the Protection of the Foreign Born [WCPFB] lost only two cases. In November 1960, the U.S. Supreme Court voted to uphold the stoolies who had testified that Hamish McKay and William Mackie were Communists twenty-five years earlier. Both were deported on the same day—November, 18, 1960—McKay to Canada and Mackie to Finland.

Hamish McKay had organized Workers' Alliance demonstrations in Chicago during the Depression. He was a carpenter by trade. When he moved to Portland, Oregon, he could hardly keep his family together because he had this Communist thing on him and people wouldn't hire him. All he'd get was little jobs fixing some steps or a backyard fence. When he was deported to Vancouver, Canada, the Immigration rushed him to an unannounced flight so that his seventeen-year-old son missed seeing him off.

But deportation was the best thing that ever happened to the guy. He was met at the border by the carpenters' union and given the first steady job he'd had in years. He was just across the border, and his family could run back and forth and see him all the time. First thing you know, he had his own home. Later on his wife, two sons, grandmother, and great-grandmother got permission from Immigration to go to Canada. He got a good pension and so did his wife. I heard from her for many years. McKay's grandfather was a Scot, famed for publishing the Bible in Gaelic, and his mother was descended from a signer of the Declaration of Independence. McKay died in Canada.

The other one, William Mackie, went to Finland. He was kind of a stupid guy. During the Depression, he had peddled *The Daily Worker* on the streets for a dime and kept the nickel. He was never a member of the party—too timid to join anything, and didn't even know what he was selling, he was so politically unaware. They arrested him. He was scared. The Washington Committee for the Protection of the Foreign Born lawyers went to him, but he wouldn't have anything to do with them. He had some money at that time, so he hired a regular lawyer. "Regular" is what we called bourgeois lawyers who didn't know how to handle political cases, which are different because the public is in on them, and publicity is part of the defense. Pretty soon McKay ran out of money and he ran out of attorneys. He was about to be picked up when he hollered to the WCPFB for help. By that time, all the options had run out—you have to appeal in fifteen days, that sort of thing. They deported him to Finland and there was no way we could stop them.

Why Finland? His parents had immigrated to this country from Finland and become citizens. When the wife was pregnant, they had visited their homeland, and Mackie was born there. So there he was, Finnish. In a couple of months, the parents came back to the United States, and that's all Mackie ever knew about Finland. He didn't speak the language. Once he had been deported back there, the Finnish painters' union kept him afloat on odd jobs. He left two daughters, an eighty-year-old father, and other assorted relatives. He'd fought [for the United States] in World War II.

I persuaded Mackie to come to Canada so that his people could visit him. While he was there, I went over to see him. I took him down to the border. All the people who live along there are spies. They're all loaded and cooperating with the Immigration and Naturalization Service if they see anything suspicious. I knew this, but I wanted him to get back into the United States if only for a minute. I asked a guy who was working in his garden on the U.S. side if I could go over his fence and take a picture of the monument at the border. He said, "Go ahead." So I climbed the fence, then I got Mackie to go over and stand in front of the monument with his back to the camera and I took a picture of him in the United States. He had been deported, and it was a criminal offense for him to cross into the states, so I wasn't taking a picture of his face.

The WCPFB kept trying to get some U.S. senators interested in bringing Mackie home. Senator Wayne Morse of Oregon introduced bills to place a statute of limitations on the Walter-McCarran Act and to bring both Mackie and McKay home. Sixteen years later it passed, and Mackie finished his life in Portland.

APPENDIX 6

"Hazel Stories"

HELEN ENGLE
Board member, National Audubon Society
Founder, Tahoma Audubon Society

We had a major issue down here in Pierce County—the Nisqually Delta. We desperately needed a strong environmental voice, and birds were going to be the cornerstone of the whole effort to save the delta.

In the fall of 1968, I contacted Seattle Audubon for the names and addresses of the families in Pierce County that belong to Audubon—I would organize a subcommittee of Seattle Audubon for Pierce County. Hazel called me back and said, "Don't mess around with a subcommittee. Have your own chapter." Then she came over and more or less organized us the way she does—"Now, first, we need someone to be president. Helen would be good. Helen can be president." *Pho-o-om!* Pretty soon, there we were.

Two or three women came over from Seattle Audubon to our charter meeting in January 1969 and complained. "You can't do this. You can't take away from Seattle. You'll destroy Seattle Audubon."

I said, "On the contrary, we will amplify everything that Seattle Audubon does. It's not a matter of subtracting, it's multiplying."

Which turned out to be true. We had a thousand members within two to three years. People came and volunteered. I had it in the newspaper. Hazel was behind it, managing Seattle Audubon, egging me on. She laughed at those people who complained.

We fought hard for Nisqually. We had bills in the legislature year after year. We did everything. We finally won its preservation as a wildlife sanctuary.

I was just a gofer on a lot of projects with Hazel. The only people I ever knew to be irritated with Hazel were those who perceived she was overstepping her authority onto their turf. I never felt that she did. There are a couple of women out in the Yakima Valley who think, "Oh, that bossy old Hazel." A lot of people helped Hazel get the Wenas Campground for Audubon, but she made it happen, and she got quite a bit of press about it. Those women would have liked to have gotten the notoriety. They're the kind of people who go to an art show and say, "I could have painted a painting like that." Yet they didn't.

DAVE GALVIN

President, Seattle Audubon Society (1980–82)

Right from the very first meeting that I attended, Hazel was together and in charge. People looked to her with respect and trusted the information she gave.

She was the office manager for the Seattle Audubon Society, integral to the day-to-day operations. When I was president, she worked closely with me and the Executive Committee to make appointments to the board and to make sure the show was running well. Getting Protection Island set aside as a national wildlife refuge[1] and fighting the Northern Tier Pipeline[2] were big issues back then.

Typically for Hazel, she found out I was temporarily unemployed, and before I even knew what was happening she grabbed me to help her with the layout of the Federation of Western Outdoor Clubs [FWOC] newsletter, of which she was editor. We spent many a fun day doing that. She is clever like a fox in terms of getting people to do what she wants them to do. She has this way of going right up to people and cutting to the chase—

"I need your help"—living at that moment and literally seizing people by the arm. The next thing you know, you are involved for hours, or years, of your life. I watched her one time from the corner, where I was working on the books. A salesman came in. Before he knew it, this guy, who happened to walk in for a minute's worth of business, was standing there helping with the address labels for half an hour before he finally said, "Oh my God, I've got to get out of here."

She grew influential in Audubon by being the midwife to the formation of new chapters. She is very good at getting people together, even a handful of people, around some issue, and basically empowering them to get on with it. Then she steps out of the picture and goes on to organize somewhere else. She would facilitate a meeting in somebody's house locally so it wouldn't be her meeting. She'd start by promoting the idea of local control, of doing things for the environment in their own area. Then she'd go around the room and get them to pick up tasks. "Oh, Arlen, you could contact the newspaper, couldn't you?" "You know, Bob, you could do a first mailing, at least." And before you knew it, she had cobbled together a half-dozen people who, whether they wanted to or not, had made a commitment to do one thing. That became the core of the new organization. I've seen her do it for Audubon, and I've seen her do it in the peace movement of the late 1970s to mid-1980s.

Hazel is the only person I've ever met with the skill of not letting conflict bother her. She has this tremendous ability to let any kind of conflict or interpersonal issue go right off of her, like water off a duck's back. Because of this, she's practically stress-free. One year we were strapped for money, scrubbing every line of the budget, and we came to the dues to the Federation of Western Outdoor Clubs, which was Hazel's child. We voted not to pay our dues—to relinquish our membership in the federation. She lost that particular vote after a lot of debate. It went over to many meetings. That was one time when she didn't get her way, and I was nervous about how she would react. She just said, "It'll work itself out." Within two years, we had some funds in our budget, so we voted to come back on the federation. In the meantime, Hazel had never taken our name off the masthead of FWOC. Instead of dwelling on the past, she's always looking to the next cause that she's going to rally the troops for. Never twiddling her thumbs. I've heard her have words with people, but never yelling. She has very strong opinions, voices them, and lets it go. She looks to the longer view and probably figures that eventually things will work out her way anyway. She has that absolute conviction that leaders have to have.

STEVE HALLSTROM

President, Seattle Audubon Society (1992–94)

When I came on the Seattle Audubon board, in 1992, Hazel struck me as a very efficient person, disciplined, a person of few words. She didn't participate in the discussions if they were not leading to any valued place. She would tune out and sit there. Yet she hadn't lost contact, and when something important came up, she would be back in. Or if a discussion went on too long, she would re-engage and stop it. Her bluntness would startle the board members. They assumed she was being offhanded or making a wisecrack, but there was always a lot of thought and wisdom behind those comments.

I can remember the time that she took me to the woodshed for not behaving properly as the president. The woodshed was her apartment. She told me it was a stupid thing I'd done, and she told me why, without going into a lot of detail.

I said, "Is it going to have serious consequences for my being the president?"

She said, "No. But it was bad. You would have been more effective if you hadn't done it."

It was a very positive way of saying, "You didn't do right, but it's not the end of the world. I'm upset with you, but I'm not angry with you."

Underneath, she has this tremendous understanding of what's important, so there is very little room for equivocation. You could spend a lot of time trying to argue, and you would find that you get nowhere. So you accept it, and you try to work from there forward. She's able to do that with a lot of people. If she cares for someone, she will spend the energy and the time to teach. She's passing on wisdom, an understanding of the value of depth in thought and style. She's so successful because she's right.

PETER BERLE
President, National Audubon Society (1985–95)

Shortly after I was appointed president, in 1985, I attended a large dinner in Seattle where I was seated next to a small white-haired lady about whom I knew nothing other than she was very important in the Audubon world. Throughout dinner she gently, persistently, and insightfully probed me about the environment and causes I had been involved in. The interrogation, laced with good humor, was never threatening. It became clear to me that she was taking my measure. By the time the meal was over, she knew everything there was to know about me, and then some. Since she had been so artful in stimulating my proclivity to talk about myself, I knew nothing about her except that her name was Hazel Wolf.

I soon learned that in the Northwest there is a special coherence to the Audubon chapter effort. There are the usual conflicts between those who watch birds and those who save the world. But there is a culture of activism that is pervasive. It is a culture that puts a high premium on gathering the facts and organizing everybody in sight. Through persuasiveness, persistence, and presence in every forum where testimony is heard and decisions are made, the Audubon chapters in Washington State are respected and effective agents of change. I am convinced that part of their energy and outlook stems from the fact that twenty-three of twenty-six Washington state chapters share the same DNA—they were all founded by Hazel Wolf.

Hazel's effectiveness as an Audubon environmental missionary is without parallel. Numerous new Audubon members have been recruited by Hazel because they happened to sit next to her on an airplane, train, or bus. Hazel told me that whenever she travels, she spends the first part of the trip watching her seatmate, seeing what he or she is reading or is interested in. She will start a conversation and arrive at a topic on which there is agreement. Only after that will she get to Audubon or the environmental subject of her current attention.

I had occasion to meet Hazel at the airport after a transcontinental flight. While we were waiting for her baggage, a couple vacationing from Holland came up with pencils in hand to get Audubon's membership address. Apparently, this time Hazel had run out of the membership forms she always carries with her. She gets people in her camp before they can think they may disagree with her, standing in sharp contrast to many who take a position and blast away until the adversary is either demolished or both sides are exhausted.

Unlike many environmentalists, Hazel sees people as part of the environment, not apart from it. She has an acute sense of process—figuring out how to convert or pressure the key players, through resolutions and publicity, to come out in the right place. She has been unrestrained by political correctness about who you should talk to, setting up dialogues with everyone from Communists to corporate executives.

BROCK EVANS

President, Federation of Western Outdoor Clubs
Executive director, Endangered Species Coalition
Former staff member, Sierra Club and National Audubon Society

In 1967, I left my law practice forever to be in charge of anything the Sierra Club did, from the North Pole to California—six glorious years traveling around, organizing, and fighting for wilderness. There were just tons of battles going on for the North Cascades and the Glacier Peak Wilderness, and that's the context in which I first met Hazel. She was very active in Seattle Audubon, sharing a house with Emily Haig, a great saint of our movement who fought on behalf of Olympic National Park, and a heroine to Hazel. I remember folding-licking-and-stamping parties, and conversations with Hazel on Emily's front porch in Seattle.

We all knew Hazel as a wonderful, strong figure who would not back down. Hazel was the one who said, "You've got to work with labor. You've got to reach out to Native Americans and minorities. There aren't enough women doing things." She was our gadfly, our conscience. "Come on, come on. Do better, do better, do better!" She took me to meet Joe De La Cruz over in the Quinault tribe, for example, back in the seventies.

When my political campaign[3] really got going, in 1984, she became my treasurer, and all the young people working with me idolized her. She was eighty-six and would jog up to the headquarters in the morning, then jog out with the books underneath her arm at night, saying, "How's everything going?" The day after I lost, we all had to go over to [former Rep.] John Miller's headquarters and concede. It was like a wake, like a death ride over there. Hazel cried. We all cried. It took me a year and a half to get over that. Hazel was a rock all the way through. That's what cemented our bonds in a personal way, more than just the professional things, and we're as close as we can be, living across the country from each other.[4]

The Federation [of Western Outdoor Clubs] has always been one of Hazel's power bases, first as past president—that's clout, and it gives me some cachet, too, back in Washington, D.C.—and second as editor of the newsletter. She can write all she wants to about labor, about Indians, about Nicaragua, and no one complains, partly because she's Hazel, and no one's going to argue with Hazel, and partly because she has this powerful position. *Outdoors West* doesn't have a tremendous amount of influence as far as what the president of the United States or Governor Locke will do, but it has some. I would say that Hazel is a driving force of the Federation of Western Outdoor Clubs. She keeps it alive with money from her speeches. I only became president because she asked me.

She flew out to my wedding and danced, and then wore my wife's wedding dress to her 100th birthday party. I'd do anything for Hazel. Nobody says no to Hazel.

We were all at a FWOC convention in Bozeman, Montana, in August 1981. I said that I wanted to hike in the Spanish Peaks Wilderness nearby. Hazel heard about it and asked if she and a friend could come along. Hazel was eighty-three at the time, and her friend was in her seventies. I didn't want to be hobbled by these two old ladies, but I couldn't say no.

Ken Baldwin, one of the old-timers in the movement, and about as conservative as you can get—he didn't smoke, drink, or swear—drove us out there. As soon as the plume of dust from his pickup was out of sight, Hazel took out a jug of wine, and we took a couple of swigs. We found a trail and took off. After a few more stops and a few more pulls on the wine, I picked up my pace.

Three or four miles ahead of them, I sat down to wait. Well, I waited for two hours, and they didn't show. Then I panicked. I ran back, calling and shouting—it was grizzly country—thinking I was responsible for their destruction. Out of breath, I finally slowed down, hearing voices around a bend. There they were, lying on the flat rocks, taking in the sun with their shirts off, the jug of wine two-thirds empty beside them. We floated down the trail.

She always surprises me. . . . I went to Israel to teach law at a kibbutz. She discovered I could get a fax out there, this little place in the desert. So I get this fax on April 6, saying, "Brock, your article for the president's message in *Outdoors West* is due by April 15. Please make sure I get it." April 16, another fax from Hazel. "You missed your deadline. Here's the editorial I'm writing for you. If you want to make any changes, let me know."

JOE DE LA CRUZ
Former president, Quinault Indian Tribe, Northwest Affiliated Tribes, and National Congress of American Indians

I came about meeting Hazel in the mid-seventies, right around the Boldt decision.[5] I was coming from an NCAI [National Congress of American Indians] conference in Denver, and a young lady—at that time Hazel must've been in her seventies—sat down next to me on the airplane, and we got talking. I told her that the different environmental organizations kept passing resolutions targeting the tribes, damning the tribes.

About a year later, we got hold of Hazel and told her that we'd like to get some of our chairmen together with some of the environmental leaders. We basically had a lot of things in common, but nobody was talking to one another.

The Northwest Affiliate Tribes was meeting in the old Davenport Hotel in Spokane. It was springtime, and the Federation of Western Outdoor Clubs was meeting out at Fort Wainwright [also in Spokane] the same week. We arranged to go out there and meet. It was a nice sunny day, and we sat around in a circle on a lawn. We talked about what our concerns were and our traditional feelings toward Mother Earth. We had many more things in common than most people realized, and from that point on, we went into a coalition with Hazel and the Federation of Western Outdoor Clubs and some of the Sierra Club.

When the tribes were catching a lot of bad media after the Boldt decision, Hazel wrote articles that clarified some of the complex issues, and the normal media don't do that. They do the sensational thing—who's catching what, or who's beating on who. For a period of time, almost every newsletter of the federation covered tribal issues. I've been one of the speakers at her federation, and I've brought her to many of our events.

She didn't get involved in the environmental community until late in her life, and I noticed that her contribution is seeing that people get together. For her 100th birthday celebration, which was attended by seven hundred people, Seattle Audubon organized a tribute to her. She just thinks the world of me, and I think the world of her. I've met a lot of people in my lifetime, but nobody that I know of has Hazel's longevity, her little persistent, unique way. Anywhere she takes an interest, she makes a difference.

W. RON ALLEN
Tribal chairman and executive director, Jamestown S'Klallam Tribe
Former president, National Congress of American Indians

Ann Sargent and her brothers lived just up the street from me in Port Angeles, and we played like children play, but I never got to know the family. In my college years, all of a sudden, Ann's grandmother, Hazel Wolf, shows up at the doorstep of an apartment I was renting over at the University of Washington to let me know that she's been watching me.

Watching me—it made me think about what I was doing, kind of an eerie feeling. It crossed that threshold from the pragmatic world that you live in to the spiritual world that you think is out there, but you're not quite sure.

I said, "Wow, who are you again?"

She wanted to encourage me to be an active participant wherever I found myself. The experience of her visit was stunning. It's etched in my memory. A kind of messenger.

As my career evolved, Hazel was regularly there, a mentor-guide, popping up out of the blue just to say, "Hi. How are you doing?" After we sorted through how I was doing personally, she would ask what I was doing as a leader, spur me on, usually in environmental issues.

Joe De La Cruz, Billy Frank Jr. of the Northwest Indian Fisheries Commission, and Mel Tonasket of the Colville—these are the acknowledged leaders. These are the people who worked extensively with Hazel and with the environmental community for many years. Her name and her political contacts to advance our agenda are trusted. She can pick up the phone and talk to people, connected at almost any economic or social sector. Her outreach is beyond most people's awareness. Whenever things happen that affect Indian leadership and the environment, without a doubt she is always right in the middle of it.

People thought that sooner or later she would start to run out of energy, but she never did. She doesn't own a TV. The more I become aware of her personal lifestyle, the more I realize that she is a woman who is always mentally engaged.

A few years after I hired Ann Sargent as a secretary,[6] all of a sudden it clicked—Hazel's granddaughter! Then Hazel gave me a hard time. "You got a diamond here. You better be taking care of her."

The divine spirit has to have a medium through which it sends energy. In this case, I believe that Hazel was certainly one—don't try to deceive this person, she'll look right through you. She was like the North Star, the one that keeps you focused.

I went to the Audubon Society in downtown New York, and who do we end up talking about? Hazel Wolf. All of us who worked with Hazel for all these years recognize her as not just having an Indian heart but having that Indian spirit—having that same reverence for life and for the world around us.

1. Protection Island is in the Strait of Juan de Fuca off the mouth of Port Discovery Bay, on the northern beaches of the Olympic Peninsula.

2. No Oilport, Inc., of Port Angeles, joined by numerous Audubon Societies and environmental groups, led the legal battle against the Northern Tier Pipeline Company's proposal to build an oil superport at Port Angeles and to construct a four-hundred-mile pipeline under Puget Sound and across the Cascade Mountains to the Great Plains; see "The Intertribal Conservationist Coalition," in Part V.

3. For U.S. Representative from Seattle's 1st Congressional District.

4. Evans lived in Washington, D.C., while working with the Sierra Club.

5. The decision handed down by Federal District Court judge George Hugo Boldt on February 12, 1974, stating that the Indian tribes of Washington State were entitled to 50 percent of the harvestable salmon running through their traditional waters; see "The Intertribal Conservationist Coalition," in Part V.

6. See "The Intertribal Conservationist Coalition," in Part V.

Hazel Wolf's Speech to the Graduating Class at Seattle University, June 1997

In giving me this honorary Ph.D. in the humanities—and I have truly been honored—I was asked to speak to the graduating students. It was hinted that my speech should be inspirational. However, I was not told what I was to inspire you to do, so I am on my own.

There are lots of options. I could try to inspire you to plant an herb garden, or to learn how skillfully to manipulate a skateboard, or to become anthropologists and carry briefcases, or join the Audubon Society—this is a commercial—to help reestablish the depleting ozone layer, or, better yet, sell spotted-owl T-shirts in a timber-dependent community. There are, as I said, lots of options.

I'll start by giving advice on the traditional route toward reaching your goals, if you have any, that was cooked up by some remote Chinese philosopher. He or she said—in Chinese, of course—that to go one thousand miles, one must take the first step. Unfortunately, he or she didn't say what to do next. We are left with one foot in the air.

Maybe the best I can do for you is to give you a lot of unsolicited advice. If your goal in life is to be happy, as mine once was, my advice to you is to stay right where you are. Just keep on going to school as long as you can get away with it. Then, if that becomes impractical, just move in with your folks and stay there.

If they lock you out some night, then get married and move in with your in-laws. This may not work out, but you can try it. I wish I had someone give me this advice when I was young, because, let me tell you, it is really rough out here. In all my many years, I haven't yet adjusted to most of the things I have run into, such as answering machines that say, "For other options, press 1," expired credit cards, running out of gas on the freeway during the rush hour, dead batteries, unremitting toil on some forty-hour-a-week job, heavy rain on the Fourth of July year after year after year, and, finally, preparing phony résumés. I could go on, but I must keep an eye on the clock.

Also, since I have run out of inspirational ideas, I will fill up the time left to me by telling you a story. You most likely have heard it before, because I first heard it many years ago in Bellingham, in a cafe, having lunch with a drama student who had a part in the *Mikado.* Do you go in for that sort of thing at Seattle University? Here is the story.

A couple of dedicated baseball players were worried about the hereafter—that is, whether they played baseball in Heaven. They agreed that whoever died first would come back and tell the survivor if they played baseball up there. One died. A couple of weeks later, the survivor heard his friend's voice: "It's me, Bill. I have good news and bad news. First the good news. Yes, we do play baseball in Heaven. The bad news is that we have a game scheduled for next Friday—and you're pitching."

I know that upon graduating with you, I will probably be known as Dr. Wolf. However, you can all just call me Doc.

Notes

Part I / Ready for Adventures

1. Hosea 8:7.

2. Hazel Wolf: "My mother spanked me often. She never drew blood or bruised me—no whipping or caning or strapping on the palm of the hand—but she turned me over her knee and slapped me very good. It stung and it hurt, so I'd cry, but it wasn't child abuse as we understand it now. I don't think children should ever be spanked. I don't think you should strike anybody, especially somebody who's as helpless as a child. But that wasn't the prevailing method of bringing up children in those days."

3. The term *tomboy* is no longer needed to explain the behavior of active girls, though it was in 1910. Since the late sixteenth century, the English language characterized Hazel's active behavior as that of a tomboy—according to the *Oxford English Dictionary*, a "girl who behaves like a spirited or boisterous boy, a hoyden who trespasses against the delicacy of her sex."

4. Rather than see her three children taken to orphanages and foster homes, the usual treatment for children of poor widows at the time, Hazel Wolf's mother determined to hold the family together by working at jobs allotted to working-class women: factory operative, laundress, nurse, domestic, boardinghouse operator. She was one of the "unfortunates," as they were called, a working-class woman who did not fit into the acceptable categories for female circumstance and behavior. Women who worked were supposed to be between the ages of eighteen and twenty-five, their pay called "pin money," to be spent on clothes and coiffures for attracting a mate.

After that, they were supposed to be married, at home, raising children, taking care of a husband, going to church. The ideology of true womanhood, which presented an image of women as pious, pure, submissive, domestic dependents of breadwinning middle-class males, made millions of working-class women invisible, especially those like Hazel Wolf's mother who, as a single parent, defied the middle-class norms of the period in several different roles in order to preserve the freedom of her family. See Barbara Welter, "The Cult of True Womanhood: 1820–1860," *American Quarterly* 28 (1966), 151–74.

5. The IWW was a radical labor organization founded in 1905 in Chicago, but its stronghold was in Washington State and the Pacific Northwest. Called the Wobblies, the IWW opposed organizing workers into craft unions and aimed instead at creating one big union of workers worldwide.

6. Prior to the women's movement of the 1960s and 1970s, the one power position allowed to women, from elementary school classroom to union to boardroom, was the office of secretary.

7. In 1685, Louis xiv of France revoked the Edict of Nantes (1598) granting toleration to French Protestants. Called Huguenots, they fled under persecution to various parts of Europe and America. The DeFraynes migrated to Ireland, where they evidently joined forces with the Irish Catholics, who were under severe repression by British Protestants. Several generations later, in Hazel Wolf's speculation, her grandfather crossed the Atlantic from Ireland.

8. Hazel Wolf: "The four Frayne siblings were a quartet, and they used to sing all over the place. My mother had a really beautiful soprano. Sally was an alto. And Bob could go down [into the bass register] and sing, 'Many brave souls are asleep in the deep,' from 'Larbord Watch' [an old sailors' song]. So Howard must have been the tenor. I can remember them singing together when we were kids."

9. Ezra Meeker was a colorful early pioneer, also from Indiana, who settled in Washington Territory in 1853.

10. When George William, Hazel Wolf's grandfather, ran away to join the navy, he took his mother's maiden name, Anderson, as a disguise. Afterward, he didn't want to lose his family name, so he just moved the "Cummings" back in and called himself George William Cummings Anderson.

11. Hazel Wolf: "I've always favored women, by and large. I think they're better people. I could be prejudiced about that, but of course I am one. My granddaughter Ann is a very spirited person. She grew up in a neighborhood of boys. Her two siblings—the one above her in age and the one below—are boys. All her friends were boys. She must have been four or five when it dawned on her that she was a girl, and that she was excluded in certain ways. She said to me once when I was visiting, 'You

know that I'm going to turn into a boy?' I thought, 'Uh-oh, it's hit her.' I acted shocked. I said, 'Think it over. We've got nothing but stinky little boys in this neighborhood. You're the only girl we have, and we don't want to lose you. Please don't turn into a boy. Please don't turn into a boy.' She solemnly promised, and she never did, because her grandmother was so shocked at the idea of losing this only girl in the community."

12. William Cowper (1731–1800), "The Winter Walk at Noon," bk. 6 of *The Task,* l.560, in H. S. Milford, ed., *The Complete Poetical Works of William Cowper* (London: Oxford University Press, 1907), 231.

13. Prostitutes demonstrated the economic reality underlying nineteenth-century marriages, in which husbands prohibited their wives from paid labor: by demanding payment for what middle-class women gave for free in exchange for social status, prostitutes took control of the economic side of the transaction. In both cases, women were recognized and supported by men only as sexual objects. Surveying the conditions of working women in the 1870s, the Massachusetts Labor Bureau concluded that low pay drove women into vice, and that it wouldn't be eradicated until women could support themselves on their wages. The Progressive-era prostitute, who could earn about five times what a factory worker could, saw her profession as a choice for upward mobility rather than as submission to economic oppression. Prostitutes maintained pride in their choice to avoid the menial tasks and humiliation that marriage often entailed. Many were educated—excellent role models for Hazel Wolf when, later in life, she too determined to live independent of men. Widows, prostitutes, and nuns: Hazel Wolf lived among women on the edges of society, who bore the brunt of sexist attitudes and economic discrimination, but who could, to some extent, run their own lives. See Friedrich Engels, *The Condition of the Working-Class in England* (Moscow: Progress Publishers, 1973); Charlotte Perkins Gilman, *Women and Economics: A Study of the Economic Relations Between Men and Women in 'The Yellow Wallpaper' and Other Writings* (New York: Bantam, 1989), 154–55; Agnes Smedley, *Daughter of Earth* (New York: The Feminist Press at City University of New York, 1987), 142; Nancy Woloch, *Women and the American Experience,* 2d ed. (New York: McGraw-Hill, 1994), 234–35.

14. St. Anne's Convent school, one block from the Empress Hotel, near Victoria Harbor, now set aside as a historical landmark.

15. Sir John Suckling (1609–42), "Ballad Upon a Wedding" (1641), in B. J. Whiting, Fred B. Millett, Alexander M. Witherspoon, Odell Shepard, Arthur Palmer Hudson, Edward Wagenknecht, and Louis Untermeyer, eds., *The College Survey of English Literature,* vol. 1 (New York: Harcourt, Brace and World, 1942).

16. From canto 1 of Scott's "The Lady of the Lake: A Poem."

17. For help with this anecdote, thanks to Paul Rogat Loeb, *Soul of a Citizen: Living with Conviction in a Cynical Time* (New York: St. Martin's Press, 1999), 222.

Part II / Fighting for Survival

1. Ella Dalziel, one of Wolf's closest friends, had five brothers: Jim, Harry, the twins—Ted and Bob—and Buns. Young people gathered at the Dalziels' to sing and plan adventures.

2. Edmund Burke, *A Philosophical Enquiry into the Origins of Our Ideas of the Sublime and Beautiful* (London: R. and J. Dodsley, 1757).

3. Out of 600,000 Canadian soldiers mobilized in World War I, more than 60,000 died and 113,000 were wounded; in all, 3 million from the British Empire (including Canada) were killed and wounded, 6 million from France, and 7 million from Germany, compared to 250,000 U.S. soldiers.

4. Hazel Wolf: "I had started to smoke when I was eighteen. No health problem was ever raised. If I'd had any idea smoking was harmful, I wouldn't have started, because I was an athlete. To me, smoking was a moral issue, and what I think about moral issues is, you've got to take them on. When I got pregnant, I quit smoking and I quit sex. Just didn't think they would be good for the baby."

5. Hazel Wolf: "I took the name Nydia from the Englishman Sir Bulwer Lytton's classic *Last Days of Pompeii*. Nydia was a blind Greek flower girl, a slave who led the hero and heroine out of the burning city, then later committed suicide. *Nydia* is also the Greek word for 'hope.' The name traveled by way of the Greek Orthodox Church to Moscow and became very popular as a diminutive for Njerska. Lenin's wife was named Njerska. Most Russian classic novels, such as Tolstoy's *War and Peace,* have a Nydia."

6. Hazel Wolf: "I don't know why more mothers don't board. They'd have much more time with their children and not be interrupted with all this housekeeping business. I think that's the way families will go in the future. They'll begin to share accommodations, people of like thinking, people with common interests moving into these larger groupings. Now, I suppose I lack some of those so-called womanly traits, like knowing how to mop a floor. Another bad thing about it for me is that I never learned to cook. I didn't want to anyway."

7. Crown Zellerbach was one of the Northwest's largest landowners and timber producers.

8. See "Nydia Levick, Hazel Wolf's Daughter," in Appendix 1, "Family Reminiscences."

9. Timber cruisers survey timberland to estimate costs and potential profits of harvest.

10. Hazel Wolf's trip to Barter Island, 1979.

Part III / Communist

1. Report of the Committee on Unemployment Relief of the Seattle Municipal League, *The Administration of Relief in King County* (Seattle: Seattle Municipal League, 1933).

2. Who would do the "social work" of helping the unemployed? The government hesitated. Unions, their treasuries emptied by unemployment and wage cuts, also hesitated, for fear that strikes might cost them the few jobs that remained. Communists, by contrast, acted immediately in solidarity with the workers, providing leadership for spontaneous strikes, raising funds for soup kitchens, organizing a national network of unemployment councils, and using the slogans FIGHT! DON'T STARVE and WORK OR WAGES. On March 6, 1930, the Communists organized a demonstration simultaneously in Washington, D.C., and in every major U.S. city, which drew nearly a million workers; see Fraser M. Ottanelli, *The Communist Party of the United States: From the Depression to World War II* (New Brunswick, N.J.: Rutgers University Press, 1991), 28–31. They began to overcome their reputation, inherited from the 1920s, as a small sect controlled by Moscow's puppets who squabbled in foreign tongues about irrelevant theories. With revolutionary rhetoric muted, the Communists in the 1930s built a reputation as imaginative organizers who paid attention to people. The Communists were largely responsible for creating the perception that unemployment was not the workers' fault but rather the consequence of a worldwide economic disaster.

Behind this local flexibility and responsiveness, the Comintern (the international arm of the Communist Party, in Moscow) continued to maintain control of the "party line," which, despite wildly disparate conditions in each country and continent, was supposed to determine uniformly the activities of Communist Parties worldwide. Fortunately for the CPUSA, the Comintern changed its line, abandoning its adamant antigovernment stance and advocating the Popular Front of democratic forces against fascism, a policy that supported neighborhood and union activities that were ongoing in the United States.

3. Nancy Woloch, *Women and the American Experience* (New York: McGraw-Hill, 1994), 438.

4. The Workers' Alliance was founded by several communist and noncommunist groups that had organized the unemployed. Throughout her years of activism in the 1930s, Hazel Wolf organized unions and handled grievances for the Workers' Alliance, which became a national force for the unemployed in 1935, just as she joined the Communist Party, and just as major New Deal legislation benefiting workers passed Congress (the Social Security Act, which provided for unemployment insurance; the Wagner Act, which legalized unions; and the Works Progress Administration, or WPA).

There were other groups in Washington State that organized the unemployed—for example, the (noncommunist) Unemployed Citizens' League, which established bartering services for the unemployed and influenced several elections.

5. By 1936, it was the "Red Decade," when the Communist Party got behind Franklin D. Roosevelt, and when Roosevelt, if he didn't get behind the party, certainly supported the American Federation of Labor (AFL), the Congress of Industrial Organizations (CIO), and the Workers' Alliance, in which the Communist Party was dominant. Roosevelt and the New Deal were no longer viewed as the bourgeois capitalist enemy, but as bulwarks of democracy against the looming fascist threat of Hitler and Mussolini. Very few realized that Stalin himself had already created the premier fascist state under Communism. See Ottanelli, *The Communist Party of the United States,* 28–29.

6. One of the centerpieces of Roosevelt's "Second New Deal," the WPA, founded in May 1935 and headed by Harry Hopkins, hired workers from the relief rolls at union wages, but they worked only thirty hours per week and hence didn't compete with private industry. Jobs were mainly in construction, but there were also WPA projects in the arts, theater, drama, and writing. By the time the program ended, in 1941, 8.5 million people had worked at some time for the WPA, at a cost of $11.4 billion. The WPA was the largest federal relief program in U.S. history.

7. As part of the flood of legislation during the first one hundred days after President Franklin D. Roosevelt's inauguration, in 1933, the Federal Emergency Relief Act appropriated $500 million to the states for relief for the poor, with additional appropriations in later years.

8. See Appendix 1, "Family Reminiscences," for Nydia's experience of the Depression.

9. See Woloch, *Women and the American Experience,* 455–56:

The 1930s saw an expansion of federal agencies and in particular a marked growth of opportunity for social workers. After the federal government initiated welfare and relief measures, the social work profession, which remained two-thirds female throughout the decade, grew by leaps and bounds. Social welfare leaders worked throughout New Deal agencies, serving on advisory boards and helping to draft new legislation; as a result, jobs opened up for them on federal, state, and county levels. "My studies at school didn't prepare me for this," recalled a new county caseworker who had graduated from college in 1933, in Studs Terkel's *Hard Times.* "We were still studying about immigrant families. Not about mass unemployment." Carrying large caseloads and adapting to the welfare bureaucracy, new social workers often resented the insensitivity their roles demanded. "We're under pressure to give as little help as possible," a caseworker complained in 1934.

10. Hazel Wolf's and others' objections to using state militia funds were heard. The Communists brought to Washington the concept of an unemployment security

system paid for by employers and the government. They lobbied and testified for the 1934 Lundeen Bill. They asked the National Congress for Unemployment and Social Insurance in January 1935 to bring pressure on Congress, and they were heavily involved in the compromises that resulted in the April 1935 Social Security Act. Between 1930 and 1935, by developing effective responses to the needs of the unemployed, the Communists had become part of the mainstream reaction to the Depression.

11. Communists became known for leading the fight against evictions. In scores of cities and neighborhoods, the furniture scene was played out. Once the furniture was spotted on the sidewalk, an Unemployed Council would appear with fifty or more neighbors, who wore down the will of the local sheriff by repeatedly cycling the furniture back into the apartment and restoring disconnected gas lines and electricity with meter jumps. The Unemployed Councils made it clear that these street tactics were related to the broader objective of creating a national unemployment insurance; see Studs Terkel, *Hard Times* (New York: New Press, 1995), 401–2.

12. Karl Marx and Frederick Engels, *The Communist Manifesto* (New York: Monthly Review Press, 1998; originally published 1848).

13. See Part I, n. 5.

14. Like many others, Hazel Wolf was attracted to the Communist Party by the way it combined education and action. In a collection of memoirs of 1930s organizers, Christine Ellis gives an explanation similar to Wolf's for why she joined the party: "The thing that impressed me the most was the stress on education, culture, respect for others, devotion to a movement that would by its example win the masses to the cause of Communism"; see Alice and Staughton Lynd, eds., *Rank and File: Personal Histories by Working-Class Organizers* (Boston: Beacon Press, 1973), 24.

15. According to Marion Kinney, "There was an upsurge in the Communist Party organization on the University of Washington campus because people were wandering around trying to figure out how to live, what to do about the problems of unemployment and housing—the works. The Communist Party had a good solution. Mainly, it was in terms of getting people to fight together for their wants and needs. At the time, it was no big deal to join the Communist Party. This was long before they started all the lies and warnings and red-baiting." Kinney became one of Hazel Wolf's closest friends when they worked together on the Washington Committee for the Protection of the Foreign Born during the McCarthy period of the 1950s; they saw each other regularly up to the time of Kinney's death, in early 1999. See Appendix 3, "Marion Kinney's Story."

16. See Adam Smith, *An Inquiry into the Nature and Causes of the Wealth of Nations* (Dublin: Whitestone et al., 1776); Thomas R. Malthus, *Essay on the Principle of Population As It Affects the Future Improvement of Society* (London: J. Johnson, 1798); David Ricardo, Esq., *On the Principles of Political Economy and Taxation* (London: J.

Murray, 1817). Together these authors are considered the founders of the Manchester School of classical liberal economics.

17. During the first one hundred days of his administration, President Franklin D. Roosevelt established the Public Works Administration (PWA), under Secretary of the Interior Harold Ickes, with $3.3 billion distributed to state and local governments for building such projects as schools, highways, and hospitals. In November 1933, Roosevelt established the CWA with $400 million from the PWA, to hire four million unemployed workers. The CWA was heavily criticized for the makeshift nature of the jobs, and the experiment was terminated in April 1934.

18. The yellow-dog contract was an employment contract in which a worker disavowed membership in and agreed not to join a labor union during the period of employment. A "yellow dog" is a contemptible, worthless, yellow (that is, cowardly) person. The yellow-dog contracts were so named by unions, their signers becoming "yellow dogs" to union members.

Beyond her work as organizer for the Workers' Alliance, Wolf discovered connections to the AFL, the traditional, moderate organization of primarily craft unions. This was no accident, for members of the Workers' Alliance and AFL organizers crossed paths frequently at Communist Party meetings. Wolf sought to legitimize the WPA workers as a force in the New Deal—for example, by using the WPA union to organize public school teachers who had been intimidated by yellow-dog contracts forbidding unionization, and nursing them along until they revived their own AFL union.

19. The National Labor Relations Act, or Wagner Act, was passed in May 1935. It reaffirmed labor's right to unionize, prohibited unfair labor practices, and created the National Labor Relations Board to oversee labor relations.

20. Hazel Wolf and the Workers' Alliance demonstrated to the WPA that unionization was inevitable. At the end of 1936, Aubrey Williams, deputy administrator for the WPA, finally recognized the Workers' Alliance as the official bargaining unit. In Washington State, the Workers' Alliance was particularly strong. Harold Brockway, the head of the Washington State Workers' Alliance, with ten thousand members, was the Communist Party candidate for governor in 1936. In 1937, U.S. Sen. Lewis B. Schwellenback of Washington, "on the initiative and request of the Workers' Alliance," introduced a resolution to prevent the dismissal from the WPA of anyone unable to find a private job at prevailing wages in the trade for which he was trained and fitted.

The CPUSA was encouraged by the Popular Front policy of the Comintern to engage with contemporary politics and issues rather than hold to a policy of revolution. As a result, the party was tamed by the U.S. political system. For example, despite the explicit warning of its Communist secretary that the Workers' Alliance had to "guard against becoming merely a trade union for WPA workers," it became just that. The Workers' Alliance excelled at its new task of protecting workers' rights within the New

Deal system. Every year, when Congress threatened to cut the WPA appropriation, the Workers' Alliance would stage demonstrations in major cities and threaten further "social disorder" if funds weren't restored. In 1937, unemployment was just as high as it had been in 1932, but the Communist Party and the Workers' Alliance had advanced from the streets to the hallways of Congress and the state capitols. See Harvey Klehr, *The Heyday of American Communism: The Depression Decade* (New York: Basic Books, 1984), 297–99.

21. The Washington Old Age Pension Union was founded in 1937. William Pennock became its secretary at the age of twenty-three. From 1938 to 1946, Pennock served in the Washington state legislature as a Democrat from the 35th District of King County, pursuing the extension of social security, the protection of organized labor, and the defense of civil liberties.

22. Hazel Wolf first worked with John Caughlan (August 25, 1909–April 17, 1999) in the Washington Old Age Pension Union. He was the organization's attorney. As a Harvard Law School graduate in the mid-1930s, he worked in the Seattle prosecuting attorney's office. Then, having fallen into disfavor for taking on political cases, he went into private practice. At his death, he was one of Seattle's most celebrated members of the liberal bar. See Part IV, in which he figures prominently, and Appendix 4, "John Caughlan's Story."

23. Between 1935 and 1937, the economy recovered somewhat, with unemployment falling to 9.2 percent (among WPA workers as well), and the gross national product achieving the 1930 level. President Roosevelt decided that the recovery warranted a reduction in relief programs and a move toward a balanced budget, and the WPA experienced the largest cut in its budget for the 1937 fiscal year. When, that winter, the economy slipped again and unemployment rose to 12.5 percent, Roosevelt requested an emergency appropriation of $3 billion for the WPA; hence the hiring and firing cycles in WPA projects.

24. On Black Monday (May 27, 1935), the Supreme Court killed three New Deal programs and argued against further extensions of federal power.

25. In one of the first indications that a witch-hunt was in the making, the WPA ruled administratively from Washington, D.C., in 1938 that only U.S. citizens qualified for the program. Hazel Wolf had neglected to become a U.S. citizen when she emigrated from Canada in 1923 (see "Petition for Citizenship," in Part II), and so she was foreign-born, an alien. The WPA was probably acting under the 1938 Hatch Act, which made Communist Party membership grounds for refusal of federal employment. Also in 1938, the U.S. House of Representatives established the House Un-American Activities Committee.

26. Marion Kinney: "The Workers' Alliance was helped as far as organization was concerned by the Communist Party, and the [Workers'] Alliance was quite a powerful

organization at one time. It helped unemployed and homeless people. You know, there were no homeless people on the streets during the Depression as there are now. When my husband got out of a job, and I wasn't making enough money to really do much, we went and lived with his family. We lived with my family some of the time, too."

27. An article in the Seattle press indicates that Hazel Wolf left out one dimension of her struggle—the single unemployed women she was defending were stereotyped as prostitutes:

> Workers' Alliance leaders asserted in semi-monthly public session with county commissioners late this week that homeless women seeking relief through a King County welfare employee had been told to let their boyfriends take care of them; they said they had numerous women witnesses ready to testify against the woman welfare representative in question.
>
> The charge brought an order for immediate investigation from county commissioners, and elicited an indignant statement from King County Welfare Director Kenneth Wadleigh that department policy had never required prostitution, and that the charge was "undoubtedly without foundation." Commissioners asked that specific charges be made and prepared for hearing next week, in which the accused woman welfare worker, with any witnesses she wishes, is expected to appear, as well as Workers' Alliance witnesses. Statements of both sides could then be taken under oath by the Board of Commissioners. Further objections of Workers' Alliance spokesmen to treatment of those seeking relief welfare were also voiced at the session with county commissioners ["Welfare Relief Ruckus," in "The Saturday Digest: The Essence of the Week's News," *Argus*, Dec. 4, 1937, p. 3].

28. Eventually, in 1946, Nydia was legally admitted to the United States as a G.I. bride, when she was twenty-seven years old. John Caughlan: "You got tremendously, terribly penalized if you were openly a member of the Communist Party. Take Leo [Hazel Wolf]. She couldn't become a citizen. It was becoming apparent in the late 1930s that [the] Immigration [and Naturalization Service] was going after people whose political views they didn't like, and I think she wanted to get in while it was still possible. She was denied her citizenship, not openly on the grounds of her politics, but on the grounds of her lack of morality in living in the same apartment with a man by the name of Victor Hicks. That was regarded as clear evidence of bad moral character. Her application was really turned down because Immigration was quite aware of the fact that she was what we now call an activist. She was in the middle of the Progressive movement, thus obviously a 'Red,' and thus obviously not fit for U.S. citizenship, according to the standards that the Immigration had worked out. But at that particular period of time, they had no legal grounds for denying her citizenship on that basis, and it wasn't as popular to go after people for being left or Communist as it was two or three years later. They didn't have anything else on her at the time except

that she acknowledged that she was living with a man to whom she wasn't married. I didn't represent her in 1939. Somebody in my firm of Cahan and Carmody did. Immigration is the most reactionary, backward, repressive, and regressive bureau in the U.S. government. It's something, of course, that she spent a great deal of her time wrestling with." See also Part IV and Appendix 4, "John Caughlan's Story."

29. After thirty years of teaching, Wolf's sister-in-law, Mrs. Hildur Josephine Hughes, came before the Seattle School Board to appeal her firing for allegedly having been seen at a Communist Party meeting, according to the *Seattle Post-Intelligencer* (Aug. 8, 1953). She was unable to find work. After Bill's death, she peddled door-to-door and died in poverty.

30. Maurice Raport, born I. M. Rappaport, was a Russian-Jewish Wobbly (member of the IWW) who joined the Communist Party in Canada in 1920. He was sent to direct the party in Washington State in 1933.

31. Jessica Mitford confirms Wolf's perception in *A Fine Old Conflict* (New York: Knopf, [1956], 1977), 63: "The party had recently adopted an ironclad policy against the recruitment of aliens. The reason for this was a provision of the Smith Act under which aliens were required to disclose Communist affiliation. Should the alien affirm that he was a party member, he would be subject to deportation; should he deny it, he would risk a perjury prosecution. The party met this problem by barring all aliens from its ranks for their own protection."

32. Hazel Wolf: "In some ways, I've never liked women's organizations, and not because there are women in them. I never wanted to be a man when I was young. I always wanted to be a woman. It's just that I've never wanted to be in a women's organization. I'm not saying there's no place for them. I'm very proud of NOW [the National Organization for Women] and the League of Women Voters. They get a lot of respect because they investigate everything thoroughly and don't go flying off the handle. They are responsible groups, but I never wanted to be a part of them. I like to be in an integrated organization to fight for women's rights."

33. A professor of philosophy at the University of Washington; see "Expelled," in Part IV.

34. The Travelers' Aid Society was founded in the 1920s to set up booths in major transportation terminals and stations where volunteers, mostly women, helped new arrivals make connections with relatives and friends or find shelter and a job.

35. According to Barry Hatten, law partner of John Caughlan and employer and close friend of Hazel Wolf, if Wolf didn't feel like working for a while, she would go down to the unemployment office, get an assignment for a job, and then reveal to the interviewer her membership in the Communist Party. She would be turned down for the job. Thus she met the requirement for continued unemployment benefits by "actively seeking employment."

36. Hugh DeLacy had been president of the Washington Commonwealth Federation and was a Seattle City Council member in the 1930s. A radical Democratic congressman from 1944 to 1946, he ran in 1946 without the support of the Democratic Party, which abandoned any candidates who had been associated with the Communist Party, and was defeated by the former Washington State commander of the American Legion. Shortly thereafter, the Democratic Party began the purge of Communists to which Hazel Wolf referred earlier; see Klehr, *The Heyday of American Communism,* 256, 403.

37. Under the wartime Lend-Lease Program, the United States shipped more than $50 billion worth of goods to Britain and Russia.

38. See the narrative of Nydia Levick, Hazel Wolf's daughter, in Appendix 1, "Family Reminiscences."

39. Barry Hatten: "The trial was so important to the government that they sent special prosecutors out from Washington, D.C., who told us, 'We have to convict these guys, or we're accusing our own FBI of lying.' They brought with them tape recordings of a drunken party that allegedly proved Redin was a spy, but you couldn't understand half of what was said. After the acquittal, the FBI hounded the engineer who had testified for us."

40. "Citizenship Denied Red Suspect: Judge Bars Canadian Woman in U.S. 24 Years," *Seattle Post-Intelligencer,* Oct. 18, 1947. A radical Seattle journalist published a contrasting interpretation of the hearing:

> In denying the application of Mrs. Hazel Anna Wolf, a native of Canada, the judge opined that "She [is] disclosed by the evidence to have written one or more book reviews on Russia for one local newspaper called *The New World."* The judge went on to say that membership in the Communist Party is not a reason for denying citizenship but that the applicant had not satisfied the court that she is devoted to the principles of the U.S. Constitution because she had written "admiringly" of a foreign nation. (Guess who?) If this was not enough to gag you, Judge Bowen then added that Mrs. Wolf had not made a showing of a religious affiliation and hinted that this caused him to carefully scrutinize the value of her testimony.
>
> Mrs. Wolf reviewed Konstantin Simonov's *Days and Nights* for *The New World* a couple of years ago. Many of you will recall that *Days and Nights* dealt with the defense of Stalingrad—an epic which stirred the deepest feelings of people all over the world. It moved Mrs. Wolf to write a warm and understanding review. Last week that clipping from *The New World* was waved in her face and used as one of the reasons to deny her citizenship [Terry Pettus, "Wall Street Has No Mortgage on Patriotism," *People's World,* Oct. 1947].

41. On March 25, 1947, Truman launched the new loyalty-oath program with Executive Order 9835. The order authorized the attorney general to list organizations

he considered "totalitarian, Fascist, Communist, or subversive, or as having adopted a policy of approving the commission of acts of force or violence to deny others their constitutional rights." The Loyalty Review Board was authorized to investigate government employees who were suspected of membership in or sympathetic association with such groups. About one in five Americans either was subject to taking the oath or had to receive clearance as a condition of government employment. In Hazel Wolf's view, it was Churchill's speech that had started the paranoia, and Truman's loyalty oath that had begun the Communist witch-hunt.

Part IV / Fighting Back

1. See John Kenneth Jones, "McCarthyism in the Northwest: The Example of Huff et al. vs. United States (1953)" (master's thesis, University of Washington, 1968), 9.

2. Arrests of aliens during the McCarthy period far outnumbered actual deportations, a strong indication that intimidation of ordinary citizens was one purpose of the interminable INS hearings. In the United States in 1950 there were 10.3 million foreign-born citizens, and 2 or 3 million aliens. From 1945 to 1954, 163 "subversives" were deported. In one year, 1949, 140 political aliens were arrested for deportation in nineteen states; in another year, 1951, 205 were arrested, only 6 of whom had been living in the United States for less than twenty years; in 1953 there were 300 arrests. One study, completed in 1956, revealed that of people involved in 307 political deportation cases, 60 percent had lived in America for more than forty years, and 81 percent for more than thirty years. See David Caute, *The Great Fear: The Anti-Communist Purge under Truman and Eisenhower* (New York: Simon & Schuster, 1978), 224–29.

3. See Appendix 2, "The Hazel Wolf Deportation Case."

4. The proceedings were based on a law of October 16, 1918, requiring the deportation of an alien who, after entry into the United States, was a member of an organization that advocated or taught the overthrow by force and violence of the government of the United States. In 1940, the Immigration Act of 1918 was amended to include deportation on the basis of past membership in organizations advocating violent overthrow of the government. Before the completion of Hazel Wolf's deportation hearing, the Internal Security Act of 1950 was passed. This act amended the law of October 16, 1918, to make membership in the Communist Party, prior to or subsequent to entry into the United States, grounds for deportation. Therefore, a charge of deportability on the amended grounds of membership in the Communist Party was lodged against Hazel Wolf on February 12, 1951. While her case dragged on, the 1952 Immigration and Nationality Act (Walter-McCarran Act) passed, requiring deportation of an alien if she had been a member of a subversive organization at any time in the past (that is, there was no statute of limitations). According to the Walter-

McCarran Act, an alien could be arrested without warrant, held without bail, jailed for ten years for failing to deport herself, and deported to any country that would take her if the country of origin refused. Under this law, no hearing had to be granted to the deportee if the disclosure of evidence entailed by a hearing was deemed incompatible with national security. The commissioner of immigration, appearing before a Senate committee in 1954, estimated that there were under this law some seven hundred grounds for deportation.

The Walter-McCarran Act made one guilty for acts committed in the past, even though such acts were legal and not punishable when committed. Thus the act violated the U.S. Constitution, Article I, Section 9: "No Bill of Attainder [loss of civil rights by a person sentenced for a serious crime] or ex post facto [after the fact] Law shall be passed." Wolf's hearings "established" that she was a member of the Communist Party in 1937 and 1938—that is, at a time when membership in the Communist Party was neither illegal nor a deportable offense. The U.S. Supreme Court upheld the new immigration laws with the reasoning that the ex post facto law applied only to punishment of crimes, whereas deportation was an "administrative adjustment" rather than a crime. An attempt was made to include the safeguards of due process in administrative hearings through the Administrative Procedures Act, but the Supreme Court refused to hear the argument that aliens were covered by the U.S. Constitution. See Caute, *The Great Fear,* 230.

5. Harry Bridges, president of the International Longshoremen's and Warehousemen's Union (ILWU), led a famous shutdown strike of the port in San Francisco in 1934. From then on, the INS kept him almost continuously in court with an order for deportation as a Communist. Finally, in 1955, the 9th Circuit Court of Appeals in San Francisco ruled against the INS.

6. Other front-page headlines at the time included WOMAN'S DEPORTATION DISCUSSED (*Seattle Times,* June 1, 1949), CANADIAN WOMAN, SECRETARY HERE, HELD ON RED CHARGES (*Seattle Post-Intelligencer,* June 1, 1949), and CAUGHLAN SECRETARY HELD IN RED ALIEN PROBE (*Seattle Post-Intelligencer,* Nov. 9, 1949).

7. *Seattle Times,* Jan. 18, 1952.

8. "Caughlan Aide Held in Probe," *Seattle Post-Intelligencer,* June 1, 1949.

9. One of the first tactical decisions Wolf and her lawyers had to make was what her answer would be to the inevitable prosecution question "Are you now or have you ever been a member of the Communist Party?" Although heard at the administrative level, Wolf's case was influenced by developments in criminal law. According to the U.S. Constitution, Amendment V, a citizen may not "be compelled in any criminal case to be a witness against himself." The U.S. Supreme Court had ruled in 1950, in the Blau case, that a witness could avoid being in contempt of court or Congress by invoking the Fifth Amendment on the question of Communist Party membership;

see Victor S. Navasky, *Naming Names* (New York: Penguin, 1980), 399. Nevertheless, during the McCarthy period, "taking the Fifth" implied guilt (that is, membership in the Communist Party). As late as 1960, refusal to testify was viewed as tantamount to a confession of guilt. U.S. Attorney General William P. Rogers, in a letter to Mrs. Franklin D. Roosevelt dated June 29, 1960, wrote that Hazel Wolf "refused to testify at the hearing and thus avoided being questioned under oath as to her continuing support of the Communist Party and her activity in Communist-sponsored projects," with the clear implication that she was a Communist.

10. "Women's News," *Seattle Times,* Nov. 9, 1949.

11. Ibid.

12. *Seattle Times,* Nov. 19, 1949.

13. Hearings and trials of Communists usually began with a "battle of the quotations." The goal was to convince the hearing examiner or the jury that the writings of Marx and others were not a set of vague theoretical philosophies but actually a blueprint for action, and that mere membership in the Communist Party entailed the intention and effort to bring about the violent overthrow of the government, prohibited by law; see Jones, "McCarthyism in the Northwest," 47. In order to prove the point, the INS imported experts, called "informants," who supposedly had recanted their belief in Marxism-Leninism: 83 of these were under contract to the Justice Department in the early 1950s, 35 of them full-time witnesses performing all over the United States in various anti-Communist trials and hearings. The informant network spread through the government bureaucracy, with the Internal Revenue Service, for example, paying $499,995 to 290 informants during one year; see Caute, *The Great Fear,* 119–20. Paul Crouch, who appeared at Wolf's first round of hearings in 1949, was an infamous expert witness, engaged as special consultant to the INS at $4,840 per year. He claimed that he was a Communist organizer in California who had left the party in 1942. He lived in Hawaii, testifying all over the United States but most often in Washington, D.C., where he lived rent-free; see Caute, *The Great Fear,* 127–29, and Jones, "McCarthyism in the Northwest," 53.

14. H. C. "Army" Armstrong was a leader in the Workers' Alliance and a state legislator who had secretly joined the party in 1936 and testified later that he kept his card at party headquarters instead of carrying it. Katherine Fogg was a state legislator who testified that she had joined the party in 1937 as a secret member. Wolf had never met Clifford Smith in any of the organizations where she was active. Ward Warren, a prominent local stoolie at Wolf's hearings, was a regular ex-Communist witness in the Northwest. He had been recruited into the party by William Pennock and was active in the Washington Commonwealth Federation, an organization of the middle class that influenced the Democratic Party in the 1930s to support leftist ideas and candidates. He began his stoolie career at the Canwell hearings in 1948.

15. "Three Testify for Mrs. Wolf," *Seattle Times*, Dec. 13, 1949.

16. "Women's News," *Seattle Times*, Nov. 9, 1949.

17. "Mrs. Wolf at Red Meetings, Says Witness," *Seattle Times*, Dec. 11, 1949.

18. *Seattle Times*, Aug. 10, 1950.

19. According to Barry Hatten, after the split-up of Caughlan and Hatten, Hatten went into a partnership with Sarah Loeser, Hazel Wolf became their secretary, and Hatten handled Wolf's deportation case. Some time later, Hatten split with Loeser over issues of honesty, saying, "Leo even agreed with me on that." Nevertheless, the women in the Communist Party, of which Loeser was a member, claimed that she had been a victim of gender discrimination, and they put pressure on Wolf to quit working for Hatten. The situation was an additional incentive for Wolf to quit Seattle altogether. Her friendship with Hatten remained strong, and they continued to work together in the Washington Committee for the Protection of the Foreign Born.

20. Henry P. Huff was a founder of the Communist Party in Washington State. William Pennock (see "I Got Organizing," in Part III) was secretary of the Washington Old Age Pension Union and served for eight years as a Democrat in the Washington State legislature. Johnny Shields Daschbach was chair of the State Civil Rights Congress. Terry Pettus was the editor of *People's Daily World*. Paul Miller Bowen, an African American, was a former section-education director for the Communist Party in Seattle's South End. Karly Larsen was first vice president of the Western Washington District Council of the International Woodworkers of America. Barbara Hartle was an executive officer in the Communist Party of King County who terminated her stay in jail by becoming a government witness. After the Smith Act trial, Hartle "named names" to the House Un-American Activities Committee (HUAC). According to Barry Hatten, Wolf called him during the HUAC hearings and said, "Barbara Hartle is down here lying about us. She's saying you and I were never members of the CP." Hatten said that Hartle had "turned" because she had been roughly treated by the Communist Party leadership. She had no personal knowledge of hundreds she named, but she did have personal knowledge that Hatten and Wolf were Communists. She was trying to protect the people she liked.

21. "The mammoth job of typing the Smith Act trial transcript, making an appeal possible, was achieved under [Hazel Wolf's] direction at a saving to the defendants and their supporters estimated at $30,000" (*People's Daily World*, Dec. 17, 1954, p. 6).

22. Hazel Wolf: "I remember Florence James, the director of the Seattle Repertory Theater, was present at the performance of *By Trial and Error*, and she liked it. The Seattle Repertory Theater was completely destroyed during the witch-hunt. James and her husband had founded the Seattle Repertory Theater in the 1930s. She also founded the Walker-Ames Theater at the University of Washington, which experimented with theater-in-the-round. She was subpoenaed for the Canwell hearings in 1948 and

arrested as a Communist in the 1950s. At her trial, a stool pigeon reported that she had traveled to Moscow and, during an interview with Stalin, had agreed to twist all of the arts in the United States toward Communist ideology when she returned to Seattle. But Mrs. James found newspaper clippings documenting a lecture she had given at the time she was supposed to have been conferring with Stalin. She also produced telephone bills and light bills and all kinds of proof that she wasn't anywhere near the Soviet Union at the time that the stool pigeon said she was there. The jury was afraid to hand down a decision against the government, but they didn't quite dare put her in jail, either, so they suspended her sentence. The government was so determined to frame these people! By that time, people were afraid to go to her theater, and she had to close down. She ended up being in charge of the Provincial Theater in Regina, Saskatchewan, and awarded a Queen's Silver Jubilee medal, the highest honor for the arts in Canada. That's what we lost when we lost Florence James. And all social content got wiped out of plays—and out of films, too."

23. Citizens' resistance to the persecution of foreign-born residents who had been accused of membership in the Communist Party gathered around the American Committee for the Protection of the Foreign Born (ACPFB). The Washington State chapter of the ACPFB provided the social, political, legal, personal, and organizational foundation of support for aliens threatened with deportation. As an activist, Hazel Wolf always allied herself with an organizational base that simultaneously functioned as her extended family. The Washington Committee for the Protection of the Foreign Born (WCPFB), founded in response to Wolf's arrest—she was the first of many aliens arrested by the INS in the Seattle area—filled that place in her life just as the Communist Party was being dispersed by government persecution. The members of the WCPFB were friends, family, philosophical colleagues, and political warriors. Her anecdotes about Abner Greene, Marion Kinney, and William Pennock show how intimately politics and personal friendships grew together.

24. *The Northern Light,* vols. 1–8 (Nov. 1953–Jan. 1961), is available through the University of Washington Libraries, Manuscripts and University Archives Division. In the *Northern Light,* Wolf reported on national developments and kept track of all the WCPFB cases. She was as much engaged with her colleagues' defenses as with her own, mingling their stories with hers to create the WCPFB community.

25. *The Northern Light* 1:4 (1954), 4.

26. Ibid.

27. *The Northern Light* 1:1 (1953), 4.

28. *The Northern Light* 1:4 (1954), 3.

29. Ibid.

30. *The Northern Light* 3:3 (1956), 3.

31. See Appendix 3, "Marion Kinney's Story."

32. William Pennock's death was reported as a suicide (*Seattle Post-Intelligencer*, Aug. 5, 1953). During the trial, he admitted to Communist Party membership in the 1930s and was deeply disturbed that he had lied about it during the period when the party mandated secrecy. At the time of his arrest, he was president of the Washington Old Age Pension Union, a post he had assumed in 1944. He had been a founding member of Washington's Progressive Party in 1948. A pamphlet about his life, available in the Northwest Collection at the University of Washington Libraries, was published from his responses to John Caughlan's questions when he was on the stand during the Smith Act trial.

33. Carlos Bulosan, *America Is in the Heart: A Personal History* (New York: Harcourt, Brace and Company, 1946).

34. See n. 38, below.

35. Jessica Mitford, author of *The American Way of Death* (New York: Simon & Schuster, 1963), was a Communist Party member from 1939 to 1956. She published the story of her life with the party in *A Fine Old Conflict* (New York: Random House, 1956).

36. In each issue of *The Northern Light*, Hazel Wolf reviewed the status of the WCPFB deportation cases. In the Oct.–Nov. 1954 issue, for example, she reported that of those arrested for deportation, five Filipinos had been declared undeportable by the Supreme Court because they had been classified as nationals, six had been classified as undeportable because no country would accept them, one had been classified as an exclusion case (that is, the country of origin had refused to accept the alien for repatriation), two had died, and five were termed "critical" by the WCPFB because their countries of origin would accept them once all possible court appeals had been exhausted. Hazel Wolf's was one of these critical cases.

37. For two cases lost by the WCPFB, see Appendix 5, "Hazel Wolf Tells the Deportation Story of William Mackie and Hamish McKay."

38. For more than sixty years, the sturdy relationship between Hazel Wolf and John Caughlan—as colleagues in the 1930s, as employer and employee in the fifteen years after World War II, as attorney and client in the McCarthy period covered in this section, and finally as progressive political colleagues since the 1960s—served progressive politics in Seattle and the Northwest.

Wolf told this story about John Caughlan: "In 1948, five years before the Smith Act trial in 1953, John got on the stand to testify in a citizenship hearing, and the prosecutor asked him if he was a Communist. John said no, so they charged him with perjury. I was the fund-raiser for his long drawn-out trial. The jury stood up to the phony evidence and acquitted him. I told him that he is the only certified non-Communist in the United States. When the government finally figured out how to catch him, it was many years later, in 1962. He was arrested for nonpayment of taxes in the years 1953 and 1954. I led the fund-raising for his defense and kept the law offices open for him. He was convicted, and they gave him eighteen months with time off for good behavior."

John Caughlan served an eight-month sentence at McNeil Island Federal Penitentiary, where Wolf visited him and began to make friends with the prisoners (see "With Prisoners," in Part VI). When Caughlan was released from McNeil, the WCPFB and the liberal community held a reception for him and Wolf, but Caughlan avoided any publicity about his incarceration and took a trip to Vancouver, British Columbia, instead—a small piece of evidence that government persecution did take its toll, although neither Caughlan nor Wolf admitted it; see Appendix 4, "John Caughlan's Story." On January 4, 1984, the federal government transferred the administration of most of McNeil to Washington State, which then dedicated three-fourths of the island to a wildlife refuge and one-fourth to a state prison.

39. For more details, see Appendix 2, "The Hazel Wolf Deportation Case."

40. See Appendix 2, "The Hazel Wolf Deportation Case."

41. "U.S. Deportation Order Fought by Ex-Victorian," *Victoria Daily Times,* July 13, 1957; "Last-Ditch Battle Opens to Prevent Woman's Deportation," *Vancouver Sun,* Aug. 23, 1957; "McCarthyites Plan to Deport Grandmother," *Mine-Mill [Toronto] Herald,* Sept. 1957.

42. "Deportation Protested by Canadians," *Seattle Times,* 1957.

43. See Appendix 2, "The Hazel Wolf Deportation Case."

44. "Mrs. Wolf Unwelcome," *Seattle Post-Intelligencer,* Oct. 14, 1958.

45. "Woman, If Expelled, Can't Go to Canada, Says Attorney," *Seattle Times,* Oct. 14, 1958.

46. "Seattle Woman Ordered Shipped to British Isles," *The Oregonian,* Feb. 13, 1961.

47. U.S. Constitution, Amendment III: "Excessive bail shall not be required, nor excessive fines imposed, nor cruel and unusual punishments inflicted."

48. Federal District judge John C. Bowen, who had denied Hazel Wolf's petition for U.S. citizenship in 1947; see "Patriotic Citizen," in Part III.

49. *Vancouver Sun,* May 26, 1960, and *The [Vancouver, B.C.] Fisherman,* undated.

50. *The Northern Light* 8:1 (1961), 4.

51. John P. Boyd, letter to Sen. Warren G. Magnuson, May 30, 1960.

52. J. M. Swing, appointed commissioner general of the Immigration and Naturalization Service in 1952 by his friend President Dwight D. Eisenhower.

53. "U.S. to Deport Woman of 62: British Subject," *The Guardian* (London), May 18, 1960; "Facts from U.S.A.," *The Word* (Scotland), May 1961; "A Great-Grandmother," *Daily Express* (London), May 19, 1960; "Seventh Bid to Deport Grandma," *Daily Mail* (London), May 19, 1960.

54. See "British Ask U.S. to Reconsider Deportation: Seattle Woman Being Treated for TB," *Seattle Post-Intelligencer,* June 2, 1960:

Britain today asked the United States to reconsider its decision to deport a British subject who has been living in America since 1922. David Ormsby-Gore, foreign affairs minister of state, said today Britain took the action because it learned that Mrs. Wolf has an arrested case of tuberculosis and a "drastic change in her environment could cause serious repercussions." The British government also requested its embassy in Washington, D.C., to find out whether Mrs. Wolf had relatives in the USA, and to what extent she was in touch with them.

See also "Mrs. Wolf to Ask Delay in Deportation," *Seattle Times,* June 2, 1960: Mrs. Wolf said the change of climate is not worrying her, but rather the anxiety, possible lack of nourishing food and probability of a lower economic level because she is not familiar with British law and would not be able to work at her profession.

55. *Seattle Times,* June 9, 1960.

56. See "Court Reverses Order Deporting Seattle Woman," *The Fisherman,* Feb. 10, 1961:

The circuit Court of Appeals for the [9th] Circuit in San Francisco on February 1 reversed the deportation order against Hazel Anna Wolf and directed district Judge John C. Bowen to convene a three judge court to hear the constitutional issues involved in her case.

See also "Citizenship Disputed: Seattle Woman Asks Deportation Reversal," *The [Spokane] Spokesman-Review,* Dec. 10, 1960; "Hearing in San Francisco: Hazel Wolf Deportation Affects 30,000 in U.S.," *The [Vancouver, B.C.] Fisherman,* Dec. 16, 1960; "Ex-Red Grandmother in Court: Key Deportation Law Gets First Test Here," *San Francisco Chronicle,* Dec. 10, 1960; "Woman Wins Deportation Case Round," *Seattle Post-Intelligencer,* Feb. 2, 1961; "Woman Wins Deportation Case Round," *Seattle Post-Intelligencer,* Feb. 2, 1961.

57. "[Hazel Wolf is] still under threat of deportation. Rebuffed in latest arguments before the U.S. Court of Appeals, the government is now studying its next move in the Wolf case" (*People's World,* March 2, 1963).

58. Eugene V. Dennett, a member of the United Steelworkers of America, had been president of the Inland Boatmen's Union. Called before the House Un-American Activities Committee Pacific Northwest hearings in 1954, he admitted to holding various offices in the Communist Party in 1931–34, 1935–43, and 1945–47, when he was finally expelled as a Trotskyite; see Harvey Klehr, *The Heyday of American Communism: The Depression Decade* (New York: Basic Books, 1984), 456.

59. Hazel Wolf:

The party was crushed by the McCarthy era, although the persecution started long before McCarthy ever thought about it. The members were immobilized. When I went to meetings, they would just talk about theory, which had always bored me anyway, so I didn't go very often, and then I was in California for a year in the mid-fifties, and when I came back, I just faded out, bored—I can't remember the date.

But there is a remnant—a few people like B. J. [Barbara Jean] Mangaoang, who married Ernesto Mangaoang, one of the Filipino union leaders. She's the head of the Communist Party today in the Pacific Northwest, somebody whom I like very much. I was disturbed after I left the Communist Party that it paid no attention to the environment. When B. J. Mangaoang ran for governor of Washington State in the seventies and eighties, I cooked up the environmental platform for her campaign. When the Communists finally got around to putting out a pamphlet on the issue, they asked me to critique it.

Every chance I get, a big event or an award where I can invite my friends, B. J.'s always there beside me, with a name tag showing she's from the Communist Party. Through my activities, I get her before the public. They look at her, and she seems calm enough, not wild-eyed. She has a lot of assurance. She doesn't look like she's trying to overthrow the government.

Right now the function of the Communist Party is largely educational. They put out leaflets on issues. They attend any kind of demonstration. The Communist Party is part of the growing desire of the people to get these big multinational corporations off our backs—and they need to be pushed off. I don't know how we'll do it.

60. From the decision (no. A4-671-658) of Chester Sipkin, special inquiry officer, U.S. Department of Justice, Immigration and Naturalization Service, Dec. 15, 1966:

Brockway testified that he was a member of the Communist Party from 1931 to 1945. He held such positions in the party as Unit Organizer, Section Organizer, Member of the Legislative Committee in the Bureau, and Member of the District Committee. He met the respondent sometime in 1933 or 1934 and was in contact with her until 1945 when he left the Party. At the time he met her, she was active in the Workers' Alliance, an organization separate from the Communist Party, but with "lots of Communists in it." Most of his contact with her was in the Workers' Alliance, but he saw her at Party functions and at Party unit meetings during the time he knew her. He last attended a closed Party meeting with her in 1944. . . . [T]he respondent was active in the Party. She handled literature and did a great deal of secretarial work both for the Party as well as the Workers' Alliance. She also worked from time to time at the Frontier Bookstore during the period he knew her. . . . Although the respondent attended fraction meetings, she never attended top fraction meetings. . . . When asked whether she had ever held an important job in the party, the witness stated that he knew she was an official of the bookstore, was an agent for the distribution of literature, and heard her make speeches on the importance of reading Communist literature.

61. Ibid:

Dennett testified that he was a member of the Communist Party from the fall of 1931 until he was expelled in October 1947. During this time he held various offices such as unit organizer, section organizer, unit agitprop director, district agitprop director, and member of the District Bureau. He met the respondent in 1937 or 1938. In 1937 the Seattle Unity Council was organized to coordinate the work of unions being expelled from the American Federation of Labor because they advocated CIO types of organization. He was chosen by the Party to be the Unity Council's executive secretary, and with the help of the Communist Party was elected to that position. He needed a secretary and the respondent was recommended to him by various members of the Party. She worked for him about three months. He discussed with her at least two or three times a week such things as union policies, dates for meetings, etc. He found it difficult to say whether the respondent was aware of the Party policy except, perhaps, where it was applied to a particular union. He did not know if she belonged to any Party organizations but she was active in the effort to organize office workers into a union. He felt certain that he met her at closed Party conventions. He did not recall that she ever attained high office in the Party. As the result of her tying up the office phone with personal conversations, he had to let her go and did not know what became of her.

62. Ibid:

The respondent testified that she attended meetings of the Washington Committee for the Protection of the Foreign Born. . . . She refused to testify as to whether she had ever been a member of the Communist Party. . . . Although the respondent was a member of the Communist Party for many years, no evidence has been adduced showing that she had any knowledge of its nature or that she ever attained any stature in the Party. Inasmuch as the Government has not met the burden of overcoming the possibility that her membership in the Party was devoid of political implications, the charges against her are not sustained.

Hazel Wolf wrote to INS special inquiry officer Chester Sipkin, who had rendered the decision, as follows:

As you must know the New Year brings to my family and me, through your decision in my case, the release from a burden we have carried for almost twenty years. I know that Special Examiners are supposed to do only what the law dictates and maybe should not be thanked by the benefactors of their decisions. Nevertheless, I am very grateful to you; and not only for your decision, but also for the understanding, tact, and kindness during the hearings that enabled all of us, my witnesses, myself, and I am sure Mr. Caughlan, too, to do our very best in presenting our case. Mr. Boyd [INS district director] advises that there will be no appeal, so I will now make an application for citizenship. I hope the New Year brings you and your family security and peace. Sincerely yours, [signed] Hazel Wolf.

63. Sir Walter Scott, "The Lay of the Last Minstrel," canto 6, stanzas 1–2.

64. Before September 11, 2001, the INS no longer attempted routine deportation of people for their unpopular political opinions or for their connections to certain organizations. In the 1990s, however, aliens with criminal records, no matter how

trivial, were targeted by the INS. The Walter-McCarran Act is still on the books, and in the spring of 2000 there was a case pending in Los Angeles against aliens with connections to an alleged terrorist group, the Palestine Liberation Organization.

65. Emmett Watson, "Ms. Audubon," *Seattle Post-Intelligencer,* 1976.

66. Emmett Watson, *Seattle Times,* Oct. 10, 1985.

67. The accused were acquitted of a charge of conspiracy and fraud in December 1992.

Part V / Environmentalist

1. The story of the brown creeper is Wolf's signature piece, told and published often. Described in *Peterson's Field Guide to Western Birds,* the brown creeper (family *Certhiidae*) seems like Wolf: a "very small, slim, camouflaged tree-climber," the brown creeper is "brown above, white below, with a slender decurved bill and a stiff tail, which is braced during climbing," and it "ascends trees spirally from the base, hugging the bark closely." For Wolf's 100th birthday, Tony Angell, one of the Northwest's renowned naturalist artists, painted an opaque watercolor of a brown creeper going up a fir tree. Wolf said, "I'm sure it's the only painting of a brown creeper in the world. It's so inconspicuous. There's nothing beautiful about it. It has no red tail or topknot or funny yellow legs with feathers on them—nothing like that. It's just a little brown bird like ten thousand other little brown birds." Wolf once said in an interview for *Pacific Search* magazine that the brown creeper went down the tree and the nuthatch went up. A letter to the editor pointed out that a birder like Hazel Wolf wouldn't make such a mistake, so it must have been the editor. Wolf replied that it didn't matter very much because she didn't think brown creepers read *Pacific Search.*

2. Dr. Claude Heckman, Seattle Audubon Society president from 1959 to 1962, was forever urging Seattle Auduboners to progressive activities in his *Audubon Warblings* column, "Planning for Progress." Acquisition of an office and affiliation with National Audubon heralded vast changes in membership and style, consonant with national changes in the early 1960s conservation movement. In its first step toward national political activity, in 1962, the National Audubon Society took up the cudgel for Rachel Carson's *Silent Spring* and then presented her with the Audubon Medal in 1963 (the same honor Wolf received in 1997). Citizens—anxious about the effects on human health of pollution, and perceiving human destiny in a new, global framework—flooded established conservation organizations like the National Audubon Society with applications, even though they had never hiked a canyon or identified a bird. By the late 1990s, Seattle Audubon, with more than five thousand members, was the sixth-largest Audubon Society chapter in the United States, with a board of twenty-three directors, sixteen staffers, and more than four hundred volunteers. In 1982, Seattle

Audubon had hired an office manager, and in 1994 the organization hired an executive director. Seattle Audubon was still Wolf's "family," however, and she was introduced at Audubon gatherings as an "elder."

3. John Muir, *My First Summer in the Sierra* (Boston: Houghton Mifflin, 1911), 110; excerpt first published in *The Atlantic Monthly* in 1911.

4. Earl Larrison, *Washington Wildflowers* (Seattle: Seattle Audubon Society, 1974).

5. Robert Pyle, *Watching Washington Butterflies* (Seattle: Seattle Audubon Society, 1974).

6. A partial listing of Wolf's travels is as follows: by canoe, the Boundary Waters area of Minnesota; by kayak, Espíritu Santo Island off Baja California (two visits), Scammons Lagoon at Baja California, and Glacier Bay National Park, Alaska; by sled, Barter Island, in the Beaufort Sea; by car, U.S. national parks and the Alaska Highway; by raft, the Yakima, Skagit, Grande Ronde, and Rogue Rivers, the Grand Canyon, and the Missouri Breaks area; and, on foot, countless hiking trips of one to five days in the Olympic and Cascade mountain ranges. She also made tours to wildlife refuges and cities in southeast Alaska and Great Britain and to a bird sanctuary in Costa Rica. She traveled five times to Nicaragua and twice to the former Soviet Union. In thirty-five years, she traveled to all but two biannual Audubon Society national conventions and to every biannual western regional Audubon gathering at Asilomar, California.

7. Between northern Minnesota and Ontario, in the Ontario-Superior wilderness.

8. Under the jurisdiction of the Organization for Tropical Studies, a group of twenty-six universities plus the New York Botanical Gardens and the Smithsonian Institution assist in a wide variety of field studies in Central America. The office on the campus of the University of Costa Rica maintains four field stations. Dr. Alexander Skutch lived on one of the field stations and often served as field interpreter for Audubon visitors.

9. Listed in *Who's Who Among American Women* and *Who's Who on the Pacific Coast,* Emily Haig joined the Sierra Club in 1912, was elected chair of the Northwest chapter, in Seattle, and was later made an honorary life member of its executive committee. She served as president of the Federation of Western Outdoor Clubs and on the boards of the Mountaineers, the Washington Environmental Council, and Olympic Parks Associates. She was active in the Seattle Audubon Society in the early 1950s, serving as president in the early 1950s, as trustee, and as chair of the Conservation Committee until she died, in 1977, at the age of eighty-seven. Haig's home, on Federal Avenue, provided a meeting place for the Audubon board and for the monthly meetings of the Conservation Committee (similarly, in the 1950s, Wolf lived upstairs at the home of Helga and Herbert Phillips, who hosted Communist Party meetings at their house in the University District). Around Haig's long sturdy dining-room table, projects were born and strategies planned, with legislators and officers from state agen-

cies as well as environmentalists in attendance. At a time when nonprofit organizations were prohibited from lobbying in Olympia, Haig managed to convey the fact that she spoke for Audubon without actually saying so. Respected by members of the state legislature and the state agencies during her ten years as Seattle Audubon Conservation chair, she was the "Audubon Lady."

10. Founded in 1947, Olympic Parks Associates is a citizen organization that monitors Olympic National Park, created by an act of Congress in 1938. Consisting of three rain-forest valleys leading to the Olympic mountain range and Mount Olympus, it takes up almost the entire Olympic Peninsula, directly west of Seattle and Puget Sound.

11. The North Cascades Conservation Council organized citizen pressure for creation of the North Cascades National Park, in the Cascade mountain range, which runs north to south the length of Washington State, directly east of Seattle.

12. The Washington Environmental Council (WEC) is a coalition of environmental groups in the Pacific Northwest founded by Tom Wimmer, former member of the National Audubon board. Wolf served WEC as secretary for a short time but did not concentrate her energy there.

13. Wenas Creek is off Interstate 5, west of Ellensburg on the eastern slope of the Cascade Mountains, right at the edge of the sagebrush steppe and the ponderosa pine–covered foothills, about two hundred miles and three hours from Seattle.

14. Hazel Wolf would give the following speech at the annual Wenas campout:
On my way to Wenas today, I first stopped at a national park campground. I said to the ranger, "What will the PHOEBE?" He said, "Two dollars." "That's RUFF," I said. "No, it's KNOTT," he replied. How can you argue with a guy like that?

So I came on to Wenas. Everybody had left on a field trip—not a FLICKER of anyone, not a SOLITAIRE soul in sight—no one to CHAT with, that is, until a skinhead came along with his BALDPATE.

Next, my friend Bill came by in a very bad mood. You should have heard him GROUSE and RAIL. He was indeed a CROSSBILL. I said to myself, "POORWILL."

I saw some WESTERN teenagers LOON up on the horizon, with their plaintive call "gimme, gimme, gimme." They began BUNTING a ball around. One hit a BUTEO, but it was caught in the outfield by a FLYCATCHER. One seemed to be hurt, because he was LIMPKIN. Not a PEEP out of him, though.

Then some LAUGHING GULLS came in. They were VEERY immature. They came with a big DIPPER for water. One said, "Let's PHALAROPE," which they did, and then left. What a LARK!

Next, some cats came in for a funeral and held a KITTIWAKE attended by a flock of MOURNING DOVES.

Things then got SORA bad. A woman came PUFFIN in, bent on ROBIN the camp. At the same time, a tourist from south of the border arrived, and then the thief started to fire her revolver. You should have seen that MEXICAN DUCK, and heard him RAVEN at that WILD TURKEY. It was very, very STARLING. Then the thief stole my tent, and I started to OWL, "Bring my CANVASBACK!" I muttered to myself, "If I could catch her I'd THRASHER and CHUKAR out." It is a CARDINAL sin to steal EIDER a tent or anything else in the Wenas campground.

Well, it was a real hectic day, but I'm not the least BITTERN, and have no EGRETS.

15. The Nisqually Delta, diked for farming in the nineteenth century, was proposed in 1980 as the site of an oil terminal and refinery. Then the Weyerhaeuser Company wanted to locate a deep-water port there. Tahoma Audubon Society led the fight to preserve it as a bird sanctuary. On Interstate 5 between Tacoma and Olympia, it now comprises twenty-two acres of prime habitat for 102 bird species, including 23 species of hawk.

16. Helen Engle and other friends tell their "Hazel stories" in Appendix 6.

17. About fifty miles north of the mouth of the Columbia River, and vital to the health of the West Coast's shorebird, waterfowl, and raptor populations, Grays Harbor, with its Bowerman Basin, is the last largely unaltered estuary between California and southern Alaska, and the last stop for thousands of shorebirds before they embark on their fifteen-hundred-mile journey to Arctic and subarctic breeding grounds.

18. Studs Terkel, *Coming of Age: The Story of Our Century by Those Who've Lived It* (New York: New Press, 1995).

19. "No one person has gained more members for Seattle Audubon than Hazel Wolf," according to Chris Peterson, Seattle Audubon Society executive director.

20. Joe Hill, a Swedish immigrant, IWW worker, and labor songwriter, was executed in Salt Lake City on November 19, 1915, at the age of thirty-six. He became a folk hero and labor martyr, a symbol of the American radical tradition and the quest for economic and social justice for society's disadvantaged. "Joe Hill," by Alfred Hayes and Earl Robinson, quoted here by Hazel Wolf, has become a classic of American folk songs.

21. After fourteen years of stocking Audubon's office with volunteers, books, newsletters, bird-watchers, and connections, Hazel Wolf assumed the presidency of the Federation of Western Outdoor Clubs (FWOC). Founded in 1932, FWOC is a venerable coalition of outdoor, hiking, and conservation clubs on the West Coast, a crucial link in the network of environmental organizations. When it looked as if the organization was going under, Mike McCloskey, acting executive director of the Sierra Club, asked Wolf if she would step in and rescue it. Wolf brought new blood into FWOC by installing some of her younger friends as vice presidents for each of the western states. Then she sent out newsletters to the member clubs and revived their interest in the organization. When her term expired, in 1980, Wolf became editor of *Outdoors West*, a post she held for twenty years. At her death, she still sat on the FWOC execu-

tive committee, helped plan the annual convention, and kept the organization tied in to her various projects.

22. Hazel Wolf jumped into controversies around the Columbia Basin Project in 1977, the same year she left the office of the Seattle Audubon Society (but not Seattle Audubon). At the age of seventy-nine, she took on the Grand Coulee Dam, the fourth-largest hydroelectric system in the world; only Turukhanska, in Russia, Three Gorges, in China, and Itaipu, at the border of Paraguay and Brazil, are larger than the Grand Coulee. The dam and its irrigation system, called the Columbia Basin Project, have taken the work of several generations, and the project is still unfinished. Wolf can take a small part of the credit for that. It was conceived in the late nineteenth century, born in the Great Depression, and constructed with the populist rhetoric of New Deal democracy. Looming near the Canadian border—on the edge of the Colville Indian Reservation, ninety miles west of Spokane, Washington—the dam and reservoirs were built to extend electricity (in the case of the Grand Coulee Dam) and irrigation (in the case of the Columbia Basin Project) to the desert of eastern Washington.

23. Named after an engineer, the Bacon Siphons draw water from behind the dam into the Columbia Basin Project's system of pipes and canals, which deliver water to the central Washington plateau. The first Bacon Siphon sends water to the west side of the plateau. Hazel Wolf opposed construction of the second Bacon Siphon, to water the east side: it would have cost more than $2 billion, and Wolf figured that the water would degrade the land, for the sole benefit of corporate farmers.

24. Renamed the Washington Department of Fish and Wildlife in 1994.

25. Bombardier beetles (family *Carabidae,* species *brachinus*) have the habit of ejecting from the anus a glandular secretion that is foul-smelling and irritating and serves as a means of protection. Darking beetles (family *Tenebriodidae,* species *eleodes*) run about with the abdomen raised at an angle of about forty-five degrees. They emit a foul-smelling black fluid when disturbed. Each type of beetle characteristically stands on its head, and each is abundant in eastern Washington.

26. The folksinger Woody Guthrie worked for the Bonneville Power Administration, which administers the Grand Coulee Dam, for twenty-six days in May 1941. He completed twenty-six songs about the Columbia River, the Dust Bowl, the Depression, and the hopes small farmers placed in electrification of the rural West.

27. See Sandra Postel, *Pillar of Sand: Can the Irrigation Miracle Last?* (New York: Norton, 1999), chap. 1.

28. In theory, the sale of electricity generated by the dam was to pay for the irrigation of the Columbia Basin. In practice, the planners forgot to subtract the electricity needed to run the irrigation pumps when they estimated how much electricity the Grand Coulee could generate for sale. And, of course, the actual cost of pumping water out of the lakes and onto the land was higher than the estimates.

29. The issues of the Columbia Basin Project turned on the cost-benefit analysis. A 1981 executive order by President Reagan, designed to curb environmental regulation, promulgated that "regulatory action shall not be undertaken unless the potential benefits to society from the regulation outweigh the potential costs to society." For example, if General Motors were asked by the federal government to spend $100 million to install antipollution devices, a cost-benefit analysis might show that the devices prolonged twenty lives for one year at a cost of $5 million per life, whereas the same funds could buy ambulances and save five hundred thousand lives per year. From an environmental point of view, the cost-benefit analysis introduces the "tyranny of illusory precision"; see Philip Shabecoff, *A Fierce Green Fire: The American Environmental Movement* (New York: HarperCollins, 1993), 220. Both costs and benefits are defined as economic quantities, easy to calculate and inflate in either direction, whether or not they relate to the actual costs to nature, accrued over decades and centuries. In this story, environmentalists turned the tables by using the cost-benefit analysis to oppose a government boondoggle.

30. With the election of Ronald Reagan, in 1980, the environmental movement lost support at the federal level. The Reagan administration returned to the late-nineteenth-century robber-baron philosophy distinguished by federal giveaways of water, coal, timber, and grazing rights and expenditures of public funds to build dams for agribusiness. Reversing the policy of two decades, the new administration decreed an end to research on alternative energy sources, thus increasing U.S. dependence on oil and adding to the negative balance of trade. Meanwhile, James Watt, Reagan's notoriously conservative secretary of the interior, used his power to transfer public lands and resources to private entrepreneurs. Environmentalists complained that regulations weren't enforced. Pesticide contamination increased, acid rain and global warming soared, the national parks and refuges deteriorated, clear-cutting continued its rampage, environmental agencies lost their best people, and judicial appointees flaunted their antienvironmental views. Watt tarred environmentalists as "subversives."

31. Dixie Lee Ray served from 1976 to 1980 and was the first woman governor of Washington State.

32. Article II, Section 1 of the U.S. Constitution: "No person except a natural born Citizen, or a Citizen of the United States at the time of the Adoption of this Constitution, shall be eligible to the Office of President. . . ."

33. The popular screen actor and director Robert Redford campaigned for Massachusetts governor Michael Dukakis (1975–79, 1983–91), the 1988 Democratic presidential nominee, who lost to Vice President George Bush.

34. In Victoria, during World War I; see "Leaving Home," in Part II.

35. In 1977, the Federal American Indian Policy Review Commission encouraged Indians to gain legal control over their own resources, to drive environmentally dam-

aging mining and energy projects off reservations, and to plan for self-sufficiency. Reservation Indians have pursued this course, sometimes encountering fierce opposition from environmentalists who opposed any development on reservation land, and sometimes forming coalitions with them. Since 1985, for example, Native Americans for a Clean Environment has fought Oklahoma's Sequoyah Dump with no help from environmental groups, while in Ward Valley, California, five different tribes have built a successful coalition with townspeople and environmentalists against a low-level nuclear-waste facility proposed for their desert neighborhood. Hazel Wolf judged her coalition-building activities as her most significant contribution to the environmental movement.

36. The conference brought together tribal chairs and leading environmentalists of Washington State. On the conference steering committee were Bernice Delorme, Elizabeth Furse, Russell Jim, Joan LaFrance, Ellie Menzies, John Platt, Rudolph Ryser, and Hazel Wolf. The twenty-five conference sponsors included the American Friends Service Committee, the Seattle Audubon Society, the Point No Point Treaty Council, the Samish tribe, the Steilacoom tribe, the Sierra Club, and the United Indians of All Tribes Foundation. Other conference participants included Lillian Basil of the Union of British Columbia Indian Chiefs, Bill Bradley of Yakama Nation, Maria Smythe of the Columbia River Inter-Tribal Fish Commission, Frank Bennett of the Lower Elwha Klallam Tribal Council, and Tom Wimmer.

Hazel Wolf, as cited in Paul Rogat Loeb, *Soul of a Citizen: Living with Conviction in a Cynical Time* (New York: St. Martin's Press, 1999), 221: "I remember Russell Jim came in late and I asked him, 'How come you noble savages are staying at a motel, when we whites have to sleep on the cold floor?' I reminded him, 'You know, we're all nonsmokers, so it's no use dragging out the peace pipes.'"

37. The four-hundred-mile, forty-two-inch-diameter pipeline was proposed for placement under Puget Sound and across the Cascade Mountains, to serve customers in eastern Washington, Montana, Idaho, and the Great Plains.

38. John Dennis Spellman, a Republican and the eighteenth governor of Washington, served from 1981 to 1985.

39. Formerly Ken Cooper.

40. On February 12, 1974, Judge George Hugo Boldt handed down a decision that the Indian tribes of Washington State were entitled to 50 percent of the harvestable salmon running through their traditional waters. His ruling also made the Indian tribes co-managers of the state's fisheries.

41. In the Northwest, fish are the major resource over which Indians seek control. Indian-white relations came to a dramatic pass with the 1974 Boldt decision on Indian fishing rights. During phase two of the Boldt decision's implementation, Hazel Wolf persuaded her environmental network to make common cause with the Indians.

In her letter addressed to "Friends" of the Federation of Western Outdoor Clubs, dated March 1, 1979, Wolf wrote:

> It is the federation's belief that the Second Phase, to which our brief will be addressed, is of concern not only to the Indian tribes but to non-Indian fishermen and conservationists on behalf of the general public's interest in the preservation of the environment. Efforts by Indians to identify the environmental causes may not get the credence they are entitled to because of the Indian's obvious economic stake in the matter. Expression of these views by an amicus [curiae] brief filed by the Federation having no such direct economic stake will help to focus attention on these serious questions. We also believe that our amicus [curiae brief] will contribute to changing the widespread misconception of this as a racial conflict. The successful outcome of this lawsuit would provide a new source of environmental control of value to the entire community [cited in Fay G. Cohen, *Treaties on Trial: The Continuing Controversy over Northwest Indian Fishing Rights* (Seattle: University of Washington Press, 1986), 140].

42. The Reagan administration considered nuclear war not only thinkable but winnable, unleashing a public debate on the concept of "limited nuclear war." At its December 1981 board meeting, the Seattle Audubon Society responded by calling for a bilateral freeze on the further proliferation of nuclear weapons and by forming the Ad Hoc Nuclear Committee, chaired by Hazel Wolf. She also represented Audubon on the Seattle Nuclear Weapons Freeze Campaign, the local branch of a national organization of churches and peace groups fueled by mass antinuclear demonstrations in Europe. Wolf's committee hosted educational events (for example, a lecture on nuclear freeze at the University of Washington). A little over one year later, in January 1983, Seattle Aububon petitioned the National Audubon board to support bilateral negotiations to halt the further manufacture, distribution, and deployment of nuclear weapons (that is, a nuclear freeze). In February 1983, the board of National Audubon refused to support the freeze concept.

43. The conference, called Long-Term Biological Consequences of Nuclear War, was held October 31–November 1, 1983.

44. In her speeches, Wolf cites Frederick Engels, *The Origin of the Family, Private Property, and the State* (New York: International Publishers, 1942, 1973), 261: "Thus at every step we are reminded that we by no means rule over nature like a conqueror over a foreign people, like someone standing outside nature—but that we, with flesh, blood and brain, belong to nature, and exist in its midst, and that all our mastery of it consists in the fact that we have the advantage over all other creatures of being able to learn its laws and apply them correctly."

45. Hazel Wolf: "Many years ago, I was visiting Pinky Tippy at Lake Sawyer. Next door lived some Catholic women who had displayed a picture of Pierre Teilhard de

Chardin [1881–1955]. I was so taken with his face that I got his books and read them all. Some were too theoretical for me." Among his major works in paleontology, evolutionary biology, and Christian mysticism, Teilhard de Chardin's *The Phenomenon of Man, The Divine Milieu,* and *The Future of Man* are perhaps the best known.

46. Among dozens of books on ornithological subjects authored by Alexander Skutch, such as *The Imperative Call: A Naturalist's Quest in Temperate and Tropical America* and *Orioles, Blackbirds, and Their Kin: A Natural History,* two are in a broader vein: *Life Ascending* and *The Golden Core of Religion.*

47. John Robbins, *Diet for a New America* (Walpole, N.H.: Stillpoint, 1987).

Part VI / One Neighborhood

1. The term *contra* is short for *contrarevolucionario* (counterrevolutionary). It refers to the opponents of the Sandinista government, who took power in 1979.

2. When she spoke to her audiences in Seattle about this experience, Wolf would say, "I want you to hear that bell," and she would play her tape recording of the tolling bell.

3. Sponsored by the Tahoma Audubon Society, the conference, called War and Environment, took place October 5–6, 1984.

4. Nick Allen, Joseph Collins, and Frances Moore Lappe, *What Difference Could a Revolution Make? Food and Farming in the New Nicaragua* (San Francisco: Food First Books, 1982).

5. David Brower (1912–2000), called the Archdruid of Conservation by John A. McPhee in *Encounters with the Archdruid* (New York: Farrar, Straus and Giroux, 1971), founded three environmental organizations and in his lifetime was probably the most respected U.S. conservationist. With Steve Chapple, Brower wrote *Let the Mountains Talk, Let the Rivers Run: A Call to Those Who Would Save the Earth* (San Francisco: HarperCollins West, 1995).

6. Asociación de Biólogos y Ecólogos Nicaragüense.

7. Six years later, at a 1993 gathering of forest activists in Oregon, women, without warning, interrupted the program to discuss their concern that the convention and, in fact, the entire environmental movement, both mainstream and grassroots, were dominated by men. They drafted the Six Ashland Principles, embodying the ideas that women, in contrast to prevailing stereotypes, are not caretakers and men are not aggressors, that women and men are natural allies, and that women and men are all leaders in the environmental movement. See Mark Dowie, *Losing Ground: American Environmentalism at the Close of the Twentieth Century* (Cambridge, Mass.: MIT Press, 1995), 231.

8. Nicaragua had expelled twenty U.S. diplomats and one hundred other U.S. employees in response to a U.S. search of the Nicaraguan embassy in Panama, a violation of diplomatic immunity.

9. Rudyard Kipling (1865–1936), "Recessional."

10. Vice president under President George Bush (1988–92).

11. Homero Aridjis (1940–) is internationally recognized as the premier poet of his generation in Mexico. In 1985 he rallied one hundred Mexican artists and intellectuals to petition for government action against air pollution in Mexico City. The petition gave birth to the Mexican environmental movement.

12. UNO candidate, and widow of Pedro Chamorro, editor of *La Prensa*, who was assassinated in 1978.

13. Under the Reagan administration, the U.S. invaded Grenada in 1983; under the Bush administration, the U.S. invaded Panama in 1989.

14. After she returned from Managua and the First Central American Conference on Environmental Action, Hazel Wolf used every opportunity to generate support for Nicaragua, including her ninetieth birthday celebration, in 1988. Four hundred people from all phases of her life attended a fund-raising dinner and donated $4,500 for medical supplies for Nicaragua. Wolf gave the funds to Seattle's St. Mark's Episcopal Cathedral, which bought an X-ray machine and an infant respirator for a rural hospital.

15. See n. 14, above.

16. Within a week of returning to Seattle, Wolf raised $1,500 to match the $1,500 the Nicaraguan Episcopal Health Assistance Project had already collected for another respirator.

17. Through her participation in the Fourth Biennial Conference on the Fate and Hope of the Earth, in 1990, Wolf met many indigenous people and became deeply impressed with their power, as the weakest of underdogs, to withstand the globalization of corporate capitalism. Her conviction that native peoples, especially the women, were the backbone of the global environmental movement inspired the next phase of her activism and linked her back to the coalition with Native Americans and to her Seattle neighborhood.

18. The Gwitch'n Nation of Northern Athabaskans follows the caribou herds of the Porcupine River through four hundred miles of the Yukon Territory and Alaska. Sarah James lives in Arctic Village, one hundred miles above the Arctic Circle, in northeast Alaska, but travels often to international conferences, to Washington, D.C., and to the lower forty-eight states to lobby for protection of her homeland. In 1988, the proposal to drill for oil in the Arctic National Wildlife Refuge occasioned the first meeting of the Gwitch'n elders in more than a century. Refusing to let larger coalitions speak for them, they formed the Gwitch'n Steering Committee, filed suit against the

U.S. Secretary of the Interior for the right to a subsistence way of life, and became leaders of the global environmental movement of indigenous peoples. See Mary Joy Breton, *Women Pioneers for the Environment* (Boston: Northeastern University Press, 1998); Jan Schwab, *Deeper Shades of Green: The Rise of Blue-Collar and Minority Environmentalism in America* (San Francisco: Sierra Club Books, 1994).

19. Wangari Maathai of Kenya, now an international eco-hero, is the first woman in east or central Africa to have earned a doctorate. She taught veterinary anatomy at the University of Nairobi, Kenya. A strongly patriarchal government prevented her from sitting in Parliament, so she devoted herself to the Green Belt Movement, a hugely successful effort by women to reforest the country.

20. Wolf's friends in the Lummi tribe, near Bellingham, Washington, brought K'in Bor and Manuel Chan Bor of the Lacandone people to the United States. The group traveled to the San Carlos Apaches, the Tohono O'odhams, and the Hopis. Back in the Northwest, the delegation held press conferences, addressed dinners, meetings, and receptions, talked on the radio, and hosted a conference at Daybreak Star Indian Cultural Center as part of a fund-raising effort.

21. A play on NIMBY, the acronym for "not in my backyard," coined to describe residents' typical response to government's proposals for siting various forms of waste disposal. The acronym is often used in referring to people who generally favor something (such as low-income housing) but don't want to live next to it themselves.

22. A manual of parliamentary procedure first published in 1876 by Henry Robert, an American army general. Hazel Wolf, having spent her life in meetings, was shocked to discover in the 1990s that *Robert's Rules of Order* was considered a tool of oppression. In her view, parliamentary procedure allowed for decision making through an orderly, democratic process of majority rule. *Robert's Rules of Order* had framed her life as a successful organizer with the Communist Party, the Washington Committee for the Protection of the Foreign Born, and Seattle Audubon Society. For someone like Wolf, who was eager for action, parliamentary procedure guaranteed that, one way or another, a decision would be made.

23. Alan Forsberg, CCEJ board member, 1992–99: "It took the CCEJ board six months to come up with a vague and meaningless mission statement. A few years later, we needed one for a grant application. Also, we had a general membership meeting and elections coming up, and we needed to tell people about the organization. Going through old filing cabinets, we ran across the mission statement Hazel had written in five minutes for the 501(c)(3) documents. It was clear and concise, and everybody loved it, but only I knew it was hers. I didn't tell some of the other board members that Hazel wrote it, because they routinely dismissed her ideas and contributions to the founding of CCEJ. I think they simply failed to respect her great age and wisdom."

24. As of 2000, CCEJ has a small staff, a stable board, an office in Seattle's Central

District, a ten-page quarterly newsletter, and a schedule of community events. CCEJ is a recognized member of Seattle's and Washington State's environmental network.

25. Williams's autobiography, out of print.

26. The one-time federal penitentiary that later became a Washington State prison; see Part IV, n. 38.

27. The Jefferson Award is a prestigious national honor that recognizes individuals throughout the country who perform great public service, largely without recognition. The award is given in five categories and is nationally sponsored by the American Institute for Public Service, in Washington, D.C.

28. In the 1930s, Dave Beck was an organizer for the Teamsters and a dominant personality in Northwest labor. From 1952 to 1957 he was national head of the Teamsters Union and in the 1960s was a respected citizen of Seattle, sitting on the University of Washington's board of regents. At the pinnacle of his career, in 1962, he was convicted of income tax evasion and spent thirty months at McNeil Island Federal Penitentiary.

29. Brownie (Darrell Brown) had spent time in state prisons in Oregon, Washington, California, Utah, Nevada, and Idaho, and in federal prison at Alcatraz. Later he was transferred to McNeil Island Federal Penitentiary, where Wolf met him.

30. A member of the board of the National Audubon Society; see "Putting the Bee On," in Part V.

31. Ed Browder, letter to Hazel Wolf, Dec. 29, 1994:

Thanks for all the calls and for worrying about me . . . it is nice to know that one is in the thoughts of others . . . Love, Ed.

32. Ed Browder, letter to Hazel Wolf, Dec. 26, 1991:

Some people get their fantasy and facts mixed up, and try to make fantasies come true in real life. I think I did indeed have a natural bent or talent for the wayward path. When I was young, we played Cowboys and Indians, never Cops and Robbers. I was always an Indian and well aware it was fantasy.

33. Ed Browder, letter to Hazel Wolf, Feb. 17, 1994:

My grandson had a major battle with his live-in girl friend or whatever you call them, and he moved out and felt so badly he was ready to quit his job and maybe wander off. I spent two days giving him some advice, but then you know it is almost useless to give advice to people obsessed by what they think is LOVE and being young and inexperienced adds to the problem. However, I am hopeful he will listen to me, his sister, and my son—his father—all of whom are telling him to forget the spoiled brat and get on with his life.

Hazel Wolf, letter to Ed Browder, Mar. 5, 1994:

I pity any young person, or older person for that matter, who gets caught up in the "love" trap. It is purely chemical and people are so helpless against such power. If they get married it is quite possible that they can find themselves friends and live happily ever after. Unfortunately, that is rare. That is one of the reasons I am a hard-core atheist. What kind of a god would create a creature with such an inborn trait? Some people are driven by this trait; I am one of the lucky ones who isn't, yet I've had my share of the grief of unrequited love. I hope your grandson comes out of it. Tell him for me that two years from now he will have forgotten what his adored one looks like and feel lucky to have escaped from a foredoomed relationship. By the way, this "live-in" arrangement is called "live-in companion." That covers heterosexual, gay, lesbian, or platonic situations. Love with no chemicals, Hazel.

Ed Browder, letter to Hazel Wolf, Mar. 5, 1997:

I am trying to get out your way in June, as I am to get my final discharge papers from the DOJ [U.S. Department of Justice] on 11 June. It has been a long twenty-five years (plus two which they added on when I was in that Mexican hoosegow), and so twenty-seven years and I will have paid off the stain on my escutcheon imposed by Judge Solomon out there in Portland on June 11, 1970. Never thought the time would roll around, but due to your friendship and warm letters and visits, it has been made much easier. Love, Ed.

34. During her trip to Decatur, Alabama, Wolf gave speeches, planted trees, and attended receptions in her honor. At a parting ceremony, the mayor gave her the keys to the city.

35. Former Republican U.S. representative from Georgia, leader of the "Republican Revolution" of 1996, and speaker of the House (1996–1998).

36. Studs Terkel, *Coming of Age: The Story of Our Century by Those Who've Lived It* (New York: New Press, 1995).

37. Liberation theology is a group of Catholic doctrines that emphasize the liberation of poor people, people of color, and women from oppression.

38. See Appendix 7, "Hazel Wolf's Speech to the Graduating Class at Seattle University, June 1997."

39. William James (1842–1910), American philosopher and psychologist.

Index

Hazel Wolf, born Hazel Anna Cummings Anderson,
gave herself the nickname Leo in early adolescence.
After her mother remarried, Hazel was often called Leo Hughes.
She was known as Hazel (or Leo) Dalziel after her first marriage
and as Hazel Anderson Wolf after her second.
In this index, her name is abbreviated as HW.